Intermission

.

Anne Baxter

Intermission

A TRUE TALE

G. P. Putnam's Sons, New York

Fifth Impression

SBN:399-11577-3

Library of Congress Cataloging in Publication Data

Baxter, Anne.
   Intermission.

   1.   Baxter, Anne.   I.   Title.
PN2287.B39A32   791.43'028'0924 [B]   75-45285

*This book is respectfully dedicated
to Mother and Dad, with love*

I am deeply indebted to the following friends:

Edith Head Ihnen and Wiard "Bill" Ihnen, for the key to their aerie;

Charlotte Hawthorne Gill, who must have used a built-in Rosetta Stone to translate my penciled hieroglyphics into type;

The encouragement of Jo Lathwood, Whitfield Cook, J. Watson Webb, Jr., Mr. and Mrs. Kenneth S. Baxter, Mr. and Mrs. William E. Aull, Randolph Galt, Christopher Isherwood, the late Bennett Cerf and Anne Slater, who read the first manuscript, written in 1964;

Long-time friend Kay Brown, who unearthed it in 1973;

Phyllis Jackson, for suggesting G. P. Putnam's Sons;

John Dodds, for editing with a cold machete;

Amelia Haygood and Carol Rosenberger, who reinforced my spirits if not my syntax;

Patricia Donahue Wendling, for deciphering the final, final rewrite; Joseph L. Mankiewicz, for inspecting it; and to Lieutenant D. E. Edwards, ex-Girl Guide, and D. K., both of whom know why.

Contents

No other country offers less assistance to first settlers.
—Captain Arthur Phillip, who founded
Sydney, Australia, in 1788

An adventure is only an inconvenience rightly considered.
—G. K. Chesterton

It was the best of times, it was the worst of times . . . it was the spring of hope, it was the winter of despair, we had everything before us, we had nothing before us, we were all going direct to Heaven, we were all going direct the other way—

—Charles Dickens

Truth is stranger than fiction but not so popular.
—Anon.

Intermission

1

Curtain Down, Houselights Up: Late January, 1959

WHAT luxury, I thought, kneading my bare shoulder blades into the sandy bank. The bank slanted sharply to the smooth, silent river, and I lay on my back upside down, like a cat in the sun. Better watch it, you'll burn, you're white as a grub. The blood began to pound in my head. I kicked my legs and sat up, brushing the sand off my back and out of my hair, and swiveled on my bikini briefs to face the river. It flowed by like cooling molten glass. No wider than Wilshire Boulevard, but still Australia's largest river. I listened to birds high in the eucalyptus trees and realized how much Australia smelled and looked like parts of California. Among other things they shared eucalyptus trees. Only here they were called gum trees. I stood up groggily and stretched. What time was it? Edwina said they'd come back and pick me up at half-past four. I remembered their amazement at my wanting to be alone on the banks of the Murray River. Like too many people they thought making a movie was a kind of game. They certainly had no idea what a sweat this one had been. Reaching high, I plucked a frosty blue, sickle-shaped leaf and crushed it. It turned green and sticky. I sniffed it deeply and felt a shocking bite of pungence up my nostrils. I threw it in the river, grabbed my nose in pain, and sneezed. Stickybeak, I thought, smiling at a marvelous Australian word for someone nosy, and walked back to my patch of sand and sun.

I lay down again, this time feet pointed toward the river's edge. Gravity tugged gently at my body. Through half-closed

17

eyes I watched the sky and thought about those last long weeks of work. The heat had been unbearable. Angela Lansbury and I had wilted in it. So had John Mills and Ernest Borgnine. The sets were steam baths. The perspiration poured off us but the beer wouldn't come out of the tap in the pub scenes. Too hot. The spigot just foamed at its mouth. I hoped the picture was good. *Summer of the Seventeenth Doll* was thought-provoking and dealt with people who could but would not grow up. I thought it had captured the raunchy, seamy side of Australian life. We'd shot in cramped little tenements and a squalid amusement park; filmed a three-night-long sequence on the greasy harbor ferry, and had quickly become steeped in the beery, brawling side of Sydney.

How different Torumbarry was. Peter and Edwin Baillieu were charming and relaxed. Their station (we would have called it a ranch) was in wild untidy country, but Torumbarry's house was very different. It was a wide, handsome building made of limestone, with high ceilings and tall windows and spacious rooms. Australians had been enormously kind and I'd had many refreshing country weekends, but this was the last, and the best.

I dozed blissfully in the warm silence, delighted that tonight's dinner party had been canceled at the last minute because the American who owned the neighboring cattle station had gone to the Philippines and could not join us. Thank God. I was hardly in the mood to entertain a stranger.

My suitcase was half packed for the trip home tomorrow. I'd discovered that for an extra fifty dollars I could fly back to California through the Orient, a part of the world I'd never seen. Friends had armed me with letters of introduction and I was hungry for the whole adventure. The high points would be Angkor Wat and a stay in Tokyo's Imperial Hotel, which my grandfather had designed in 1923. Frank Lloyd Wright was my mother's father. She was his favorite as a child and he used to call her "Taffy." She was beautiful and saucy and thoroughly individualistic, all of which he loved. But when the family broke apart she'd understandably sided with her mother and there had been many painful scenes. He and I had no such ravines between us and had discovered deep affection easily. He en-

18

joyed my career and I revered his genius. We laughed a lot together. He taught me to mistrust façades and always to observe life beneath its surfaces; to find excitement in a seed pod or beauty in a carpenter's hammer. He gave me other inner eyes. I gave him pleasure as a lively audience and as his favorite Taffy's daughter.

I heard the Land Rover growling in the distance. I sat up quickly and peered around for my scarf. My hair looked as if I'd combed it with a wooden spoon.

There they came, Edwina, Peter, and their rosy children, bounding along the sandy track, ready for a swim.

"Edwina! I'm having the most lovely time—can't tell you how I've longed for doing nothing in the sun—thank you both!"

"You didn't feel abandoned?" She smiled anxiously.

"Heavens no! You've given me a gift!" She laughed in that way people have that implies actresses are crazy.

"Have you had a swim?" said Peter as he strode toward the river bank.

"Nothing so athletic, I'm afraid." I smiled. "But I'll dunk myself now to wash off the sand."

Edwina settled on the bank with her roly-poly little girl and opened a huge pink parasol; Monet should have painted them in its glow. Peter, five-year-old Petey, and I fell into the silky water. Curling around in the river, I thought, how civilized. Miles from anything called civilization thrived unhurried life and love. What was it Patrick White had said about Australia? Something strange. John and Mary Mills knew him from London and we had all shared a Japanese dinner together in our stockinged feet during the filming of *Seventeenth Doll*. He was a brilliant Australian who wrote brilliantly about Australia.

I couldn't remember. The inscrutable aura surrounding him was almost palpable and so oddly forbidding I could hardly hear what he was saying. He and his remark mystified me. Watching the free and easy Baillieus at play reduced his vaguely sinister comment to a dinner quip and I tossed it aside.

"So sorry Ran isn't here," called Edwina from the shore.

"Who?" I asked.

"Ranny Galt, our American friend who was supposed to come to dinner."

"Don't worry about it, please, Edwina," I called back, treading water. "Besides," I said, laughing with secret relief, "I look and feel like the bashed-in carnival doll in the film."

Darwin was 103° at three in the morning. I got off the plane, just because I wanted to stand for a moment in so remote a place. When we landed at Jakarta all Caucasians were segregated, a startling feeling. Non-Caucasians enjoyed the warm breezes or air conditioning with iced drinks. The rest of us sweltered in a cement room sipping tepid orange-colored water.

At Bangkok I was met by Australia's cultural attaché and his wife: we found an instant rapport and they ladled great helpings of Aussie hospitality.

When could I go to Phnom Penh to see fabled Angkor Wat, and could they possibly go too? They could get me there but couldn't guarantee I'd get back, because of the growing war on the Cambodian border.

It was a terrible letdown but an impossible chance to take. They knew how keenly disappointed I was and suggested side-trips around Bangkok with a Thai guide and friend named Manas Manasaputr.

Manas was part German and part Annamese. He was massive, Buddhalike, and missed nothing. In three short days I tried to learn all about Bangkok and thanks to Manas I almost did. On my last night he took me to have my fortune told. We visited an elderly Buddhist priest he knew behind one of the hundred temples made of broken china. It was steamy dusk, and young acolytes were sluicing their orange robes with buckets of water and hanging them like banners to dry. The priests' room was marble, long and low; a monkey and a puppy chained on silver chains were playing together. The priest was in his golden shrine in an alcove. Manas spoke to him in Thai and interpreted, but I swear I began to understand directly. The priest spoke of many things, among them vast changes to come into my life. Some comments about the past were eerie with truth.

We left and wandered down Bangkok's dimly lit streets and heard gay music and hubbub in the courtyard of yet another

20

temple. People were milling in excitement, a red-draped funeral was in progress to the left, food of all kinds was frying over charcoal fires. A dozen or so small bamboo cages, one gray bird in each, hung over one little stall.

"What kind of birds are they, Manas?" I asked.

"Wild ones. You buy a bird, make a wish and set it free." He smiled cynically. "The owner will catch them again tomorrow."

"Let's give two of them a free night." I bought two, closed my eyes, and wished:

—a fine man for me;

—a father for Katrina;

and out they flew. It was all so silly and such exotic fun.

Hong Kong was cold and I grew anxious to get home; Okinawa was tropical and I was more anxious than ever. Japan was shivering on the brink of very early spring. I was ushered into the lobby of the hotel it had been my lifetime wish to see, only to find I'd been housed in the "new" non-Frank Lloyd Wright wing, a tasteless glass box. I threw a polite fit, and with abject apologies the management changed me to one of Grandfather's elegant small suites. Of course it was small-scaled, Grandfather had designed the whole place for the Japanese people, not rangy overgrown Americans, for God's sake. He always said anyone over 5'10" was a weed. Grandfather was 5'10".

The army of occupation had painted cheap gold paint in between every poured concrete design. Awful. What a legacy. Never mind, that romantic building still triumphed over earthquakes and armies.

And now home. Home and Katrina, my seven-and-half-year-old. I wanted to have some days alone with her before we went to Grandfather's for Easter in Arizona.

Taliesin means "shining brow" in Welsh; Grandfather had named both his homes Taliesin (Tal-ee-*es*-in). Easter celebrations at Taliesin West were unlike any in the world. Arizona is dramatically beautiful in spring, and Grandfather loved drama. He had designed a theater for me when I was three years old— sowing a potent seed.

Mother, dad, and Katrina and I drove down from Northern California. I had sold my house in West Hollywood and had taken an apartment near my parents for the time being. They

21

were living in Menlo Park while their new house was being built south of San Francisco and had been in charge of Katrina during my stay in Australia.

We drove out across the Paradise Valley on the dirt road to Taliesin. That Easter morning was soaked in blinding desert sun. The sweep of buildings cut clean lines into an intense blue sky, as married to that rock-strewn desert floor as anything he'd ever built.

"Look at the balloons!" cried Katrina, her green eyes flashing. They were marvelous, straining straight up on their strings, shouting with gay color in windless air. Everything and everyone formed kaleidoscopes of multicolor. Desert flowers festooned the long tables. Young men and women apprentices from the fellowship moved to greet the arriving guests; we embraced other Wright family members; of the six in Grandfather's original family, three were there: David, Lloyd, and Mother, each with children and grandchildren to join the celebration—not only of Easter, but of their father.

There he came, arm in arm with my step-grandmother, who wore a bright straw hat with flowers in her hair. Though almost ninety-two, he walked with small panther-smooth steps, the most graceful man I ever knew. He was dressed in white linen, a dashing soft-brimmed straw hat shaded his merry eyes, and he exuded geniality and delight.

We greeted one another with joy. The quality of our time together had been matchless and we both savored that rare fact.

The apprentices sang songs, from ancient Gregorian chants to spirituals, and we all deeply felt the perfection of those sun-drenched moments in another world. Or was it the quintessence of the best of this one: an atmosphere conceived by a magnificently creative spirit, whose explosive, husky laughter infected us all with ebullience?

The day ended with more music; a concert by a fine young pianist named Carol Robinson. Music was something else my grandfather and I shared; it was a necessity to us both. How he loved to play grandiose Beethoven-like chords on finely tuned pianos! As we all walked down the steps to the car that evening, Katrina looked up at the glittering desert sky.

22

"Is that the Big Dipper, Mommy?"

"Yes, dear."

"It's pouring out!" she exclaimed, gazing up. She was right, the Dipper was almost overturned above us.

"What do you think it's pouring, Katrina?" I asked.

"Oh—all kinds of good things." She leaned sleepily against me as we walked away.

A few days later Grandfather fell dangerously ill. An operation was performed and he rallied with incredible stamina. Two nights later I wakened from a peculiarly distressing nightmare: in a vast twilight valley and a great dark bird with mile-wide wings bore down upon me, roaring with speed. Cold with fright, I snapped on the light. It was three o'clock. I tried to calm myself reading and as I turned out the light an hour later the phone rang; it was my mother.

"Anne—Papa died an hour ago." I comforted her as best I could, put down the phone, and wept.

A thousand comments were made about Grandfather's extraordinary genius, his stormy life, his work—all to do with his public self. San Francisco's educational television station planned a memorial show, as his last building was being completed just north of the city. They called and asked if I would talk informally about his more private self, his early family days. Mother and I discussed it, and it seemed to help her to talk about the helter-skelter Wright family and the fun they shared, as well as the hardships. With her blessing I said I'd contribute what I could to a truthful image.

The show was beautifully done and very moving. Grandfather's roots were so vibrantly American that just speaking about him made you believe all over again in native American space and beauty and tenacity and daring.

When it was over, I walked away shaken by emotion and oddly aimless.

"Miss Baxter?" I turned.

"There's a Mr. Peter Baillieu calling you—he's on the phone."

"Pete Baillieu?" I repeated in astonishment. "For heaven's sake. Is the call from San Francisco?"

23

"I think so—didn't sound like long distance."

"Right—where's the phone?"

He pointed to a phone on the wall by the sound stage door. I hurried to the phone, stepping over a mess of cables, thinking, Pete—what was he doing here? Why wasn't he in Australia? And how did he find me? Perhaps he and Edwina were on their way to Aspen; they'd mentioned wanting to go.

"Hullo . . . Pete?"

"Ah—" said a soft voice. "This is Ranny Galt."

"Oh?" I replied rather frostily. Games like that irritated me. Why had the man lied?

"I was afraid you wouldn't come to the phone so I used Pete's name," he went on. Now I knew—this must be the American cattleman who never materialized for the dinner party at Torumbarry.

"Edwina told me I might call you but I didn't have your number. Then I saw your name in the paper and that you'd be on TV about Frank Lloyd Wright and I thought I'd try to catch you."

"I see." At least he had initiative. "Are the Baillieus here?"

"No, they're in Aspen. Would you possibly have dinner with me?"

Damn. The Baillieus had been wonderful to me—*they* liked him and he was their neighbor, very important to them.

"Well, perhaps we could have a drink right now?" That would get rid of him neatly and at least I would have been polite.

"Ah . . ." he hesitated, and I was sure I heard restaurant sounds; clinks and conversation. "Sorry, I can't do that—but what about dinner tomorrow?" Damn again. Remember Torumbarry and that weekend of heavenly rest.

"Tell you what," I said, thawing slightly, "I'm coming into town tomorrow for a baseball game. Could we have an early dinner?"

"Wonderful!" his voice warmed and strengthened. "Could you come to the Clift Hotel?"

"Yes, I know it well. What time?"

"Whenever you say." When did baseball games end?

"Seven o'clock?"

24

"Couldn't be better. Look forward to seeing you."

"Thanks very much," I said coolly and hung up. Damn. Damn. Damn. I railed at myself. Involved in a blind date at your age. Dear, kind Baillieus, this is only for you and that happy weekend at Torumbarry. Kind of a cheap trick using Pete's name. On the other hand, he was right. I wouldn't have come to the phone if he'd used his. Funny, wasn't it, I thought, my Grandfather's death had brought a stranger from another world into mine, however briefly.

I drove the forty miles home wondering what sort of dress I could wear to a baseball game that would look right for dinner. Relax. A dinner was just a meal.

2

Meeting

THE Clift Hotel was comfortable, respectable, and nice. No more. No less. The doorman grandly escorted me to a chair on the outskirts of the lobby. Coming out from under a screen of newspapers stretched long trousered legs. Smoke rose over the top. The doorman cleared his throat. "Mr. Galt!" he announced. The newspaper crackled and down it crashed. A nimble hand yanked a long cigar out of a face that reminded me of a newly opened window in a stuffy room. Randolph Galt stood up smiling. I felt my chin tilt. Everybody's tall to me, but he was taller than most. Younger than I'd expected. Not precisely handsome, but I was glad I was slim and in my favorite red knit dress.

The doorman bobbed delightedly as he palmed his tip, and served me a flashy "Nice to see you here, Miss Baxter!" as he wheeled to go.

"Well done, Mr. Galt," I said, amused at his minute arrangements. "I'm glad I didn't have to search for you—wouldn't have had a clue what to look for and it's no fun being at sea in a large lobby."

"It's Ranny. And frankly I was afraid I wouldn't recognize you either." My eyebrows must have twitched. "I don't go to movies much," he said with quick grin, softening what was almost a retort.

"I thought we'd go to Trader Vic's," he went on. "That suit you?"

26

"Fine—I'd love it." It was an excellent restaurant and I enjoyed his decisiveness.

"You mind walking? It's only two blocks straight up."

"Not at all," I enthused. "Be silly not to, it's a lovely evening."

He took my arm and strode with me out the big doors as if we were heading into a high wind, although there wasn't even a zephyr. Trotting alongside him my ego wondered if he'd even seen me in a film. Probably not. It was certainly a subject I'd leave at home, like my dark glasses.

The steep blocks disappeared as we chatted with the briskness of two strangers in search of a subject.

"Are you from San Francisco?" I asked, as I stretched my stride to keep up.

"No—Honolulu. I was born in the Islands." So. That explained those shoulders, surfing and swimming. And his skin, whose color was less tanned than irradiant à la Gauguin from years of tans.

"How long have you known Pete and Edwina?" I asked.

"About four years, off and on. My property's near theirs in the Riverina, but I don't actually live there. Pete and I raise Santa Gertrudis cattle."

"So he said," I answered. "He showed me some of his herd—first time I'd seen Santa Gertrudis since a visit to the King Ranch years ago. Do you know the Klebergs?"

He looked at me curiously. "No, but Pete does."

"They're old friends of mine; that unique Brahman–long horn cross should be terrific in Australia's dry country."

It was fun tossing out a remark I knew would surprise him and I looked ahead blithely. I felt him glance over, intrigued that I knew one cow from another; it lit his eyes. Shining no-color eyes, like water in a country puddle, slightly hooded by deep curved eyelids under neat peaked brows.

"Absolutely—they're a new breed to Australia, not that popular yet, but we think they will be." Our unexpected conversation seemed to amuse him. A crowded eyetooth showed when he smiled. He had roundly sensual lips; his nose was short and almost delicate for that taut oval face. What was Galt? Danish?

We were suddenly there. Trader Vic's was already crowded. Evidently our table wasn't free and we were ushered into the bar. His clothes were a confident mix-match—Yale, I bet myself. His brown hair was thick and crisp and bits of fractured silver broke out around the edges; the forehead was unusually high, or perhaps the tide was going slowly out.

As we sipped our drinks I noticed one of the captains my family and I had known over the years peeking into the bar. He greeted me with raised brows and lifted chin, and conferred with the other headwaiter, who nodded and hurried to us.

"Your table is ready, Mr. Galt. Nice to see you, Miss Baxter," he said, smiling and bowing.

"Mr. Galt" eyed me as I rose, and I wondered exactly what he was thinking. We were led to an excellent table. Had I been hopelessly pigeonholed under "Hollywood" actress? Maybe I could somehow erase the "Hollywood." I'd pigeonholed him under "playboy" sight unseen—and had quickly crossed out the "play."

Dinner was delicious, we shared a penchant for unusual food; and I was right about Yale, but didn't expect a History of Art major. Nor did he expect my passion for deep sea fishing or the natural world in toto. I guess the best of that dinner was its ease. It was so easy. Subjects presented themselves with a magician's sleight of hand. He was enthusiastic about a great variety of things; it burnished his eyes. Or, I wondered, was he simply being a good listener and responsive date? What did it matter? I'd probably never see him again anyway. His total lack of cynicism, ease, and easy laughter led us both out of our private cages into fresh air. He asked cautiously if I'd care to go on to a nightclub. Just as cautiously I retreated into "If you like," and we went on to some dim, pinkish place. It was clear he pigeonholed dancing under "supposed to." I was suddenly tired from a long day, and the evening ran down like a toy.

He took me to my car and after polite good-byes I drove the empty freeway home and thought about open windows and stuffy rooms and not a whit more. Except how exhilaratingly different he'd been from what I'd expected.

It was years before I found out he'd had a ticket to Australia for the next day. He called in the morning and we dined again, because it had been so easy the night before. This time he rented a car and drove south to Menlo Park, and the third night I

28

remember I cooked a very simple meal that seemed oddly festive, candles or no candles, because we laughed so much. We crossed a thousand bridges of laughter, back and forth. He met my family and my small Katrina. As we said good-bye that evening the laughter halted, and so did we. We just stood staring, transfixed by a startling fact in our eyes, and fell in violent love at third sight.

Who can describe that most private earthquake? I was more afraid of it than most and carried well-hidden scars. It was as if I'd fended off the whole world with my eyes squeezed shut, only to open them and find another unarmed child like myself. Paralyzed with fright, I stood still while the earth rocked and roared. Then we turned to each other as one turns to the sun.

Ran (for some reason I couldn't seem to call him "Ranny") left for Australia ten days after we met. All dressed up for some inane premiere, I drove him to the airport and memorized his face for a last time in the wordless seconds before he turned away. I felt dead sure I would not see him again, and even more sure I should not. We were totally unlikely together, and all my instincts told me to run back to the safe reality of acquaintance. He was gone like a diver into a sea of people and porters and shouts. I wiped wet mascara off my cheekbones with shaking fingers and tried to light a cigarette, hit the car into drive and ran away. I heard a plane high overhead that could have been his, and thought a final, decisive good-bye.

The next night, when Katrina was safe in bed, I sat in the dark studying the hot coal on my cigarette. It was over. Much the best. All I had to do was forget the way I felt, or the way he looked when he talked about some new property he wanted to buy called "Giro" (Ghee-ro). It was green and rolling he said, not flat like the Riverina. There was a fine wild river too. It was north of Sydney. How far? I thought he'd said around 180 miles. I knew that fifty miles from a city could be wilderness in Australia. As he talked of Giro his eyes burnished as they had when we first met. He was the only man I'd ever met with irrefragable, innocent charm. That's what I had to forget. Maybe it would help to enumerate for the hundredth time all the good reasons against our improbable duet.

One—I started with myself. I am six and one half years older—five months of the year, anyway. That would be there like days of the week.

Two—I knew nothing much of his world; he knew next to nothing of mine.

Three—He can't carry a tune in a steam shovel; music is part of the fabric of my being.

Four—History of Art at Yale notwithstanding, he wants to live life with his hands, not his head; my life had been mental, although I adored the natural world.

Five—He treasured anonymity. I was branded by exposure.

Six—

The phone rang. Honolulu! I sensed it. Don't answer. Again it rang. I could feel that cable vibrating fathoms deep. And again. No, NO!

SIX—Australia means making new friends, his. It rang again like a living thing. Don't *answer*. Again! NO! I mashed my cigarette and jumped up to pace. He feels at home there, you'd be an outlander, even to him. Again! NO! I wrung my hands and crouched on the floor, holding on to my knees. Where's seven—

SEVEN—Where are you seven? I need you. *RRRing!* I couldn't bear it and capsized on the ninth ring. His warm soft voice reminded me of late April talking to early February.

He told me he was coming back to California and me. Love had been a shattering surprise. I still felt as if I'd been left in pieces on the floor.

This was the first of many calls. They kept us alive. It was unbelievable; to have been crisp strangers on the phone such a short time ago. And now to know that a word or a look from him, or none, could plow me like a field.

"You putting down roots in Australia, Ran, why not find a girl who understands it?" I pleaded, torn by an inner voice saying, *And someone younger, someone without another man's child, someone not burned and twice-shy, and certainly not an actress!*

"I don't want some other girl."

We had endless talks like that, and they always ended the same way. He was incredibly persuasive. He charmed my common sense into nonsense. He was coming back to California and me in June. It's hard to let go of joy.

30

Mother and Dad were wary. I was their only child and my career and impulsive life had forced them to swallow many a bitter pill. Australia seemed a banquet of pills. They were polite and cordial to Ran but increasingly silent at the mention of that faraway place.

Katrina was the only one who penetrated our June haze. We had good times. She watched Ran out of cool eyes for symptoms of affection, and unbent as she spotted them.

She'd barely known her own father. John Hodiak and I were divorced when she was only fifteen months old; he died tragically a little over a year later. Her memories of him were few but of the purest pleasure. She used to peek out of her closely guarded self at the various gentlemen escorting me during my seven years of single life. But no one was invited in. She'd had to share my time with a possessive profession and she had become possessive in self-defense. Not healthy perhaps but I understood. When she was four and a half she came home from school and said accusingly, "Why don't you pick me up at school like the other mothers?"

"Because I work," I replied, "and I love my work. Besides, I need to work to give us food and clothes and a nice home to live in, and your fine school. I hope you find work you love some day, darling. It'll make you happy and free."

With that she stated flatly, "Your job is to stay home and take care of me."

I wondered then if I could ever make her understand. I don't believe she ever has.

It's almost impossible to be a normal mother when you're an established actress. It's an endless agony of priorities. I'd tried to console myself with the belief that our quality of time was a cut above the harried quantity of time dispensed by more available mothers. But was it? Guilt remained a resident devil.

Her attitude was watchful toward Ran and me. After all, she'd bided her time before, and her life with me had gone on undisturbed, except for my work, which she took like medicine. She continued to bide it, but suspected this was something new to face. Fortunately for us both she was horse-mad and his talk of Giro and its wild country beckoned her with the possibility of her precious dream—her very own glorious horse. Ran played with Katrina more like a much older brother or young uncle and could make expert outdoor fires. Most of my gentlemen friends had been indoor plants. She stood slightly to one side and watched our every move, as if we were jet planes with motors ajar: would we take off or go back to the hangar?

I wondered what his mother and father thought. He spoke of them with glowing warmth, his sister too. There were obviously close ties between them. His father belonged to one of the celebrated old missionary families of Hawaii; his mother enjoyed an active social life and was involved in philanthropic causes.

"Because I've been a film actress, doesn't your mother think I'm some Hollywoodsy form of grass-widow spider?"

He grinned across his cigar. "She wants to meet you."

"I'd be delighted."

"What about yours, now that you bring it up? What do they really think?"

"She thinks I'm insane. Nothing new. Australia sounds like the moon to them both."

"That's because they haven't been there—mine have. Mother's in New York and is coming to see her brother and sisters in Los Angeles. Would you come to meet them?"

Ran stayed at his aunt's house in Bel Air. I stayed at a hotel in Westwood. He met his mother at the plane; she and I were similarly dressed in navy blues and white. Her figure was trim; she had flair without flash; her eyes were bright as spirit lamps. An altogether charming lady.

After lunch I asked if we might have a private conversation. And so we did. She sitting in the sun by her sister's mountain-top pool; I cross-legged beside it in a red bandana suit wet from a swim.

It was a serene and beautiful place, bowing with tropical greenery. A strangely curving palm bent far out over the jewel of a pool. All was as warm and impeccable as Mrs. Galt and her sister. Looking up at her, my eyes squinted in Bel Air's bright, blue haze. I'd left my sunglasses on the table next to her and wasn't about to put them on. If we were going to talk we should be eye to eye.

Something told me Ran's mother had cut her trip short for this meeting.

32

"Anne?" She said my name with a delicate exclamation point.

"Yes, Mrs. Galt?"

"What can *possibly* interest you in this *boy*?" Excellent, I thought, we're not going to mince a word. I leaned forward, clasping my hands around sundried knees.

"A great many things that will be hard to explain. But I'll try." I smiled back at her.

"Please do," she urged, watching me carefully.

"Has Ran mentioned anything about marriage to you?"

"No."

"He has to me. And I want you to know that, however strongly I feel about him, I don't think it's a possible idea." There was a small silence.

"Why?"

"You first asked me what could interest me in 'this boy.' I am six and one-half years older than Ran."

To my total surprise she burst into laughter.

"That *couldn't* matter less!"

"I think it does," I protested, taken aback. "Maybe not so much now, but later on it could matter a lot."

She studied me with faint amusement. "Anne!" Again she said my name in a dramatic whisper as if about to impart a secret. "You've done so much in your life; Ranny's just starting, really. How can you find him interesting?!"

God, I thought. What a huge question. To have to explain to a man's mother why you were in love with him. I stood up and moved to the chair opposite her at the glistening glass and wrought–iron table.

"Mrs. Galt," I began, my back and face very straight, "my father has always been the measure of a man to me. His enthusiasm for life; his supreme ethical sense; his sense of the ridiculous; and, above all, his unshakable integrity and lack of guile have always been my yardstick. Even so, I've made some bad mistakes in judging men. My fault. I'm an emotional person; dangerously so. I think Ran has those qualities, and I admit I'm completely captured by someone so utterly different from the men I've known. You know perfectly well I'm in love with him. Whether that's good for either of us I do not know. It is a fact. We have a thousand strikes against us. The age differ-

33

ence you toss aside is only one of many. Marriage alone scares me to death. But, if at some time in the future I ever feel I might be able to make him happy, I'd like to try." I sat down hoping to God she hadn't noticed my damp eyes. Could've been the sun after all. Her eyes never left mine.

"Ranny says you've been to Australia?"

"Yes. I made a film there."

"He's never actually lived there, you know. My brother has interests there and Ranny and I invested in some land in Western Australia a few years ago."

"He loves it there," I said.

"I know." She smiled. We both knew how he ignited when he talked about Australia.

"But, Mrs. Galt." I spoke very directly. "That's all I know. What he eventually plans to do there I don't know. He's interested in raising cattle. He says he's found a cattle station called Giro. I think he's still in the midst of discovery. Aren't we all? I'd hate to think we weren't."

"Possibly," she answered tentatively. We were silent for a moment. How exquisitely feminine she was, except for the ice cube of diamond I'd noticed on her right hand. Usually women who wore those needed to. She obviously didn't.

"Mrs. Galt," I said gently.

"Yes?"

"Makes me feel funny probing Ran's thoughts when he's not here." I grinned. "He wouldn't like that."

She laughed with a marvelous lilt. He was so real in that moment he might've been standing there; a vivid link between her planet and my spaceship.

"What about your career?" she asked.

"That would be one of the larger problems. I'd have to give it up, even though he's amazingly vehement that I go on. And he's never even seen me on the screen." I laughed. "Probably just as well, considering some of the parts I've played." I wanted a cigarette badly, but I'd left them with my clothes. It was absurd. I suddenly felt as if I were talking to Ran's former wife. Someone who'd loved him deeply, whom he'd divorced, but saw frequently. The crazy thought made me drop my eyes.

34

When I looked up she was gazing at me with a mixture of admiration and rue.

"He has no money, you know."

"Frankly we've never discussed it," I stated truthfully. "Nor have we discussed many things. There hasn't been that much time. I think you mean so much to him he simply wants us to be friends."

She looked away and when she turned to me again she sparkled. He had her eyes.

"Wouldn't some iced tea be good?" It sounded as if she'd suggested a nice visit to Tahiti.

"What a delicious idea!" I sighed. "My back is roasting but my bathing suit's clammy. I'd better change. Besides, Ran may think we've been at each other's throats." She laughed and we rose together to go inside. As we parted, I to the pool changing room, she to order the tea, she asked about Katrina.

"She'll be eight in July," I answered, and disappeared to change.

Much was left unsaid. Rightly so. At least she knew I was honest, was aware of my strenuous doubts, and also knew that if I ever thought I could make Ran happy I'd like to try. Nothing more. Except of course that he and I were not quite sane.

I wondered why she'd mentioned money. Surely he had enough, or how could he have been in Australia at all?

Ran had trained to fly jets in Phoenix, Arizona. We touched on the subject when he joined us that afternoon, and Mrs. Galt mentioned her fascination with Taliesin West and Grandfather. I described his discovery of the Paradise Valley in 1934 and how he was told there was no water out there. He'd scoffed at the local wiseacres, remarking that saguaros grew there as well, so there must be water. He then bought a large hunk of desert; is reported to have pointed his cane like a divining rod, saying "Dig here." They went down 800 feet—but water they found and he began to create one of his most magnificent dwellings out of massive sunburnt rocks, wood, and canvas.

Mrs. Galt was on fire with curiosity to see Taliesin. I felt drawn there by a yearning to once again be where his genius reverberated. The students would have gone north to Taliesin

35

East in Wisconsin. Only a few hardy caretakers would be there. June could be fierce, and Grandfather never air-conditioned the free-flowing desert air at Taliesin. The three of us took off for Arizona. No wonder she and Ran were close, both so full of life, so eager for fresh experience.

It was, and was not, a success. Mrs. Galt and I became friends, but Taliesin was unutterably depressing to me. He was gone. The spirit was gone. The genius loci had gone. Only the stones were warm from baking desert. Later I wandered off alone. Ran found me standing in the gloom of the empty theater where we'd all had supper and chamber music at Easter. He gathered me in his arms without a word.

"We shouldn't have come," he said after a moment.

"I'm OK," I muttered into his shirt. "I had to take one more look. Thank God you're with me."

I took a farewell look and never went back to Taliesin again.

We'd rented a car and, sensing my solemn mood, Ran changed the subject as we drove back to the sprawl of Phoenix.

"When I was here in the Air Force there was a joint that made fabulous Orange Julius. Bet I could find it!" An hour later his mother and I were in hysterics at his determined wanderings through street after street peering for Orange Julius. When Ran wanted something he was singleminded. Only hunger pains made him give up in disgust and we gratefully ate huge steaks minus Orange Julius.

Ran's father arrived from a Yale reunion and the Galts flew up to see friends in San Francisco and to meet my parents the next week. Mr. Galt was as large as Mrs. Galt was petite; a smiling, jovial person who'd been a football star at college. He laughed easily and heartily and plainly adored his wife.

My mother greeted us while watering the shrubs she and my father would take to their new home. Their interim apartment had a long deck crowded with plants that flourished under her eagle eye and legendary green thumb. I sensed it was difficult for her and my father to make a to-do over anybody connected with transplanting their only child and only grandchild 9,000 miles away.

But it was all very pleasant socially. My handsome mother and father were perfect hosts as usual. Golf, Oriental Art, and people fit the puzzle pieces of conversation nicely. Australia was a subject barely patted on the head. Dad, the diplomat, steered carefully around that pothole. Perhaps it would have helped if Ran and I hadn't been sitting there watching them play doubles.

We all enjoyed one another in a guarded sort of way. We dined together and the Galts left for San Francisco—and Hawaii. Time had begun to hound us. There was so much to do: finding a house for Katrina and me; filming a television show; Mother and Dad finishing their house and moving; Ran seeing to his Australian interests and researching the property called Giro. Everything seemed to close gently but firmly over our private emotions. Even simple geography. More airports, more difficult good-byes.

I thanked God for Ran's letters, and that incredible lifeline, the overseas phone. He bought Giro in July and said it was his place in all the world and that he couldn't wait for me to see it. His enthusiasm poured out on paper and reached out for mine over the phone. That ardent impulse to share made me love him even more.

3

Unmoored Balloon

HE came back to California in September; this time to Los Angeles, where I'd finally found a secluded house in a canyon of burly sycamores for Katrina and me and my five Japanese screens. Home was extremely important to me, specifically graced with a touch of the Orient; Mother's and Grandfather's influence. My dramatic screens, Katrina, and a Gypsy camp of things stretched luxuriously in every room. Ran was delighted by what I'd created in so short a time.

We were unbelievably happy in the euphoria of constantly rediscovered love. He talked about Giro with tremendous excitement. He said the house was awful, but a lot could be done with it. I instantly pictured something like a tumbled-down Torumbarry, with its spacious tall rooms, and found the pictures in my head tempting beyond words, though I cautiously didn't say so. Something kept tugging me back. Fear. I was sickeningly afraid of failing again at marriage. Especially since Ran had never been married. I had loved John as much. But we'd eventually congealed in the longest winter in the world. Daily estrangement. Things unsaid. Even a fight would have warmed us. To my shame, I'd picked one at last in order to unfreeze the word "divorce." Slamming drawers, running around our silver-ceilinged bedroom, and avoiding his motionless eyes. No one else came between us. Just us. And a lot of that us was me. It had shaken what faith I'd been able to muster in myself. John's tragic sudden death woke guilt up. Later, a disastrous costly affair made me all the more certain of my emotional instability. Thank God I had fought shy of marriage with that rapacious gentleman. But avoidance is not a way to live. Nor to raise my girl.

Katrina seemed at ease with Ran; especially compared to the usual polite short shrift she'd given my other men friends. Her own life, new house, new school, new neighborhood friends, engulfed her. He'd never made the mistake of bringing her expensive presents, always suspect to a child no matter how they respond at the time. She knew how he and I felt about each other and that he wanted to marry me. Her comments ranged from, "If you get married to Ran would I get to be in the wedding?" to, "Well, he wouldn't be my real *father*."

My reply to that last was, "No. Your father's dead. He would be your daddy."

"OK."

She knew none of the difficulties of my decision—they were inexplicable to eight years old. I was her compass. As long as that was not threatened her world rolled on.

He pressed marriage more urgently. I wondered if he saw the dream that began to form in me. My only visions of Giro sprang from his lively descriptions of untrammeled nature, and memories like the rosy glow of Edwina Baillieu's parasol on the bank of the Murray River. Inexorably the dream grew. Would it be barely possible that he and I could dare to make a private world gleaned from all the worlds we'd known? His well-ordered island world and unruly Australian ones; my salty theatrical world and gentler domestic ones. Australia might be a gateway to foreign worlds; Oceania, New Zealand, the Great Barrier Reef—the gorgeous Orient—even the South Pole, unknown worlds to explore together.

Nothing seemed impossible as my imagination took off. On and on it flew, an unmoored balloon. Ran's dream of Giro had cut it loose. What a great adventure and challenge to help build the finest American-owned property in Australia! It needed hard work and terrific discipline, but my profession had trained me in both.

Before, my fears of marriage had effectively punctured the runaway balloon. But my wise flock of fears faced a flock of

39

Ran's; all rams and silver-tongued. Unfair advantage. Who says love is fair?

One night after steaks and wine we sat lazily in chairs in the open center of my house, watching stars and sycamore leaves flicker in a desert wind. He delicately broached the subject of my coming to Giro. It worried him that I hadn't seen it, that I wouldn't like it, that if we might marry I'd hate living there—that it might affect my decision about us.

"But, Ran," I said, "you didn't ask me to marry Giro!"

"I know—I know—but I still wish you'd come. It would mean the earth to me to have you see the place. And I think it is important to us both," he pleaded, his face very serious. "Mother and Dad are coming down in November." He watched me intently.

I stood up and put my hands on his shoulders. "Darling, if I ever come to Giro I'll have made up my mind. I'd be marrying a man then, not a place."

As the time came for him to leave we were miserable.

"Anne, come to Hawaii with me. I have business to do there on the way back. The family'd love to have you."

I was silent for so many reasons; only to feel the dream balloon rise higher and higher, and myself plunge deeper and deeper into love. "Yes, darling, I'll come with you."

His eyes drained of anxiety and shone in their astonishing way. For once the airport didn't mean a painful good-bye. We flew to Honolulu together.

Mr. and Mrs. Galt met us, draping us with fragrant leis and delighted smiles. The Cadillac drove smoothly up to an older residential district above the fast burgeoning city, on the way to the sheer mountain cliffs separating Honolulu from Kaneohe Bay. Nothing much was seen from the quiet winding streets except the rooftops. Privacy reigned. The sun came out. Everything was instantly sequined with droplets of water. Rainfall near the Pali pass was 60 to 80 inches a year as opposed to 5 inches at Waikiki or Kahala. Two worlds twenty minutes apart.

The big square house had a haunting Hawaiian name. Spreading arcs of giant monkey pod trees canopied its calm geometry, and tons of water pouring off the steep Pali boiled over rocks deep behind it.

Whenever I think of that house I hear rushing water. A constant choral background to the life within it. Mrs. Galt's magic touch was everywhere. Daringly arranged flowers. Art books enticingly displayed on a huge teak table under one generous window. A 1,200-year-old Tang horse. An exotic gilded and mirrored Siamese highboy; pure white cotton rugs, gleaming floors; simple, comfortable couches and chairs. A Modigliani nude over a French gray marble fireplace mantel opposite a fine old Japanese screen in gold leaf with pure white chrysanthemums. A carved green velvet chair, and at every glance one looked out onto ordered friezes of living green. Not many rooms, but all tall and large and open to one another. A party of two or 200 equally welcome. Moss tinted the balustrades of the terrace on all sides. I walked slowly out feeling perfumed leis cool against my neck, and stared enthralled at the waterfall coursing far below. Ran came up behind me.

"It's perfectly beautiful," I said.

"Yes, Mum's done a lot of work inside and out, but she loves it. Just keeping growth under control is a job up here."

I was amazed. He'd already changed into khaki slacks, cotton shirt, and bare feet.

"Don't you want to change? Your bags are in Dawn's old room. Come on. I'll take you up. Mother's out hassling with her cook. He's very Japanese and very temperamental."

I stayed in what had been his sister's room, very feminine with French windows. He was in his, which was as crammed with his clothes and belongings as if he'd never left. But had he? He had bought a furnished apartment in Sydney but did he actually live there or merely occupy it, like a territory? This extraordinary house must still be home, I thought. No wonder Giro meant so much—it would become a first place of his own. That I could help realize came the tempting echo.

I was changing into a silk shirt and white pants and was fiddling with hair growing limper by the minute from the humidity when I was startled by gales of laughter and crashing mambo music floating up the curving staircase. Good God, don't tell me they were having a party and guests had already arrived. I glanced at the clock on the lace-covered French bureau. Four o'clock. A tea dance? Hadn't been to one of those since the Plaza Hotel in New York, aged fourteen. Bare feet came pounding up the uncarpeted stairs.

"Sweetheart?" It was Ran.

I poked my head out. He stood wreathed in smiles, brandishing a cigar. "Come on down."

"What's going on?" I asked warily.

"Mother's having her dancing lesson."

I looked astonished and relieved. "How marvelous!"

"She's great." He grinned. "They both are. Started as exercise and now they win national contests."

My sandals clattered as we hurried down the glassy stairs. Bare feet stuck better.

He was right. She was sensational. Mrs. Galt and her teacher were flying around the terrace off the dining room to throbbing rhythms. Mr. Galt was a beaming audience; he knew a star performer when he saw one.

Dinner was utterly delicious; she set a table as charmingly as she danced. Obis flung down the dull white lacquer table. Baked breadfruit, to surprise me; a rich chocolate torte she'd made herself to please Ran. Candlelight, icy wine, and water falling off the mountain peak outside.

We left the table as the Japanese cook's diminutive white-clad wife staggered to the living room terrace with a loaded silver tray of various coffees. The air was soft as whispers in a rapt audience.

I stuck my nose into the steam off my demitasse and breathed luxury. If I knew Ran at all, he enjoyed this but chafed under it. Too finished a civilization. Nothing was needed but maintenance. He was watching me closely. As if to say, I've had this. It's perfect. It doesn't belong to me or to us. We can be free in a new land.

They retired early and we walked alone, in bare feet, down to the water. He held me in his arms and we didn't have to say a word.

I awoke to mourning doves and slivers of rain. What time was it? I craned at the clock across the room—eight fifteen. Was that late here? Not knowing, I scrubbed my face, brushed my teeth and hair, and donned a short robe in pink checked cotton with crisp ruffles. Pale lipstick and brown mascara was as far as

I should go, I warned myself. Opening my door and pinching my cheeks with the other hand for a rosy glow, I tiptoed down those noisy stairs trying hard not to clack my heels.

It had stopped raining by the time I'd crossed the dining room tiles to what I could see was breakfast in progress on the terrace.

"Good morning—I'm late!"

"Of course you're not," cried Mrs. Galt. "What a pretty robe!"

"Thank you," I replied, noticing she was dressed. Mr. Galt stood as I came to a table glowing with yellow linen and white china.

"Don't tell me Ran's not up?" I asked, surprised not to see him.

"Heavens yes. He's out and gone and is coming back for breakfast. He's doing some shopping for dinner. I thought it would be fun to barbecue at Kahala with Dawn and Bill tonight. Ran loves to barbecue."

Yes, I thought, and he's very good at it. I was smart at canned soup.

"What would you like for breakfast, Anne?" She went on, "Papaya, strawberries, peaches, grapefruit?"

"Papaya would be lovely."

Mrs. Galt rang a little silver bell. The tiny Japanese lady scuttled in, her thick glasses throwing rainbows in fresh sun. "Fumiko, Miss Baxter will have papaya." And off she scurried. I thought I heard the front door open and close. And the crackle of paper bags far away. And the slap of bare feet? My ears are devastatingly good.

"Ran?" Mrs. Galt left for the kitchen.

"Hope you slept well," said Mr. Galt as he scraped his bowl of breakfast.

"Very," I said with a smile. "Only the doves woke me and they were discreet."

He laughed. "They're all over the islands."

The air bounced as the swinging kitchen door opened. Ran followed his mother over the tiles to the terrace.

"Hi," he hailed me as I turned.

"Hi." I smiled. "I'm disgustingly late, I hear you've been up for hours."

43

"Not really," he said as he sat down. "Everything opens early here—and quits early. Even banks. Mum's got a great butcher but it takes time to butterfly a leg of lamb.

"Darling," interrupted Mrs. Galt, "roast beef or a nice hamburger?"

"Some of last night's rare beef would be delicious, Mum."

The silver bell was jangled again. And so it went.

As it turned out, the Kahala house belonged to the Galts too. They used it as a guest house or an escape from their dripping mountain climate. Ran's sister and brother-in-law lived down the Kahala lagoon a half-mile. I met them there late that afternoon. Ran's sister was a vivid girl, brimming with gay assurance, quick banter, and abiding love for her husband and three small children. Her husband had been Ran's roommate at Yale. He was unceremonious and had an impudent, ribald sense of humor. The three were great companions. He gave me one of the few nicknames I've ever had: Banana. A formalization of Annie Bananie. It must've knocked the possible perch out from under movie actress for him.

They welcomed me warmly. I entertained them with stories of Darryl Zanuck being shaved in a barber chair during cocktails at his house in Palm Springs; Sonny Tufts getting swacked in a deep sea diver's suit at a press photographer's fancy dress ball. It took four men to pry him out as he floundered to the men's room in desperation. And Clifton Webb doing an elegant imitation of the ballet, *Afternoon of a Faun,* one midnight while standing on my Chinese garden seat. His mustache never even twitched.

Bill and Dawn told wicked tales of Ran's wildness as a boy; to say nothing of escapades with a commendable variety of females. Made me wonder if I was simply the latest on the list of happenings. He might have read my mind because he cut the raillery short, saying, "I hate to break this up, but we're due down the beach, and I'm chef tonight!" He led the way down to the Galts'. The four of us waded in and out of the lagoon formed by Kahala's roving outer reef, the everpresent sea wind bellying loose clothes and flinging hair in our eyes.

Though he obviously loved it, the island seemed to make Ran

44

increasingly restless. A day or so later he said, "Let's take a picnic to Alii (Ah-lee-ee)."

"Where?"

"Mother and Dad's bungalow on the north side of Oahu. Should be great swimming this time of year."

"O.K. What do I bring?"

"Just a bathing suit, maybe a cotton sweater. Sometimes it can be cooler and stormy. You never know over there—it's different and a lot less *formal!*" he said with vague irritation. "I'll bring some steaks. Mother and Dad can join us for supper. Maybe we'll spend the night, although it's only an hour away."

It was a fascinating drive and showed me more than vestiges of what Hawaii used to be. Taro plantations, crazy-quilt huts on stilts in riots of flowers, clustered orange papayas on tall stalks under their leaf umbrellas. Careless, slow-moving people in bold colors and patterns. A town with four a's, Kaaawa. And to be alone was the best.

Later, at Alii, it struck me like the silence in a storm's eye as I washed lettuce for our lunch. I froze. He was cutting cheese beside me at the sink.

"Ran?"

"Yes?"

"I'm not sure you need what I have to give," I said, looking at him long and hard. He let go of the knife. I turned away and was staring at nothing. His arms came around me.

"What made you say that?"

I shrugged, suddenly discovering my throat had tightened down alarmingly. He turned me to face him. It was hard to look up.

"Why don't you let me worry about that," he stated with an impervious grin.

That afternoon as we walked a surf-beaten beach I asked about children.

"What about them?" he said, peering down into a tidal pool.

"Maybe I couldn't give you as many as you'd like. Your sister plans on five or six."

"How many did you have in mind?" he asked in mock dismay.

45

"That's not what I meant!" I replied vehemently. He stopped and studied me tenderly. "I wouldn't care if we didn't have any!" he said firmly, turned, and threw himself into the surf. I guessed he was conscious of my concern about our age difference and had again flicked it away like a thread on a sleeve.

I watched him lunging through the jelly-green waves. He was completely at home in that water. As restless as he was. No matter how much he loved this island, it confined him. Stamina, I mused. I could give him well-tried stamina in a new unpatterned life. My God, how I longed to help him pull away from measured patterns into open ocean! The pattern in my own life had begun to grate and wear thin. I'd worked and studied and worked and sweated for almost twenty-four years. I'd had unusual varieties of success. Our lives had been vastly different, but that wasn't all bad. Wasn't I resourceful enough to mine all the creative energy I needed from building a life with a beloved man and a beloved child in unknown patternless country? My Welsh forebears were pioneers—wasn't there one in me somewhere?

Shaking his wet hair, he was wandering out of the water; it flowed over his thighs in shining capes as his knees rose and fell. I heard my mother's voice fuming, "What will you do for intellectual stimulation way out there?"

Read! I thought an impatient answer. Read all the things I've—

He shouted to me, "Don't you want to swim again?" and paused, foam sizzling around his ankles.

"Right now!" I yelled and ran and dived in. To hell with my hair; looked like a wet bathmat anyway. I could slick it back tonight and stick plumeria blossoms in the rubber band. Side by side we concentrated on the next wave.

Hosing off the salt near the kitchen door, I asked casually, "Your father's retired, isn't he?"

"Yes. My grandfather started the Trust Company but Dad always hated it. He retired when he was only sixty."

Somehow I had to bring up a prickly and boring subject. Money. It was an oddly cloudy area. Ran never carried cash to speak of. I'd had to cash a check at the Brown Derby in Beverly

46

Hills to get us into a movie one night; and yet he'd bought Giro. And flew his own plane.

Alii was refreshingly informal. Lots of old bamboo furniture, matting on the rambling floors. Closets full of battered toys from Ran's sister's children; windows filmed with salt spray. A healthy, freewheeling place. The Galts arrived while I was swearing at the sticky stem of a plumeria that I couldn't push through the rubber band holding my wet hair. No time to talk now; nor should I mention what his mother'd said about money. This was our private business and I instinctively knew he'd bristle at her comment.

We all decided to stay the night and Ran and I strolled sleepily along starlit sand, both full of steak with bourbon sauce, a prized recipe of his mother's. I broke the silence sharply. "I want to ask you a very straight question."

He chuckled. He always laughed at me when I revved up and went full speed at any subject. "Fire away, madam."

"Ran, I'm serious," I replied quickly, planting my toes in the sand.

"You don't say?" He looked down at me with great amusement. A tree watching a squirrel worried about where to put her next nut.

"Could you support Katrina and me? You must've extended yourself greatly by buying Giro. Why should you take on new responsibilities now? You tell me all the things you want to do there; they all cost one devil of a lot of money." In spite of myself I was getting emotional, a doubtful refuge under stress. He was the opposite.

Calmly he put his hands on my shoulders, saying, "You're a worry wart."

"Yes," I admitted in a thick voice.

"Please don't be. I couldn't handle a household like Mum's but there's enough to handle you and me and Katrina and Giro." His hands lifted to smooth my hair. "You look very pretty," he murmured, "even though you've lost a blossom."

I reached a hand to the back of my head. "I knew that damned rubber band wouldn't hold."

We kissed with startling passion.

"Dearest, will you come to Giro? I leave day after tomorrow.

47

It would help so much to know you'll be down in a few weeks."

"But love," I answered, "I told you—I won't come unless I've decided. I won't let what Giro is or is not decide me. That isn't right. No one should marry some place. They should marry someone."

We kissed again and I knew that in the few hours ahead I would have to make the decision. For me, for him, and for my child.

Our last night we'd had another pleasant dinner with his parents and were finally alone on the long terrace listening to the falling water far below. Black and silver boulders were heaped against a backdrop of bamboo alive with wind.

"Anne, will you come to Giro?"

I leaned against him. We both felt far too much to think any more. What lodestars men and women can become to one another.

"Can you? In November?"

Lost in the tunnel of love, I heard only yes and more yes.

"Yes, Ran, if you really want me to."

We clung in passionate relief, and the balloon soared on.

In that one sentence I'd said I'd be his wife, had cut away years of personal ties, and canceled a career. He'd never insisted on the latter; quite the opposite, but I knew that the remoteness of Australia would finish it. I had become one of the billions of women who'd dropped their lives and followed love. Very old-fashioned, and very real.

I wasn't the only actress who'd done it, God knows. I vividly remembered a talented young girl I'd admired: Jane Bryan was her name. She'd left her career at its first crest and never looked back. Greer Garson had married and gone off to Santa Fe, New Mexico. Susan Hayward was living in Georgia with her lawyer husband. Others had done it. By that I mean left a career and married totally out of their world. But this was different. They had married established men in established lives. I'd said I'd go to an unknown place toward an uncharted life. Katrina would be ecstatic.

Our seeing each other had been a well-kept secret. I'd told only intimate friends, and as an actress the only intimate friends one dared have were veritable clams. What if I ap-

48

peared in Sydney? Even briefly? The press have itchy fingers. That's their business. If I dreaded that exposure, it would spell anathema to Ran. I'd warned him about that. But like a great many other things discussed between two people in thrall, unvarnished actuality vanishes before that heady fact.

"Ran?" I broke away from him gently.

"Yes, sweetheart."

"The press will be all over us like a tent the minute I step off that plane in Sydney."

"You really think so?"

"I know so. Look—United Artists wrote me asking if I'd be coming down for the premiere of *Summer of the Seventeenth Doll*. Cheapskates. They didn't even offer to pay my way. But I could say that was why I was there, and give them one day of publicity in Sydney to ease my conscience."

"Why not?" He agreed it was the perfect smokescreen.

Leaving him the next day wasn't as hard. November wasn't far off. And love had now grown from feverish to factual. Even so, longing for him rang me like an unanswered phone.

Jessamyn West says, "Love is not what you think." She's right. It's what you feel. But it's not enough to feel a marriage. You have to realize it.

4

Giro and the Muster

AS the plane landed in Sydney I emerged from my kennel in Limbo. After seventeen long hours in the air, I was furry-toothed and poached of eye at seven A.M. somebody's time, somewhere. I disembarked eagerly, searching for the balm of his particular face. Where was he? I peered around desperately. My God. Not there. Not anywhere. I paused, aghast, greeted only by Customs and the whir of the beady-eyed press beyond glass doors. Someone touched my elbow. I jumped in surprise and was handed a sterile envelope. Tearing it open I read, "Darling Anne, someone I know was in the waiting crowd. I pretended I was meeting a business friend and left. Call me. All my love, Ran," and a telephone number. Keep going, I thought, just keep going. Customs was quick. I pushed through the glass doors and the press rose like a Chinese New Year's dragon and had at me. I smiled and smiled and fenced and parried.

"Premiere of the picture I'd made there—" "No romance!" "*Heavens*, no! Just reacquainting myself with some *charming* Australian friends, just a *friendly* visit, just *fun!*"—and for God's sake let me out of here. A small knot of confused and delighted studio publicity men pushed through the crowd, hoping I had come for the opening—although of course they hadn't heard a word. The airline must have told them I was aboard. Hemming and hawing, I promised to do a day or so of publicity for the picture after happy "visits" to "friends" who'd been so *friendly* while I was there filming. Where? Oh, well, kind of all *over*—here and there. Bless them. They kindly bustled me into a studio car for deposit where? I frantically remembered Ran and I had decided on a just-in-case; the Australia Hotel.

Of course, there was no reservation of any kind. At quarter to eight in the morning with last night's makeup, conning one's way into a small room ("No, I wasn't sure how long I *was* staying.") "No *suite*, Miss Baxter?" "No, thanks!" Just a door I could shut, a phone, and a jigger of hemlock.

I was shown to a room done in exquisite contemporary nothingness, whose beds were still turned down for a night that had never come. Closing the door on the mystified well-wishers from publicity, I eyed the telephone. I was afraid to pick up the receiver. What if— I nursed disaster. When I did pick it up, Australia's irritatingly insistent double *BRRRing-BRRing! BRRing-BRRing!* at the other end of the line almost destroyed me. No answer at Ran's apartment in town. I hung up. How was I going to make a reservation 8,680 miles back without stir? I remember looking out that tall, grimy window, withered curtains moving in the November spring air, and crying without a sound. Moments later the phone rang.

"Where are you?" he said.

"What do you mean, where am I?" I choked.

"Dearest, I've been waiting for you since seven A.M. in that damned lobby."

"Oh, God."

"Where are you?"

"I'm in 209 and haven't even unwrapped the soap."

"Where are your bags?"

"Here."

Pause. "I'm coming up."

"OK." That American storm-port, OK.

I had exactly two minutes to despair over sat-in clothes and crumpled hair before he was there. What can I say? His presence would have toasted the dark side of the moon. We grabbed each other like life preservers. He smelled so good. Distilled outdoors. I was sticky from recent nerves and hours of travel. Distilled indoors. His hands still gripped my arms as he held me away.

51

"How in hell do we get out of here without a fracas?"

"Don't they have freight elevator, darling?"

"Fantastic." He grinned.

The freight elevator creaked and Ran's huge shoulders tossed my lead suitcases like handbags into a small station wagon with "Giro Pastoral Co. Pty. Ltd." written on the door. Pale blue. We didn't have to talk much after the initial shocks, and drove and drove.

Out of the maze of Sydney we sped, crossing inner harbors, the summer homes of Palm Beach, New South Wales, and on up the coast. The country smacked of California at every glance. Dry scrubby hills and cliffs; eucalyptus or gum trees in every conceivable variety feathered strange horizons with familiarity. They were messy but indestructible trees; hard-core bush Australians, I was to discover.

Lunch was stifling. Australia had its own kind of roadside luncheonette: very antiseptic, *lady* waitresses in rubber-soled shoes, food like stewed sawdust, and so quiet you couldn't talk. Terrible.

Skirting the industrial monotony of Newcastle, we left the beach-strewn coast and wound inland on narrow roads. The countryside was quilted with small, spareribbed farms. Sparse and characterless except for beautiful flowering gums and wattles (acacialike), all completely absorbing. I hardly noticed Worcester, Giro's nearest town; just another Pop. 2,500, one paved street and one hotel. The pavement stopped five miles out and the real road to Giro began.

Still a few fences and cattle guards, but fewer and even more pieced-together homesteads. Ran worried about the road's effect on me and I knew it, so I visibly relaxed and let him see I was enjoying the whole experience especially the three river crossings.

We slid through water flowing like corn syrup over wide ribbons of cement.

The river was utterly lovely, clean and rippling over stones and boulders. Lithe, Rapunzel-like willows softened every bank with grace and green. I fell in love with them at first sight. They were the simplest of Giro's gifts.

The road roughened and hardened; the ground swelled and

52

trees fell away as if the land had been stripped and chastened. Ran described the imported and exported Chinese labor gangs who'd cleared it for grazing, too much, too hard. Erosion was a creeping thing, since too many trees had been ring-barked, left to die, and either burned or abandoned to corpse the landscape with gray bodies.

My reverence for nature was offended.

"I hope Australians aren't as hard on people as they are on trees," I remarked uneasily.

"They're a bit tough on horses out here," Ran answered casually.

"We don't have to be, do we?"

"No." He smiled over at me.

"Good." I smiled back, linking eyes with him.

If I'd been beside a stranger I'd have been more than vaguely alarmed by what I'd seen. The land looked so harsh, so empty, so callous. Beside Ran I felt almost safe. He was not only far from a stranger, but American, not Australian, and that gave us a snug strongbox of shared attitudes. With him I felt I could greet the hostile unfamiliar without a qualm. Tiredness began to usurp my excitement. He must have seen my eyelids droop.

"Anne?" he said, nudging me gently, "we're coming up to Giro's boundary gate. It's still quite a way to the homestead, but Giro Station begins up there." He pointed ahead with his chin.

I snapped to attention and looked up eagerly as the little blue wagon struggled through young gum forest and up a groaning grade to Giro Gate. He cut the engine, jumped down, and moved to the tall wire gate. The silence was heavenly. I opened my door and stumbled out to listen. My legs had been bent so long they fizzed. It was unbelievably quiet. He stood at the opened gate, watching me, terribly pleased to see that this was as great a moment for me as it was for him.

"No brass band, but welcome to Giro," he said in a soft clear voice. We looked at each other for a long time and embraced as if the wolves of civilization were at our heels.

Giddy with anticipation and lack of sleep, I leaned forward as we bumped up the last hill above the homestead. We paused on the crest, I looked down, and there it was. My God, I thought, it's like a bunch of used toys. There were a few trees near the irregular center house. From our view the buildings were dwarfed to dice in vast treeless space. The landing strip cut a long sandy swath, marked by one lone tree beside it. We jounced over a badly eroded stretch going down a long boggy pasture. Ran opened the gate to the strip, drove through, and closed it.

"Had to fence the strip," he said, climbing back in. "The animals like to wander all over it." We sped down the strip past the tree and drove through the weeds to the right of the house.

"The manager lives right there." He pointed to a small cottage. "I'll move them down nearer the river someday."

Ran's mother and father welcomed us gaily. His mother's eyes twinkled. She'd met Giro. I hadn't. She looked perfectly turned out in faded blue cotton jacket and trousers possibly left over from a visit to Western Australia where Ran had bought land a few years before. Certain women have an easy talent for the right look at the right time. Never too much, never too little. My wardrobe had a tendency to veer one way or the other.

"Anne—you must be exhausted!" she exclaimed as I followed my bags into a dim little bedroom.

"Not really." I smiled over my shoulder. "Too excited."

Ran put down the bags. He seemed to fill the room just standing there. We beamed at each other.

"I can't believe I'm here, Ran."

"Neither can I." He laughed. "Your bath is in here." He opened the door to a little linoleum place. I noticed a brandnew pale blue sheepskin on the floor.

"Did you put that there for me?"

"Only costs a few more cents to go first class," he said with a flourish, looking at his watch. "Five thirty. We'll eat in about an hour. Meals aren't very thrilling around here but they have to be on time. The housekeeper runs the show." I stepped into his arms for a beautiful moment and he left me alone to unpack. Love may be temporary insanity, but what a glorious way to be nuts.

As I rushed to unpack I tried to collect my first impressions of Giro homestead. At first glance it had seemed so small I couldn't believe it. Not that I'd pictured a mansion, but that group of tacked-together crates huddled in tiny eddies of defunct shrubbery was a shock. It looked petered out, as if its slip were showing. But, so what? Didn't everybody's? That sagging veranda, the pinched cement walk that ended in an arbor matted with vines through which one surveyed miles of empty land. A bushy Victorian eyebrow cocked at Wyoming.

As I tried to unpack I suddenly realized there wasn't room for three-quarters of my things and decided to leave most of them in the suitcases. The small standing wardrobe was full. Nary a closet. Mental note number one.

Washed, and in fresh clothes, I wandered outdoors. The shabby-genteel yard spread away from two ancient orange trees, one half-naked in near death, and a good-looking tangerine. Each tree rose from a cemeterylike mound of earth bordered by stones like baked potatoes. Among dowdy stone-edged shrubs lurked a busticated out house, a collapsing grape lattice, and a screened cage about eight feet square.

"That was the old meathouse," called Ran as the veranda screen door banged behind him.

He joined me, and as we strolled I heard a commotion beyond some tall, ratty-looking trees.

"Do I hear sheep?"

"You do. Take a look in the tennis court."

"*Tennis court!*" I laughed in disbelief, and saw a high metal fence beyond the tree leaves. An erstwhile court was now a juicy mud pie full of milling sheep.

"They're killers," he said.

"Killers? Sheep?"

"You kill them, they don't kill you. Standard local joke for city types like you."

City type, my foot. I'd show him.

"When the weather's warm we change from beef to lamb. Keeps better. Let's go back and have a drink before supper."

"Sounds positively civilized," I replied, glad he didn't know all I was thinking.

Supper was boiled à la Australia except for dessert, which was passion fruit with boiled custard. We all chatted between entrances and exits of silent Mrs. Taggart, Ran's part-aborigine housekeeper. She scared me too.

Ran and the station hands were trekking up to the Myall

55

country on horseback early the next morning on a cattle drive. Would I be too tired to come? No, I would not, was my foolhardy answer. How could I refuse a long look at the rest of Giro. His mother and father were going up in the Land Rover.

After dinner his mother led me around what seemed a labyrinth of tiny rooms and sleeping porches. "But it looked so small!" I said, looking into room after room. She and I counted twenty-three, sans halls, more halls, and the skinny back veranda. All rooms to clean—I forgot to think.

As I followed her I suddenly wondered how much she knew. Had Ran told her I'd said yes? She'd said not a word about us as such. I felt like a welcome guest, no more. It bothered me.

As we came back to the two men sitting on the veranda, Ran searched my face for reactions.

"Would you like a short walk before we turn in?

"Love it." We strolled off together, all of me wondering what time it really was.

"I told you the house wasn't much."

I began to laugh. "Would the budget fall apart over a couple of closets?"

"I'll take it under advisement," he answered. "You've got to realize it's been a manager's residence," he explained eagerly. "You should've seen the mountain of beer and whiskey bottles out the back."

"Ran, please stop. Giro homestead is hardly the rest of my life—you are." I kissed him and added, "If I don't go to bed soon I'll fade away like an old soldier."

Later I lay in bed too tired to sleep. Why is everything always so different from what one expects?

No, I did not expect The Manse. I admit I'd had frequent flashes of convict labor cutting blocks of limestone, a dark cool cellar, and big old musty rooms. I couldn't help remembering Torumbarry's high, wide, and handsome space.

Walking in off the veranda was like sticking your head in a cardboard carton. Giro homestead at first glance defied me by default, not by what it was—by what it wasn't. I redecorated every wall, door, window, and floor as I looked. The collection of twenty-three boxes with a pleated iron hat went in and out of twenty periods and a hundred colors in a matter of moments.

Paint, hammers, and carpenters slashed, banged, and peopled it. Poor old Giro—it was never to feel a thing but my scruffy hands and greasy coats of off-white. I turned over, trying vainly to switch off my mind.

If the house looked like a hobo showing his teeth, the furnishings were a cheap sandwich filling between iron and boards. The living room sofa and chairs had succumbed to many a crushing behind and were belching stuffing. I never knew green could be so compelling. That green would have depressed Santa Claus. The not-quite-wall-to-wall carpets were splattered and exhausted bouquets of dirty pink flowers. All sorts of tottering little tables; a lumbering black city phone that didn't work, sporting a muscular cord; and in a room 13 x 16 there were three doors, two windows, and two pairs of French doors. With a 10½-foot ceiling, it reminded me of the boxes I used to punch holes in for my caterpillars. I sighed and tossed again.

Ran said the place had been born a cabin in 1901. A procession of occupants had tacked on room after room, letting the outside in. The only windows that looked outdoors were on sleeping porches, but they were banked with louvers in no-fair-peeking bathroom glass, shutting off any view of anything and probably inhaling stifling sticks of air in summer, freezing drafts in winter.

A cramped "fibro" closet in Ran's bedroom and two wardrobes stood around to complete storage. Any of the three would have upchucked from my Japanese kimonos alone. Meeting Giro was a reverberating collision.

I finally slept like lead, was rapped up at five thirty and staggered awake.

Years ago I'd filched a pair of blue jeans boiled to suede from Twentieth Century-Fox and a button-down blue shirt. Both were a speck too tight, but appropriate, or so I thought. My Texas hand-sewn boots were resplendent with leather and butterflies. It only took me six red-faced, blue-aired minutes to stuff me into them.

We were to muster a bunch of 300 heifers to the Myall, nineteen miles up to the top of the station's undulant valley. I'd been learning to ride in fits and starts since camp, motion pic-

57

tures had trained me further in a haphazard way, and I was game, but horses always flash the white of an eye as they crane to watch me mount. My legs are tough, but short, and I need a well-aimed leg-up.

She was whitish and freckled, and halfway through that arduous day I named her Sparkle Plenty. She had a neat walk that got places, a jagged trot, and a smooth canter. We got along fine. Australian horseflesh is thoroughbred, though an occasional draft horse is fed into that fine stream to give it heft. The station horses were admirably surefooted, at least Giro raised ones were. They plowed through rivers without a qualm, crunching over rocks and glancing shoes off underwater boulders.

I was caught by the difference in cattle-goading sounds between countries. I don't know what gauchos yell, never having been to the Pampas, but American cowboys use a ferocious falsetto "Kah-hah!" Australians use gruff talk, shrill whistles, and impressively bright dogs in two breeds—kelpies and blue heelers, heeler meaning they nip heels. I loved hearing them urge and cajole those acute, mangy-looking creatures.

"Naow—Beauty— Gaow gittah! Gittah naow—Git the caow girl—Gittah! Stope ah—stope ah naow!" And off a scruffy little bitch would run, well and truly flat-out, belly to the ground, ears laid back, flying over the stony hills, nipping savagely at heels, swerving and cussing them back to the sloppily moving group.

One man, one horse, and one or two good dogs, and the Australian stockman has a world and a living. He can herd thirty or forty erratic heifers alone.

On up the valley we went, leaning into the hills, hanging on for dear life, so hungry by ten thirty you didn't think you could bear it.

We reached a gate, Lemontree Gate, and paused for a bite and the inevitable tea. A fire lit from nothing, neck lamb chops—one aromatic bite per chop—and such a convenient handle to grasp, the perfect picnic protein. I tried not to remember killer sheep.

The scrubs of dogs whined softly at a polite distance at the

58

odor of meat. I couldn't resist and threw a couple of chops, which they gobbled, bone and all. I wished I'd had more.

Bread, thickly buttered. Australians butter and jam their slice of bread into an easy half-pound apiece. At the end, billy tea. Every stockman carries a quart-pot, or billy, in his saddle-bag. Encased in leather, it's no more than an oval (for saddle lie) smoked-blackened tin can with a lid. You fill it with river water, hang it on a stout stick up across the coals, and lay a green stick across it so as not to smoke the tea. When the water is boiling furiously, you throw in a fistful of tea and take it off the fire. After it has steeped for a good three minutes, you grab its handle, swing it in a great arc three or four times to shove the tea leaves to the bottom, and pour the best, strongest tea in the universe. Very heartening.

By three o'clock the plane trip began to tell on me, caressing me with exhaustion. I wandered in my excellent Australian saddle and Sparkle Plenty dragged along more or less under her own freckled power.

Just before the push to final pasture, Ran rode back once more to see how I was. I answered him with a look and a weary smile. He dismounted and, lifting me down, guided me to a white cedar tree, dead still in the afternoon heat, and said quietly, "Wait here. I wish I could wait with you, but we won't be long."

He kissed me. I watched him go, wondering why everybody didn't look like that in a faded blue shirt. A gentle man is a scarce animal, I thought drowsily, as eyelids met and I slid into warm red dark in the sun.

5

Curbstone Funeral:
A Picnic and a Lamb

THE next morning I could hardly stand on heart-shaped legs. Fortunately Ran had to get something unusual done to the Land Rover, so he took me with him to "Town." The Land Rover reminded me of a big dog, tough but friendly. I secretly nicknamed it Rover. Not to be cute. I'd been subject to animatism since childhood. Even my dresses had names. Big toes and scuffed shoes had faces—cars always. Perhaps too many children's stories with engines talking; or just an only child peopling her solo world. My first was a Maroon Buick named Beulah. She bucked at stoplights like a rocking horse. Ferdinand was next, a secondhand Cadillac coupe, black. Faultless creature. I cried when he had to go. I named an original model T-Bird after him. Good Time Charlie was a placid, sturdy station wagon, slow to anger and clearly a Christian Scientist. Nothing was ever wrong with him. Gorgeous, the Lincoln Continental, was a real witch, was towed five times in a month, once in the pouring rain and once in the Christmas rush. Goldilocks, secondhand Pontiac superwagon; high-powered but ate oil like an oilaholic. Crumby Buttons was an old roué of a Chevy—looked like a shark in drag and leaked his brake fluid on the sly. Stinker. Almost killed us coming out of Bel Air one day. Babar, or 2 Big as he's now licensed, is a well-trained Indian elephant. Four-door Cadillac. Dependable if obsolete. Our seven-year-old family pet as I write. We all have our secret vices.

It was good to sit down. Worcester was thirty-four miles away over that scenic dirt road, a road to rumple your kidneys and make you reach for handholds and a camera. Australians are not that familiar with mountains and thought the road was hair-raising. It didn't bother me because, knowing our Sierra Nevadas and Rockies, I figured a 5,000-foot mountain for a foothill. There were some precipitous drops, however, and never a fence, which gave a certain fillip to high curves. The willows trailed their veils on one side, then the other, as we forded the meandering river. Thick bottlebrush sprang after them, flaunting vermilion bristles, and gnarled wild lemons were a surprise. Nature runs around with her shoes off in Australia. Unkempt and unfettered, she's always pulling oddments out of her sock and tossing them about to see what'll happen. With that much space and so few people, she can experiment.

Ran explained that soft woods weren't indigenous and pines were only grown on purpose, but that there were false pines or she-oaks. I could never remember whether it was she-pines or false oaks. Upwards of 300 varieties of gums, cedar (white and red), mahogany for fence posts, sassafras. White cedar had a poisonous berry much disliked by farmers because it killed pigs. The magpies spat the seeds out into the pigpen, spelling curtains for the inmates.

And always the spangled river coiling and uncoiling beside us through heaving country that made me think of fat nudes asleep under camel's-hair robes. Bearded mountains rose on either side of Giro's mounded valley, indigo in distance. Flowing out from the groins above each mountain's thighs came a darker, more succulent green. Ran said they were the rain forests, and took a turn to show me.

We plunged into a jungle where light penetrated in shafts, and vines looped the loop through the trees.

"What are those, darling?" I cried, pointing to a tree with large heart-shaped leaves, some carmine colored.

"Stinging trees. As bad as nettles only bigger. Don't touch."

We lurched slowly into muddy ruts and roots, swaying from side to side. Suddenly a mossy black-red column shot up high out of the jungle roof to spread in the sun. Its base ran out on the earth in four or five thick spines for several feet.

"And that?"

"Rosewood."

"You mean like furniture?"

"Exactly."

Transfixed, I pictured the rich pink heart of those massive trunks, sliced, honed, and polished into the sophistication of antiques. Ridiculously out of place—like me? I smiled to myself.

Rover crawled back onto the dry road, whining plaintively and resumed his usual mazurka in disgust. Rover wasn't so hot in the rain forest. Next came dairy farmers, who don't give a hoot. Ran deplored their dilapidated farms: rusty iron flapping, new wire clawing decayed wood, peeling paint, and careless litter—animal, vegetable and mineral.

Past these blots on the bush escutcheon, to pavement and Worcester. To me most Australian country towns, Pop. 2,500, looked as if they'd flourished once: Pop. 5,000, business brisk, but things hadn't gone well, and what was left was sitting tiredly on a bench reviewing the lost race. This was not true, just an unkind thought.

One paved street and one hotel with its inevitable pub. Women weren't allowed, but I peeked in as we drove by. The interior was shiny white tile, as inviting as a men's room, which in a way it was. Three dry goods and grocery stores, a vegetable and fruit store or two, a smattering of hardware shops, two drugstores, a couple of variety-newsstands, and Dr. Burke's shingle on a rambling house.

Worcester's location was extremely beautiful. It lay beneath the shadows of an outcrop of sharp-toothed hills called the Worcester Buckets. Some lunch-hungry giant must have bitten chunks out of their tops, leaving a striking silhouette above colorless cluster of buildings.

Rover breathed his irritated sigh as we pulled into the garage, a quietly demented array of hubcaps, decaying vehicles, wrenches, screwdrivers, metal signs, reclining bikes, ratty-looking tires, rags, and men; all liberally frosted with oil and grease.

A man's chat in that eminently male world can last anywhere from one to twelve hours, but I didn't know that then. After forty minutes it got hot. After an hour it got hotter. I finally crept out of my seat for air and wandered disconsolately among the rubbish, feeling like the dented hubcap I saw tossed in a corner. I was suffering from a severe case of wilted ego. Another forty minutes later, I had sidled to the curb to sit in nervous dejection. I believe if I'd had an Australian pound or two on me and an ounce more courage, I'd have jumped ship and gone to Sydney. There was a train we'd passed at the tiny station. What was I doing sitting on a curbstone in this incredibly faraway half-horse town? Love, of course. But where was he? And why didn't he wonder about me? Hauling myself to my feet, I wandered out among the little fenced houses above the town, singing to myself in French, German, Spanish, Polish, and Burl Ives. Worcester had gone home to lunch. The dusty unpaved streets were deserted.

My stomach growled. I was thirsty, too. I wondered what would happen if I knocked on one of those curlicued aluminum screen doors and asked for a drink of water—in a French accent? The sun cooked my head as I sank once more to the curb. Forty pictures in six countries, seven plays in two, a drama trio in forty-two states, sundry narratives, speeches, boat christenings, plaques, statues, and certificates, radio and TV not counting—and here I was on an afterthought of a curbstone. Hungry. I thought of lying down for a nap. Maybe they'd pick me up for a—tramp? Not a vagrant; that was something else. Might be fun to see the inside of the Worcester jail—or was there one? The place didn't look exciting enough for a criminal.

I stretched out dreamily, hands behind my head, and tried to think what my life in Australia would be. Living here would prune me like an overgrown tree. Any American woman—certainly me. I sensed it would be as painful as unspoiling a child. What was hard to understand was just how spoiled I was. Perhaps even my necessities were luxuries here. Could I take it? For him, for a shared goal, for love—yes. Although for a moment there, it was a damned good thing I didn't have a penny on me. I just might have boarded that train. My ears pricked up at Rover's groan. I looked up and Ran looked down.

"Where in God's name have you been and what do you think you're doing?"

I slowly picked myself up and busily brushed dust off the back of my pants and sweater. "Around."

"Don't you want some lunch? It's almost two o'clock."

"Yes."

I climbed into the seat, a lesson learned. This was truly another world, this Australian world, and it fitted Ran like a glove. I now suspected it could chop me down to size.

In principle picnics are fun, including ants. My first picnic at Giro took place the day after Town, and was planned to perfection by my mother-in-law-to-be, chaperone extraordinaire. Ergo, I didn't even have to remember the salt. All was organized.

Ran had chosen a place across the river, and after several rearrangements of everybody and everything, off we went, and inside of five minutes were nicely stuck in the river. Rover was peculiarly apt at finding hidden boulders and running his abdomen onto them, leaving helpless wheels spinning like overturned beetles. It was really quite peaceful because there was nothing you could do but play island and wait, with knees drawn up out of the water coursing over the floorboards, while Ran walked back to the station and got the tractor to unglue you.

It was all very calm and interesting. I looked back at his mother and father, they looked at me, and we broke into helpless laughter. His father's laugh was especially infectious. We felt so silly hunched up out of the river flowing through beneath the seats. His father was a large man and simply couldn't fold himself in two for long. He pushed open the door and waded off to shore, soaked to the hips. Ran's mother's eyes danced as if life were always a new game to be played.

"Well," she said, smiling drily, "here we are!"

"We certainly are." I laughed. What a superior place for a private conversation, I thought. She and I always seemed to have our talks near water.

"You know I have said yes," I began, turning sideways in my seat to face her.

"I wasn't sure," she replied lightly. "What do you think of Giro?"

"In a funny way that's why I'm here. I wouldn't have come if our decision was based on a place instead of on us."

"I understand," she said with a quizzical smile. "But what *do* you think of it?"

I paused. With so much in my head it was hard to answer. "It needs closets."

We laughed again in singular rapport. She didn't seem to think it was at all strange Ran hadn't confided in them. He was in many ways a fiercely private, elusive being.

"Would you think I was totally mad if I painted the dining room?" I asked.

"Isn't it gloomy," she agreed.

"Maybe a nice fresh blue?"

"Anything would be an improvement, Anne. I'm sure Ran would approve," she replied in amusement.

"The country's so beautiful and I'm in love with the river and the willows!" I went on, glowing with enthusiasm.

"Did you see the Queensland firewheel tree?"

"Yes, it's gorgeous! Maybe I could cut some blossoming branches for the living room tonight. Bank them in corners—all red and orange and deep green!"

We chatted on about the house. I wanted to take measurements and she offered the elegant blue writing paper she'd brought down and said she'd help. We had a happy time sitting in the middle of that river. After all, we happened to love the same young man.

Eventually the tractor and various two-legged brawn arrived where Ran's father stood drying himself in the sun. I looked over my kneecaps down the river and caught sight of what looked like a miniature rowboat. One of the men shouted. Ran plunged through the current to us and stretched a dripping arm into the back of the back seat to extract a long gun. He grinned at me.

"Come on, Banana. You shoot." Bill's nickname had stuck.

"Shoot? Shoot what?"

"The duck! Look." He pointed to the baby rowboat.

"But—"

"Go on."

I hated guns. Over my protests about being a rank amateur, he put the cold stick in my hands. Squinting my eyes the way I'd faked in three Westerns, I pulled hard on the trigger. *Bang!* Eyes stil half shut, I winced. My collarbone was obviously bent.

"Here," he said grabbing the gun. *Bang!*

Men came storming into the water, churning individual

waves. Much unintelligible conversation and here came Ran, gun held aloft and carrying a wet bundle.

The tractor started up in a blue cloud, chains rattled, and we clutched our seats as out we lunged, a surfacing hippopotamus.

Hearty noises were again exchanged and Ran got in behind the wheel once more, this time in bare feet, quite sensibly, I thought.

The picnic spot was beside a smooth flow of river curtained with willows and bottlebrush. Lunch was laid out in small piles on flat rocks.

"Shall we have roast duck?" said Ran.

"Marvelous idea!" I burbled, not really tuned in.

"Fine. Want to pluck it?"

I blanched as he proffered me the damp bundle. All I could see was a tiny lolling head and sleepy eyes.

"Are you squeamish? Would you rather not?" he asked, concerned.

"No, no—happy to do it," I assured him, as a dissonant chord played me sharply.

The body was still warm. Its feathers were starting to dry in sticky points. Cradling it in frozen nonchalance, I sauntered stiffly to the riverbank, ostensibly to dispose of the feathers but actually to hide. I opened my hands to look. The complicated beauty of its coloring stunned me. Feeling numb, I ripped and jerked the feathers, which fell in soundless tufts on the pulpy bank. I pulled every single one, dreadfully nauseated, but like the would-be surgeon, I could scarcely faint at first blood.

The bird was naked now, skinny and pocked, dead as any murdered corpse, and so was I.

I brought it back to be trussed on a stick and cooked above the crackling fire. In minutes it was charred to a grimy kink and I felt years older and very tired. Ran said it tasted fishy from the river.

You are what you are. It's all a matter of emphasis, I suppose. Damn my highly colored viewpoints, anyway. The fact that they were highly colored was an irrevocable personal fact, with which I was never able to deal in Australia. Nor was exasperated Ran. He thought I wasted emotions. For me they were the essential tools of my profession and always at hand. He used his emotions as a last resort, like dipping into capital.

66

The fourth morning I awoke to a superb chorus. It had rained in the night and always, if they're around, the magpies deny their shrewish name and sing about it. Never have I heard anything like those pure intermingled chords; miniken pipe organs playing natural cantatas. Hearing is believing that delectable music. I didn't know then that they wreaked havoc in the corn, but I'd have forgiven them anything and planted fields of it to assure their golden throats after rain.

The sheep were still mired in their oozing tennis court, and Ran called me to come and see a newborn lamb tremulously finding its toothpick legs. We clung to the high fence and watched. The rags of afterbirth were still in evidence and the ewe stood quietly staring into space through her companions. The lamb gathered its legs together and moved to her like a mechanical toy improperly wound.

"It's trying to find her milk," Ran explained.

The lamb rocked uncertainly and stumbled toward its mother's flank. As it lifted its searching head almost within reach of her teats, the ewe turned sharply, leaving the befuddled creature facing, not a first breakfast, but Mama's dark eye.

Again the lamb made a heroic effort to reach the bag—again the ewe wheeled to avoid it.

In quick anger I pulled Ran's sleeve, saying, "What's the matter with her, Ran? Why doesn't she help it?"

"I don't know, dearest," he said. "Sometimes they're bad mothers—one reason I hate sheep."

She'd done it again.

"But can't we do something?" I implored. "The thing will starve to death if this keeps up."

"Don't worry. I'll keep an eye on it and if things aren't better tonight we'll take it out and feed it by hand."

I looked back, partially reassured, but confused by a newfound flaw in nature.

It grew cold and had rained again. Ran loomed up to the veranda about four o'clock looking so elegant I was speechless with admiration. A thick white sweater, beaten jeans shoved into knee-high heavy oiled boots, a flat, wide-brimmed digger hat and, draped over all of him like Napoleon's cape, a dryza-bone, or Australian stockman's raincoat. It was stiff and oily and had a high generous collar ending in a shoulder cape. The rest fell in folds to the ground. A glowing cigar completed the ravishing sight.

"How about a walk up the strip?" He grinned.

At that moment I would have said yes to anything he suggested, certainly a walk.

"I'll grab a sweater," I answered, smiling foolishly, glad he didn't know what I was thinking.

We strode through the thick wet grass and up onto the strip for the first of many such silent strolls. They made me feel as if I'd just quenched my thirst.

As we came back we saw the sheep being driven to their mud prison and Ran's expression cooled. They had trouble getting through the narrow-gate—pushing and shoving in heavy-breathing excitement. I looked eagerly for our lamb, but he was nowhere to be seen in the crush. Ran scanned the flock and looked increasingly stern.

"Where do you suppose it is?" I said with a worried expression.

"I'm not sure. Sometimes they trample the young ones getting in," he finished, avoiding my face.

"Oh, God," I whispered.

With that, the last dirty gray bottom forced itself through to the court and there it was, a twitching, broken toy.

I shook and stared.

Ran dashed to the house, plowed onto the veranda, and was back as I listened to his steps. He had a rifle on his arm. Out of the corner of my frozen eyes I saw it rise. The broken toy leaped once, twice, three times as the bullets struck it. It jerked once more and was still. Tears ran down my face as I turned to hide them, ashamed to feel so much.

Ran trudged back to the house ahead of me.

I never wept again at anything like that. Avoid it I did.

He said I'd made it harder for him—clearly I was wrong and he was right. What I felt was my affair. Showing what I felt became his affair and somehow that was wrong. I'd have to learn to lock a Pandora's box of powerful emotions. That would prune me harder than lack of luxury any day. Maybe I could learn his mother's attitude: life as a new game. But wasn't Giro awfully big for a game? And I was lousy at games. The idea of having to edit my emotions cowed me. But that was what I began to do. I began to shut up. Is there always a moment in love between a man and a woman when one or the other starts to omit important reactions? Catholics have the sin of omission. They are correct. I don't mean the little white lies that protect. I was mortally afraid of some of the emotions in that Pandora's box. There were infantile tantrums in there, suicidal depressions infested it, violence and craven fear bulged in corners.

But it was also rich with sexual passion: and a skinless actress. The raw spectrum of myself, Dead End Kids, et al. An explosion in that box could bring down the house.

I'd cleaned up some of my Dead End Kids for him to meet. He had a few of his own. But that day turned the key on mine, which I pocketed deep. If I dared to trot out an emotion now it'd better be edited and rehearsed. Otherwise I might lose him. And that was more frightening than what hid in any Pandora's box. I neglected to face the fact that my work had provided vital airings for the explosives inside. Acting had been healthy catharsis all my life. Never having been denied it, I took it for granted. Every aspect of Giro spelled openness. Our drawing together spelled love, not constriction. It never occurred to me that behind the word "edit" hid the word "amputate."

6

Mind Furnishing

I PAINTED the dining room, ceiling and all. Ran's mother encouraged the operation and even wielded an occasional brush. The shade of blue was unsettling, but as she'd said, anything helped.

In ten days Ran and I had ridden all over the station—up to faraway boundaries on horseback drenched in sudden rain; groaning over rocky hills and through rivers in Rover. I'd even made passable billy tea to my delight and his. The sharing of that wild, raw place was unforgettable and awakened the latent pioneer in us. Giro's remote reality seemed to weld us closer and closer. Our very separate worlds fell away as we stepped into Atlantis. We changed our days to suit the weather and ourselves.

He'd only skimmed Giro's mysteries since July. We meandered from discovery to discovery together. We were in cahoots in a mutiny against the cement, cardboard, and chatter of civilization. Even the fact Giro had to generate its own electricity seemed fun; seemed to heighten a feeling of independence. Although the generator noise certainly dented country evenings.

I came away from that rarefied atmosphere convinced that I could do it all. Transform the homestead. Fill it with books, flowers, music, and new friends. Armed with true love, energy, and hubris, nothing seemed impossible. Even a small chapel leaped into my mind. A stone house someday, with sweeping views. Katrina grown and married in her own place somewhere in those thousands of acres. And Ran's children-to-be of course. And all the books I'd never had time to read or music I'd never had time to play—he'd said my piano could come down. He'd catch me staring raptly into space and say, "OK. What wall just bit the dust? What room did you just redecorate?" He'd gibe at me fondly, knowing I had been as completely captured by Giro's challenge as he. I knew I'd have to squander myself to do it all, but I'd done that many times before for *less* reason and had always recouped. Purblind of ego, I soared on, and the whole of Giro took on an old master's glaze of permanent possibility. The homestead must have snickered behind its rusty screens.

Ran had a big twin-engine plane then, and flew me into Sydney. It was keenly satisfying to sit back and watch him perform something he loved to do, and did well. He was a damned good pilot.

I gave the studio the interview and appearances I'd promised and flew home in a daze. There was so much to do.

Marrying a man and going to live in Australia are an earthquake apiece; when they happen together, cataclysmic. Trumpets blared as I attacked headlong in a revolution dismembering one single private life and one child-sized one.

A houseful of furniture had to be deployed in Giro's patchwork of twenty-three rooms, a glittering wardrobe had to be mercilessly slashed to the knucklebones. My whole existence became a twenty-four-hour rummage through attic after mental attic. I crouched in the midst of everything I'd ever bought, been given, gotten stuck with, loved, worn, sat on, hung on a wall, cooked in, swum in, paraded in, lain on, read, enjoyed, collected, and worked for; like an anxious octopus, tentacles swarming and fingering, discarding and hoarding, tossing out, putting back, eyeing and sighing, burning and storing, giving away and regretting, sweeping clean; and pawing ruefully over the pile of trash in the corner. I lost a few tentacles in the process, but felt lighter for it. Books were the worst. I kept only art books, finely bound ones, or those that could stand the test of rereading. Katrina's panoply of toys, came too. She was to come later at the end of her school year.

Before leaving Giro I had scribbled measurements on sheet

after sheet of pale blue stationery while Ran's mother held the other end of the tape. A clever architect cousin deciphered a floor plan from those hieroglyphics, allowing me to shove and fit furniture and belongings all over Giro without a muscular qualm.

Opposite is the roofless plan of Giro as a kookaburra bird might have seen it.

If you can't read floor plans, I'm sorry. I hoped you could.

Why did I haul it all 8,680 miles, entailing gargantuan problems and expenses? Because I like my own things. I thought it would be an unnecessary strain on our new family to travel back and forth to Sydney, no mean jaunt, where home furnishings were an unknown grab bag anyway. Moreover, I hated all my excellent and comfortable things being buried alive in storage. I hated the thought of paying storage. Why not use my things to spark Giro into a fabulous island in the bush? I absolutely could not have lived in it for long the way it was, and Ran agreed.

As for my wardrobe, I'd been acting professionally since I was thirteen, I loved clothes, and never having been beautiful, I always expected them to counterfeit that illusion. My weight varied ten pounds. I was never really sure what to wear when and had every conceivable just-in-case; long, short, up to here, down to there, tinsel, no tinsel, prisms of color. Last and worst, I was penny-wise and had collected a greedy dressmaker's dream in to-be-altereds, save-for-laters, and good-fabric-may-come-back-in styles.

The whipped cream on this banana split was a $3,000 trousseau, something nobody ever needs, but brides often have one foot in the loony bin. Just to put me in with both feet, my pal Edith Head steered me straight at Juel Park's custom-made trap in Beverly Hills. The day I tiptoed over Miss Park's elegant gray threshold I realized I'd entered an intimate underworld literally whispering with silks, satins, and secrets. Juel had been designing underwear and night undress for famous ladies and probably a few gentlemen since the diamond-studded twenties. Norma Shearer, Carole Lombard, Marlene Dietrich, Betty Grable, Lana Turner, and Elizabeth Taylor, to name a few. Alongside those fables I felt like a brown wren among birds of plumage, but jolly Juel and I got along famously.

GALT RANCHO
GIRO STATION - AUSTRALIA

73

First, she talked me into a nude satin nightgown, saying Dietrich insisted it was sexiest. Pretty hard to refuse that one. Next, over even feebler protests, hot pink chiffon frosted with white lace over the breasts, under a snowy coin-dotted net peignoir with billowing sleeves, butterfly bow, and price. I breathed deeply and sat down. Had I said Ran liked blue? I had. Woe is me, I had. "Then why not," she chirruped, "a crystal-blue French satin and lace nightie, half-slip, bra, panties, and merry widow?" (A strapless, boned contraption peculiar to 1959.) She giggled. "Worn under your wedding dress there's your something blue!" Why not, indeed? And why not that same luscious quintet in white, Dietrich-nude, and lascivious black? Especially since the black merry widow would sport a small red heart with my initials hand-embroidered in teensy—I had to put my foot down—teensy lower-case script—"abg" appeared on absolutely everything in teensy lower-case script. Evidently Lana's and Liz's many trousseaux had also been relentlessly monogrammed, only far more grandly. I think Juel said EF was on everything twice intertwined when Elizabeth married Eddie Fisher.

Juel had made hundreds of her most gorgeous creations in utter secrecy, often filling simultaneous orders for a producer's wife and his latest side dish. Nor would she have batted one hair of one false eyelash. Juel was a juicy encyclopedia of Snappy Stories, but she never revealed current names or confidences. It plainly would have put her out of business. She hurriedly unrolled a pearly bolt of candlelight satin for the wedding-night gown and suggested a simple chiffon matching coat edged with coffee-colored lace. And how about a black chantilly lace peignoir over a black satin gown, nude crepe lining the lace over the bosom for the third anniversary, and a pistachio-green crepe de chine coat and gown because my hair had red lights, etc.? All I could do was nod. I finally found my voice and pleaded hoarsely for at least one washable nylon. Over a slightly curled lip she said, "Three—and I'll doll them up with a touch of lace and of course your monogram. Let's take your measurements," she sang brightly, flinging a tape under my armpits. And moments later a fast-molting brown wren tiptoed out in a daze.

74

The linens were in the same vein, different colored monograms on each room's sheets, special-order blanket covers, special-order blankets, special-order Hawaiian quilts; they never fit *any* bed. Since "Giro" means "Black Satin Bower Bird" (which no one's ever known except aborigine ghosts and Ran and me), I had the towels done from a picture in *Living Birds*, the blue-black male for Ran, the olive female for me. They were faithfully stitched by the talented fellows who made Marlene Dietrich's beaded show gowns.

Curtains were labeled as per each room and sent with their brass poles, rings, brackets, and instructions for hanging. Rugs were cut to fit, marked, and rolled for instant luxury.

Two unheard-of-sized beds in Australia, king and queen, were ordered and sent; nor could I resist lamps nor large linen lampshades nor anything for that matter. Resistance was nil. The trumpets were sounding and I leaped on my prey, Giro. I marched into antique stores and pounced. How could I possibly do without one witch doctor's purse? Two early American barber poles? One Spanish four-poster bed—with golden pineapples? Or one Ute war drum, one African elbow rest, one Wyoming coyote skin, two Chinese garden seats, and one Mexican Adam and Eve? And then there were my things. I was tough with myself about the Japanese screens and brought only one. Twelve feet of horses. Forgive me, Giro. You and me and our taffy-pull of ambivalence.

7

$\mathcal{T}$he $\mathcal{W}$edding

MY mother and father felt I was making the mistake of my life. It was a breach that would take many years to heal.

The moment I got back I was offered a picture called *Cimarron*, an ambitious remake of one made years before. Ran had wanted us to be married January first. *Cimarron* wouldn't finish until the first week in February. Another crucial decision. It was a good part in a huge picture. I badly needed the money to leave a clean slate behind me. Transport alone was astronomical.

We'd probed the career dilemma at length. Ran felt it would be a mistake to halt a profession I'd studied for and worked in for twenty-three years, and I knew you couldn't pursue a career 8,680 miles from its wellspring. Not to mention Broadway, 12,180 miles away. Impasse. I knew in my soul I'd have to be willing to relinquish even the possibility, whether he agreed or not. That was hard. But no one has any right to a marriage with one foot out the door. That was when I still thought being an actress implied something you did, not something you inherently were. He was wiser.

Knowing Ran's penchant for privacy, I'd repeatedly warned him about its inevitable invasion. I tried to explain that a relentless obligato plays beneath any film career. Exposure.

At the thin-skinned age of sixteen, when Twentieth Century-Fox met me and I it, the studio publicity department had trained its worldwide guns on my exposure.

I'd had an early inkling, and still smarted from the first words David O. Selznick ever spoke to me. I had come out to Hollywood at fifteen to make exhaustive tests for his and Mr. Hitchcock's *Rebecca*. Rooted in panic to Mr. Selznick's plush office carpet, I watched him descend on me, bend at the knees, peer glassily at my lips, which promptly froze shut, and say, "Lemme see your teeth!" Exposure *ne plus ultra*. Especially since a chipped front tooth had just been patched.

Fox ran a close second with my first session in the portrait gallery. Whispered words were bandied behind hands, and the publicity woman took me aside. Would I mind removing my bra? They'd stuffed my baby fat into a red and white rayon jersey creation for a cover shot. Desperately wanting to be sophisticated, I chirped, "Of course not!" but felt as if I'd been looted. I still have that shot somewhere. It appeared on the cover of *True Romances*. My red-waxed grin would have thrilled an undertaker, and what resembled two 150 watt bulbs protruded that cheap jersey. They thought it was great exposure. Theater doesn't cut the mustard. You can be a hit on Broadway in letters twenty feet high and cabbies will ask, "Whatcha doon in Noo Yawk, hey?" Film, not theater, is the acme of exposure.

Ran laughed at it all. One giant funny story. Fortunately, filmmaking had lost some zest in recent years under the pressure of swelling costs and television. The people I worked for were apt to be thin-lipped and short-tempered, poring over schedules and costs, sexing up simple scenes to "sell." Acting is the hardest play in the world. I revere it. It is more fun and more agonizing sweat than anything I've ever known. But I'd begun to feel square. It's a slap in the face to discover halfway through a picture you're the only thickwit who cares about the material at hand more than the paycheck.

Ran was bitterly disappointed about the postponement. The rebuke was silent but palpable. Letters stopped. Mail after mail bringing no letter from him rang me like a warning bell. Not that he'd been overtly angry, but a dangerous silent tide went out.

He came up just before New Year's. We were constrained for the first time. Work was so hard to explain. Too often outsiders thought you were just showing off and getting paid for it.

77

I was still shooting the film, but I never knew when. The director often wanted the entire cast dressed, made up, and ready from eight thirty on, freeing him to shoot anything anywhere. Late the night before was the earliest I'd ever known about the next day. Furthermore, an actors' strike was brewing, which threatened to string out the picture weeks past its finish date. I didn't mention that last dark cloud. Ran was disgusted that an expensive film was run like original chaos. Our agreement on that helped us join forces. Nothing like a common enemy to forge links.

"Darling, please try to understand," I begged. "I *had* to do this damned movie. I have to pay bills; I have to go to Giro without strings! As it is this house is now a mammoth problem. It must be sold, and I've barely bought it!" Reluctantly he understood, and love swept in like the tide that had ebbed.

New Year's Eve I'd made a late champagne supper and had just put a bunch of parsley down the disposal when he grasped my arms and gently bent them behind me. I felt a ring pushed over wet bits of parsley onto my finger as he kissed me into vertigo. I brought my hand around to behold an emerald flickering serenely in its dewy parsley frills. How did he know it was the only gem I've ever cared a bean about?

Of all the times in life, the week before your wedding begs for privacy. I was on the verge of shambles. Nor did my previous warnings help as the horror story that followed began to unreel.

First came a wild letter from a demented fan to whom I'd merely given an autograph three years before. The man had pursued me unmercifully by mail and phone. Obviously he was unbalanced, and our engagement announcement evidently crashed his scales. He threatened to stop the wedding, to shoot Ran, and wired Hedda Hopper and Louella Parsons to that effect. He brandished a pistol under my agent's nose, my dear friend Arthur Park, and was removed by the Beverly Hills police force. I suppose if he'd killed poor Arthur they'd have incarcerated him, but he didn't so they wouldn't. Next he sent a letter to Ran's mother and father with a snapshot of himself holding a very large baby, saying, "Has she told you about *us*?" It ended by saying he'd find me in Los Angeles, follow me to

Honolulu, etc., etc. Exposure was now hawking and spitting on my prized personal life.

A detective watched in the pine shadows outside the small engagement party I gave for Ran to meet old friends. *Cimarron*'s solicitous press corps carefully escorted us to the plane for Hawaii. The next morning his father arranged a visit to Honolulu's police chief, regarding surveillance of incoming boats and planes before we signed our marriage license to the smack of flashbulbs. I writhed with apologies for the whole mess.

Ran was stoic and everyone was kind and I wanted to bolt. The local papers and Australian press wanted all sorts of informal shots. We did the polite minimum but it was still an intrusion. Giro swam before us, a blessed mirage.

Edith Head was a longtime friend. She had kept our secret and designed the wedding in three shades of blue. It was to be very small. Since John Hodiak was no longer alive I was considered a widow and we were to be married in St. Andrews Episcopal Cathedral, whose bishop was a close friend of the Galts'.

My first wedding had been in Mother's garden. Feeling as they did my mother and father did not come to the second one. They did not dislike Ran. It was the idea of Australia they hated. Ran's mother offered their smaller house at Kahala for a wedding breakfast. The lanai, or glassed living room, opened onto a large center patio of grass and foliage. On the opposite side it slid open to a wide lawn bordered by the clumps of sea grape which masked the sandy edge of the lagoon. It was airy, pretty, and had lots of room for an extra-length table. Ran's favorite ginger blossoms were out of season so I chose water lilies for the table. Champagne was ordered, caterers alerted, and I had brought real maple sugar for a newfangled pancake pie I thought Ran might like.

J. Watson Webb, Jr., one of my oldest and dearest friends, had been invited by the Galts for the week before the wedding. He was staying there at the Galts' Kahala house. Watson had liked Ran immediately when they met in California and had agreed to stand in for my father. Watson helped me over some bad moments during those days. It seemed all wrong to be designing my wedding in the Galts' house, the Galts' church, using the Galts' florist. All of it. But Ran dearly wanted to be mar-

79

ried in the islands, and considering the emotional situation surrounding me it seemed the best solution. Ran's sister was to be my matron of honor; her husband Ran's best man; and Katrina couldn't wait to be flower girl. I'd even had a few wedding portraits taken of Katrina and me by the best photographer in the history of Hollywood, John Engstead, while Ran was in Australia. Nothing had been conventional, really. But neither were we. Neither was life. A convention was an assembly, wasn't it? We were certainly going to have one of those.

The wedding was at nine in the morning. Katrina worried that everyone would think Ran's sister was the bride. She looked beautifully fresh in Edith Head's French-blue mousseline de soie. Katrina wore robin's-egg blue and a halo of forget-me-nots. I looked nervous and pale in layers of both shades. There were only nine of us. My enduring friend, Watson, gave me away. His quiet face and tennis-muscled arm guided me to the altar. He knew I felt cast away like spindrift on the wave of the week gone by. Ran was narrow in the face from all his thousands of miles of travel. I wasn't sure I was there.

The cathedral rose on and on above us like a primeval forest. Ran's silvery silk tie gleamed in the dusky, cool light. What were we doing here all dressed up? I felt absurd and alone. But wasn't I? No family. His. One friend of mine, plus my kind secretary, Helen Freeman, who'd take Katrina to Kauai for a vacation while we went off for a few days. The organ stopped; silence held echoes at bay.

The bishop's deep voice asked us to speak directly to each other. I turned to Ran. His eyes blazed with candor, telling me I was there and why. Words came out weighted with the sum of two full lives and Katrina's brief one. As we embraced I realized he was tense as a phone wire, too, and forgot about myself. Arm in arm we turned to go and I saw my beautiful child smiling shyly over her bouquet. I stepped to her and pulled her close. How could I have felt lonely moments before? Music and voices broke into wavelets of sound. Outside the church clumps of beaming observers, many of them Oriental, clapped and murmured in delighted gusts.

Mrs. Galt looked stunning in emerald green and blue. Mr. Galt marshaled us all, wreathed in smiles. At windswept Kahala there was the traditional Hawaiian Queen Louisa's cake, which we'd all stirred for luck at the big house the afternoon before; and my lavender-and-white water lilies, curving down the long table, and the champagne I'd selected, and the maple sugar pancake pie. Watson snapped pictures without seeming to do so. He'd been a film editor at Fox for fourteen years, which is how I'd met him, and was expert. Dawn's children and Katrina played on the grass by the lagoon.

Bill's parents joined us. It was a gay party; filigreed with champagne toasts to the three of us, to Giro, to the future. Watson eyed me with a knowing look. He knew that the sunny morning was flawed by the aching absence of my family. So did Ran. Unspoken but there. The last to rise and give my toast, I directed it to Ran, raised my glass, and said, "If I can live what I feel, Giro will be the happiest place in the world," sat down, and blew my nose.

Pelted with laughter, emotion, and Rice Krispies, we drove off to the big house to change for our trip to the other side of the island, in accordance with a barbaric custom. The honeymoon.

Ran's family had loaned us Alii's many-bedroomed bungalow on the north edge of Oahu. He'd chosen a hidden bedroom for us with its own entrance. I'd deposited my bulging suitcase full of trousseau in a room off the living room, embarrassed to let him know its magnitude. That night, arrayed in all my finery, I tripped blindly over hummocks of grass trying to find my way through the dark to our nuptial couch. Wet sand and salt, soaked and stained candlelight chiffon, and coffee-colored lace. I remember cursing softly, vainly trying to wad my train up out of the dew, and hearing the surf on the reef shout like a far-off football crowd. Denim over bare skin would have been far more appropriate in the simplest of bedrooms and plainest of beds. Prophetic. I in my Astor's pet horse of a trousseau. He in apropos nothing.

We took quick trips to the outer islands, fished for marlin off Kona—it was all charming, but only marked time. Life would begin in Australia.

The wedding had been so intimate that Ran's mother gave a reception ten days later for 300 on their wedding anniversary. I don't know how, but I remembered all 300 names. There's a hint of politician in an actress.

Ran had a habit of large anger at nothing much. I'd asked him why on one of the trying days before the wedding. He'd smiled slightly, looked into distance, and said, "I have no obstacles." That left me speechless, having faced so many. Perhaps he meant Giro was the steeplechase he craved.

Katrina and I hugged goodbye; she'd had a windfall vacation in Hawaii during the wedding and after and had thoroughly enjoyed ditching school. Ran and I went to sea in a runcible pea-green sieve at one A.M. Honolulu time, March 1, 1960. It was a long way to Giro, our longed-for Nepenthe.

8

Arrival #2: Climate Terrible

WE arrived in Sydney on March 3 at nine A.M. Australian time, embarrassed by some of the clothes—seventeen bagsful. It was very, very hot and sunny, and our edges were severely deckled by the time they let us out of the plane, in which we had not slept for eleven hours.

The furnishings—O Understatement, I love you—took quite some time to arrive, but sundry lampshades had erroneously been sent air freight in 3 foot by 3 foot cartons at frightful cost. Customs were in a lather about us and our rocky stream of luggage, but that was nothing compared with those damned lampshades. Customs simply wouldn't believe that's what they were. A lampshade in Australia was Granny's rose silk hat and not much bigger than that. Ran gritted his teeth as I lamely chuckled my way into intricately sealed cartons. "See," I trebled, "ah—we makeum *big* in America." They all gathered around us in amazement and threw sympathy at Ran like peanuts.

Next came the press. I'd warned Ran they might greet us and hoped they'd forgotten. But not that much happened in Sydney with so theatrical a flavor, nor did Americans make migration to Australia a habit. The combination was fatal.

We innocently pushed our perspiring way out of Customs to land in a buzzing wasps' nest of press, cameras, gaping onlookers, tape recorders and, I registered dully, *My God*, TV. Ran turned livid and I plastered my damp face with a teeth-drying smile. Hell took a back seat as TV cameras trundled toward us.

Ran was cornered into an interview on camera about ranching in Australia, and when I dared a look at him with my plaster smile, he was frightening. His head seemed packed in dry ice. He spoke in a voice like sand on a windowpane; a stranger with the gas flame of murder in each glazed eye.

Somehow, trickles of warm fluid crawling around inside our clothes, we burrowed out to the kind face and car of a friend of Ran's. Muttering epithets too numerous to print, Ran squeezed in beside what was left of me and we drove off, the wasps tapping hungrily on the windows. They followed us, they stopped us, they hailed and hounded us, cameras dangling. Damn, damn, damn careers and newspapers. Damn them all. I could have expired under a pebble.

The luggage traveled to Ran's bachelor apartment in two cabs. The apartment was on a hill above Sydney's heavenly harbor, but was three flights up *after* you'd climbed a flight of stairs outside.

A crumpled mass of persona non grata, I struggled behind three men up those dingy stairways. The apartment was a moist little tomb, its eyes tight shut on the most superb view, which I let in at once. Even that shining sight only focused a room teeming with cabdrivers, husband purple and sweating, husband's friend carefully expressionless, and suitcase after suitcase after suitcase. It made your shins bark just to watch them tumble up.

I overheard the friend say through the crackle of sizable tips, "When are you going up to Giro?" Ran answered with a glance at his impressive flyer's watch, "Just as soon as *she* repacks."

She? My ears ricocheted. *She*?

They went on discussing the limited capacity of the plane and how long *she* would take as I wildly tried to remember where and in what, which was. It was decided I could take two bags plus a cosmetic case.

Looking what I desperately hoped was crisp and efficient, I opened the nearest bag. Ball gowns. Snap, snap. They marked time and concentrated on avoiding my red-faced pantings, crouchings, and snappings. Mumbling a wifely "Excuse me, dearest," I stumbled into the bedroom for hangers. The standing wardrobe was full. So were all six small drawers. Not an

84

inch of space for anything. Fighting an impulse to bawl, I pointed to two unopened bags and said they'd be perfect, hoped the
plane wouldn't sink, and wondered whether I'd chosen anything useful. Nor had I even had a chance to look at the apartment.

I never was able to undo the tangle of that terrible day. The
apartment was always fruity with clothes shoved into crushed
sandwiches of lace, satin, leather, and wool, and my eventual
allowance of three small drawers choked on fancy step-ins, evening bags, gloves, stockings, scarves, belts, etc., etc., three years
later. Whatever I needed in Sydney was at Giro and vice versa.
A vice, indeed.

After the curtains and blinds were pulled down on the jumble of costumes and child's blockhouse of suitcases, we lunched
on tepid oysters and wound through Sydney's hydra-headed
suburbs to the plane and Giro.

Ran had exchanged his twin-engined plane for a smaller single-engined one and I sat alongside him. Flying in a machine
that small was like spreading your arms and zooming. I liked it.
We landed about four in the afternoon. It had rained a little
and was still and gray. As the propeller whirred to a sudden
stop I could almost pet the silence. It had been noisy for such a
long time. Dogs barked in the distance, augmenting the hush. I
pointed my toes and slowly slipped out of my seat to the
ground. How good everything smelled. I sniffed ecstatically.

"Anne?" Ran called from the veranda. He seemed hurried.
"Where do you want these?" He had a suitcase in either hand.

"Wherever there's room, darling," I answered. He hesitated
a moment and disappeared into the room I'd occupied before.
There certainly wasn't room in his for anything but us.

I walked through wet stubble, carrying my cosmetic case, up
the cracked cement walk to the veranda screen door. New awnings, I noticed. Loud red and green stripes. Their newness
wasn't flattering. Ran had already changed to boots and I
watched him stride down the hall toward the kitchen, headed
for the side door exit. He heard me come in off the veranda
and turned in the dusk of the late afternoon house.

"See you later, sweetheart," he called as he banged out the
door and went across to the manager's cottage.

Standing in that boxful of shadows, I felt like a schoolteacher the first day of school; poised before bedlam. The magpies warbled. What exquisite music! A screen door slapped somewhere. I heard deliberate footsteps. The kitchen? The steps stopped.

"Mrs. Galt?"

"Yes?" I saw a ghostly figure behind the kitchen screen door.

"What time will you want to eat?" It was Mrs. Taggart, planted in the distant gloom.

Pick a time, any time, but say something firm, Mrs. Galt, warned an inner voice. "Six o'clock" I said.

"Right." She turned and vanished shutting yet another wooden door behind the screened one. Remarkable how many inside doors had been outside doors in years gone by.

Horribly early to eat, I thought, but this was the country. The generator was a capricious beast. What engine wasn't? I'd already learned it was to be used only after the last drop of daylight or for welding. No lights until six o'clock anyway. I'd wondered how Mrs. Taggart saw to cook. Maybe she glowed in the dark like fireflies. I walked into the little bedroom I'd stayed in before. Nothing had changed. Yet. I sat for a moment on the worn bedspread's cotton tufts. An upsurge of frustration welled. Damn it, Giro, I'll get you yet! I sighed. How empty the house felt, or was it me? No. I was uncomfortably full of unimportance. A chill ran down my spine. Had Giro subtly begun to cut me down to size?

The Baillieus gave a handsome party for us in Sydney a week later. I wore my short, simple wedding dress and tried again to remember reams of names. Flying back to Giro, dizzy with new faces, I dreamed of parties in the Giro I so wanted to create. Of course we were a trifle far away. Surely a solvable problem.

It's astounding how little I understood.

9

Not Fairs

WE married like anybody else; we started life together like anybody else; and were buried under an enormous pile of unsuspected unexpected.

Ran, as an American living in Australia, was a curiosity; an American actress was curiouser and curiouser; he and I together became Sore Thumbs.

After spasmodic attempts at "settling" we were dumbfounded by a steady stream of mail from all over Australia. Mr. and Mrs. Rudolf Golf, Mr. and Mrs. Anne Baxter, Mr. Roger Golt and Wife, Anne Basker, Movie Star, etc., etc. There were Warm Hearty Welcome letters and Good Luck Newly Married cards, but the lion's share asked us to open things.

March and April plunged Australia into paroxysms of town and country fairs; the countryside shouted in the throes of harvest. Some of the town names sounded absurd to me (our Indian names are just as peculiar, but I was *used* to Penobscot, Pottawatomi, or Massachusetts). Would we come please to the yearly celebration at Goondiwindi? or Wagga Wagga? Toowoomba would be delighted if—Bugilbone or Wollamumbi wishes you to. Fascinating.

Ran had decided we should do only a very few, and those limited to our area—open the town show at Mittleton, fifty miles east, and perhaps appear in Worcester at a fund-raising drive for the municipal swimming pool. His second mistake was a thorny one; both happened on the same day.

Small bush towns move with surprisingly heavy feet, and many letters and phone calls were necessary to make what should have been simple arrangements. Ran was to fly us to Mittleton at eleven in the morning and land on the golf course; they'd drive us to the fairgrounds for a look at exhibit halls and animals; then opening ceremonies in the grandstand, and fly back home early afternoon. Time for a nice breather before Worcester.

The Worcester arrangements included a visit to Giro by two members of the Shire Council, one of whom I'll call Salty Barleycorn, a classic rapscallion of a smalltown politico. Salty was a purist in cuspidor cupidity. I saw their dust as they caromed up the road and scuttled in to put on my other head, the one they wanted to see; which meant a complete face, gold jewelry, Thai silk shirt, slick trousers, and laughing repartee. I was a smash. Old snaggletoothed Salty hadn't seen eye shadow in the daytime for *all* seventy-four years. He flapped at his distended belly with both hands in leering, winking relish; he gloated over me like a prize pig, licking his lips as he gazed—imagining luscious chops? He gave a pompous speech about the pitiful youth of Worcester limping along with only a river to swim in, drank a big beer and, wheezing juicily, left with his silent sidekick.

The great day dawned wet and dangerously misty for flying. I got up at five thirty to roll my washed-last-night hair and finally decide what to wear. I chose a green suit, stacked leather heels, leather bag, a favorite French scarf, and knit leather gloves. When I got there the ladies were all in print silk, openwork white gloves, white shoes, and flowered hats. It was always that way. I was always underdone, like our meat.

After frantic phone calls from Mittleton: Could we fly out?—"Misty, but clearing . . . going to be fine later, positive . . ." they'd say. Ran took a chance and threaded the plane through wicked low clouds, ending in a hotshot landing on the nice green grass in a fine steady rain. He really was a superb bush pilot. Our arrival was a sensation. On we charged into group after group of people. All very, very kind, dispensing tape recordings, photographs, and interviews in the mud-printed clubhouse. My teeth were already dry from smiling, an occupational hazard I knew well. Harassed Ran was already looking grim.

The fair took place around a white-fenced racetrack, no grandstand, just bleachers on one side and people massed at the fence. The other exhibits (besides us) were in halls, stalls, and tents. Lunch was in a long wooden barracks, and the sun came out to cook us during it. I was suddenly made of wet felt and thought of hiding out in a ladies' room to get away from those hundreds of perforating eyes, but there wasn't one handy.

There are two parallel lines of conversation at Australian country gatherings—prescribed female, and exclusively male. Not counting the one *you* may be having, which in my foreigner's case, was heterosexual and tended to set me aside like a dinner salad. I began to play a game. One ear was tuned in on the ladies' pastel pavane, the other dialed in on the men. It required well-honed concentration, but I was trained to it and grew proficient, in self-preservation. Talk's cheap in America, but a precious item in the Australian bush. It's a lifeline and one treads water in a Sargasso Sea of dailiness waiting to grasp it. Female talk was simply more seaweed, the lifeline appeared to be exclusively male. How can a bottled peach compete with animals, or inventions, or station catastrophe? But I sensed I was an unwelcome visitor in the men's conversational kiva—any woman was.

I studied the big raw beef of a man opposite me. He had pale, rapacious eyes, moonstones set in cherry leather. His harsh jocularity with the men contrasted sharply with bored grunts at the wife, or the women. He wasn't sure whether he should lump me with the ladies or with the hot numbers he knew in Sydney.

Loose custard, fruit, jello, ice cream, and tea of iron arrived for dessert. Afterward all of us ladies were led through warm mud to the Arts, Crafts, and Food Pavilion, and the men surrounded Ran for a trip to the machinery and animals.

I was awed and touched to see display after display of infinitely painstaking work. Hours and hours and loving care expended lavishly on bottle after bottle of fruit. I could see those ladies miles from anywhere tenderly lifting boiled fruit from

89

kettle to jar, dreaming of glorious recognition. They must have used forceps. How else could they have managed a cherry in the pineapple slice at the bottom?

Homage to cross-stitched dresser scarves and crocheted baby sets, beribboned gladiolas, delphiniums, roses, wilting in the heat; ornately decorated cakes, meringues, and drying biscuits sitting on blue satin with "First Prize" in golden letters. I fell in loving respect with the Australian countrywoman standing in the sawdust of that ugly pavilion. Pin those prizes on your heart, dear Madam; you've earned them and many more, because I know now what else you do. Many times hoping only for a lofty pat on the head or peck on the cheek or another pair of plastic earrings as the men saunter off together.

The sun had gone when we emerged, and a heavy rain began to pour. Various men with badges appeared with umbrellas and dry-za-bones to throw over Ran and me as we slogged to the race track.

In its center was a heavyweight flattop truck, on which perched slatted wooden chairs and a microphone. People were pasted thickly against the white rail beyond the track, now puddling with rain, some hanging out of pickup trucks and cars, some holding newspaper shelters, some holding babies under sparse trees.

The mike whined in protest as we were boosted onto the truck to sit like soggy chickens. "Just a few words!" That's what they always say, "Just a few words!" But they'd better be the right ones. I agreed heartily with "few." The applause started, then paused as we sat. Raw Beef throttled the mike in a red fist and shouted a five-minute introduction: "*Privilege* . . . Pleasure . . . We all know who . . . Glad to have our great yearly event . . . Australia's best . . . and . . . needs no introduction." Five minutes is a long, long time. Somebody punched Ran and hissed, "You first." He looked taut— "Mr. Randolph Galt." (Applause)

Ran got up and spoke slowly, clearly; said every word I'd thought of saying; looked ill, and sat down, eyes glittering with relief. Mr. Beef collared the mike again. Only two minutes this time. Rain blackened my shoes, my bag, my spirits.

Here it comes: "Needs no introduction—here she *is*!" Applause and whistles. As I thanked again for a welcome to a new life in a new land, etc., I saw Ran leaning over and two badges whispering eagerly. I heard a horrified "*What?*" from Ran and hurriedly finished my few words.

Ran looked a book at me as they explained to me as well, that since they'd promised everybody a good look at us, would we be driven around the track so they all could? What does one say to all those hungry eyes?

Never could I describe that ride. Clinging to those rickety seats, feeling my new husband's raped dignity emanating like steam, it might as well have been a tumbril, and I prayed for a well-oiled guillotine. My teeth were the only dry place on me, though why they didn't get rained on I'll never know.

The flight home was perilous and late. We could barely see the strip at five fifteen.

As we dragged onto the veranda I made fervent apologies.

"Ran, I can't begin to tell you how sorry I am about this whole blasted thing. It's all my fault and it's put you through hell!"

"Never mind. I'm the one who said yes," he replied tersely, tearing off soaked clothes and shoes.

"But I knew more about what it could be like. I should have stopped you and it never would have happened if I didn't have two heads."

"Look, darling, it's too late now. Forget it, and if we don't hurry we'll never make Worcester. The road'll be a bloody mess, and it's an hour and a half flat-out."

"Can't we call them—say the river's up or something?"

"No. Go on and change."

Miserable, inwardly kicking my exposure to a pulp, I tore into dry clothes. I replastered my face and stuck eyelashes on it; screwed up lank hair into a fancy cowpat, threw on short red chiffon, satin shoes, my white mink cape, cut two or three triangles of yellow cheese, and climbed into Rover.

We were due at seven. We hardly spoke; too much to say and no time to say it. Talk is pointless in the hub of a horrible mistake. The night was black and dripping. Geysers of mud rose in our slimy wake; there were seven gates to open and shut; my ankles wore spats.

Ran drove like one possessed. Mad at circumstance, at me, at

91

himself, at Salty Barleycorn, at exposure such as he'd never known. We skidded half miles on the bias, we switched Rover's tail like a horse who hates flies, we went through swollen river crossings with eagle wings of water—one hell of a trip.

A rendezvous three miles from town yielded no one. After twenty fuming minutes and swallowed cheese, a car rolled up full of fresh faces and jollity, looking askance at mud-caked Rover. It was decided we should wedge ourselves into their car for the arrival. We were deposited in a cement building whose floor looked as if chocolate syrup had been danced on, while Salty, in dazzling floodlights, introduced us.

Salty was far more lurid than Mr. Beef: "Privilege . . . Pleasure . . . Hollywood . . . Australia . . . Needs no introduction . . . Hollywood in our midst . . . To think that . . . Worcester . . . swimming pool . . . Australia . . . Welcome . . . All the way from Hollywood . . . Worcester . . . America . . . Randolph Galt . . . Large landowner— cattle station—municipal swimming pool . . ."

My eyelashes itched.

"Like you to meet Mr. and Mrs. Randolph Galt!"

Up we climbed onto Salty's makeshift platform, braving blinding lights, rain, and a sea of upturned faces. They'd come from thirty miles in every direction. Children who should have been in bed polka-dotted the crowd. To a roar of applause and whistles Ran was hugged to the microphone by the hangman. All was silent. He started to speak in clear, slow tones, but to our toe-curling dismay there was a whale of an echo.

"I'm very glad—*I'mveryglad*—"

Ran paused, wondering whether it would happen again.

"To be here with—*Tobeherewith*—

"So many—*Somany*—"

It was a midget crucifixion. Ran was so shaken by this incubus of sound he couldn't stop. Word after word fell out and reverberated. At last he found a key word and got off. Applause.

As he sank to his seat jaunty with relief, he jabbed me with an elbow. "Keep it simple," he admonished with a ventriloquist's stony lips.

I stared back through my threadbare sense of humor and

92

recognized a newly minted speechmaker. Ran was drunk with the heady wine of bitter experience.

Salty sprayed again through those ratchet teeth: "Hollywood . . . Needs no introduction . . . Very graciously . . . Our cause . . . Here she is!"

I kept it simple all right, but no one cared. Every eye was busy gobbling up white mink and scarlet chiffon and their one and only glimpse of a movie actress; what was left of her.

They left us at our chariot with beaming thanks. The night had freshened and was starry, and after endless miles of gumbo and gates, we mutely fell into bed, each other's arms, and Giro's blessed anonymity. Nirvana.

10

Projects X, Y and Z

AFTER our disastrous honeymoon with community projects, I hurled my battalion of one into Projects X, Y and Z. All of which were designed to prepare Giro for the onslaught of things slated to arrive in May. To say nothing of Katrina in June.

Project X meant all floors bared and/or scrubbed. Some wore peeling linoleum; some were cheap, unfinished flooring; the rest, six in all, were covered with almost wall to wall carpeting whose sleazy patterns were all but obliterated with years of dirt. The "almost" had left an inch-and-one-half trench around each edge, a humdinger of a catchall for mashed flies and other insect husks, powdered mouse droppings, and human litter. No tack strip. The carpets had been pinioned to the floors with thousands of nails.

Grasping a honey of a three-foot crowbar, I had at it, and for days became a hunchbacked predatory animal with a long iron snout, a voracious nail-eater with snarled, thatched head. It was acutely soul enriching to do something at once so *destructive* and *constructive*.

I could take the puffs and clouds of desiccated animals, minerals, and insects, but to my disgust all rugs had been nailed through a matted mass that seemed made of gummy hair combings and which clung in tufts to the rows of nails. Most of the time the rotten carpeting tore away, leaving a picket fence of hairy nails. Giro homestead, my tramp, had rusty teeth.

94

Once rug tatters were up and dragged foot by moldering foot and out-of-doors, I had to go back for the fine work of extracting nails. The heads came off. I threw the hammer across the room and went for a "cuppa."

I vividly remember giving Mrs. Taggart wide berth. I'd heard all the stories about the bachelor's housekeeper walking out as the bride is carried in. Beyond that, Jean Taggart commanded her own peculiar awe. That day, as I stepped into her kitchen, pouring with sweat, she remarked evenly, "You're going to kill yourself." She left the "you damned fool" unsaid and handed me a marvelously sugary "cuppa" cha (tea), for which I thanked her. Jean's cuppas were always heartening—perhaps because they and she were surprisingly strong.

I watched her through the steam from my cup. She was a quarter Aborigine, or so I had been told in undertones, which may have accounted for the total absence of pink in her skin, a certain rich liquidity of eye, and full, flat, lavender lips. There was an aura of quiet sex about her that gave the merry ha-ha to shapeless dresses. I never saw her in a flap. She had swift inner rhythm, but never hurried; and when she looked at me I thought I heard a typewriter.

No one knew much about her origins. Her husband, though I doubt Jean had bothered about such ceremonies, worked for the station. Jack had blue eyes and sandy hair. He was caved-in thin, and wore rimless glasses. He'd been hurt driving the tractor and was convalescing on the government; or rather on the floor of the back veranda hour after hour, day after day, watching the sun age, minutely rolling cigarette after cigarette. I never saw a man do utterly nothing with such absorption. She'd bring him his supper, but noon after noon he'd walk into the kitchen and make himself the same sandwich without a word. It took him a good half hour and was done as meticulously as his fags. Paper-thin slices of onion, one, two, three, four; thick bread slices heavily buttered; medium thin slices of tomato, one, two, three, four; and the shaking on of the salt was a snail-slow, bent-over ritual. It fascinated me, all of it. How little they talked, those two, but how perennial their relationship.

Jean's emotions stayed locked away. I only knew what she was the opposite of. Jovial, for instance. Or cute. But she could

95

hate. She hated the manager and, I heard, had attacked him once with reptilian venom. He never *ever* spoke to her.

Setting down my empty cup with a sigh and daring to bleat mournfully about decapitated nails, which disintegrated me, she penetrated me with a long look. "Hang on," she said.

As usual Jack was spread-eagled on the back veranda. With an earsplitting "JACK!" she guided him slowly in, put a pair of pliers in his hand, and Jack sat quietly in my wake, yanking nails out by the roots, an expressionless country dentist.

The "lino" came up like peeling sunburn. It had its own share of archaic filth and bug morgue; fast work, though, and "very fun," as Katrina would say.

The living room held buried treasure. Beneath the moribund carpeting lay Giro's birth certificate. Here were the honest ten-inch cedar boards of Giro's original cabin, built some seventy-five years before. It had become the kitchen as Giro aged; blue and white lino in time-honored stencil formed an old-fashioned island in the center. I was thrilled and rubbed my hands at the thought of my creamy Greek Astrakhan rug on wine-dark boards. Of course the lino would have to go.

What they used for glue in 1900 I do not know. Four broken paring knives, two gallons of scorching paint thinner, sixty kettles of boiling water, six pairs of gloves, and one and a half days later I had doggedly taken off a strip ten feet by eighteen inches, just enough so my rug would hide the rest. I quit and went back to work on rugs or scrubbing floors.

Hard as it was, that kind of work was amazingly gratifying. It had a tremendous purpose; to make a home for my husband against all odds, to serve as healthy penance for all the hue and cry my career had dragged into our marriage. God knows the movie-star label burned away like my calories. Ran never knew, but the metamorphosis of Giro hid a tacit apology behind its back.

He'd come in at odd moments to battle with the ancient phone. The manager gave orders within the station, but the outside world was Ran's problem. The herd was sorely in need of new blood; bulls had to be found at a price; barren cows culled and sold, or butchered to feed the station. I sensed he had as much to learn as I did; and no time. Frost was on its way.

He'd come in unexpectedly and catch me in some odd room looking like a dirty pirate. We laughed at each other as I saw his boots and straightened up, out of breath.

"Take it easy," he chided. "You'll pull the floors up with the rugs!"

"Listen, darling," I wheezed, gasping for breath, shoving ropes of hair off a sticky forehead. "I know you'd thrive on Henry Mancini once a month, but I really am starved for music. We've got the little portable machine and I've got five or six records with me. Could I, please, only an hour a day, I promise?"

"You mean you want the generator?" he interrupted, neatly arranging his face.

"Only an hour a day! To paint to?"

"It's not in good shape." He looked dubious. "We're going to have to get a new one. Damn it, expensive."

"Oh, OK."

"Tell you what. Machinery's breaking down all the time. We need electricity for the welder. We'll let you have it whenever possible."

"Terrific." I grinned. "Thanks, love."

"I have to fly out and see some cattle for a few days."

"Sure. Could you possibly order me a few gallons of off-white from Yates and Twomey in Worcester before you go?" I thought I saw his eyes flash dollar signs. It was new for me to ask someone else to buy me anything. I'd always paid my own way.

"How many?" he asked, suddenly cautious.

"Oh—five?" I had no idea how much I needed.

"That's a lot of paint."

"But one coat won't do a lot of places, Ran. And some four-inch brushes? And thinner?"

He looked preoccupied.

"You're sure you need that much?"

"I don't see how I can do with less. Maybe four for a start and then if I need more—"

"OK. Four," he replied quickly.

"Thanks very much, darling!" I would have ordered six and

97

kept any leftovers. Opposite attitudes. Or was Giro already in tight straits? Money again. Or was it yet?

The phone rang; loooong–short, loooong–short. He hurried to answer and I overheard a conversation with our only neighbor, ten miles away, Tom Biddeford. He'd become a kind of pragmatic mentor in the first months Ran was at Giro.

"Tom, what kind of seed you think we ought to have for the lucerne? George thinks—" And he closed the office door. George Peckett was Ran's all-hallowed cattle broker. I bent over my crowbar again and thought what a dead loss a Yale degree was in the bush. But then, so was Stanislavski's method. What did it matter? We were into it now up to our eyebrows.

As I lunged at the floor yet again, I smiled to myself— God, that man can light me like a candle or snuff me, just like that!

So as my extravagant salary I wheedled the engine for music to paint to. Bach beat a pulsing morning hoedown, Scarlatti bridled an afternoon hour; or Bartok quartets when cranky. What earned bliss.

You can cover absolutely anything save a corrupt soul with enough coats of off-white. Giro wasn't worth a surgical facelift, so like lots of women I just applied another coat of paint. And another. And another.

My war with Australian wallboard, or fibro, started with Project Y. Fibro is used for the same reason corrugated iron is in the bush. It's cheap, cheap to transport, and a medium-trained chimpanzee can bang up walls, ceilings, and doors with wood strips, a hammer and a mouthful of nails. Most walls and ceilings at Giro were made this way and precluded paint rollers. I don't guarantee the monkey. Katrina's room-to-be and the kitchen were rough-sawn one-and-one-half-inch boards, hers varnished nastily in unprintable brown. The hall walls and doors were outdoor slabs of cedar and had been thickly repainted off-white for years. They were chipping like a bad manicure.

Fibro resisted paint to such an extent that my technique became exactly like slapping someone in the face from side to side with occasional pokes in the eye. That last in paint parlance is called stippling, a pantywaist word for what I was doing. And

98

no matter what I did, every brushstroke showed like a pattern in old Irish damask. Another coat, sometimes three. How I loathed fibro! Couldn't put a nail in it to hang a picture; it split like lightning; there'd be jagged holes covered with brown paper and tape against winter cold. You could put a foot through in half a second but never a nail.

Ceilings meant being precariously perched, melting like cheap wax, and the fumes in those box-tight rooms sent my nostrils cowering. One night, early in Project Y, I decoded a new ache from among the recent throng: my hands. Oh, God, I worried! Bloody arthritis is setting in. Thirty-seven years old, May 7, no chicken, quite right, but arthritis! Four-inch brushitis it was, but flamboyantly worth it.

A rising tide of clown white poured over Giro. Higher and higher it lapped, drowning trillions of flyspecks, veils of dirt, and sticky whorls of cobwebs. I left it viscous enough to fill nicks, pits, and gouges; like frosting a mammoth cake. I knew what was underneath, but like the rats above and the snakes below, what you don't see you don't have to look at. From the smell, I'm sure paint is antiseptic as well. It almost kayoed me.

Ran and the manager were hounded by murderous days and nights of plowing for fifty acres of alfalfa, "lucerne" they called it. They plowed in shifts far into the night, the tractor light cutting a path through the dark in a race against frost.

I'd heard ominous angry words out the back. Something was brewing between the Taggarts. I never knew what went on, but in the midst of painting they moved out in a secondhand trailer. No visible hard feelings. I suspected ingrained restlessness and a final searing contretemps with the manager.

Mrs. Taggart came to say good-bye, immersed in private dignity. I really hadn't expected her to.

"Mrs. Taggart?"

"Yes?"

"Would you like to have one of my records?"

She watched me, not a flicker in her eye. "I like that sad one."

I knew the one she meant. She'd mentioned it before. "You mean the Scarlatti, I think. Just a minute." I ran to my room

99

and found it. It was an album called *Songs for My True Love.* Salli Terri and Laurindo Almeida and a flute. I ran back. "Here. Enjoy it," I said.

She smiled briefly, as if to say, "You poor slob, why are you doing this?"

"Thanks." She turned her back and the door slapped with finality.

I could see her swinging unhurriedly toward the jerrybuilt trailer they'd bought for their trek. Jack gunned the engine on a car of uncertain lineage and the dust powdered their wake. I was glad I had, in that instant, touched the mystery of her world.

Surfacing out of sleep at midnight, I'd see a man carved out of dust with white spaces for eyes treading wearily to a shower, and would wonder uneasily what kind of elbow grease would rescue those clothes now that Jean Taggart had gone.

I fell apart after twelve rooms and two halls. Some picayune form of pneumonia from being bathed in perspiration in the hot winds of April. I fell into bed nursing a temperature of 103°. Cough syrup came out with the mail in an unlabeled bottle. When uncorked, the clear goo gave off a flattening whiff of chloroform. Just what I needed. But it kept coming back up in the shape of the spoon. Three days later I went back to my paintbrush, coughing like a sick leopard, until Ran called a halt and found a Mr. Bates to finish the job.

Mr. Bates is pronounced B-i-t-e-s. Aussie is not an accent, it is more like the spike in a hot punch. The less formal education, the more spike. Mr. Bates spoke it so well I'd get lost in *how* he was saying something rather than what he said. I became an indefatigable hunter trying to tie down that savory kangaroo: the sound of Aussie. "Nile" for "nail," "mile" for "mail," were a snap. The rest wasn't that easy. There was a fascinating lack of cadence—like doing a snake-hips rhumba with no shoulders moving. Those gravel monotones captured the freedom ring of hard-bitten insouciance.

Remember Harry Belafonte's calypso tune "Oh, My Marianne"? That's what Mr. Bates sang, whistled, and hummed while he painted the rest of Giro. Only when he sang it, accompanied by hollow brush thumps and beats on fibro it went like this: "Haow, Haow, Haow, Maw Mirrienne, Haow, Haow, Haow, Maw Mirrienne." He wore coveralls the texture and color of diploma sheepskin. They were sugared with slabs of paint, and as he walked down the hall he sounded like someone reading the Sunday papers. You know those deliberate fish in city aquariums who, as they propel themselves toward you, fix you with a particular eye? When I told Mr. Bates I wanted the ceilings the same color as the walls ("You see, these rooms are *masonite boxes*, Mr. Bates! We must paint them *out!*") he would float, fin-still on his side of the glass, and fix me. "The Biddefords had everything a different color," he would counter.

After I had not convinced him at great and fervent length exactly what I wanted, just as passionately did he not convince me that I was crackers, thereby establishing the perfect relationship between painter and paintee. And the fish moseyed away from the window.

Sage green to match a rug sample for Anybody's (our guest room) was a crisis. The gallon can opened on a cross between pea and pippin, white alone wouldn't budge it—it just got soupier. After watching dainty smidgins of this or that and silent stirrings, I exasperated.

"We're going to have to kill it with black, Mr. Bates."

"Black?" A fishy eye adhered to mine. "You'll only muddy it with black!"

"That's exactly what I plan to do. Muddy it!" I smiled ferociously.

He rattled to his feet and the eye washed its hands of me in disgust.

Pouring over the paint pots, I plopped in black. An opaque eye settled on the nape of my neck. Another fine stream of black trickled in. Mr. Bates sucked in his breath with a searing hiss. The green was relinquishing its noisy ghost.

More black. A really violent hiss. A blob of white. Five drops of chrome. Terrible hiss and the eye clamped shut in pain. It was a wrestle of wills, but I won; a perfect match. The eye opened, pearly with the dawn of respect!

Wonderful fun was Jack Bates despite our skirmishes with Wedgwood blue in Ran's bath and Olympian gold on his sleeping porch. Four coats each.

"Ran?"

"Yes?"

We were off to the strip for a short walk before bed. The engine still racketed on, hacking peace and quiet into lumps.

"Tell me about protocol," I asked.

"What do you mean?"

"Well, Mr. Bates is such a blessing. Would it be OK if I offered him a beer when he finishes? He's cooking for himself; it must be lonely."

We walked up onto the strip, Ran's cigar glowing orange as he strode along.

"Why not? An Australian once told me, the Aussie would rather wash your car and join you in a beer afterward than be paid two pounds for it; and then, only if he feels like it."

"That's what I thought!" I smiled, pleased at a right instinct.

The generator began to run down like a clapping audience after the last curtain. Lights went down and out.

"You cold?" He threw an arm over my shoulders.

"No, feels marvelous." I was struck by the intimacy of two human voices in that virgin dark.

"No stars; might rain tomorrow," he remarked softly. Weather was far more than a safe topic in the bush. It was the crux of it.

"Good," I answered. Rain was almost always good.

So Mr. Bates and I quaffed a frosty beer at days' ends and off he'd go to have a smoko and open tins in the decrepitude of the former shearer's quarters.

I'd watch him go, uneasy at how much I counted on our peculiar companionship. In a way, he knew more about what I was doing than Ran did. It was his job, of course. But I had replaced a career with this self-selected job of mine. It struck me hard that I was used to that kind of daily camaraderie because I had been an actress. You almost married a particular company of people making a film or rehearsing a play. Hours and hours of concentrated time, like a bunch of greyhounds after the

102

same rabbit. Faces flew before my mind, not always with name attached, but every one important in their way. Grips, electricians, camera boys, cameramen, camera operators, assistant directors, wardrobe women and men, makeup artists, hairdressers, fitters. The Mr., Miss, and Mrs. Bates of that world. They would be present and concentrated on the actors' emotional contribution. They'd be moved to tears or laughter or riveted silence by what all of us were shooting for. It bound us together for weeks or months. You knew a lot about their daily lives. Like Mr. Bates and me. More than their families did in some ways. But you knew about those, too. It brimmed your day's work. I not only liked Mr. Bates, I needed Mr. Bates like hell: for simple human contact. My love for Ran was enormous. But it was suicide to live in his pocket. He had a right to his world. I just wished he'd share a bit more of it with me. Some women were bored silly with men's worlds. I'd lived in a world based on men and women all slaving away together in a thousand fields, for the same hope-driven result. Fine entertainment. Fine performance. You could kid the pants off what you were doing, but underneath you knew you took a joint risk. A going forth into battle for the possibility of excellence; and of recognition of that excellence. Now, now, I chided myself, you've been all through that a hundred times. It's all here. Look for it. See into life. Don't just look at it. Grandfather had said that. You have love. You have freedom of a rare kind. Where is your mettle? Or was it metal? Damn. Start dinner. I'll need a flashlight in twenty minutes. What I wouldn't give to hear Aaron Copland's "Appalachian Spring"! I heard my mother's penetrating voice saying, "Where's your intellectual stimulation?" Shut up, Mother. I have been given everything I ever wanted. It's up to me.

Mr. Bates had been swallowed by the shearers' quarters. The air was sweet filtering through the kitchen screen door. These windows had to be washed. Surely there were ladders around tall enough. I walked out, so stiff with aching muscles and paint I sounded like Mr. Bates' newspapers. Which did I do? Pick dinner's salad or get clean and lovely for my man? I grinned— what a choice! "Do I have caviar or champagne?" I laughed out loud and banged out the door, running for lettuce, sun-drenched tomatoes, onion ribbons, and parsley. Squinting in the dusk, I found four neck chops in the kerosene refrigerator and mashed them in pepper and olive oil, I dashed down the hall for a bath. The engine went on as I scrubbed my toes. I'd left "Appalachian Spring" on the record machine. It revved up with the engine. Oh, glorious, Oh, how perfect. A gift had been given.

"Anne?"

"Yes?" said I, shouting out of my bath.

"Would you like a dressing drink?"

"Yes, oh, yes!"

"G and T?"

"Yes!" I called.

"Instanter," said he. I'd done it right. Sequentially I mean. Nice to come home to a woman relaxed and in the bath with perfumed oil. And dinner under control.

Project Z was child's play. Not that a tot could have done it, but neither could I, so Ran and Sam Pugh, the station's giant groom-gardener, hove to.

How could all my things get in if Giro still bulged with battered paraphernalia? A station family took the dining room; we ate in the kitchen. The living room went, we sat on the veranda. Pooped-out mattresses and bedsteads flopped everywhere; one pair of chrome beauties crashed tinnily into Anybody's. Two more landed in Katrina's, one pretended couch on a sleeping porch. We used a bedraggled double bed until our king-size would rumble in, the other went with the living room set to a tiny cottage we were furnishing for future help. A few more vanished into the maw of what had been the shearers' quarters along with various cracked chairs and tables, never to be seen again.

The last scrimmage was with floors. The miles of paint-tattooed floors took to dark oak like a wino swilling plonk; it just slithered on and held, glossy and spruce. Ran was really impressed by the gleaming floors.

"Unbelievable!" he exulted. "Too good for boots. I'll have to walk around in my socks."

"You do that anyway," I snorted.

104

"Insults will get you nowhere, Mrs. G. I didn't expect you to turn the bloody place into a temple—not sure I should even live here!"

"Oh, shut up." I laughed. "It's not that bad!" And I puffed like a courting turkey. Ridiculous to care so much about mere paint and varnish. Or was it? The ultimate fun was that no one really shared Giro's before and after but us.

I love an old Jamaican saying I heard once. "When socks have hole, only shoe know." Giro's ragged and dirty sock had been shoved into a shiny brown and white shoe. Eureka. We camped in empty splendor waiting for my sea shipment to show sail.

11

Three Blind Mice

IT was the one thing that hadn't been done. The living room. I'd gotten lazy about it because one 14-foot wall would prance with 12 feet of Japanese horses, and one wall had been knocked out for two cabinets to come. The ceiling was temporarily held up by two 4 × 4's until my two barber poles arrived. What needed doing was the fireplace and its fibro wall and bits and pieces around the bedroom door and French windows.

I stood in the middle of that room early one morning, chewing my nails. There was just enough off-white and dribbles and dabs of other colors to mix a really fascinating no-color. That was it. Put everything under the sun in it without Mr. Bates breathing down my neck. Mother of Pearl! Whistling energetically, I gathered all the paint pots, shrouded my varnished floor, and squatted near the rickety ladder, lost in concentration. Footsteps were coming with unaccustomed lightness down the hall. Sock-footed Randolph. I looked up.

"Don't worry, I don't need any more paint. Just have to freshen this last room and cancel phony brick fireplace. OK?" I spouted defensively. He approached me like a twenty-foot putt.

"Sweetheart?" He was so calm and fond I wondered what was wrong.

"Sir?" I inquired suspiciously.

"George and Julia Peckett are coming up."

I leaped to my feet. "What? In this mess?" George was his magician of a cattle broker.

"Now, cool down. I've been trying to get him up here for weeks This is the only time they have. As it is, Giro will be a sidetrip on the way to Toowoomba in Queensland."

I took a deep breath. "When?"

"Sometime later this afternoon."

This afternoon? Oh, Ran! For God's sake, we don't even have anything much to sit on. And those awful wads of beds—"

"Sweetheart!" he said sinking a perfect putt into the cup. "Not to worry, they couldn't care less. Julia's been through all sorts of rough stations. It's really important to me to take George around. Don't worry about cooking, I'll take care of that. Maybe we can even barbecue."

I'd had it. I knew I'd had it. One more try:

"But, Ran, I'd hoped the place would be attractive when they came and—"

"Really, darling, forget it. They're terribly easy."

I fumed, and fumbled for a cigarette.

"Well, I mean, why not ask the Biddefords and have an old-fashioned empty-house ball?"

He answered pleasantly surprised. "Would you mind? I've been wanting Tom to meet George."

My shot at sarcasm had bounced off a bulletproof vest. I gave up. "And the manager and his bride, of course?" I said saucily.

He hugged me.

"Yes! Will you quit looking so stricken? I promise I'll help."

Momentarily mollified, I indicated my paint pots. "What'll I do about this?" I spread my hands in exasperation.

"Will it dry in time?" he asked. "Don't knock yourself out. Why don't you forget it until after they leave?"

"But, Ran, I've almost got the perfect color. It's early, I can do it. It'll at least look fresh."

He looked wary and wasn't about to be partner to my possible martyrdom.

"Suit yourself." He shrugged. "I'll go see what we've got in the cold room and call Tom."

Unlike most men, Ran always made our social arrangements.

Half an hour later I'd hastily conquered the fireplace and its dingy wall with a strange nacreous color. As I was turning on top of my teetering ladder, ready to climb down and move

107

quickly to the next bits, an elbow hit the can of paint and down it clanked, flinging the last of my forever unmatchable white all over the room. It was a busy day.

We decided on a roast, which I didn't know how long to cook, and a buffet-style veranda picnic. It didn't matter, really. The men were oblivious to anything but station and cattle talk and the ladies were quite happy with their chat. Kath Biddeford didn't get out much and thrived on the gossip, however stale. Her dark-haired good looks were visibly heightened by human proximity.

The phone rang as I deposited the last of Giro's mismatched plates by the sink. Ran yelled "I'll get it!" and hurried down the hall, mightily annoyed at the interruption.

"Yes? What?" he barked. "What? *Brisbane?*" The phone always developed a bad case of croup at night from the engine. "Who wants to speak to her?" His voice had perceptibly deepened.

Her. That must mean me. I came to the kitchen screen door.

"Mister *who?* James Polano? I can't get you, operator. Would you spell that?" he complained, shifting his weight in irritation. "Ess-tee-ay-gee-ell? Operator—are you sure you're right? Gee-ell-eye-ay-en-o?"

I lit up. Stagliano—Jimmie Stagliano, my mad California Italian pal from the Boston Symphony! Ran was out of patience.

"Just wait a minute, I'll see. Anne?" He leaned out of the office and spoke in a lowered voice. "You know a James Stagliano? He says he wants to speak to Anne Baxter. Shall I just tell him you're not here?"

"Yes, I do. I mean no, don't. He's an old friend."

"You'd better take it." He proffered the phone. I smiled sheepishly and came out, reaching for the phone, and trying to be casual. He rushed back down the hall to the men.

I was beside myself. Jim was a fabulous musician, first French horn player of the Boston Symphony Orchestra. And wonderful fun. He said he'd asked the operator in Brisbane to get him the very well-known Hollywood actress Anne Baxter somewhere in Australia. She'd said, "What? You mean the Queen of Australia? No problem." I collapsed with laughter. Five min-

108

utes later she got me at Giro. Neither knew my name was now Galt.

The orchestra had been on a world tour and was on its way to concerts in Sydney. Could I come down? I said I'd let him know at his hotel in Sydney and hung up in an astounded glow. To hell with the dishes.

"Ran," I called, running out onto the veranda. "That was Jimmy Stagliano. He's first French horn of the B.S.O. He's going to ask Munch for his tickets. They're sold out. Can we go? Sunday night?" This was Friday. Heads turned to me. I suddenly realized I might as well have been talking a foreign language. There was a heavy pause. "Ahhhh, maybe." Another pause.

I sucked in my breath and plunged on. "He's . . . well, he's really a great guy, and I think it's the best orchestra in the world. Munch is *sensational*. I met him at Jimmie's house at Wellesley." Words kept tumbling out into what I began to realize was an embarrassed silence. It stopped me.

"You're sure you have to leave tomorrow, George?"

"Yes, Ranny, we've got to be in Moree tomorrow night and Toowoomba Sunday."

Ran turned to me, all eyes were watching us both.

"Don't see why not," he said magnanimously. Smiling from ear to ear, I breathed, "Terrific! Coffee, everyone?" And I left to a chorus of "Rights!" and "Pleases," hoping they wouldn't mind plain jelly (gelatin) for dessert. *That* I could cook.

James the Sybarite thought his medium-grade hotel was a fleabag. He told us Charles Munch had literally searched through all his pockets for tickets and found two. "Only for *you*, Cheemee." We met Jim before the concert in the Green Room. He had two other friends waiting, the second and third French horns, and several groups of other musicians. We met them all, and at a wink from rotund, pink-faced Jimmie, he and his horn players formed a trio and serenaded Ran and me with a dulcet rendition of "Three Blind Mice." I was in ecstasy. Ran looked as if he were tolerating a slight case of claustrophobia rather well.

Munch was in superb form. Brahms' Second was to me what

body surfing must have been to Ran. Then they bit into Samuel Barber's *Medea* until I almost couldn't bear it, nor could I bear it to end. Later, as a final encore, Munch narrowed his hypnotic bedroom eyes and put the strings through a performance of "Air for the G-String" I've never heard the like of. It was a technical masterpiece. The crowd roared themselves hoarse.

It was over. We saw Munch, terry towel around his sweating neck, and thanked him profusely. Jimmie asked us back to his fleabag to have a drink in the room he shared with Sammy Mayes, the brilliant quarter-Cherokee cellist who had been with Eugene Ormandy since he was eighteen, and who had auditioned for Jimmie at thirteen. Sammy's ambition was to someday make Jimmie audition for him.

We all got slightly squiffed and Jim waxed more and more Italian. With a hot-eyed look at me he addressed himself to Ran seated opposite him on the twin bed. "What are you doing with this gorgeous, sexy lady way out there with no competition but the bulls?" Ran laughed, and I lapped it up like a cat at a dish of cream.

12

Elephants and "Groceries"

NECESSITY can come up with some pretty creative ideas. Jean Taggart's kitchen castle had seemed impregnable while she was in it; now it became mine. No more tiptoeing over Jean's freshly mopped kitchen floor with a murmured "Excuse me!" Mine all mine. When she went, my common sense said, jeeringly, "So you used to throw Cointreau on the duck and brandied chestnuts on the ice cream? Let's see you cook!"

I promptly shoved myself into the center of Giro's kitchen, felt six eyes boring into the back of my neck, and turned slowly to face the biggest, blackest stove I'd ever seen. I thought I saw white porcelain handles turned in a sneer and heard a faint gravel monotone growl, "Bet you can't," and named it Bertha. She was fueled by two five-foot silver bombs which stood outside the seven-foot-high dirty window beside her. Porta gas, Ran said. He'd let me know in no uncertain terms it was a real privilege to have gas. Most bush cooks had to deal with coal or wood. Early mornings he'd disappear with what looked like a machete into our small coldroom, where the Station meat was kept, deposit a shapeless mass of meat on the kitchen table, and wave good-bye.

"Thanks, darling," I'd cluck, bustling with phony confidence, "looks lovely." And I'd stare in utter dismay at the outsized purple amoeba before me.

Cuts of meat at Giro were like nothing I'd ever seen. After the initial kill, the carcass was quartered, unchoice slabs re-

111

moved for corning, and the meat distributed day by day to the Station stockmen and their families. A station "keeps" its employees, meaning meat and milk, or rather meat and a milker or two.

We were unusual in that Ran had installed a small but impressive coldroom. We generated our own electricity and ran the engine an average of five hours a day. Hopefully, once cold, the room would maintain daytime temperatures between 40° and 45°. During the night temperature in the coldroom dropped 10 degrees after the engine was switched off by virtue of eutectic plates. I never did understand how those worked. With insulation low temperatures held fairly well in cool weather, but the variance was much greater in heat. A beef carcass could last the Station two to three weeks. Hot weather determined how soon it stank.

You get used to practically anything, though. The coldroom door opened into a narrow pathway between our drinks table and the linen cupboards and there were times when that smell a lot more than wafted through the house, but you just got so it didn't bother you much.

The meat was fair, and occasionally good. The good carcasses I began to call Josephines. As Ran explained, a station can hardly kill prime cows, and steers were not grown. We sold weaners—seven to ten months old. So barren cows were chosen whenever possible; hard to be sure, though, and it was always a minor tragedy to kill and find an embryo in good condition. That bothered me. I flinched for a kindred female. The ugly fact of killings was ever present. I only went near *one* by mistake. A penned animal sensing danger is devastating to hear and see; its frantic screams and terrorized rushes at freedom were more than I could take. Butchery is so violently human, so coolly necessary. As a carnivore one is helpless, so I'd shut my eyes and turn away, wishing I were deaf. Those cracking shots buckled me. For a split second I became that cow.

Staring at that meat the first day, I immediately thought of hamburger. But hamburger in Australia was called "mince," and was actually chopped into small pieces, not ground. Nor did we have a meat grinder. So I chopped it, or rather hacked it, to bits and fried it. Ran was very patient, and though he loved good food, was willing to eat unbelievable quantities of chopped beef in my hours of trial. Onions from Sam Pugh's Station garden helped, and tomatoes and salad greens. Broccoli was a dull thud. By the time I got through with it, the trunks stayed tough and the tops were limp. Where, oh where, were my cookbooks. I knew I'd be able to follow directions. As an actress I'd been known as a director's dream, but the cookbooks were on the high seas with everything else I needed.

Twice a week the mail car's dust rose down the valley at noon. It was always a thrill to drag the big, locked leather bag into Ran's office, fetch the hidden key, and greedily sort the contents. Santa's biweekly sack!

Ran had come back to lunch one mail day as I had proudly graduated to cheese and onion sandwiches fried in butter.

"Banana!" he shouted from the office as he opened an official-looking envelope.

"What?" I yelled back through smoking grease and the kitchen's screen door.

"It's here!" He came in brandishing papers from his customs broker, stating my things had docked and he was working to free them. What a moment! I did a jig in front of Bertha, the stove, howled with delight, and burned the bottom of the sandwich.

"Madam, I believe this calls for a cold beer." Grinning from ear to ear, he stalked into the coldroom for a bottle of Melbourne Bitter, excellent Victorian beer, like champagne to us.

Australian Customs were unusually understanding, and in a few days Ran got a call saying my things were on their way in the biggest available truck.

I was on tenterhooks. Would anything fit? Would what I'd laboriously planned look wrong? Could I figure out the curtains? Could I lay the fluffy bathroom carpeting? Would the toilet seat covers fit? (They didn't.) How would I hang anything on that damned fibro? Would things be in smithereens? Most of all, would Ran approve? *Please Lord, let it all work.*

All hell broke loose in Worcester. The truck had rolled into Town, but we'd had heavy rains and it completely bogged five miles out. After twelve hours of monumental effort, they debogged the leviathan, but definitely decided they'd never make

113

our road, and deposited the three lift vans on the railroad station platform in pouring rain. Two 5,000 pounders and one 2,500 pounder. A lift van, in case you've never moved overseas, is about the the size of a one-car garage; its pine boards are lined with waterproof tarpaper and abundantly, maddeningly, nailed. The smaller "van" contained, among other treasures, my washer and dryer which Mrs. Boris Karloff had told me to take. She said, quite rightly, that American appliances were bigger, better and cheaper than what I'd find, even though we'd have to order a transformer; Australian voltage is on a different cycle.

"Ran," I worried. "What can we do?" I kept picturing twelve thousand five hundred pounds of my belongings deluged with rain.

"Not to worry," he said. "Stay loose. I'll see if I can get Mrs. Munro's boys." Meaning two fellows in Worcester with a flattop truck, whose mum ran the business. I studied him as he went into action. He'd begun to catch fire. This was an enormous obstacle and he obviously loved it. He hated piddling details; this needed broad strokes and he ate it alive. But the river was up; even mail couldn't get through for a week. We broiled in frustration and opened cans. The vegetable garden was awash.

Ten days later the three crossings were thought to be better than chancy. Mrs. Munro's boys got two lift vans on and struggled toward Giro.

Ran jumped onto the tractor, a D-4, and roared around the back, scooping out a large ditch in order for the flattop to back in and hit level ground; he planned to pull the vans off on makeshift log rollers with the tractor. Mrs. Munro's boys had a crawling, hair-raising trip. Kath and Tom Biddeford, our neighbors ten miles away, cheered them through the last crossing, and Tom gave a helping hand with his light tractor. They'd almost gone over the palisades at Peach Tree Cutting.

I prayed again, following that trip mentally, and remembered the sad story of the first family to live nineteen miles up the station in the Myall country. They'd pulled their furniture in by bullock sledge and the whole shebang went over a cliff. The sledge still sat halfway up, a tattletale wreck.

"Ran! Thank God! Here they come!" I yelled, banging out

114

the veranda door. I can hear that truck now, moaning and gasping in labor as it fought and floundered down the last lap.

Ran gave them a wave and a victory sign and leaped onto the caterpillar. I was beside myself with joy, and my heart swelled at the thought of Giro, swept clean and ready for final transformation.

Still shy of me and the recent goings-on, the Station people watched from a distance, obviously dumbfounded at the sight of those house-sized boxes.

Getting them off required many gesticulations, a great deal of shouting back and forth, conferences and mopped brows with motors chattering. The ropes gave way on No. 2 after a mighty heave, and chains were hunted and lashed anew. The noise was deafening as the tractor snarled and screeched at the last 5,000-pound haul. Done! There they sat, dim dinosaur rumps in the fast-fading light.

My belongings. *Belong belong belong belong.* Bell sounds. Solid communal churchbell sounds. Women and their things. How many times I'd heard women say, "I'll feel better when I have my own *things*"? Novelists knew it. The cliché of the small girl arriving at the convent door clutching her few precious belongings, or Mrs. Pioneer, watching anxiously as her precious sideboard was inched into the wagon for the trek west. I could hear my mother's voice shouting, "Be careful!" as lumbering movers extracted her favorite teak cabinet from the van.

What was it about women and their possessions? Any age, any nationality. John Hodiak had come to our marriage with a suitcase. Ran parked his duffel bag anywhere and felt at home. There were men who reacted the female way, but they were apt to be accused of just that. Standing there in the dusk, I was aghast at that hulk of things. My mind nosed the subject again. Perhaps the word explained itself: I had my belongings, therefore I belonged? That desperately longed-for state: the ancient illusion of the uniform making the soldier, clothes the man, or possessions the woman.

The air cooled for the night as I stood staring at 10,000 pounds of nest material. A star popped over the corner of one great box. If I could have snapped a finger and made them vanish I just might have. I felt sick to think I needed all that to feel secure. All wrong, but don't think anymore. Too late. Gigantic efforts have been made, don't muff the finale.

Mrs. Munro's boys killed two quarts of Dirty Annie (Resch's dinner ale) and slam-banged down the road, lighter by 10,000 pounds and ready for steak and eggs. Ran and I toasted each other grandly; it was hilarious and dreamlike, the whole operation, all of it. Us. Giro. Those hoosegows waiting to be opened after three and a half months and 8,860 miles. Alas, we'd overlooked one glaring omission. No movers. They were back in Sydney drinking paychecks. No one, just Ran and I, two hammers, and my trusty crowbar in the ring with two elephants. "Sic'em!" I hollered, feeling my beer. We sicced 'em.

It was a tremendous job, but again I recognized what Ran really relished—ropes, chains, machines, and men. Big projects to wrassle were his meat. It's a wonder he married me. Five foot three and three-quarters in stocking feet.

After supper he climbed a ladder and hit one elephant in the ear with a crowbar, I hit it in the toe with a hammer, and away we went under a star-spangled sky. They were packed like wisdom teeth, magnificently so, but what a backache of a task! I suppose that's why nothing broke—no room to rattle. What was miraculous in the days to follow, everything fit: rugs, tables, chairs, beds, chests, china, towels, everything. I was overjoyed, and so was Ran. Rolled inside the two bathroom carpet pieces were a carpet knife and tape, as requested. It had paid lush dividends to move scale furniture on paper. Is there any better feeling in life than to work really hard at something impossible-sounding and have it turn out right, with someone you love that much?

Three days later Mrs. Munro's boys brought the 2,500 pounder—a "piece of cake" compared to the others, so they said. Ran flew into town and picked up a livewire of an electrician, who rewired all the lamps and hooked the washer and dryer to the fifty-pound transformer. Everything worked. I couldn't believe it.

My two hands could carry only so many things from here to there and it took ten days for the excelsior to clear. Sam Pugh and Ran carried in heavy stuff in no time. On a brilliant wintry June morning I wandered from room to room, sipping coffee and shamelessly preening one slightly beaten chest.

116

Ran loved it all. That was the best. He already had three favorite chairs—a black-and-brass campaign chair in the living room, a flaring wing chair in luscious red leather in his office, and a wide rattan veranda chair. There were two of those, so I got one too, in that all-important screened room.

I'd successfully broken the living room and dining room boxes with curves. Disgracefully pleased, I sat in one of the low curved chairs on either side of the curved couch facing the fireplace, whose cheesy brick veneer I'd painted out. Setting my coffee down on the skinny teak table in front of the couch, I leaned back and admired the six panels of Japanese horses covering the wall opposite the fire. A small fire was still going from early that morning. Mornings were chilling fast. Ran thought the screen was perfect. Six different horses in six different positions in six stalls, full of rhythm and in horse colors—palomino, sorrel, black and white, bay, dapple gray, and roan, with a glow of gold leaf top and bottom. His leather campaign chair in the far corner, black and gold tea canister lamps, and loosely woven linen curtains on brass rods completed the effect. It was pretty hot stuff at night, with a crackling fire flicking flashes of gold off this and that, and my Diego Rivera watercolor in earth tones. A homemade nightclub. And the goat-hair rug foaming like fresh cream all over the floor was irresistible in bare feet. The fleas would agree, but I didn't know that then. I'd muffled color in most rooms since they were so small. Natural linens and textures underlined with black here and there worked like charms.

Ran liked blue. Any blue. So I'd thrown deep blue over the acre of king-sized bed and a Persian horse caparison over that in blood reds, golds, and blues. That gorgeous gewgaw was what horses wore to parades; an overgrown bib hanging down their fronts with tassels to kick as they pranced. Those damned tassels—I had to comb them with my fingers every morning. Ran thought it looked terrific. The mahogany hatrack from some Barbary Coast brothel was already draped with Ran's hoarded torn workshirts and shorts. Two French carriage lamps and a Mexican *santo* (I thought we'd never hang the shelf for it on the fibro) were above the bed.

The second front bedroom became the "Four Poster" because of its handsome Spanish bed. It was between the bath I used and the future closets Ran had promised me. I wrote letters there and sneaked a cigarette the nights I couldn't sleep. He hated my smoking.

My bath had towels appliqued with the female bower bird in olive on sky blue, sky carpet, massed Mexican bottles in turquoise, a black lacquer table, and from time to time, live frogs in the toilet.

Ran's bath had the male bird in blue-black with a red berry in its mouth on beige towels and rug, a Moroccan stool, massed Mexican bottles in royal blue, and from time to time, live frogs in the toilet.

There was an evil black hole in the fibro directly over my bathroom window. I painted a big blue eye around that pupil, arched brow, lashes, and all. A haughty reminder not to let myself go to pot.

The passage to the massive coldroom door had a rainbow rug from Oaxaca, Mexico, and a teak drinks table, I painted "El Bar" with a swag of red rope and tassels on the door into the hall, and plastered the walls opposite the linen cupboards with Mexican bullfight posters and crossed *banderillos.* Not that it was light enough to see them.

The phone rang in Ran's office—Loooong–short–loooong–short. I rushed down the long hall.

"Yes?"

"Mr. Galt?"

"No, this is Mrs. Galt."

"Oh. Well, I'll try later on, thanks."

"Thank you!" Sometimes I wasn't even trusted with messages.

The master of Giro or no one.

The office fire was almost out; it could be such an icy cubbyhole. I was glad I'd toasted it with red. My Ute war drum was the red leather chairs' companion. Gold and red striped sisal (for the mud to go through) was fine on the floor, but I noticed the substantial cranberry picker was already collapsing from *Queensland Country Life, Country Life N. S. W., Weekly Variety, The Hollywood Reporter, Cattleman, The New Yorker,* the international editions of *Time* and *Newsweek,* old Sydney papers, and catalogues, much of which we never had time to read. Ran's desk was a plug-ugly in factory steel, so I coated it olive and sat a red East Indian drum lamp on it.

I went back for my cold coffee and smiled as I came down the hall again to the kitchen. That screen door was my happiest canvas. The bottom half was fibro and now flaunted Giro's crest: a mustard shield with cockroaches rampant and a German proverb, "Be careful what you want. You may get it." In German. I didn't want to scare everybody.

We both loved the two-inch-thick oak table in the dining room. I'd had it stripped to honey color and the curved pigskin chairs around its solid disk were comfort itself. The ceiling was tall enough for my four foot by five foot Toulouse Lautrec poster and for the black tin chandelier whose candles, I was to discover, either blew wax all over us or relaxed into a bouquet of wilted phallic symbols in the heat. A Tibetan chest in faded reds, golds, blues, gingers, and greens leaned against a wall for storage. With black-iron candleholders, it took thirty candles to light that room. The Australian bush had gone from kerosene to neon; candles were scarce. They sold them in pairs—for bodies at wakes. Expensive, too.

I'd painted Katrina's furniture thick white, added flowered quilts and brass headboards; her toys and pictures would do the rest. Anybody's (the guestroom) stuff was also coated white; lime pillows complemented Mr. Bates' and my sage green.

Someone was knocking at the kitchen back door. I opened it and saw Mrs. Mackendrick, known always as Mrs. Mac. She and her husband and family had been working at Giro forty-odd years through a procession of owners and managers. We could not have managed without them. She smiled timidly from the shadows of her battered hat.

"Mrs. Galt?"

"Yes, Mrs. Mac." I smiled back.

"Mr. Galt will be home a bit late this evening. He went up the Myall. Told me to tell you."

"Thanks, Mrs. Mac."

"Here's a bit of cream for you." She held out a can of impossibly thick cream.

"Oh, how marvelous. Very kind of you!"

"Right. Anytime," she murmured and was gone.

119

He'd be late. I'd have time to really cook a meal—he deserved a feast after what I'd been serving. The day's beef lay in a flabby heap on the silky-oak table I'd stripped of paint. My American cookbooks were stacked on one of the gay, flowered Mexican chairs. Better mop the veranda first. That dark finish was printed with boots yet again. I mopped by two carousel horses rearing on either side of the veranda screen door and around two four-foot-high raw wool baskets I'd unearthed in the old sheep-shearing shed. They were great for boots and extra saddle gear and dry-za-bones. I'd skated them to the far end. They were indigenous and cheerful, especially when a bright Turkish saddlebag spilled over. Or my Texas butterfly boots. Or a Navajo saddle blanket. And Alexander Calder's mobile clanged above.

I wrung the mop, picked up my bucket, and stretched.

Nobody down there believed any of it. One craggy codger from Worcester kept toeing and raucously admiring our "mat"—meaning the Greek fur rug. "I'd like to have that mat." Over my dead body!

Wandering in that honeycomb of rooms, Giro rose like a Phoenix bird from the ashes of Projects X–Y–Z. Hallelujah.

My lucky day was the day my June Platt cookbooks were unpacked. I'd had a perfection of a cook for nine years in California, and she and J. Platt were unbeatable. All I did was plan menus, or, rather, steal them from Mrs. Platt.

She wrote for idiots like me. "Walk into the kitchen, get out a bowl x ″ by x ″ and x ″, don't worry if what you're making looks awful, it's supposed to, everything will be hunky-dory later on," etc. Thank God for June Platt. Ran joined me in obeisance. He loved to eat.

Start with stew. I had to start somewhere. My first attempt was "beetifoo," as they pronounced it, the second more delicious, better and better. I was Duchess of Stew, and confidence flooded me with joy. Kitchen Sinks I called them finally. They had fantastic things in them as my imagination took off, always anchored solidly to stew by Platt. I had at last found a stage on which to perform. Stew conquered, to my ego's avoirdupois; I flipped on to further triumphs *au Giro.*

I learned pie. Apple pie. Granny Smith green-apple pie, an unparalleled cooking or eating apple, I might add. Platt's crust was hellish to work with and I knew blank about pastry. It took many anxious tries, and Bertha was a burned and smoking mess. But what pie! I eschewed cinnamon in favor of lavish butter, sugar, and lemon; and when we could rescue peaches from flying foxes, fruit flies, birds, and the wet, we had warm, fresh peach pie cooked with peach kernels and a whisper of almond flavoring in Mrs. Mac's smooth, cool cream; or tart-sweet plum tart; or Ran's favorite, garden rhubarb shortcake.

Bread was my *enfant terrible,* and the page under Oatmeal Bread has craters on it like the moon, from dough-draped fingers. It was discouragingly difficult, but it satisfied my soul to smell a house filled with the fragrance of baking bread. Kath Biddeford threw up her clever hands and wailed that I'd set her back twenty years.

To say that food in Australia is bland is a euphemism. Even the salt is less salty. You have to double the dose every time. As a result, we hankered after highly flavored and spiced dishes.

One unique find was what they called a pumped leg, or corned leg of lamb. I was taken aback when I learned they simply pumped the thing full of saltpeter with a syringe. Not knowing what else to do, I roasted it, with herbs, ginger, and garlic. They were shocked. Boiling is the correct procedure. In fact, boiling was the procedure period for almost everything, but I got huffy and wouldn't.

Along with her other magic talents, Mrs. Mac was the station angler: perch, catfish, and mullet abounded. She knew precisely where they hung out; plied them with bread a couple of mornings, then helped herself. Not exactly kosher, but it provided a welcome shot in the arm to a diet of beef, corned beef, mutton, lamb, and beef.

Bertha and I became the friendliest of enemies, filled with intimate knowledge of each other's idiosyncrasies, mutual distrust, and respect. She was a tightwad about simmering. It took a magnificently controlled wrist and four asbestos pads on a burner to reach that tenderest of heats, and I sport the scars of her blistering, ton-weight oven doors. Never mind, Bertha's ovens could sear a roast to its ultimate in juiciness.

But man cannot live by bread alone, or meat, or pie. I had to learn Groceries. Groceries was a good game on our nine-party line and it was nip and tuck with all the shire ladies playing, too.

First impressions are not to be trusted. I thought the telephone was cute. Jean Taggart knew what she was about and used to assail it with a voice like a microphone on the fritz:

"Helloooooo? Helloooo? Are you therrre? Helloooo?"

Earsplitting caterwauls and buzzing cranks. It's a wonder the operator didn't hear her without benefit of the wire.

It had a little crank just too small for convenience and two big rusty bells, often muffled by a wad of Ran's cast-off undershorts. Our number was LOOOONG–short, LOOOONG–short. Bedlam without the underwear.

Barnard's emporium opened at eight fifteen; at eight sixteen you grasp the little crank and grind. Place receiver on ear, hearing sounds resembling a dog chewing Grape-Nuts inside a large tin can. Bang down receiver. Grind and crank again, jerk receiver to ear noting welcome sound of underwater voice, "Yes? Worcester here."

"Working?" Local lady horns in, trying to elbow you out of game.

I crisply shout: "Yes! Working!" back at her. Angry click. Score point. Underwater voice: "Worcester operator here."

Enunciating as to one hard of hearing: "May I have Barnard's? Worcester 214, please?" Operator translates your American accent: "Wanting Bahnuds, did you sye? Woostah two wan foh?"

"Yes, please!"

"Right."

Pause. More Grape-Nuts. Male underwater voice grumbles: "Barnard's here."

And on you go rattling off your list. Woe betide the player who waits until eight thirty-one. One crank and you're in a flock of irate "Workings!" You can't quit, though; that list has to get in before the mail leaves. Edibles came out to Giro twice a week, and the pickup left town by nine thirty A.M. If the ladies were just "chatting" you could always shout a frantic "Working!" as a hint and hope they hang up. A good gambit.

We didn't need drum telegraph in the bush, not with that telephone. Everybody knew all. One dairy farming couple had

122

earphones hooked up near their bed and tuned in on the line for entertainment.

Calls coming in from Sydney were a mind reader's delight. You were given every fourth word as clues. Sometimes the telephone would play dead, which meant a long wait for the medicine men, but by the time they'd arrived it would cackle awake just to winnow us.

It had been a public phone once, with a room of its own labeled TELEPHONE in big baked enamel letters. It never forgave us the fact we demoted it to private property, and when we'd attempt a call home from a rare weekend in Sydney, the operator joined the enemy.

"Sorry, too early for the switchboard at Guyra, not open yet!"

"Look, operator, it's Giro, not Guyra, and it's a private phone. It's our home, we *live* there. Please ring Giro one."

"Sorry, there's no Guyra one. No such number."

One day it tried to kill me. I knew it was suicide to call while a thunderstorm bombarded us. The telephone siphoned lightning and jangled its bells through every storm. Thinking I was scot-free that afternoon when a brusque storm had passed over the hills, I rang Worcester and was waiting on the line when it blasted me to the office floor, leaving me flat on my face, bugeyed and giddy. Giro's infernal gazebo.

13

A Day in the Life

THE performance after opening night is always a little flat, even after rave reviews. I felt like that. The house was more or less done and I'd automatically been moved out of the sun and into the shade of routine. No matter what I did, our lives remained separate. Ran's was out, mine was in. After six A.M's. tender good-byes, I'd see or hear him joking and talking with the manager and men to the refrain of running motors or snorting horses and off they'd go in all directions. Silence settled in the house like the motes of dust minutely snowing in the rising sun. I'd stand stock-still and listen, afraid to look into the corners of my mind. Something hid there worth dreading and I didn't want to know what.

Here I was surrounded by all my pretty things and an outdoor world redolent of animals and salty men and nature. A picnic to which I was not invited. Come now, I thought to myself, the day is yours. Freedom. Between what? answered the waiting silence. Don't think. Shut up and make the beds.

Today was mail day. What time was it? I absolutely had to win Groceries today because I'd made up my mind to try chicken paprika and had been saving Mrs. Mac's cream until it grew green fur for home soured cream. Our chickens were for eggs. Chickens to eat came from Town.

The kitchen had an old alarm clock. Only six thirty. Time to clean the place and make a real effort to mop backward from the hall kitchen door to the back one, catching the pantry and laundry on the way out. Pantry first so I could dump the bucket in the laundry tub. Maybe my herbs would come in this mail. I'd ordered them from an ad in *Women's Weekly* and was working on a special space for them where the old meathouse had been. The tennis court had gone. Ran loved to rip things out and tear things away. He never seemed to have enough space around him.

Quarter of eight—watch it. Groceries was imminent. Wonder if he'd come home for mail, and if so, what did I have for lunch? He'd had steak for breakfast. Maybe the chili would reheat once more. I decided to roll up the hall and office rugs, sweep, end up by the phone ready for Groceries. Win Groceries, and wet-mop both places. Then laundry and ironing. I clenched my teeth—how I hated ironing, mostly because I was so lousy at it. I threw the hall rug out on the side cement walk in a cloud of splinters and dirt and banged the screen. Shirts. I never knew where to start—back, collars, sleeves, or what. Throwing the office rug out, the door banged again. Sheets. Too damned big for the laundry. I'd given up ironing them. They always ended with gritty rims; couldn't keep them off the floor. "Rough dry" sounded nice anyway. Like Rupert Brooke, "the rough male kiss of blankets, etc."? I stopped and jeered at myself—ironing my foot. No engine! Can't possibly. Goody! I swept everything including the office hearth and attacked the phone with a vigorous crank.

"Working?"

Crankcrankcrank.

"Working?"

Grape-Nuts told me the line was at least alive.

"Worcester operator here?"

"Two one four, please."

"Right." The day had begun. I watched a fresh breeze make waves in the young lucerne out the office window.

Around eleven I went out to face Sam Pugh, who hated women, especially me because I picked his young onions.

"You'll never have onions that way, Mrs. Galt!" he shouted furiously. He never got closer than fifty yards.

"But, Mr. Pugh!" I shouted back sweetly, "I don't want so many big ones. Mr. Galt likes the scallions!"

He glared out of his tiny red eyes and stalked off in disgust.

He was bent over a row of cauliflowers as I approached warily, keeping my distance.

"Mr. Pugh?"

"Yes." He spat at a nearby cauliflower.

"May I pick some onions?"

"Only over there!" He jerked a thumb over his shoulder at a thick-stemmed row.

"OK. Thanks." I pulled some beauties as he moved as far away as possible into the rhubarb.

"Mr. Pugh?" He kept his back to me but was listening, I knew. "I'm trying to plant a herb garden. Where's the best place to get topsoil?"

"Well, you can't take it from here!"

"But where?"

"I'll have to tell Mr. Galt!"

Boy, oh, boy. Indoors was female, outdoors was male. Not even a barrowful of dirt. I clutched the grimy globes of onions and was back to the laundry to rinse them when I heard the plane. I looked up in surprise, knowing it couldn't be Ran. But who? I ran into the laundry, dumped the onions, and washed my hands, wondering what to do. It must be planning to land on our strip; too low for anywhere else unless it was in trouble. Like a country bumpkin I ran out the back and watched the strange plane circle for landing.

"Anne? Anne?"

It was Ran from the hall. I looked out front and saw the dusty Station jeep with its door open and motor running.

"I'm out here," I called.

He poked his head out the left side door of the hall. "Listen, I've got a hunch who's in that plane. Go hide in the garden till I call you."

"What? Why?"

"Just go ahead and hide!" He was gone. I could hear him pounding through the house and out the front veranda.

Mystified, I beat it to the broccoli and crouched. It maddened me not to be able to see what was going on. I saw the plane land and roll down the strip until it was hidden by the homestead. Sam Pugh was nowhere to be seen. He had probably seen me

126

coming and vanished. As I hunched over, chin on my knees, my mind wandered around Sam Pugh. He was the perfect Giro gardener. He washed every other week; walked through the river wearing his shirt, shorts, *and* shoes, and drank beer all day Sunday, a snazzy solution to a day off at Giro for a loner. He must have shaved once in a while because he maintained the identical amount of tough graying stubble. Since he hated women, I didn't dare to ask what his secrets were. Never have I eaten such vegetables. Even oldmaid cauliflowers became Lillian Russells, cooked in three minutes to succulence, each stem of each snowy floweret grass-green; capsicums (bell peppers) like spring hats; rhubarb so handsome I arranged it like iris; tomatoes so tight and smooth you couldn't resist stroking your cheek with their coral satin. Cucumbers bold with flavor, tender smiling baby lettuces, corn so nubile you ate cob and all.

Sam complained bitterly all the time, a real sorehead. I was always smoothing angry feathers from afar—the manager, the bugs, the rain, no rain, *women,* the wind, seed, bugs, the manager, dogs, the manager, *women.* We knew he didn't drink on Sundays only—his eyes were like a boiled owl's on Thursdays as well. I shifted on rapidly cramping haunches. What in hell was going on out there on the strip? Or were they in the house, whoever they were? And what was I doing here, hiding in a bunch of broccoli clinging to the underside of the world? I began to giggle, always a feeble solution, but the whole thing was so silly. I glanced at the vegetable beside my nose. Sam's broccoli was really beautiful close up, dwarf baobab trees, silver, blue, and green.

The stranger plane engine revved, so at least it wasn't in trouble. Who were they and why were they leaving so soon? Fascinating! I fell back onto my buttocks and ducked my head. These pants would need a wash. What didn't? Bloody laundry.

"Banana!" Ran was leaning out the kitchen door.

"Can I come out now?" I begged. "What's going on?"

"Wait a minute till they take off," he said in a lowered voice.

"Who?"

"Press from Sydney."

"You're kidding. You mean they just flew up without calling?"

"They did. Wanted all sorts of photographs of you, me, and the house. One guy was from a magazine. Never mind"—he smiled evilly—"I got rid of them."

The plane roared up the strip and went up, up, and away. Ran scanned the departing intruders with great satisfaction. I've always wondered exactly what he said to them.

"Come on out. They can't see you now." He motioned to me.

"I have become intimately acquainted with broccoli," I remarked, straightening up painfully, shaking the knots out of my knees.

"Are you home to lunch, darling?" I asked hopefully.

"No, I'd better eat with the men. Only came back when I saw the plane. See you." His head popped back in and seconds later the jeep bumped away along the rutted road.

The mail came just as I'd hung a wash. It was always a tantalizing tonic. No herbs yet, but a lovely batch of letters from home. Mother's was studded with disaster as usual; sharp reports from life's battlefield. My brilliant mother was as up-to-date as tomorrow, and as Victorian as a starched lace cap. She always enclosed clippings designed to bolster my moral fiber if not my morale. After one of her letters, you needed those clippings as you got up off the floor. I longed to see her, but she would have hated every second of what I was doing. So would my beloved father. Perhaps when Giro was everything we hoped it would be they'd come down for a visit. There was a short sweet note from Katrina, and a nice enthusiastic letter from Jane Fyfe, who was to bring her down and would take care of her lessons. They'd be here in two weeks. What a long two weeks that would be for me. I couldn't wait to see my vibrant sprout. Only two more letters. I'd better save those for dessert, I thought, and lugged two crates of groceries into the kitchen. After hurriedly putting things away, I grabbed a leftover chop and a napkin left from breakfast and sat, reveling in human companionship.

Chewing on my cold chop, I read a newsy letter from Edith Head full of current doings and follies in Los Angeles. We never called it Hollywood; there really was no such animal. That interior suburb was just another neon hive of third-rate shops, restaurants, and tourist traps.

128

Edith was undisputed queen bee at Paramount, and, as such, got stuck with Elvis Presley, one of their big moneymakers. The latest was called *Blue Hawaii*. Outside of weaving pigtails in the grass skirts or more sequins on Elvis' bucking crotch, she admitted her scope was somewhat limited. She'd have to fly to Honolulu, via red-carpet treatment, which she loved. I glanced away to dream a little. So near and yet so far. Only five thousand miles or so. Wouldn't that be smash if she'd fly the coop and come down under for a visit? I bent over her inch-high script once again.

She went on to say Hitchcock's new film, *Psycho,* shot in black and white and in no time flat à la television, was going to hit the jackpot. She'd seen it at a private screening and had overheard Hitch planning a startling ad campaign. And that he and Alma would be at most worldwide premieres, including Sydney, Australia. Wow. I tipped my head back and studied a cruising fly the size of a bumblebee. It lumbered through the air like a B-52 ready to drop its load. Not bombs. Maggots. My heart thumped. Maybe Ran and I could fly in to Sydney to see them. If only I knew when. I'd write Alma and hope. I shifted in my kitchen chair, looked down, and read on

Marlon Brando's first self-directed film, *One-Eyed Jacks,* was giving his moneymen fits. It was reported to have cost over eight million. They might sue. Egad zooks! I whistled; that's one expensive horse opera. Gold oats or something.

It was Edith's picture, cowboy outfits and all. She said Brando had shaken the wardrobe's workroom into blushing titters. Women usually fitted without a stitch. Men never. Edith walked in for Brando's first fitting and there he was, resplendent in jockstrap, period. She never batted her black-rimmed spectacles, but the fitters went up the mirrored walls. Edith agreed with Brando. Nothing like starting from scratch.

Edith's architect-designer-artist husband, Bill, was doing miraculous things to their old Mexican colonial house, including a study for him and a capacious new dressing room with storage space galore for Edie and her unbelievable cache of cachet. That reminded me, I'd absolutely have to ask again about wardrobe space at Giro.

She and Bill sent much love and said they'd decided to put all

129

six cats in the huge three-story former aviary. I giggled aloud, picturing all those big bird holes with a Cheshire cat grinning in each. As I read her towering signature I sighed again. Don't shut up, dear friend, I can hear myself think.

How I longed for a juicy chat with Edith and Bill, my ever-ready friends. My utterly sophisticated churchmice. Or with Peg McNaught, who'd written at length last week. She was at Fox when I first came, in charge of fashion publicity. Nobody did that anymore. The studios were breaking up like river ice in the spring. She free-lanced now and was a tried and true confidante. I shut my eyes and let myself dream again as my fingers folded the letter. Of picking up a dial phone and making a date for lunch. Cold salmon in aspic and warm conversation.

As I came to after a moment, a large envelope caught my eye. It was from MCA, still my theatrical agency, and contained five week-old copies of *The Hollywood Reporter.* They came every week. A bright lady agent of mine had offered to forward them free, via the mail room of MCA's famous antique-filled building in Beverly Hills. I'd accepted eagerly, but hadn't read them much. No time, for one. And inclination had oddly faltered as the weeks went by. I'd stepped off a high-speed carousel and found it harder and harder to keep climbing back on, even mentally.

I pulled the MCA envelope to me. Unbending the metal fastener, I reached in and slid out one of the thin shiny red, white, and black industry Bibles.

Page One. Pamela Tiffin was the latest candidate for sex symbol. Never mind, I cracked to myself, never mind. I see she gets to work with Elia Kazan. *Splendor in the Grass* with Natalie Wood. What was it? They still fell for it. "She photographs like two million dollars; now if we can only get her to act." If anybody could get her to act, Kazan could. I'd always yearned to work with him. Only met him once at Fox, about playing *Pinkie.* They said I didn't look "negroid" enough. Hell. I'd have puttied my Irish nose. Anything. Kazan was electric, and *liked* actors. It's a wonder he wasn't drummed out of the local corps. The story line was the only thing that mattered to Darryl Zanuck.

Geraldine Page was set for *Summer and Smoke.* Be perfect.

130

Costumes by Edith Head. Also set was Laurence Harvey. Wasn't crazy about him. I'd seen him do a pretty-boy singsong Romeo on stage. I flipped to Page Two. Vivien Leigh, most beautiful of all beautiful creatures, shooting *The Roman Spring of Mrs. Stone* in Rome with Shirley MacLaine's brother, Warren Beatty. MacLaine was nominated for *The Apartment*; damned good in it, too. Siobhan McKenna cast in *King of Kings*—the Samuel Bronston monster being filmed in Spain. Extremely original actress I'd greatly admired.

Lee Remick to do Faulkner's *Sanctuary*. Ran drooled slightly at the sight of Lee Remick. I didn't blame him. Eyes like chunks of sky. Etc. She could also act.

They were going to remake, or was it rehash, *Back Street* with John Gavin and Susan Hayward. His name used to be Jack Galenor, spoke impeccable Spanish; was incredibly handsome and much thinner that night friends brought him to my house. He'd tossed off a remark to the effect that he thought he'd try acting—such easy money. That was a while ago. He'd probably made the money by now. Wonder why he hadn't tried acting yet? Bitchy remark. But I felt bitchy. Why did that daily Tower of Babble make me feel as if I'd just been fired? I suppose when you're fired at fourteen you don't forget it. Ugly feeling with nausea in the wings. At least I was fired from among the best. Philip Barry wrote it and Katharine Hepburn, Joseph Cotten, Van Heflin, and Shirley Booth studded *Philadelphia Story* when the Theatre Guild produced it for Broadway. Said I was too old. I was, too. Overdeveloped in front to boot. As that jerk said on the Fox lot one day: "Here comes Baxter with a blouseful of goodies." Grit. I was already an old hag of sixteen and a half. And what about Phil Silvers' introduction as I walked onstage for an Army camp and hospital tour show: "All that meat and no potatoes." I could have died. And a year later, during *Magnificent Ambersons,* Orson Welles, drunk on Joe Cotten's Machiavellian martinis, secretly sending his chauffeur home and pleading no transport, would I drive him? Gad, what a drive. I prayed for a policeman. Six feet four, 250 pounds, and what seemed like six hands in my shirt. All he kept saying was, "Oh, the beauty of it, Oh, the beauty of it." In tears of rage I finally shoved him out at Sunset Boulevard, threw my tattered

131

bra in the gutter, and gunned up the hill to home and Mother. Poor Orson. I always wondered how long it took him to get a cab. Best director I'd ever worked with. What did he say about *The Method?* "The only thing wrong with it was the 'The.'" Touché. Or Georgie Jessel's flailing little paws in the limousine taking us from Milwaukee to Chicago for yet more tub-thumping for a Fox picture called *You're My Everything.* When I was sixteen, Jessel sent orchids to my mother, trying for a date with me. Even my own agent had chased me around his desk, gasping, "Don't worry, honey, my wife understands me!"

I was shaking with laughter now, head bouncing helplessly on arms folded across the table, mussing up the nice *Hollywood Reporter.* In Tinsel Town, as the fan mags called it, even the birdies go cheap, cheap, cheap.

I rested my head on my arms and felt hungry. Rolling my eyes, I spotted the same heavy-bellied fly lowering itself drunkenly onto a damp dishrag. I rose slowly, stealthily rolled the manila envelope full of *Reporters,* and swatted it. Green apples were in the pantry. I went for one, throwing the mashed blowfly in the trash on the way. Opening the refrigerator, I broke off a couple of inches of yellow cheese and munched from apple to cheese as I sat back down at the table. I wondered wryly if *The Hollywood Reporter* had given me a sneaking case of sour grapes. Maybe. I was human. There were times when I'd try to figure how long it would take for Mrs. Randolph Galt (actress Anne Baxter) to become Mrs. Randolph Galt (former actress Anne Baxter). And, finally, Mrs. Randolph Galt (didn't she used to *do* something?).

Clearly Ran preferred the last. And yet he'd married an Anne Baxter; not a nonentity, though often to his chagrin. Would his interest and respect flag as I became plain Mrs. G?

I blinked out of reverie. Was I crazy? Being Mrs. B. Randolph Galt, wife of the man who would mold Giro into a great station, was a full-time job and worth every ounce of effort in me.

Getting late. Had to bucket my far shrubs and pines, wheel up two more barrows of rich dirt for the herbs to come, do the bathrooms. But the mail won. I reached for the last precious letter. It was from Ross Grieve Sweetapple, a charming Australian girl I'd met through Angela Lansbury during *Seventeenth Doll*. We felt very close. I'd boldly told her to go ahead and marry Dr. William Sweetapple, and by gosh she did. The marriage was a great success. Bill was a top-notch anesthesiologist.

What about doctors, I puzzled. What happened if you really got sick out here—or hurt? Farm machinery could be vicious. Of course there was a Dr. Burke in Worcester, perhaps he'd come out. I'd heard nasty tales about a dubious surgeon the district called Butcher Monahan. Maybe Ran could fly someone to Sydney in an emergency. Better be daylight, though, light planes weren't allowed in the air after dark, a good way to lose your pilot's license.

What time was it? Two thirty. Nice breeze. Laundry might be dry by four. I'd scrub up Ran's bath, pick a salad when Sam Pugh wasn't looking, pick something for a centerpiece, there might be a geranium or two. The lucerne was flowering in shaggy lavender balls but using them as a centerpiece would send Ran through the roof. I smiled to myself. Lucerne was far too precious as cattle feed to be used for decoration. Might even have time to get to Giro Creek for some watercress, though it was getting sparse as we neared winter. What should I wear tonight? My clothes still hung in cardboard wardrobes from the shipment, out on sleeping porch number three. I wondered when to bring up the subject of closets again. *After* supper.

The light was fading fast as I took down the wash, too dark for watercress, I decided. I'd have a bath by candlelight. Sounded almost sexy. Ran had ordered gas heaters for our three bathrooms. What fantastic luxury that would be, and no undue strain on the new engine. The old one had finally given out, and engine people had been with us for three days the week before. They'd been open-mouthed at the house and couldn't get over the monograms on our towels and sheets. My pie was admired and our cut crystal beer mugs, and what was that thing on the veranda? That thing being the Calder mobile, which made them shake their heads in bewilderment. But it was solitary doing dishes while the males chatted by the fire. Depressing, although it was better to be out of the way. I noticed they

133

immediately switched to awkward small talk in a female presence. Or was it me? Probably both, with the accent on female.

The wash was folded, things to iron piled on an ominous heap of things to iron. The table was set; I'd found one red and one orange geranium and stuffed them in lots of leaves. Clamping my chin on the pile of laundry in outstretched arms, I cautiously toed blindly down the step from the kitchen screen door to the hall and smelled a familiar smell. Damn. The carcass was beginning to go bad. No more chicken. Beef, or else, until we used every scrap. For some reason we got sicker of beef than lamb. Too bad. Lamb was for summer unless I pampered our menus from Town. Must remember to ask Ran to have somebody cart the garbage to the dump; it was starting to crawl. Wonder who would turn the engine on and when? I was afraid to touch it for fear of bollixing it up; Ran agreed heartily, which was rude but correct.

I could hardly see to put the laundry on the shelves beside the coldroom door. The lemon verbena leaves hadn't worked, drat it. I'd picked them fresh for homegrown sachet, but they'd crumbled all over the sheets and lost their fragrance. Brushing them out, I closed the cupboard with a snap. God, it was quiet. It froze me for a few seconds.

Out on the drafty sleeping porch I fingered through clothes and chose a beige mohair sweater, a long plaid skirt, a pair of gold shoes, and carried them to my bathroom. The eye I'd painted stared. Peek-a-boo, I replied soundlessly. One bank of louvers was open and I could look past twenty acres of lucerne to the willows. The sky was the color of a ripe peach from hidden sunset; sunrise and sunset were thwarted by hills if you lived near the river. Who was that? I peered out; had the men come back? I strained my eyes at a horse and rider. No, it was Mrs. Mac—I knew that hat. She awed me simply by being the legendary Mrs. Mac, the lone female to bridge both worlds; the men's secret society and home sweet home. I watched her ride out of sight toward the cottage she shared with her husband, Old Will, and their sixteen-year-old, Willie. Her daughter, Sheila, was married to Corey Blackburn, the stockman who was in charge of Corroborree, the midstation, and lived nine miles up toward the Myall. From that distance Mrs. Mac looked like an eleven-year-old boy, a mite of a woman. A dried leaf with wire veins in a man's wide-brimmed hat and maroon cardigan, pants tucked into Wellington boots.

I watched the sky become a bowl of green tea and fumbled for a match to light the candle, closing the louvers with a shiver. The little room turned from black to blue in the flame. I turned on the tub tap and poured bath oil into a growing oval of rusty water. There was something impudent about a patch of luxury in this raw place. Smiling to myself, I skinned out of muddy shirt and trousers, shoved them under the basin with a bare foot, shucked bra and pants, and stepped into the tub with a sigh. The river water heated just as well as any other even though it did have weeds. I reflected about Mrs. Mac as I soaped. She'd been known to run down a dingo on horseback, a fantastic feat; yet their yard was a sanctuary to orphaned or hurt creatures being nursed back to health. She loathed dingos for the tortures they inflicted on calves, chewing them alive so badly they had to be shot, and set traps for them. But she was heartbroken when a wallaby or bandicoot got caught by mistake. Absolutely nothing she couldn't do; mustered as well as any man; could dig the hole for the gas pump one day; make marmalade; do a mountain of boiled washing; plant potatoes; and ride out fence-checking the next.

Inevitably, I'd been labeled "American Owner's Wife"; actress was yet another tag, and both had put me behind an invisible picket fence. My shoulders were getting cold. I pulled the plug, got out grabbing a towel, and dried energetically to keep warm. I supposed that was why Mrs. Mac and I were always a trifle formal. She set the tone and I followed at her safe distance. Between words I'd search her fine-stitched face for answers to the unanswerable bush. She'd watch me from her brim-shadowed eyes for clues to another planet. We touched hands one day over her ulcers, cruel offspring of her tender heart. I'd run in and gotten some American pills to give her. The next morning she'd brought me her superlative cream in a tall bottle. Thereafter we shared homemade jam and pleasantries and knit brows over illness. I'd watch her ride off, a brown twig on a brown horse and wondered if she knew my jar of jam had a whole career in it.

135

Dressed and warm, I wiped the steamy mirror and looked. My hair was a fright wig. A good brush and chiffon scarf would help and *very* small eyelashes. Greta Garbo once said the only makeup she couldn't do without was eyelashes. Ran didn't mind as long as they didn't show.

Picking up the candle and my dirty clothes, I put the clothes in a bag on the sleeping porch, set the candle on a shelf below a small mirror, did my hair in its light, and took it to the kitchen with me. As I walked by El Bar throwing shadows like black fans, I was tempted to make myself a drink. No, not a good idea, I warned myself. Don't start drinking alone in the bush. What time was it? The kitchen clock said six thirty. Nonmechanical or not, I'd have to learn how to turn on that blasted engine. The dogs barked. Somebody was back. The engine started up with a throaty *bongettah–bongettah,* and lights grew steadily from orange to lemon. Music—quick, music! I blew out my candle and rushed back down the hall to the machine to put on some records. Nothing like a smooth beat and harmony to make a house come alive.

I often thought I'd like to have had a pedometer at Giro to see just how far I walked in a day back and forth through that warren of a house. I used to get fed up with the sound of my own footsteps. Back down the hall to start dinner. Ran drove in front around quarter of seven. The manager must've turned on the engine. A pretty good fire popped in the living room. I was learning to make them like tepees. I heard boots on the veranda.

"Hi," I called out from the kitchen, slipping chicken into bubbling butter.

"Hi," he answered, thumping boots off onto the veranda.

I watched him come in the living room French windows in stocking feet.

"I need a shower," he said. "Would you like a drink?"

"I thought you'd never ask," I replied smiling. Ice. No ice. I'd forgotten the ice again. "Wait, darling, I'll get some ice!" Ran liked a drink with his ice, a hangover from tropical Honolulu.

As I hurried to the little kerosene refrigerator a horrible thought struck me. Shower. He liked fifteen-to-twenty minute showers; I'd done two washes and enjoyed a lavish bath. Usually about this time of night the water boiled all over the roof if there was plenty, sounding like gorillas in tap shoes. I grabbed a fist-sized wild lemon from a crate on the floor and banged out the kitchen screen door to deposit the ice tray and lemon on the drinks table. Quickly I tiptoed out the side door into the chilly night to check the fire in the donkey engine of the water heater. Not a wink of flame. Damn. When the men were gone I'd simply have to practice splitting kindling and keep the thing stoked. I stole back in and heard him clanking ice into crystal. Should I tell him? Yes, I thought with a sigh. It was not always good to be surprised rather than disappointed.

"Darling."

"Yes?"

I stood penitently in the doorway of El Bar. "I'm terribly sorry but we might be near the end of the hot water; the fire looks out and I've been using it."

"That water heater. I'm going to order a new one—oil fired."

"There might be enough for a short shower, sweetheart," I added encouragingly.

"Don't worry about it," he said kindly, handing me a delicious gin and tonic with a half lemon in it.

"What time is dinner?" he asked as he padded across the living room.

"Any time you say."

He looked at his watch. "Seven thirty?"

"OK."

And he disappeared.

The chicken paprika was a triumph and a chocolate mousse I'd tried. Bertha was in great form.

He went through the mail as I finished the dishes.

"Anne?"

"Yes?" I came to the kitchen screen door.

"Found somebody to make your closets."

"Really! Sounds like Christmas!"

"Maybe next week."

"Terrific. I can get things stashed away before Katrina and Jane come."

"And I think Tom Biddeford's on to a pony for Katrina." He went on passing out good news like after-dinner mints.

137

"Ran, how wonderful! She'll lose her mind!"

"Tom says it's had a lot of experience with children."

"Should we save it for a birthday present? She'll be nine July ninth?"

"We'll see. I don't think it matters. She might as well enjoy it if we can get it sooner."

I laughed in anticipation. "She'll be beside herself."

"Have you heard from Jane Fyfe?" he asked.

"Yes, the letter's in here. Flight numbers and times and everything."

"When are they arriving?"

"The fifteenth."

"Good. I'll do some business in Sydney when we fly in."

Nothing special really. But what was *it* about out there?

Dining by candlelight in hard-won atmosphere was a little like being on a ship rolling along an unknown sea, sealed off from the world. That was good, I mused, and that was dangerous, said the secret corner of my mind I didn't want to examine.

As I lay in bed I heard the engine run down, watched the lights dim off, and listened to the silence until he came in the back door. His flashlight swayed as he strode through the house. The living room rug muffled his footsteps for a second or two. Then the boards creaked again as he crossed into our room. I was wearing Juel Park's sheer long-sleeved blue number and what I thought was my subtlest come-hither look. Not that he could see either. He yawned like the MGM lion and disappeared into the bathroom, a thoroughly married man. Giro slept. After a while so did I.

14

Katrina

KATRINA was on her way at last. We'd thought it better for her to almost finish third grade before uprooting her. She was being brought down by our first experiment in education at Giro, Jane Fyfe. Jane was Scottish and had lived in California with Angela Lansbury for four years and had done all sorts of things: been in the army in England, run hotels in Scotland, taught lessons to Angie's two children and, wonder of wonders, had been to Australia, though not exactly to the bush. Her hair was bobbed pepper and salt, her face strong and wide, she laughed with ease, and had a most musical burr. She called Ran "the Lairrd" and we were most fond of her. She was to continue a program of American instruction outlined by the headmistress of Katrina's school, workbooks and all. The perfect solution, because we wanted Katrina with us at Giro and the only alternatives were Australian boarding schools (they actually sent them as young as six) or my teaching her through the government school, correspondence from Sydney, and I knew that spelled disaster in gothic letters. I pictured tearful squabbles in math, tearful exasperation in English, in short, a ramshackle education.

Off and on I wondered about Katrina and playmates. The Biddefords had three children, but Dan, aged eleven, was the only one still at home. Perfect for Katrina, I thought, shifting maternal gears. I'd only met him once but what a fine boy. Very independent, a crack rider, and a great help on his father's station. What a refreshing change for Katrina to meet a boy who could really do important things instead of some of the spoiled brats she'd known in school, the ones who could quote television commercials verbatim and little else. But who else? I must say I couldn't wait to introduce her to Freeda. Freeda was the biggest pig I ever saw. Her first litter was well grown. Ran got talked into the pig business just as I arrived at Giro after we married.

He'd phoned around for a suitable boar, burly enough for Freeda, who was mammoth, but agile enough for her four daughters. A lusty Tamworth Sandy was found and presented with a squealing seraglio. The ladies' enthusiasm was such, he escaped a week later and ran for cover across the river, his deflowered harem oinking back in the pen. It took Ran in the jeep, Errol, our current unpaid jackeroo (station trainee), me, and two horses to catch him. Obviously a sated sultan.

The litters came thick and fast: twenty-five piglets, from four new mothers, and *grande dame* Freeda—she had nine. That was the end of the pigpen and the four young matrons were sent out to forage in the wilds with reluctant hubby.

All efforts to keep Freeda and her nine vaudeville acts in line failed. Not a fence fazed them. Ran tried everything, but I always thought electric fences were a cheap thrill to Freeda; they buzzed her serried bosoms as she'd hoist over with a secret smile. Piglets ducked under.

It'd be fun for Katrina to empty slops if I could con her into feeding them to Freeda. She was a disposal with four feet, but temperamental. Absolutely no squeezed oranges. Anathema. She'd scatter them over a good quarter mile in fury. Three-week-old orange rinds aren't fun on the way to a swim. Heaven to Freeda consisted of pancake bits, cornbread crumbs, sugared oatmeal, bacon curls (damned cannibal), apple peels, onions, beer, a whisper of gin and tonic, jam, dead toast, fried egg edges, spoiled stew, cheese, ancient chili, sour cream, sour milk, and pie heels.

And then there were the dining room rats; Katrina might like them. They were Giro's elite. For some reason they moved frequently. It fascinated me to hear them wending their way between the dining room walls, only an occasional discreetly

140

squeaked altercation would penetrate. Where they moved to is still a mystery. Under the house was suicide. Giro was famous for the nest of snakes under it.

The rest of the house rats were bare-faced shanty Irish, and the reverberating regions under Giro's rambling iron hat were their tenement and playground, featuring raucous brawls and thumping bodies at three A.M.

We were without an attic, just corrugated iron roof, haphazard wooden supports, and a disheveled jailhouse of pipes; the ceilings were tacked on fibro. There was one access, a miserable eighteen-inch-square door in Anybody's ceiling. Ran, the pest control man, driven by sounds of nocturnal revelry, braved that stygian place armed with fresh, they had to be fresh, arsenic Wheaties, which he piled in deadly heaps here and there while trying diligently not to put his size twelves through the fibro. I held the ladder and worried.

This wasn't much fun for anybody, including the rats. So after listening to persuasive talk from country wiseacres, we incarcerated a hungry cat from five P.M. to six A.M. After a peripatetic night cringing in our bed beneath the deafening rattle of pipes, boards, the cat, and rats in flight—back to arsenic Wheaties.

Then there were the frogs. Combined with the rats, Giro homestead must have been considered a four-star restaurant among snakes. The frogs were about the size of a butter plate and just as slick. They appeared to be freshly enameled in apple green. They lived in the awnings, which were already gaudily striped in red and green. Very Christmasy. I could imagine Katrina gleefully unrolling them to hear them plop out. I only did it by mistake or in filthy wet weather, which they loved. Westerly siroccos blew for weeks at Giro, cracking the earth dry, and not a frog anywhere. But a single thunderstorm and they'd all be back in business at the same old stand. *Wraawk, wraawk—wraawk wraawk!* Those frogs would have silenced a going cocktail party. If we were away at all they'd find their way into the toilets and cling to the undersides of things. The snakes used to crawl up the awnings after them. A shuddering experience to look up at shiny frogs legs kicking in death throes, the front half disappearing down a long, dark gullet with eyes.

141

Practically a child's petting zoo, I thought, smiling ruefully. Then I laughed out loud above the dishwater because a ramshackle education was probably exactly what Katrina hoped for—pigs, rats, frogs, snakes, cows, dogs, horses, more horses, and all. My child, the city-hater, had always been nature's girl.

It was terribly important to me to look right to Katrina, perhaps because I knew she much preferred me as a mother, not an actress. I always tried for a cross between Mother Machree and Joan Bennett, neither of whom I resemble in the least. Her plane got in nine thirty A.M. We buckled ourselves into Ran's plane on a beautiful morning at seven.

"You ready?" Ran asked. He never failed to ask that before takeoff, and I couldn't help hearing, "to die." He'd clearly explained that takeoff and landing were the most dangerous moments in flying. I wasn't scared, I just believed him, and up we went with a burst of power.

"Ran?" I lifted my voice over the plane's roar.

"Yes, dearest?"

"Is it going to be hard being instant Father?"

"I don't know why—Katrina's fun. She'll have to mind her P's and Q's around the Station."

"Don't worry. I'll see to that!"

Worcester looked picturesque as we flew over. I'd never driven into Town, although I had my license; that would be a trip for Jane and Katrina and me, I thought, full of new plans. I would've been nervous driving Ran, not that he'd have let me unless he were incapacitated.

"Ran?"

"Yes?"

"If we can always present a united front on any problem with her it'd be good."

"Couldn't agree more!" he replied earnestly.

"I'll always clue you in. We can discuss anything out of her earshot but not in front of her, OK?"

"Absolutely OK."

I smiled back over at him, feeling very close.

"Maybe Dan Biddeford and she will hit it off."

"He's a great boy," Ran answered with enthusiasm. "You wouldn't believe how much Tom depends on him even at his age."

142

Being a parent is a long, complicated process. I began to feel Ran might even enjoy it. As we flew toward Sydney I kept picturing Katrina's lovely face.

"She'll probably be shy with you, darling—it's been a while."

"Don't worry, sweetheart, we'll be fine." He was right. It would either work or it wouldn't. Trying too hard would surely queer it.

"Hope Jane won't be too lonely."

"Well, that could be a problem, always is as far out as we are." He flipped his radio on as we neared civilization. "She could always take a break in Sydney. Doesn't she know people there?"

"One or two, I think. From the time she was here with Angie and her children during *Summer of the Seventeenth Doll*."

"It'll work out."

"Hope so. I just can't see myself teaching correspondence school like Kath Biddeford."

Twenty minutes later I looked down on Sydney Harbor, bristling with sailboats like whitecaps on the shining blue. Then red-roofed suburbs—Sydney was a red, green, and blue city. Ran picked up the radio mouthpiece and requested permission for Romeo Bravo Golf (his call letters) to land. My excitement mounted.

Had she grown taller? I wondered. It happened fast at her age. Jane was a real prize; there was so much we could share. Katrina's pony would arrive in a few days, I smiled inwardly at what I knew would be a great moment in her life. I'd have to warn her about Freeda. Freeda was hardly a nice, fat piggy to pat. She was a surly sow to be fed at a cautious distance.

The plane was on time, its door opened, and there they were. I waved wildly, so did they, laughing and shouting greetings too far away to hear. I turned to Ran and said breathlessly, "Hope they don't get hung up in Customs. Jane's bringing all sorts of canned Mexican goodies and two bags of pinto beans!" Ran thought a minute and then told me the cans wouldn't be a problem but the beans might. Australia was very sticky about plant diseases. He was right, those beans are still being fumigated for all I know. We never saw them again.

We walked inside to wait for them to come through the all-too-familiar glass doors from Customs.

"There she is!" I laughed, pointing at Katrina's small navy

blue figure as she burst through the door and into my arms. She felt so good I couldn't stop hugging her. I looked up at Jane through tears of joy and relief.

She was laughing and telling Ran all about Customs and the head shaking that had gone on over the pinto beans. Katrina was home with us at last, and had shyly begun to call Ran Daddy, which touched me more than I could express.

Jane looked a bit keyed up, but Katrina took the small plane in her stride and fell asleep on the way. But then, that's Katrina. She wrote me a letter once when she was six.

DEAR MOMMY,
I hop you are well if you aren't I'm sorry.

Love

That is distilled Katrina. There's a certain matter-of-factness about her, like her sole comment about Giro meals: "Mommy's food looks awful but it tastes good."

She has large green eyes, a luxuriant crop of cinnamon-brown hair, and could get anybody to do anything she wanted for her—except me, when I'd been pushed too far.

Whenever we missed one of the young jackeroos, or occasional workmen, around Giro, we'd hear hammering, a small, clear voice, and discover Katrina and her current cohort behind some hedge, where they'd be building bird traps, cages, doghouses, saddletrees, or whatever she needed at the time.

To my regret, playing Grease Spot took so much time I couldn't really explore Giro's natural world with her. We'd lived in cities and suburbs and finally here was the country on all sides, but Mother seemed fated to be an indoor girl.

The night she got her horse was an indelible moment. Tom Biddeford and Ran had found a ten-year-old dapple-gray Galloway, about the size of a very large pony or small horse. He'd been trained for children and was without vices, with the exception of sloth and obstinacy. He'd do pretty much what was required, but you had to make him. The only thing you got for nothing was a neck-cracking trot.

Under cover of dark Ran sneaked him in and came down from the barn to give me the word. I beckoned Katrina, saying "Daddy wants to see you." She disappeared with him and after what seemed ages she stepped into the living room; stood stock-still, white, and shaken. I studied her, concerned, and out came a hoarse whisper, "I never thought I'd have a horse of my own." She really did look ill. Smiling in sudden realization and relief I put my arms around her. "Isn't it wonderful, sweetheart?" Ran came in, obviously touched by her stunned reaction. Thank God we hadn't waited until her birthday.

"And Daddy gave me a saddle and a blanket for him and I fed him some oats. He ate right out of my hand but you have to hold it flat—like *this,* " she said breathlessly, color beginning to come back in her face, and stretching out her small taut hand, "His name is Bluebottle," she said with reverence. My eyes stung more than a little. After many years, a man she could call Daddy had given her wide open spaces and her heart's desire—there'd never be a better moment in her life or mine. I looked up at Ran adoringly. The very idea of an embryo family unit moved me deeply. He felt it too. Katrina had recovered herself enough to grin at Ran and ask about the next muster, and could she go. She was sure she and Bluebottle would be a great help. He said they certainly would as long as she obeyed whoever was in charge. Jane came down the hall, pretending she knew nothing whatever, saying dinner was ready and waiting. Thus, gracefully giving my child a fresh audience for her skyrocketing surprise. What a night that was. None of us will ever forget it.

If you wanted to get a rise out of Katrina all you had to do was ask how Bluebottom or Beerbottle was. She bit every time.

"His name is *Bluebottle!*" she'd fume in fierce loyalty.

About four days later Jane Fyfe and I made lunch for a Sunday picnic across the river. I drove Rover; Katrina plodded behind on Bluebottle. I had whacked Rover into four-wheel drive and had triumphantly made it across a shallow spot. We looked back and there sat Katrina with a face that looked as if someone had taken a monkey wrench to a tomato.

She shouted to us in a voice thick with tears, "He won't *go!* He won't go in the *river!*"

Bluebottle's feet were smugly stuffed into the gravel bank.

"Kick him!" we yelled over the water.

"Get a stick!" called Jane.

She kicked and kicked and kicked, her short legs glancing off the saddle only. Bluebottle never felt a thing.

"*Make* him do it, darling. You've got to *make* him go across. He's bamboozling you, Katrina!" I shouted.

I swear that pony smirked.

Gulping tears and sobs of helpless rage, she went for a stick. Bluebottle waited, his reins hanging, playacting the well-behaved horse.

Getting back on was a major operation. She was far too short-legged. She pulled him awkwardly down a path, so she could stand on high ground, but everytime she'd lift a leg he'd move away in blithe unconcern. This went on four or five times until, as a final insult, he just kept going back to the barn. It's the only time I ever saw Katrina have a bona fide tantrum. She flung herself onto the grassy bank and beat it with clenched fists, legs kicking furiously, bawling in frustration and lacerated ego.

I wrestled Rover around at the water's edge, hit him into four-wheel drive, again, and crossed my private Hellespont to reach her.

"He doesn't *love* me! *He never will!*" Katrina wailed, exposing the real wound.

I climbed out, prepared to glue her back together, when Ran trotted into view on his mare, leading the culprit. Ran took over, got Katrina back on, gave her stern instructions, thwacked the pony's fat behind, and Bluebottle plowed into the river with supreme ennui.

From then on Katrina bossed that pony and rode him as if she were a born princess. Bluebottle taught her a lot more than I ever could. Cheap at the price.

Jane was a great help, although she suffered from the cold. It was so dark early in the morning we had to use the engine to be able to see breakfast. I've never been crazy about candlelight breakfasts. She'd have a roaring fire going in the kitchen fireplace even before I got there. She and her fires were wonderfully cheering.

Still, housekeeping for four took a lot of time, especially without electric, frozen, or packaged shortcuts. If you wanted vegetables you put your boots on, grabbed a basket, walked out the laundry door and all the way to the back fence, went around that and on past the old Number 3 rainwater tank; down aways more past the garbage, on down farther past the clotheslines and on into the garden; found what you wanted, dug them or picked them, carried them back, washed them in the laundry tub, pulled off your boots, took the beets, beans, carrots or whatever into the kitchen and peeled, cut, and cooked them. And you'd better mop the mud in the laundry or it walked through the house.

Whenever I could manage it, Katrina and I escaped my homemade prison together. One golden late afternoon remains perfect in my mind. The river was plump with rain, and we wound our way alongside it through thicket tunnels of bottlebrush to a secret pebbled place where the willows wept. You longed to run your hands along the smooth folds and satin ribbons of water. One bough of a venerable willow reached out way over the rushing water, made to order for a nine-year-old girl. Chortling with excitement, she wormed her way out onto the big branch and lay like a panther cub, those water-green jade eyes a deadringer for the river rushing under her. I sat on my haunches and watched her, wondering what magic had given me so miraculous an animal. The heavy water skirted a boulder beyond her branch and Katrina said ecstatically she'd like to live on that rock forever. I wished she could.

It grew chilly and since she loved fires, we made three or four miniature bonfires in full blaze five inches across. We'd start with stiff hairs of dried grass, then a twig (a yule log to us), then another, and another in tepee shapes with a lizard's-tongue of flame darting out of the top. They were perfection, and I watched, enchanted, at her tangled mop head frozen in concentration against the noisy beauty of the water.

Nor did I have time to ride with Katrina much, and Jane wasn't much on horseback. It absolutely exhausted her, and because she avoided it whenever possible, it made her muscles sore as boils when she did. We only tried a family ride twice; showing off Giro's views meant climbing up steep hills and down steep dales; we almost lost Jane several times. Although she'd driven trucks in the Army, it was obvious she had sidestepped the cavalry. Moreover, the whole operation was far too slow for Ran. Many times he'd think he saw a dingo on a hillside and tear off at top speed to chase it, out of boredom. So Katrina had her greatest fun riding out alone or with Dan Biddeford, or mustering with Ran and the men. We let her ride anywhere within sight of Giro homestead, and since the house sat in the open like a shag on a rock, she had a lot of leeway.

Wonderful Dan, as I dubbed him, was a fine character, an excellent Australian lad. Although he was only eleven, the Biddefords had taught him to drive a tractor and he had long since become an expert at milking, forking hay, and building fires. Dan and Katrina used to exchange weekend visits, riding the ten miles cross-country, one or the other of them riding partway to a meeting place.

Of course, I worried. My head used to reel with gory pictures of Katrina lying in a pool of blood, broken bones protruding, or lying half dead from snakebites or horse kicks. But what can you do? You can't keep a child on a chain like a dog, and I strongly disapprove of chained dogs. Giro's dogs drove me mad: miserably chained on bare dirt, hardly fed unless they worked. But I was told that's how they were trained to love cattle work. Their work gave them freedom, food and excitement. They were gaunt and spiritless between musters.

In December heat Katrina and Dan would ride their ponies into the river in faded bathing suits, their lunch makings stashed in the crotch of a tree. Wonderful Dan built fireplaces of carefully selected stones and they'd eat like lords and ladies, as royal they were. Freedom is a royal gift and those two savored it as all too few American-raised children have.

What a losing battle to recapture that dazzling land, fresh with freedom, fenced with adult protection and supper's ready; a siren land, lethal, beautiful, and barely met.

I envied them as the screen door slammed.

15

Jane and the Trip to Town

I WISH it had been a light winter, perhaps Jane would have stayed, though I doubt it. Poor Jane. She tried, we tried, Katrina tried, when she wasn't on a horse or wishing she was on one. But Jane had made two mistakes. She'd been spoiled by California's glorious climate and creature comforts. She hadn't realized she was running away from magnetic ties with a family that had become her emotional life.

Poor Jane. She was so *cold,* and Giro was punishing cold that June, often below 30°. A forty-frost winter as they say. One dressed for letter writing as *pour le ski*—fleece-lined boots, heavy socks, cashmere at skin level, sweaters on top. My feet and fingers would numb minute by minute sitting with a wavering candle for light at nine A.M., pushing a pen. The sun warmed outdoors slightly by eleven, but who was outdoors? Giro's threadbare fibers practiced osmosis: they let cold in but never out—65° out in the sun at noon, 45° to 50° inside.

Jane finally confessed to me that she pined for her adopted family, especially the children. My heart sank. We bought her an electric heater and gave her carte blanche on the engine. She slept in the guestroom and Anybody's windows were beaded with steam from Jane's attempts to re-create sunny California. But it would have been insane to run the engine twenty-four hours a day and when it went off at night, the cold crept in and took over the house.

I'd brought a couple of flannel nightgowns and wore them to

rags that winter. It was a shivering dash across the living room obstacle course to our bedroom from my bath. I'd grit my teeth and scream as I hit sheets that felt like a skating rink, and rapidly pump my legs as on a bicycle to warm them and, incidentally, me. Ran would call from a bathroom, steaming from his hot shower.

"How are the sheets coming along?"

"F-f-f-ine!" I'd shout back through chattering teeth, bicycling savagely. "B-b-b-e almost h-h-uman in a m-m-m-inute."

Fortunately Ran's basic temperature seemed warmer than normal, at the very least 99.6. It was like sleeping with a Nuremberg stove.

We had one rowdy day before Jane decided she couldn't stick it out. To celebrate American 4th of July, we three, Jane, Katrina and I, went to Worcester in Rover. We went to Town!

Rover's doors had been removed for summer heat and were still off. I had my Aussie license, but had never driven on the left side except once up the station, but I'd had the road all to myself and used the middle.

It was a dry, sunny day with a crisp wind. Bristling with synthetic confidence, I grasped Rover's helm and away we sailed. Ran did it in an hour and a half; why couldn't I? I secretly avoided thinking about the river crossings, as getting Rover into four-wheel drive was almost more than I could do, and the margin for error on the slab of narrow cement was nil.

There were some really uncalled-for curves, fallouts, ratty wooden bridges and hairpin turns, one after the other; which neither Rover nor I seemed prepared for. However, I think it was sneaky of Rover to lift his back wheels and come down with such abandon. It was as if he'd just been let out of stir. We had to hang on for dear life without the doors. The first river crossing was like an opening night on Broadway. Pale and shaking, I beat and beat at the lever with the bright red knob to force it into four-wheel drive, hoping the motor wouldn't die. We made it, riffling through the current like a ferry.

Intoxicated, I roared on. No traffic so far. Lulled by success, I forgot about staying on the left side. Ran had warned me. "Please watch it, darling," he'd said. "In a spot you may swerve the wrong way."

The other river crossings were a crumb brushed off my newly

150

professional shoulder. We bulled our way through on my new-found confidence. I was a bush native; I knew the ropes; I might join the ACWA (Australian Country Women's Association). That is what I was, wasn't I? Crash—pause—thump. Rover leaped over a sharp dip before a long, large hill. Up we raced. Rover ate it up. He bared his grille and coughed up dust and speed.

Jane saw the truck first. It rose like grinning death out of flying pieces of road. Instinctively I cut right and faced him head-on. No, no, Rover, no—the wrong side! I wrenched the wheel and the truck thundered by, Rover's wheels crunching up onto eroded hillside. Jane laughed softly. "Good for you!" Her Scottish burr was stronger than I'd ever heard it. "We never had roads like this in the British Army!" Or drivers like me, I scolded myself.

Swallowing and trembling, I gathered speed again, clinging to the left like a train to a track; we made it in an hour and a half. Just out of town the dirt road changed to pavement. What a feeling. Rover felt like a lean and hungry Bentley coursing through civilization. Just think—2,500 people; 5,000 legs; 5,000 eyes; cars, real cars. No four-wheel drive, though, I sneered, impossibly pleased.

We all grew cocky with relief and began to sing "Scotland's Burning," the best of all rounds, Katrina's clean voice striking precise harmony. Music belonged to her. Down the road we bellowed, chugging into town on the wrong side of the street. I hardly heard the honks, I was so glad to be there at all, and swung Rover left out of everybody's blasting horns where he promptly died in front of Mrs. Dare's Green Grocery. We laughed in a heap and climbed out.

Worcester was so unusual it was fun. Looking at canned goods on other people's shelves was a rare pleasure. Strange brand names and corny slogans intrigued me: "Drinka Pinta Milka Day," or "Panel Beating," on a garage. That last always made me picture whole families backed up, their bottoms raised, waiting for a weekly spank.

And all those people. No one mentions the herd instinct with the same emphasis as self-preservation or sex; it ought to be next in line at least. Or perhaps I just missed people.

It seems we were as refreshing to Town as Town was to us.

Prowling around the General Store, I became conscious of whispers and nudges. People would group, stare into space, and smother sniggers with covert eyes. On the street, they frankly gaped in bunches. Silent as we passed, assiduously unconcerned. Willy-nilly my other head had come along.

The crates and boxes were loaded, Katrina was full of candy, and Rover haggled about going home. A seedy fellow leaned out of the Town pub as we churned by and yelled, "Hi, Anne!"

I waved and home we pointed, the sun spearing our eyes with javelins of light. Bad, very bad. The wind spiraled dust into that stark light, blinding me on every hill; I couldn't see the road or dropoffs or anything but shimmering dust. We crawled nervously. The crossings weren't important anymore, if I could only see. Blowing dirt stung our eyes. If only someone had remembered to put the doors back.

It was a tense trip for greenhorns. Giro was a lamp in a window through whirling earth as we came down gratefully into our valley.

Ran was silhouetted on the veranda and came to meet us. I pulled up in front and stopped. Katrina hopped out and ran to check Bluebottle.

"Boy, what a trip!" I sighed wearily.

"You're a little late. Have any trouble?" asked Ran.

"Well—" I glanced at Jane, hoping she wouldn't tell on us. I'd tell him myself. "We made it to Town in an hour and a half, but, wow! Coming home was hell on wheels, without doors. The sun was in my eyes and dust, too. Very scary!"

"You remember to stay on the left?" Jane never moved a muscle.

"Only forgot once. But I damned near hit a truck. I won't forget again." Jane smiled at me and got out dusting off her jacket and pants.

"That's the worst road in the world," she said. "I couldn't've driven it half so well." I could have kissed her.

Ran held the door for us and gave me a penetrating look as I passed him. "An hour and a half?"

I looked straight ahead. "Yup!"

"That's too fast."

"Yup. Sure is," I replied and went to fix dinner.

152

As fond as I was of Jane, or perhaps because of it, I keenly sensed her unhappiness. Ran did, too, I think. She and I had a very straight talk and I urged her to write Angela and to go back to her world. Shining and blinking at an unsolicited reprieve, she hugged me hard. And that was that.

Depressed that Jane wasn't going to work beyond August, we took the lid off another kettle of fish. We decided to try the PNEU. That spells rubber tire in French, but means Parents National Educational Union in England and is an organization that has sent teacher-governesses, armed with lessons from London, to students in every corner of the Colonial Empire since 1870. Very impressive sounding and I had hedged our bet by filling out sheaves of applications.

While Jane graced us with her smiling Scottish dependability, Ran and I could go off together here and there. We were in danger of becoming parallel lines. I suffocated under a junk-pile of things-to-do-today that only had to be done over again tomorrow.

Somehow I had to go outdoors and play. Not with a child's furrowed concentration. I'm told that when I was three years old, I'd leaf through magazines in utter absorption, barking, "Don't busturb me!" at the slightest interruption. Not like that.

Play that knows it's playing. The flourish of the human plant. Gay and purposeless play, like horseplay or loveplay or play-at-random, true recreation. Re-creation, to create anew. Two people in love needed that like air and water every day. A man has a right to a helping of playmate. Helpmates can be boring as woodpeckers. But I was too tame for him, I think. He'd always pick the toughest, rockiest, or boggiest places to roam in Rover, and we'd end up four hours later with a winch inching us free as the sun sank. Or we'd have to walk our horses down slopes so steep it felt as if they'd stumble over us. We never rode enough for my behind to be conditioned to thirty-eight miles on horseback, which was what it took to the Myall and back, lovely as it was. Even Sparkle Plenty would upchuck her recently quenched thirst halfway home, from fatigue. Here and there Giro's landscape was munificent. Once, out in Rover, we heard sounds like a distant Niagara. Wondering in excitement whether one of the rain forests had sprung so giant a leak, I begged

153

Ran to stop. He smiled indulgently as I sat, mouth agape, to listen.

"It's the *wind,* darling."

I stared incredulously. "What? It can't be!"

"Look." He pointed to the miles of grass rolling up to young gums, and on to the great gray ones up top. He was right. It was the wind, carding and combing all that mass of growth. I heard grass eddying and flowing over rapids of earth and almost imperceptible movements in thousands of gums that sounded like booming water.

I was proud to learn to manage the really knotty gates and stand with eyes crooked at the sun and an invisible thumb in my vest as he drove through. They were like wire puzzles backward, and I could put 'em back the way they were, too—just to spite. It was a point of Aussie pride never to really fix them. What for? they'd say with a shrug. They knew the gate twists like the back of their battered hands.

Strangely wordless those playtimes. I couldn't seem to think of much to say anymore that would really amuse or interest him. Fear of being boring might be the ultimate social disease. I wouldn't prattle. He didn't seem to need to talk. Rape occurred to me a noon or two; in the sun, by the far-up Myall River, hurtling thinly over stones. I would've been a willing victim. It would have been better than words more than once. At least we were together, if only side by side.

16

R and R

LOONG–short–loong–short–loong, must've dreamed it. No. The big bed joggled heavily. I opened my eyes. Ran was hauling himself out of sleep and into khaki pants. He'd worn only his underwear tops to bed. "Bloody phone," he muttered thickly.

"Maybe it's an emergency," I croaked. My vocal cords grow fur in the night.

"It better be. It's four thirty."

Again the phone jarred the cold black house. I shivered and dug under the covers.

"Yes? Who?" I heard his irritated shout all the way from the office.

"Who? Bock? Oh, *park!* She's not awake yet."

Park . . . Park, I thought, searching my logy brains. My God, maybe that was Arthur, my agent in California. I woke up.

"Can she call back? Right. What? I said, she'll call back in an hour or so. Right. Thank you." He was coming back down the hall. I sat up swathed in blankets.

"Darling, was that Arthur Park?"

"Yes. Wants you to call him."

I couldn't deny a certain guilty excitement. "Sorry he got so screwed up with our time."

"Yes. Would you mind telling him it may be ten thirty A.M. yesterday for him, but it's four thirty A.M. *today* for us."

"You bet, darling. I'll set him straight." People at home just didn't get the time difference. Figured from Los Angeles it was tomorrow and seven hours earlier. At least that's how I managed to remember.

Ran sat on the bed and started pulling on wool socks.

"Might as well stay up. We're moving some weaners near the yards. George's coming up for a look in a couple of days."

"Me too," I rejoined, hoping to improve matters by sharing discomfort. "I'll make coffee!" You might have known the disrupting phone call would be for me.

By the time I got dressed Jane was up, well sweatered, and hustling wood in for the kitchen fire. Katrina slept blissfully on. It was one of the best things she did.

At six thirty A.M. I called back. Arthur was out to lunch. Damn. I'd never sandwich an overseas call in between Groceries' determined ladies. Nine thirty might work. That'd be three thirty P.M. his time. Yesterday afternoon. That whole time differential underlined how very far away we were. Not to mention abysmal phone quality.

I eventually got him, squinting my eyes and smiling horridly in order to hear. Wonder why people did that. Had nothing whatever to do with ears. He outlined two television offers. One, a G. E. Theatre and the other an unusually good script with Dean Stockwell, who'd just made a splash in *Sons and Lovers* with Mary Ure. I said I'd let him know.

Now what? Ran had briefly mentioned wanting us to go to Western Australia to his other property when the new Cessna 182 arrived. (He felt it was larger and safer than our 172.) Jane wasn't staying much longer. Impossible. Still I could go and be back in two and a half weeks. I still hadn't sold my house in California and, furthermore, the finished pool had cost far more than I'd planned. Those payments, taxes, and maintenance on the house were draining my savings. And there had been Katrina's former school, clothes, and the dentist to pay for as well as my secretary's salary, gas, and food. Helen had held things together and been responsible for Katrina until she left for Australia. It was frightening how fast money disappeared when none was coming in. Also, I wasn't getting pregnant. Perhaps I could see Dr. Krohn. And Mother and Dad. And friends. Sorely tempted, I remembered my father pacing up and down over a year ago and saying, "If you marry Ran, don't be tempted to work. You might end up with half a career and half a marriage. You'd hate that, and it wouldn't it be fair to Ran. Be sure you take that into account when you make up your mind."

How wise he was. He knew exactly what the pitfalls would be. Why didn't I call Arthur right back and just say no? On the other hand, why not at least explain the offer to Ran? See what his reaction would be. We were an entity now and capable of shouldering joint decisions.

He thought I should go! I felt as transparent as the glass lady in science museums. As if he'd read my mind from his many mountaintops as I attacked chores or ate the mail alive.

I packed in high gear. Called my house-sitting cousin, Eric, and begged my house back for a couple of weeks. Called Peg McNaught to meet me, and in general went mad trying to be calm about everything. I looked at my puffed, cut, and angry hands. Hangnails like tatting. Damn. What to do about hair? Stop eating cheese, crackers, and Mrs. Mac's cream. Just stop eating. I'd gained four or five pounds.

"I'll grow a beard while you're gone," said Ran.

"Darling! Have you ever?"

"Nope." He grinned impishly. "Always wanted to. And I'll take Jane and Katrina to Western Australia for a quick look."

I felt a pang. I should be along.

"You and I can go back again when the weather warms," he went on, answering my conscience-stricken glance. I threw myself in his arms and kissed him with total abandon. What a man. What a sensitive, generous man.

I worked on the script on the plane, sipping bad champagne and smudging the pages because of the enormous amounts of hand cream I'd used on my arid hands. The Galts met me in Honolulu and I spent the night to break the twenty-hour trip. I told them everything amusing I could think of and they loved it. It was worth the trip just to tell them about Ran and Giro firsthand.

On the plane to Los Angeles I went to work again. Ronald Reagan was my costar and Ida Lupino would direct. That'd be fun. I'd never been directed by a woman, with the exception of

157

my mother. I was dying to see how Ida handled a setful of men. Ronnie was sweet, although I hoped he wouldn't bring his soapbox. Conservative politics were his consuming passion. I was an apolitical preservative.

The Dean Stockwell script was better. *Dance Man.* Couldn't wait to play it. About a lonely woman and a poisonous con man who ran a ballroom dancing studio. Ronnie, Ida, and I would have to sidestep fields of corn in *Goodbye, My Love*.

A luscious stewardess was bending over me, a mass of perfect teeth and dimples: "Anything I can get you, Miss Baxter?"

"Ummmmm—a gin and tonic with fresh lime, please."

"Sure thing," oozed dimples, and she wove down the aisle. What time was it? Eleven Honolulu time. One o'clock Los Angeles time. My brain spun. That meant it was six A.M. tomorrow at Giro. I'd be frying steak with three sweaters on and looking forward to Groceries. This wasn't a plane. It was a magic carpet. I felt thinner and vaguely keyed up. Wardrobe in the morning. We'd start shooting in two days. Strange. All so familiar. The morning ahead seemed more real than Giro. Which was reality? Suspended as I was between two opposing lives, both had an aura of fiction. It made me hungry and nervous.

Ronald Reagan couldn't have been nicer and brought not one but two soapboxes along with him: one for each foot. Ida Lupino was very good at her job. She displayed tough, palsy-walsy goodwill with the crew, but held a steel rein on every detail and knew exactly what she wanted and why. I studied her constantly. Instinctively I studied her in case I'd ever have to play her—or someone like her. Actors did that with most people, even passersby. Anytime. Anywhere. She was excellent with the camera. I wondered if I could do that. The mass of mechanical detail to solve was crushing. I don't think I could've managed. Any more than I could manage what I was doing and life at Giro at the same time. I squirmed in my canvas chair with ANNE BAXTER bannered across the back. It was costing her something too, I decided. Minute by minute, from the first day, I watched her dab fiercely at a perspiring face and neck with a chic kerchief.

California spoiled me rotten. Eric had left the house spotless. The clothes I'd brought huddled in acres of empty closets. At home my new closets were already jammed. At home. Where was that and which was true? I'd rented a car and found absurd delight in driving fast over slick roads. I gorged on fresh fruit and gave in to telephonitis. My hands had almost healed, nails grew and gleamed; my feet twinkled with a pedicure. Civilization had upended its shameless cornucopia of tricks just for me.

I'd talked to Ran and Katrina from Honolulu. The Cessna 182 was ready to be picked up the day after I left. Ran had stayed in Sydney and flown it home. By now he, Jane, and Katrina were well on their way to Western Australia, 2,500 miles west of Giro. Jane was very game but that must have been a long trip in a small plane. Katrina would have slept most of the way. Ran called from Perth as I made morning coffee at four forty-five A.M. It was a fair connection for 11,000 miles. Katrina had, indeed, slept most of the way. Jane was reasonably chipper. We began to speak like lovers desperate to touch, if only with voices. I hung up.

My kitchen light was the only one on Brooktree Road. A tardy owl whooed. Tires whirred on far off Sunset Boulevard, and the Los Angeles *Times* landed on my driveway. Then next door, then with fainter rhythmic plops, down the road. The sky was rinsing itself of night. I stared into space. Ran was living in tomorrow evening. My ears rang. What on earth was I doing here? I should have been in his heavy, smooth arms ready for bed. A distant fire engine whined and I jumped in alarm. I'd be late for work. I grabbed my script, flicked off the light, and ran to the car. Wait a second. Take the paper to read under the dryer. Imagine having fresh news, I marveled, as I wound swiftly down Sunset, headed for the Freeway. Somehow it didn't seem all that important anymore.

Everything was work. Even lunch hours were filled by fittings for the next show. The last quarter inch of Mrs. Mac's forbidden cream melted off my middle. Dinner became a rare hamburger with watercress as I soloed in a house no longer really mine. Peeling off eyelashes, I'd lay them carefully in their plastic box beside my plate, too weary and hungry to take the rest of the gook off my face until a warm shower and bed. No sound but my own fork.

I'd try to picture Ran flying, silhouetted against a blazing plane window with Katrina sleeping peacefully behind. Wonder what Perth was like, or his property at Esperance 350 miles south? Or the Indian Ocean? It was a spiritual tug-of-war living in so many worlds.

Dance Man would begin at noon tomorrow. Ran might call. I sank into quick tears. What in hell was the matter with me? Just tired. Go to bed. You'll hear the phone. Saturday and Sunday I'd be with Mother and Dad. I'd have to play down the gorier daily Giro details and be prepared for a lecture or two. Only because they loved me I knew, but I wasn't up to it.

Two hours later the phone rang. I fished for the receiver "H'lo?" I squeaked.

"Darling?" I could hardly hear. Clearing my throat I started to shout, "Yes!"

"We're back in Perth from Esperance."

"Are you all right, dearest? How's Katrina?"

"Fine. Everybody's fine. We'll fly back to Giro tomorrow. Didn't want you to worry if you couldn't get us."

"Everything OK at Esperance?"

"Pretty good. I'll tell you all about it when I see you."

"Wish I were there."

"You will be. I'll take you in a month or so. The plane's great—much more comfortable." I strained to hear. "Did you see your mother and father?"

"Not yet. I'm flying up this weekend." There was a crackling pause.

"Stay loose."

"I will, darling."

"Lots of love." My throat shut. "I miss you."

"Miss you too—won't be long now."

"Love to Katrina."

"Bye-bye, dearest."

The line echoed and coughed. An Australian voice said, "Are you through, sir?"

I curled up tightly, avoiding the vacant sheets beside me and solemnly eyed the dark. A rather cynical French proverb often settled me. "Nothing is either as good or as bad as it seems." I slept again, cradling his voice in my head.

The weekend with my parents was neither as good as I'd

hoped, nor as bad as I'd feared. Their new-built house was full of beauty and peace. Mother's garden already looked ten years old, artless and free in form. She always called plants and trees her babies and they loved her back with vigorous growth and bloom. I laughed in delight at the lineup of her disreputable garden shoes; their stubby turned-up toes caked with mud and pleated deep by the wet. Not much was said about Giro. Dad asked a few polite questions, eliciting a few thorny harrumphs from Mother when he did. It was just as well. Giro remained a sleeping hound under our reunited family table. We had a nice time.

Dean Stockwell was excellent and we worked well together. He was an overly intense and private person. Music was a mutual enthusiasm and gave us rapport. He told me he'd planned to be a concert pianist but at sixteen or so, when he'd sit down to practice, he'd get overpoweringly sleepy. Eventually a psychiatrist told him to go on to something else, that his subconscious resistance was too strong, and that psychic damage might be permanent. So he decided to try acting, his second love. He adored his exquisite little wife, Millie Perkins. She'd played to many plaudits in *The Diary of Anne Frank.*

Arthur Park came on the set to lunch with me and asked if I'd like to do a third show. That stopped me. A thing called *Checkmate* with Anthony George, Sebastian Cabot, and Doug McClure. A new series I'd never seen. I said I'd see if Ran might come up, if not I'd go home. As Arthur talked, I imagined Ran and me in my house, away from the apartheid of outdoors and in. Alone together for a week.

I finally got him at Giro. "Darling, I plan to leave the day after I finish shooting and see Dr. Krohn. But if you'd like a break and a visit to Honolulu and Los Angeles courtesy of *Checkmate,* just say so."

He came up that next weekend, beard and all. He took a cab to the house and was waiting as I came in from work, the early evening sun streaming in behind him as he raced toward me. We came together with shouts of joy, lovers again. The beard was carefully studied: very luxuriant, but itchy, he complained. Scissors were found. I clipped some; he shaved the rest. It was an altogether blissful time of R and R.

"Did you see Dr. Krohn?"

161

"Yes, love." We sprawled on the familiar chairs in the atrium of my house as we had done almost a year ago. Only closer.

"Nothing wrong. Just slightly wound-up. Thought I'd be barefoot and pregnant by now."

"What's the hurry?" he commented sanely.

"There isn't any . It's just me." I looked away. I wasn't going into my age again. He watched me steadily.

"Just you is a lot." I leaned over in a rush of warmth and kissed him.

"And sometimes that's good and sometimes it's bad, isn't it?" I said softly.

"Maybe." His eyes glinted with fun. "No complaints."

I laughed back at him and stood up. "Give me that plate—I'd better do the blasted dishes." He never moved.

"Leave 'em," he said and pulled me down into his arms.

Ran only visited the set once. He stood in the shadows outside camera and lights and watched Anthony George pretend to drive half of a car. Two sweating grips maneuvered it to match the filmed drive on the process screen behind him. Mr. George was the handsome star of the series' trio, firmly wedded to one smoldering expression used in every circumstance other than acute violence. In the sequence we'd done the day before with a maddened rearing horse, Mr. George's eyes actually widened. Ran's only comment was, "Where'd they find *him?*"

Jane would leave for America the day we arrived in Sydney. Our brief vacation was over.

17

Fatherhood

JANE was gone and the wind whistled through an empty house. She'd been a great comfort. In her unique way, she had a foot in two worlds: an umpampered British one, and through Angela Lansbury and me, a theatrical one. When she'd gone I finally dared to look in that secret corner of my mind and saw loneliness crouched, licking its chops. Jerking my mind away, I concentrated on daily minutiae and the growing certainty that I was pregnant. Don't tell Ran until you're sure, I told myself, no point in false alarms.

Katrina had liked Jane, but hated schoolwork and now had a surprise vacation with her adored Bluebottle. She avidly followed all Station doings, including butchering, which depressed me. Why didn't she recoil as I did? And was she developing the bush's calloused eye?

Ran began to assert his authority, and fatherhood grew a capital F. It started with the screens. Screened doors were everywhere. Katrina's method of opening them was at least pragmatic. She pushed straight ahead. Unhappily, straight ahead for her was smack in the upper abdomen of the screen, thereby causing it to belly out and separate from its cross frame.

"Katrina, watch how you open those screen doors, please."

"Yes, Daddy."

She'd forget. A screen would have to be replaced.

"Listen, Katrina, I'm not kidding. Stop shoving your hand into those screens!"

"Sorry, Daddy."

Then I'd chime in.

"Katrina, for *heaven's* sake *look* what you're doing to this *screen!*" I'd shout as she dodged around a corner. There were quite a few things like that. I knew she resented his discipline; I'd been the center of gravity for too long. But it was only right and I backed him up. The united front he and I had discussed. As his contribution to the cause Ran made a real effort to come home to lunch but even on good days the conversation went about like this:

"Say, Katrina, did you hang up your saddle?" Pause.

"I think so."

Another pause.

"Well"—Ran would smile slightly—"did you or didn't you?"

"I *think* I did."

Ran would know she hadn't, and would deliver a short, sharp lecture on saddle care. Sounds of forks and chewing. Long pause.

"How's our friend Beerbottle," I'd quip lamely.

"Bluebottle!" she'd say in disgust. Her sense of humor was still remote in that area.

"How would you like to help us muster tomorrow?" Ran would suggest, knowing she'd be thrilled.

"Sure!"

"Have to get up good and early," he'd warn. "We won't wait for you."

"I will, don't worry!"

"More pie, Ran?"

"No, thanks. I'd better get up to Corroborree; the Black-burns are having pump problems."

"Can I go?" Katrina'd ask.

"You may ride Bluebottle up if you like. Take some of that girth off him. I have to bring some spare parts up in the Land Rover."

The Blackburns had three children, Daisy, seven, Gordon, five and a half, to whom Katrina was an older woman (a role she enjoyed) and Lana, four.

164

On bad days I was the only one talking. I'd toss what I thought were tempting subjects across the table, to "M-mmms!" "Huh-uhs," or "Yups!" And another and another. Mail was not allowed at the table, although it would have filled many a gap with voices other than mine. Reading at the table offended Ran. It *was* wrong. But we seemed to need it out there. The mail arrived only twice a week, after all. Why couldn't we have done what was right for us, not simply what was right?

He confused me with quirks like that. Invisible cracks in a favorite record. Not paying a speck above the going rate for help was one. His utter scorn for anyone having learned French (of which I was foolishly proud) was another. That had been our first—what? Altercation? Couldn't call it a fight, he'd just shouted me down. Odd.

Ran was good to Katrina, but the role of father was a new one and not exactly well rehearsed. Nine-year-olds can insulate themselves from critical adults with great skill.

Once lunch was over, out they'd go. Outdoors was outdoors, indoors was in, and never the twain shall meet the keeper of the house. What a jumble shop my mind had become! As I cleared the table one day, I looked out at trees swaying in the wind, and heard the Calder mobile clank on the distant veranda and counted months once again. The baby would be due sometime in April. I already had an appetite like a doornail, and generally felt as if I were molting.

Perhaps we ought to forget the family lunches. Also, supper would be getting later and later as the light began to linger. I could make early supper for Katrina—she was always starved—sit with her, and eat later on when Ran came in. Might make mealtimes less stiff-necked. As it was, *I* was getting ornery from conversational blight.

Sitting by the fire that night feeling more than usually sleepy I knew it was time to tell him. I wondered how he'd react. I was excited but worried about the future. What would I do about a doctor in the coming months? We'd have to find a good one in Sydney. Perhaps Bill Sweetapple had an obstetric colleague. Ran sat reading in his big red chair as I appeared in the office doorway.

"Darling?"

"Yes?" He raised his eyebrows and gazed at me, lost in Queensland Country Life.

"I'm very pregnant."

He dropped his magazine and looked at me in amazement. "Really?"

"Really. I didn't want to tell you until I was absolutely sure."

"Fantastic." He smiled, rose, and calmly took me in his arms.

"I'm slightly nervous about the whole thing," I mumbled into his sweatered shoulder.

"Don't be silly," he replied softly, smoothing my back with a gentle hand. "It'll be fine. How've you been feeling?"

"Only medium, but that's perfectly normal. No problems."

He held me away from him and gave me a long, unreadable look. "Does Katrina know?"

"Not yet. I'll tell her later. There's loads of time. I'm not due until April."

He walked to the desk, dug a cigar box out from under a pile of papers, took one, unwrapped it, bit off one end, and lighted it.

"You'll need help," he said, looking serious. "I've got to fly to Sydney for a day or so. There's an agency that's supposed to be good, but it's tough getting people to come this far out."

I curled up in the big chair and watched him study his aromatic cigar, standing in front of embers like fire opals.

"Ran, could we possibly offer a bit more than the going rate?" I asked, knowing I was on thin ice.

He thought a moment and shook his head. "Not a good idea. The country pays eleven pounds a week. I don't think we should rock the boat."

"It was just a thought." And I backed away from a touchy subject. He was a stickler for following bush protocol in certain areas. I stared into the coals. Or was it money again? Such a mysterious subject. The larger plane had to be paid for, I'd heard him discussing it with Cessna in Sydney. Brochures were still open on his desk. Could I have offered to pay extra? No, it would have been bad form for me to suggest paying an extra stipend as bait for help basically to do with the station. I shook my head. Wouldn't do. There was a brochure from Caterpillar,

166

too, I noticed. I knew he wanted a bigger machine. A D-6. For a new road up to the Myall.

"Let's turn in. It's ten. Nobody's up but us." He flicked his cigar ash into the dying fire and came toward me. "After all, you need your rest," he kidded me with a fond grin. "Yell when you're ready and I'll go down and turn off the engine."

"OK." I got up, hugged him for a second, called back in a stage whisper, "I'll just check Katrina," and went down the fast-cooling hall.

The laundry flew like flags the next morning as I hung it in blustering wind. If we could only get help. At least I still had the Wizard of Oz, or was it booze? Sam Pugh might be soaked in alcohol, but that garden remained a treasure trove.

Anxiously awaited news finally arrived in the mail from PNEU. We got several nice letters from various ladies, ready, willing, and dying to come to Australia. We picked the one who said she was thirty-nine with young ideas. I bitchily hoped she wouldn't look like Deborah Kerr.

18

Miss Frostquilt

RAN may have expected something bird-like, but nothing prepared us for the tweedy condor who emerged from the plane. She was taller than he was and seemed larger. His face was a study in hard-won nothing.

Her name was Miss Frostquilt. I recognized her Yorkshire accent as she stoutly gave us her nickname, Quilty. They'd always called her that, she said with a condescending smile, in Indjar. We gave her a room of her own off Giro's lanky back veranda, its cheerless bathroom three doors down. I'd done the room up fairly comfortably. It had three windows, one door, and privacy for all concerned. At least our lives would be hyphenated.

I immediately saw Quilty had been a red head; her pink, mottled, paper-thin skin and pallid blue eyes bespoke it. She suffered wet-weather limp from a two-year-old broken hip, which seemed to augment during her descents into the Slough of Despond. Weekends were the worst. She didn't seem to read and was at loose ends on her own.

In the beginning, meals were shared. I watched Ran's eyes turn to lead as she knitted and "Oooo la la'd" through cocktail hour. So, after a couple of tries, I drank my drink alone at Big Bertha's scorching knees and cooked to escape. He stayed out late, or in his office, which drove another tiny wedge between us.

For such a cumbersome woman, her hand and head motions were lightning fast: a buzzard feigning sparrow. At the ends of meals she'd rivet our eyes with crumb-hunting, her head would cock suddenly and those large pointed fingers would pounce, pounce, pounce on helpless crumbs of this and that which were daintily mashed into her bared front teeth with terrifying speed; it was compulsive, like her conversation; all petticoated with vague hysteria. Her dreadful loneliness pricked my heart as she dangled her frozen self before our family fire in vain attempts to thaw a lifelong glacier. We were a curling iron held to an iceberg.

It was all more than I could bear. I knew that Ran would be outdoors even more as the weather warmed and the sun stretched longer and longer arms around Giro. Why didn't Quilty and Katrina sup at six? Katrina crowed a greedy "Yay!" And of course Ran began to cart his lunch and quart pot on horse or in jeep or Rover. Only breakfast remained family-style. And Ran avoided that when he could. Sometimes we'd inveigle a late private snack or I'd cook it and sit with him if I got too hungry to wait.

Poor Quilty. Day after day I offered the panacea of an ear and, like a victrola, she played me on and on and on. That pathetic needle grooved deeper and deeper into me. It was corrosive, but no more so than if I hadn't given that bony comfort. There was no one else to listen on Giro's castaway island.

I heard about her father, a forbidding man, a Thomas Hardy family dragon who never allowed her out, and great hams and beeves and sausages hanging in the larder. And her mother, who "never liked married life. I'm like my mother *that* way," she'd say with coy giggles, grace notes in a funeral march. And Indjar. Oh, that family in India. That world rotated around a family called Boose or Bossey, I never quite got a mental spelling. During these recitals she'd cock and toss her head, arching a large and vibrating pinkie to a sandy eyebrow, then purse her lips white in baby-dress tucks. "OOOOO-la-la!" she'd scream, cocking and tossing. "OOO! Hoo Hoo! Have you ever tasted the real Yorkshire pudding, with sage and onion?" As my fingers flashed from skillet to pots I'd say, "No. Sounds lovely, Quilty. You must make it for us!" recoiling at her performance.

We tried sending her to Sydney for a few days at a time, in hopes that either civilization or a wow of a toot would relieve

169

her raw and hagridden self. Little did we know how close to the marrow we were. I'd been aware that she'd had frequent bilious attacks and Ran had asked me what the "cordial" items were on Barnard's bill, but other than that we hadn't a clue.

Naturally, when Quilty took off, I had to take over lessons. My wavering respect for teachers became steely in the crucible of actuality. The schoolroom was a barn of a room attached to the former shearers' sleeping quarters and dirty hole of a kitchen; no stove, only fireplace and doddering sink. I'd scrubbed out the place, removed the greasy table, and replaced it with the former desk in Giro's office, really just a plank cedar table I'd sanded. I'd sent for shiny maps of everywhere and tacked them up and three desks had been found in a cobwebbed heap. Katrina's library was good; I'd added some art and reference books, and of course there were both instruction books for Australian correspondence for Daisy Blackburn and PNEU stuff for Katrina.

Why don't we realize the before and after of teaching? I thought you just walked in the door looking snappy, and *taught.* But what? Every twenty minutes or so I'd have to open two different cans of peas! Math was a lead-pipe cinch. Lists of problems. Fine. Next? Why, reading, of course. Only to my dawning dismay, Daisy couldn't read her name, she just remembered the story and attached it to the picture of what Bob and Jane were doing. Not a word did she truly read. The grinding patience required while a child sits chewing her lips in blushing embarrassment over "can" and "jumped" absolutely appalled me. My gears stripped minute after minute and Katrina was left to her own devices, which she loved; sidelong grins and shufflings made up *her* reading time.

I tried writing next. Wary now, but playing Pleasant-But-Firm Youngish Teacher to a packed house ("Gosh, Mrs. Galt is *fun,* isn't she? I just *love* it when Mrs. Galt takes over school, don't you?").

Have you ever heard of a mirror writer-reader? Well, you see, you write NO and the child smiles all crinkly, and sweating all over her pencil writes. ON. Need I go on? I began to perspire and gave Daisy single letters to practice, at which she was a mechanical genius.

170

Now what? Cookies! Thank God for cookies. I strode out for a cigarette, smoking as if the firing squad was tapping its feet. All those maps. Geography might possibly push lunch, and I could read aloud in a pinch. Or an art book, perhaps!

Geography was grand. We tested each other very happily, and noisily; I could feel the TV cameras grinding on a morning show and half expected a box of Snickers. We had a great time.

Lunch was long because Katrina rode Daisy on Bluebottle down to Mrs. Mac, Daisy's grandmother, a half mile away, and took her sweet time coming back.

I read to them after lunch and they drew pictures and pasted things. Over a huge, cool martini, I planned the next day. Flash cards. That's what Daisy needed. I became the stern educator. This pupil needs "*extending*," I expounded to my imaginary class at Columbia. "Her problem is an *unusual* one of course, but we, through the continuous excitement of newly discovered vistas, we can bring to her the increasing values of phonics; perhaps thusly, we can both extend her horizons and approach the yet deeper problem of the mirror-writer reader!" (Sincere and deepening applause.)

Ran kidded me unmercifully. He knew exactly what was going on.

"Sweetheart," he'd announce, pompously looking down his nose, "have you properly extended your eager students into the glorious realms of culture today? Is Daisy reciting Shakespeare yet?"

"Can it, Randolph! How'd you like to take over? Teach them football or something equally useful."

"Tut, tut, my girl, let's not lose our sense of proportion. Why not teach them to cook lunch? Then you could take the morning off and put your feet up?"

"All I need is those two in my kitchen." Still, that wasn't a bad idea, but first, Education. Daisy had to go home to Corroborree able to read something by Friday.

The next morning, I brought back corrected papers, full of sharp, professional-looking B's and C's and, after settling Katrina on a murderous composition with an evil glare I bathed Daisy's rosy freckled face with a tender smile and motioned her outside. We sat on a bench while I explained flash cards.

171

She looked like a patient cocker spaniel, and I went to work. Having learned phonetics while studying for the theater, I knew all about it, didn't I? Inside of three minutes I was aghast at the impossibility of getting one plain ordinary vowel sound out of that dear fresh-faced child. "O" said the card. "Aaow," said Daisy. "E," said I. "Oooeee," said Daisy. "I," said I in awe. "Oi," said Daisy. "*I*, Daisy." "OIeee," she said with a giggle. Exhausted already, I began on doubles. "OO." "Eeeooo," she chimed. "Oooooo!" I coooooooed. "Eeeeeoooo," went Daisy. "Ee, you know, dear, like 'peek'—Ee." "Paik?" she questioned in shy hope. I ran down like a clock. "A—cat." "Ket!" she chirruped. "E—bed." "Baid." "O like in home." "Haim." "Fry." "Froee." In shambles, I thrust a consonant atah . . . er, her. "Mmm," I hummed. She looked delighted. "Aim, Mrs. Galt?" "That's raht, dee," I answered, sighing. "Haowz abaowt aowah geography gyme? Aaoo Kye?" She squirmed.

End saow oi limped three-oo th' raist uv the' dye.

The coup de grace was a longwinded collection of arithmetic problems for Katrina in pounds, shillings, and pence. Totally daunted, I prayed for Quilty's twitching bulk to emerge from Rover, tiddly or not, the next noon. As far as I was concerned, she was definitely bilious and never touched a cordial, and the girls and I made brownies for Senior Professor Galt.

That mid-September, Ran had gone to Sydney and promised to search again for help. When he came back I had to tell him the news. Sam Pugh had been discovered stark naked and roaring drunk in the river at Biddeford's crossing on Tuesday, and had been fired. Australians have a rigid sense of propriety. He sued the station for vacation pay, lawyers, and all. Won, too. A real warpath juggernaut was violet-hued Sam, but fingers dipped in magic when it came to seed and soil. We never found his ilk again; and the garden went downhill fast.

Jean Taggart had been gone five months. Long enough for me to fully realize what a nincompoop I'd been not to have appreciated her more.

We hoped to find a couple; the man to do station work, the women to help me in the house some of the day. Of course the man would have to suit the manager; thereby hung a noose. Help erratically enlivened our lives at Giro; I'll just let them come and go the way they did.

The Floyds were first. Ran was enthusiastic at his success in finding the perfect couple so quickly. I didn't think it was so quick.

He was a strapping Welshman and was unfailingly protective of a tiny Australian wife. Alf looked like a bandylegged Mack truck and wore torn-off shorts in all weather. His furry knees just got redder in the cold. He cradled his scrap of a wife in every homemade luxury. He painted every wall and every ceiling in their dismal cottage a different color—bright pink, yellow, turquoise, mauve, green green, and blue blue. Mr. Bates would have approved. He made a covered walk to the outhouse and would've strewn roses if he'd had any. She'd give me three hours of a morning and wash up after lunch, but by the time I heard what terrible ailments had assailed her frail self the night before, I hadn't the heart to ask her to do much but breakfast dishes. When she ran out of migraines, rheumatism, sciatica, and lurid female troubles, she'd fall back on a corker of a nightmare replete with cold sweat. It was fun to wait for, like a clock chime; at first anyway. Later it was more like pulling out a disastrous daily telegram.

Alf helped me paint the laundry, and firm up loose boards, and lug heavy pails of water for shrubs. He was fine. But the manager thought he did far too much of that sort of thing and fudged on station work. And Alf preferred a jeep to a horse, unpopular on a cattle station.

The Floyds were bookends to a stolen gem of weekend in the big city. I knew Alf would hold the place together in an emergency. We flew in on a Friday noon in October. I collapsed into a hairdresser's arms and wallowed in luxury. Wafting out two hours later, feeling glamorous, I was asked out. My clean ears flapped forward like a hound at point. A nightclub? Oh, my God. Music? Soft lights, no engine, waiters and, oh, joy, no dishes.

As we sat relaxing over a glass of wine, the headwaiter handed me the menu with an off-handed, "And for Mother?" My solar plexus rattled under the table edge. We pretended not to hear.

We stayed in the apartment, which Ran had bought furnished. It looked exactly like Giro's original interior—same dingy flowers on the floor and hodgepodge of second-rate furniture. That could be my next project after the baby, I noted mentally. One delightful difference was a phone without a crank. Talking to friends I could hear was thrilling recreation. The view over the harbor was perfect and teeming with life. Restaurant cooking was a tonic to my pregnant appetite, or was I just sick of mine?

Next afternoon, strolling toward an orgy of oysters and a Greta Garbo movie, there grinned my exposure: SHE'S OUT FOR THE NIGHT shouted thick black headlines from the corner stand, over a photo of me and an asinine rundown of our little evening. Ran's jaws flexed. We flew back to Giro, refreshed, despite the press, to discover the Floyds had gone. Summarily fired. As Ran walked away from the plane with his face shut, I thought I noticed a growing saddle gall named manager under his hide. Our manager was top-notch, but the station was Ran's—or was it? A sore spot that. I bit my tongue. But I wished a lot, standing there in the breeze.

19

Wife? Wife

I SUSPECTED Ran was a bachelor who believed marriage was one of the possible answers to his life. His simple credo, "Stay loose," and if you go to a movie see *Gigi*. He didn't plan twenty-four hours ahead if he could help it and never batted an eye at the future.

I prefer Ingmar Bergman movies. I'm a lousy hermit.

Wife. Wife? I wanted to pack for him, dress his bed like a sultan's, oil his boots, cook him feasts, be his sunny days, his tornado, his rain, and his confidante; his shrewd small voice, his wily bargainer in groceries, his decorator, his tomboy companion, his nurse, and his gracious hostess; his gay conversationalist, his temptress. Wife. Who knows what that means? Oh, yes, and the healthy clever mother of his children. Preferably under Edwina Baillieu's pink parasol. A pink glow was so flattering.

To begin with, as I put a rolled sock in his suitcase, he blanched.

"Don't do that—for God's sake! I'll never find anything and I don't want to take all *that!*' '

As I made the bed he'd rush across to the other side and we'd work like an unrehearsed two-piano team until I fell on it helpless with laughter.

"Ran! Ran! We're like a one-acter: *Two Bachelors in Search of a Marriage!*"

When sick, he burrowed into bed like a mole and weakly wanted soup, just soup. No crackers even.

He guarded every scrap of ranch business, comings, goings, successful or unsuccessful, as jealously as a Papa Quail. I never knew anything, and consequently my conversation languished in its void.

"I scrubbed five whole floors today," is hardly in the ring with "The new bulls have torn a bastard of a hole in Lemon Tree gate and are into a bunch of young heifers next door."

The truth was I wanted to bury myself in him like a tick and must have made him very uncomfortable. What man can stand a constant eager beaver? If the great Chanel had labeled No . 5 "Eager Beaver," who in hell would have bought it?

Women, as lovers, are resistible. Far more so than men. Passionate ladies can be so implacably generous. And aren't men so relieved and grateful not to be women that they have vague fears of contamination when close to Her; any prolonged day in day out with Woman giving the male world the keen flavor of hooky, and her world the attraction of school during an epidemic of chicken pox?

I do not blame; I only wonder if.

When we first came the backbreaking projects consumed me. But as soon as the dust settled and I rolled the white of an eye at daily living with Giro and its retinue of rodents and reptiles, things changed. Any reasonably sentient female can do woman's work with her mind tied behind her. Being as inept as I was at every moronic chore, I became a fanatic fake. You couldn't call it acting. Improvisation maybe, but I knew better. Charlatan at best. I adlibbed my way through Grease Spot, Fresh-Faced Milk-Maid, Janitress-at-Midnight, Hoyden, House Painter, The Little Woman, Lulu the Jolly Launderette, Trixie the Fry-Cook—the wordless dramas were endless. But where was the audience? Being myself could be luxury, glorious in the country. What country? I overheard it, or glimpsed it over Bertha's clanging oven doors through a grimy window—or looked about me as I wrung a filthy mop. All city ploys, and slum ones at that. No: Making up melodramas in the human vacuum of Giro's indoor world was a recipe for despair.

I tried not to let Ran see the keg of dynamite inside (when I wasn't playing Martyr; Heaven forgive me), but had to lock my face to hide it. He fought the resultant grim mouth with the frightful weapon of indifference, more cruel than any mace to lovers. And there we'd stand on opposite of shores of a Red Sea foaming under raging skies, pretending it was a millpond under popcorn clouds. My needs were so desperate and many they would have turned an enemy into an acquaintance. But we were not acquainted. We were lovers. Full of passions and the startling pain that can come with the knowledge of each other's Achilles' heels.

Loooong short, Loooong short, Loooong short, screamed the phone. My feet would clatter to that gazebo:

"Hello? Randolph Galt? Mr. Corey here."

"I'm sorry, this is Mrs. Galt. Mr. Galt's not here."

"Do you know where he can be reached, Mrs. Galt?"

"No, I'm sorry I don't."

"When will he return, please?"

"I'm sorry, I have no idea. He left early this morning."

"Will he be in around six?"

"I'm sor— I don't *know*."

There'd be a pause.

"I see. Very well. I'll call back later on."

I'd hang up, shaking at the truth. I'd no idea where he was or what he was doing and certainly not when, and far too proud to ask.

The same needs that drove me headlong into anger laced us tighter than any rings or words. So I'd search for jokes and laughter we might share. He always took them from me in relief, until we could look into one another once again.

Open-eyed again. The openness of peaches eaten and trousers rolled, and lovers.

But however much I tried to softpedal myself into Happy-Go-Lucky Bush Country Wife, he'd sense the booming bowling alley in my head, close his eyes and ears in self-defense, and skirt me and my sweaty battles with women's work like a higher-minded cleric skirts the corner saloon.

I suppose Ran hoped his life would be much as it had been, but that I would be with him. To "round out" his life? Do men hope that? Do men see themselves walking a dappled path and reach for someone to join them as they walk? Like an insurance ad? And when they find themselves struggling up an uncharted

177

mountain in the cold rain, with a fifty-pound pack and some baby howls and some harried shrew yells, "Wait, Joe. Find us a cave! Egbert's filled his pants!"

Is he *that* surprised? At the harassment and disturbance of his peace that marriage is? And are all women haunted by the grub of fear in their vitals that gnaws and whispers as it feeds on her marshmallow center, the busy little fear that says he may not love you if he knows you as you are? The chilly little fear that makes her mete herself out in small doses, watching the patient for a temperature drop. How does he deal with the visible fact that she is only another lonely crossword puzzle like himself and not a Della Robbia wreath of smiles and tender fruits and ardent flowers—a hearth—a ladykins—a malleable fiction?

The cruel fact was that I had no place to go for companionship but him. Cruel to us both. Perhaps we could have rented Giro. As a sort of final exam. One year per couple. Kill or cure. One year. No birds of passage wanted. Signed, sealed, and delivered unto Giro.

20

Fire and Oranges

JOHN STEINBECK once looked over at me and said to his beloved Elaine, "She peeks over bushes." It made me catch my breath. I remember laughing uproariously, partly because I was too dumb to know what he meant and partly because it made me want to clutch my crotch and bosom as if naked. It'd bothered me for years. I knew why now. It was the truth. I wanted to know everything about everything, but not land in the thick of it. In the thicket?

Ran was disgusted with me.

"How can I help it, Ran? This homestead would go up in smoke in fifteen minutes," I protested vehemently.

"They do it all the time!" he exhaled sharply in annoyance.

"Well, at least be sure the blasted pump's on and we'll have enough *water* to turn a *hose* on it! *Not that it would do any good!*" I called out, near tears as he banged out the door. Giro's grasslands would ignite in a crawling rash of fire. Ran and the men deliberately set a match to them. He vainly tried to explain that weeks without rain turned the grass rank and unless the overgrown feed and weeds were burned off, the new growth was stifled. Cattle were fussy, almost as fussy as kangaroos, and would have none of the old sour grass. So they burned it.

Days on end Giro lay under a pall of yellow haze. I hated it. Ran scorned me for a scaredy-cat, but try as I would, each sulfurous day wrote a letter from fear to me in triplicate.

In an awful way the flames were beautiful at night, a diorama of Asia in the wake of Genghis Khan. Everywhere was fire and Giro's nineteen-mile valley was scalloped and fringed with it. The powerful west wind would smear it in one direction or another; it was so close I could hear its snapping jaws.

Ran insisted it was too green right around us to be dangerous to the homestead. Nevertheless, the fires remained a pack of ravening wolves at a garden gate. I'd walk out and alternately stare at the airstrip and the grasping, fiery fingers, praying the airstrip would act like the clearings and ditches forest rangers cut to halt big blazes in America.

Giro and I mourned the aftermath in silence. Young forests charred and twisted; hills bearing acres-wide scarves of ugly anthracite. I was wrong. The early spring rains brought a velour of green to that scar tissue like balm. I couldn't believe it.

Ran and the men had shown the land who was boss, had slashed at her with a natural weapon, and reveled in a boy's fun doing it.

I wonder what the animals thought. Koalas, wallabies, kangeroos, bandicoots, dingoes, and snakes must have panicked at the holocaust assaulting their docile world. And I wondered where we'd have gone if it had gotten out of hand. The river, I supposed. A raft maybe. I always wanted us to build one, but I never said why.

Though my current appetite hadn't helped cooking, this was going to be a great stew. I could tell. I hadn't put too many herbs in it; my stews had tended to be slightly medicinal since I'd started growing herbs. Before Sam Pugh was fired he had told Ran what topsoil I could use for my herb garden, and I'd hauled barrow after barrow that winter.

The stew simmering on Bertha's warm bosom, I was about to put the kitchen chairs up on the table for a professional mop when I saw Ran at the back screen door. I looked out at him in surprise.

"Could we use some oranges? I know an old tree across the river; the fruit's really ripe and delicious, I ate some early this morning."

I hadn't ridden in a while, but why not? It was a nice day. I

180

couldn't iron until the engine went on anyway, and I could take the wash down when we got back.

"Sounds wonderful. Just let me finish the kitchen and get my boots on!" I rushed to the sink in excitement.

He smiled through the door screen. "I'll go get Sparkle."

I attacked the kitchen floor, put another asbestos pad under the stew, and dug out a sack from under the crate of onions.

After we crossed the river, we rode about a half-mile and as we plodded toward the orange tree I realized it stood in the long-neglected yard of an abandoned cottage. The splintering hull and outbuildings were decaying and wildlife had moved in.

As we picked oranges in the sun I asked who had lived there. "The Mackendricks," said Ran.

"When did they move away?" I asked, dropping oranges into the sack.

"Two years ago."

"Two years!" I gasped, shaking my head in disbelief; if it had been forty I'd have believed it more easily.

"That's right," he went on, enjoying my dumbfounded stare. "Mrs. Mac had her children in that cottage; raised them all, too."

I left the orange tree and looked carefully around. There'd been a proper garden; zinnias, nasturtiums, and coreopsis were in bloom among the towering weeds. And grapes, a gnarled quince, barbed wire fences, a corral, and a rain tank near the lowest part of the rusty roof. The cottage was no bigger than a rich child's playhouse, but small rooms are warmer in winter with only one fireplace and one all-purpose stove.

Walking inside I sidestepped wasps' nests, crushed guano and the broken shards of much living. The dwarf living room had stamped metal walls; the three other smaller rooms were fibro. No running water. No electricity. No plumbing. When I pictured a family living there I was speechless with admiration. Living like that only two years ago, I thought. Nobody I knew could even imagine it.

"Ran, dear?" I called up to him in the great tree as he knocked some high, sweet oranges off the top.

"Yes?"

181

"What did the Mackendricks do when the river was up?"

"Nothing. They just didn't get out until it went down."

"My God," I whispered to myself. And here I was worried about having one baby in a house with nightly electricity, a phone, three bathrooms, and a plane for emergencies. I felt ashamed and very grateful.

"I put in a toilet for Mrs. Mac in the cottage they live in now; first one she's ever had," Ran said, climbing down the tree, tearing his shirtback on a dead branch. Oh, dear, I sighed. Mending, like ironing, was my weak suit.

They had a lovely view, I thought, looking down the hillside across the river to their present home. Mrs. Mac now had running cold water, electricity once a day, and a toilet, and I began to understand what impressive luxuries those were. Most Americans have forgotten. She still built a fire and boiled clothes; her wood stove was still her mainstay.

Ran tossed the sack of oranges behind his saddle and we rode slowly back the long way home.

"I've always thought Will was an escapee from a Hogarth," I remarked dreamily as Sparkle dawdled along.

"Definitely," Ran replied indulgently over his shoulder.

I visualized those sharp blue eyes twinkling with ribaldry in a seamed, white-stubbled pink face; he had a bugle of a laugh and knew every story and legend about the bush country. Old Will was an excellent stockman, farmer, woodsman, blacksmith and, for all his extra weight and years, had a lot of bite to him.

"He's doing a fabulous job on the new cattle yards at Corroborree. Hardly uses a nail, all notched and let-in logs," Ran told me.

Old Will's special domain was the forge, a strictly male hangout on wet days; blistering iron rang like bells through bursts of laughter. That tatterdemalion forge sheltered a real prize, an English bellows the size of our dining room table labeled 1906 in curling gold.

"Ran?" I called, kicking Sparkle and riding closer behind him. He liked a fast-walking horse. Sparkle Plenty had lost some shine lately, maybe she was pregnant too; I'd overheard the station mares had been bred. "How's Ned Beale?"

Ran laughed. We were fascinated by Giro's very lone wolf, who seemed to me to be an archetypal bush stockman.

"Oh, he's about the same. Said four words the other day and I thought he'd talk my arm off," said Ran drily.

Ned's face reminded me of a timid wolf, wide-set slanting eyes, long sharp nose, and a slash of mouth. He lived to himself like a wild thing in the Myall country at the top of the station.

"I've a feeling he's hard on horses," I remarked tentatively.

"Probably; he's a bit rough," replied Ran uncritically.

I'd seen him treat them like rattletrap cars, and he had even less time for cattle. Ned was in acute distress at anything vaguely approaching sociality, such as my saying, "Hello, Ned." You could feel his neck prickle and see his eyes squint shut in excruciating shyness. Bone-thin everywhere, but with powerful shoulders, arms, and hands. I could see him, knee-deep in muck, cigarette a tiny smudge on a sliver of lip, filthy hat pulled down over a blood-spattered forehead and darting between maddened, bawling cattle in a steaming yard, bang-tailing cows with a lightning-swift knife.

"Here's a good place to cross." Ran pointed down to a shallow place. We crossed the river and smelled Freeda's pigpen.

"How's Freeda?" I asked, baiting him.

"That crafty sow," smoldered Ran as he rode up the bank by her sty. "I'll sell her for a profit yet. Can't keep her in the pen worth a darn."

"Katrina's scared of her."

"Tell her to stay away from her—she's bad news."

We rode behind the kitchen, I gave him Sparkle's reins, he gave me the sack of oranges.

"Thanks, Ran. That was fun." How polite we were.

"It was. We should do it more often." He patted my shoulder. "See you later." He smiled warmly and took the horses off.

It had been more than fun, it had been the breath of life to me. Did he know that? I wondered. I dragged in the oranges and went off to take down the sunsweet wash, thinking how precious good moments were out there, and that Giro's *Who's Who* was a storybook.

Reporters asked me so many times, "How many people

183

worked on your 'rancho'?" I'd tell them, and could see them picturing jolly times, barn dances, and hoop-de-doo, all sorts of rousing social entertainments with cozy "rancho" families. Well, it just wasn't like that. Besides, can you picture Ran and Quilty in a square with me and Ned Beale? Hot diggity dawg.

What the reporters never knew was the real rub: none of these people could or were supposed to help me. They had their jobs, I had mine. But off again on again, Finnegan, there were those who did.

21

Sprits Monya

OCTOBER and spring were coming, meaning all hands out, at all hours, to monitor calving. They were often forced to use drastic measures on helpless young heifers unable to birth. The havoc and gore beggar description. Some had their dead calves dragging like ghastly trains behind them. I overheard that some had been bred to bulls too big for them. I saw less and less of Ran; perhaps my hyperfemale condition and what he saw those days turned me out of woman and into cow.

Starved as I was for mail, he still wouldn't allow it to be opened at the lunch table. I kept trying to fathom why; and used to eye that enticing bundle as conversation limped into a frigid pool of silence. I almost wished he wouldn't come back mail days. But those were often the only ones he did. The whole thing was childish. My attitude included.

Something was wrong. It was more than just the mail. I pawed through the attic in my head, increasingly anxious. Had I misread the signs? He'd said about children, "I don't care if we don't have any." I thought he'd meant to reassure me. Had he tried to tell me something far more important. And in Los Angeles, after I'd seen Dr. Krohn—"What's the hurry?" Did he want this child?

What if I were proving youth enough? And why didn't I realize a baby would shunt me further onto a lonely siding, even from Katrina. Nervous Nellie, I scoffed inwardly. Perfectly normal. Woman loves man. Woman has his child. Peak of closeness. A far more concrete fear was the ten years gone by since I'd had Katrina. I couldn't remember details, and pregnant women are question marks. Three weeks after her birth I'd had a stunning hemorrhage, which worried me a lot. You bleed in the country and you can disappear. I thought of calling Ross Sweetapple and giving vent to my growing distress. On our nine-party line? The locals would have eaten it up along with our privacy.

I grew more and more depressed and jumpy. Ran stayed clear of me those days and even fried his own meat for breakfast before I could get going of a morning. It hurt and my stomach turned as I smelled that smoking, blackened pan sitting in the sink, a mute rebuke. My disposition was far from sunny; so was the weather—it was unseasonably cloudy and wet.

Toward the end of October I'd just finished clearing up breakfast, had said good-bye to Quilty and Katrina as they went off to the schoolroom, and had walked to the laundry to start a wash when it began. I suddenly felt as if I'd swallowed paring knives the evening before, and thought I was in for Giro's well-known wog, a perverted gift that skulked in our river drinking water. I hurt too much to face the laundry tub and stole off to lie down for a moment. The four-poster was the cave I'd crawl into for short rests. The room was darkish because its twin windows looked onto the veranda, a fine spot of quiet for a nap when I could snare one. Lying huddled on the counterpane, I realized I'd gone into labor. Utterly miserable and terribly frightened, I pretended it wasn't so. Please, Lord, let it be the wog. I pulled the patchwork quilt over my head and wept for a few seconds.

My immediate terror was augmented by isolation and the fact that if we flew to Sydney the decision had to be made before four P.M. No light plane was allowed in the air after dusk. Secondly, to move anyone trying desperately to hang onto a child is the worst move, and we still knew no doctors in Sydney.

Where was Ran? I didn't know. Miles away. Quilty and Katrina were engrossed in the schoolroom. I couldn't just lie there doubled up and let it happen. Call Red Krohn. What time was it? Must be eight thirty. Damn Groceries to hell, I'd never get a call through. Another pain began to grow, slowly wringing my

186

insides like a dishrag. Please, God, help me know what to do. I heard a horse thud on the grass outside.

"Anne?" It was Ran. "Anne? You there?" I grimaced, too upset to answer. I heard him dismount and open the veranda screen door. "Anne!" I hiccuped a sob and managed a strangled "Yes." I heard him step through the door. It slapped shut. Silence. "You all right?" he said in an odd hushed voice. "No," I gasped, drawing my knees up and inching over onto my other side. Suddenly he was in the doorway.

"What is it, sweetheart?"

"I don't—I think I'm—I'm losing—the baby." I panted in misery, face mashed in the pillow.

Ran took over, and repeatedly called Los Angeles for advice from my former obstetrician, giving him embarrassingly clinical details, but the shots he said I needed were simply not given in the bush. Dr. Burke wouldn't come out that far. Countrywomen were sent pills with the mail, and so was I. They were too little and too late.

Katrina looked lost, and I tried to reassure her. Quilty was clumsily, sincerely kind, and I see her now, peering through the whitish gloom of the canopied bed. "Is there anything I can do for you, Mrs. Galt?"

I longed to say "yes"; it would have warmed her, but in my own anguish I could only say tea and thank you.

I vividly remember a blue cashmere sleeve proffered me at bad moments, and a beloved bachelor turned husband whispering, "Hang onto me."

It was all over Sunday; the embryo was gone. I flushed it away, appalled, and wondered how many thousands of women had done the same in an endless variety of circumstances. Always bad.

I was humiliated by what I felt was failure. The city mouse had failed miserably in her attempt to be a robust peasant dropping off a nice pink baby in the wheat field. On Monday I dressed early, rocking slightly here and there, and tried to fake a Welsh (which I am) farmhand by starting to bucket shrubs a hundred yards away. Ran saw me from afar and came after me.

God, he was angry. I thought he was going to strike me. His face was white as he shouted at me.

187

"I'll be goddamned if you'll do anything as stupid as this after what I've been through. Red Krohn says we have to fly to Sydney immediately and get you to a hospital for a curettement and a complete rest for ten whole days. We can leave in an hour. I'll tell Quilty to help you pack." He turned on his heel and strode off in a fury.

Ran would choose peace at many prices. His rages were infrequent, but they were marvelous.

Through a dermatologist who'd practiced in Honolulu for a while, we found the top gynecologist in Sydney, and I was in the hospital Monday night.

At seven the next morning I thought they were going to burn me at the stake, from the looks of the medieval outfit. First came a rough shirt. Flax? Next, thigh-high thick woolen stockings. Linsey-woolsey? Next, to my dismay, a half-inch-thick gray wool shirt with dolman sleeves and, over all, what appeared to be the top from a faded pair of striped flannel pajamas. Put on backward. Oh, yes, a headcloth pinned behind. Girt thusly, they trundled me off to the busiest anteroom and the narrowest leather table I'd ever seen. They stuck something over my mouth, a pint-size hypo came at my arm, and I caught a blurred glimpse of what I was sure were white-robed monks in a vast nave, rebecs sawing in the distant cloister.

Lying awake that afternoon in a room the color and slickness of putty, I was in a striking amount of pain. My interior felt raw, and I wondered if I could please have a pill for it. Certainly, Mrs. Galt, right away. Another large hypo materialized, and inside of five seconds I felt queer. In five more I knew I was dying under a bed-sized flatiron. I mumbled, "Help." Alarmed eyes popped at me and I heard running footsteps. "I feel like I'm going to die," I muttered drunkenly. There were slappings of feet in corridors miles away and muffled shoutings. Something made me desperately want an age-old remedy, spirits of ammonia.

"Sprits—monya—sprits monya," I murmured.

The first nurse must have heard me. Through a fine mist I saw her run out as I struggled for breath, and come galloping back with a half-gallon jug, which she uncorked and shoved to my nose. I groped for it and sniffed weakly. It proved to be instant help and, I later found, the perfect emergency antidote for morphia allergy.

My pulse had dropped instantaneously to forty-three the moment the morphia was given. No wonder I felt dead. I damned near was. Funny thing was, the lady anesthetist was called down from operating and stomped cheerily in an hour later to laughingly state, "So *she* was allergic to morphia, too! Ha, ha, ha!" Then why in frozen hell did she give it without checking first?

Ran came and warmed that sepulcher of a room. The sight of any American would have dissolved me in bathos. He was Gabriel in the flesh.

The tabloid press in Sydney behaved like hyenas. They snuffled and drooled around that hospital for gossip like offal. The hospital was furious and helped me to a darkened cab hidden out back at ten thirty that night. We were driven to Ran's apartment while I hid, stretched out on the floor of the back seat.

The obscenity of all was a cameraman and presswoman, notebook poised, knocking on the apartment door at seven A.M. And I will try to forget the obsequious phone calls. Ran was in a towering rage for days. They made up what we wouldn't give them and splattered it like three-day-old bandages all over the papers. Not endearing. Giro seemed a haven.

22

$\mathcal{R}$oast $\mathcal{P}$ig

AFTER the hospital had presto-changed Giro into a haven, our very first visitors came from America to reinforce that flimsy illusion. Ran's sister and brother-in-law, who'd bought the property he'd owned before Giro, came up from a weekend there to visit.

His sister lit my spirits like a city transformer. She showered me with compliments. All my efforts and attractive things flourished under her enthusiasm, which poured down like a desert cloudburst. What a girl was Dawn. Ran glowed and we had the time of our suddenly conjubilant lives. What an audience.

We'd been eagerly awaiting Dawn's and Bill's arrival, and Ran had been eyeing the slowest of Freeda's nine missiles for a fatted calf, or rather a suckling pig. He'd gotten pretty big while we waited, thirty-five pounds or so, but it sounded like a splendidly festive idea. I was a trifle squeamish about apples in mouths and prune eyes. Nevertheless, I got carried away on the crest of enthusiasm and Dawn and I pored over all my cookbooks for stuffing. As I said, number nine was overgrown. (Suckling, my foot. He ate everything twice.) So we settled on a twelve-pound goose stuffing, double recipe. Loaves of bread disappeared into that recipe, pounds of this and pounds of that, port wine, apples; we bawled over a pile of onions.

I finally had to stopple my ears at the screams of that wretched little pig. He gave them a savage run, but an hour or so later the shot rang out. Old Will knew all about pig killing, and a gasoline drum, full of boiling water, was steaming away over its wood fire under the great Moreton Bay fig tree. You have to debristle them, it seems, and nothing does it but a searing bath.

Ran and Bill had rigged a barbecue pit near the dining room porch and coals were forming. Into the kitchen it came, and away we stuffed. Stout cord bound it all in. They ran it through the spit and stood around drinking beer, feeling like Lords of the Manor.

Now, I don't know much about pork except it has to be well done or you can keel over with trichinosis. Frankly, my eye was jaundiced about the whole thing after so violent a death, but I'd go out and look once in a while with a queasy stomach. The cord burned, of course, and they couldn't turn the thing much because the stuffing kept tumbling out.

At five o'clock Dawn and I knew that pig wasn't cooking and said so, to beery protests.

At six we planted our feet and said, "No oven, no pig." And into the kitchen it came again, an oozing black mess. We measured. No hope of fitting. I walked away while Ran sawed and cleaved it in two, and Big Bertha's two doors clanged shut on each half.

Fortunately it was too out of shape for the apple, a great disappointment to the men. All they needed was a few reclining wolfhounds catching bones on the rush-covered castle floor. It now looked like two colossal pork roasts.

I stood on the dining room table in stocking feet and lit the tin chandelier and twenty-two other candles. Suddenly it was all startlingly handsome—candles waving and shining, crystal gleaming, Toulouse Lautrec's Aristide Briand eyeing us, orange and pink wild flowers glowing in brass on a black and white linen cloth. A wine cork squeaked and I staggered in to a triumphant chorus of American voices, bearing one-half of the pig.

No, never, ever, has there been such pork; perhaps old hat to Henry VIII, but to us a famous experience. Ran's fingers were slippery from snitched cracklings, and he dropped the razor-edged knife down the side of his good pants, slitting them like a vertical throat.

We had fun. There's a lot to be said for the fun people have with each other in faraway places. The mean temperature of friendship rises against the penetrating cold of an alien world outside. Shipboard romances bear me out.

Ran flew Dawn and Bill into Sydney to catch their plane to Honolulu, and while he was there, made another valiant attempt at finding help. I was feeling fairly well, but still had to push myself.

He came back and said with reserved triumph, that he'd found a single lady, and thought perhaps we ought to give her Anybody's. Suggesting she use the guest room meant, I supposed, she was a cut or three above the Floyds in education. Being in severe need, I thought, OK, fine. But I was leery of an invasion of privacy. Life together might well deteriorate into sneaked kisses behind a curtain made of Swiss cheese. Quilty was heavy-going but discreet.

She came by train, and I will call her Miss P. We flew in to collect her from the train. November was warm already; warmer than usual for late spring.

As she stepped off the train, I knew. Absolutely wrong. Wrong, wrong, wrong. But this far away, we had to play it out like a bad performance, until the curtain fell.

I'm a shoe looker-atter, a smallish club. Her shoes were a brochure on Miss P. They were of the thinnest, cheapest leather in a lunar fawn, a color considered impeccably genteel among shopgirls. The top edges were sharp and looked as if they sawed at even that bony instep. The heels pierced the cement like thrown daggers, quivering as they hit; the points were vicious and made one's toes curl at the thought of what must be inside. They were very new and jampacked with snob value, as inelegantly pee-elegant as was Miss P.

She was a white-eyelashed blonde, and her hair stood up stiffly in a brush all over her head like an overdue crew cut. I had a mad impulse to unscrew her head in a trice and give my dusty clothes a whisk. Earrings jumped on either side of a dry, pebbled oblong face, lightly scrubbed with orange cake rouge.

192

The total effect in a beige print dress was unsuitable-albino.

The AML and F, Australian Mercantile Land and Finance Company, Ltd., Ran's cattle brokers, drove us back to the field of stubble known as the Worcester strip, where the plane cooked snappishly in the buzzing noon heat. As we crawled out of the car, there was an injured yelp from Miss P, whose faun stilettos had sunk into the melted mess of tar at the road's edge. She fussed over them like babies all the way to the plane.

"Tiny little thing, isn't it?" she twitted between looks at her tarry heels, earrings bobbling busily as she stork-stepped into the back seat and nervously chirped, "High adventure!"

Flying back, the air grew cobblestones in the rising heat. She peeped not. Neither did she spin, I thought nastily. She talked very little, anyway, a blessing, as her Australian accent was so strong that I had trouble understanding her.

We gave her Anybody's and hoped she'd navigate down halls, through the living room, down more hall, and to the right to the bathroom when we weren't around. I never got used to someone marching through our lives clutching a sponge bag as they called it; private cleansing matter in a peek-a-boo bag.

We rearranged the linens that afternoon. It was windowless and dripping work in El Bar and after twenty minutes she fixed me with minicamera eyes and said, "Do you always work this hard?"

"That's right. Lot to do, you know," I gnashed.

Surprisingly, she was up at seven, long earrings, heels, and all, like candy before breakfast. In summer the afternoons were ovens in the house, so I expansively suggested she have a rest after lunch. I'd planned spinach salad, and chops for supper. She disappeared at one twenty. At four, after a long look at Anybody's silent door, I thought I'd better pick dinner, and at four thirty I dumped the gritty greens in the laundry sink, wishing for a swim. At five I said to hell with it and washed the spinach. At five thirty I really worried. Anybody's could cook a Thanksgiving turkey if you left it in there all afternoon. Maybe she'd passed out. Sue us or something. Like Sam Pugh. I hunted up Ran. We'd swim, he said, then come back and knock. If no answer, break down the door. At five fifty we found her, heavily perfumed, complete with earrings and heels, twinkling around the kitchen.

She left the next day by mutual consent: "Not at all what I'd expected," etc., etc. "Not used to this kind of work, really," meaning, I suppose, me, flying around Giro like the head rabbit, warren-checking.

She went back to town in plebeian Rover and we discovered three things after she'd gone. She'd been a free-lance writer for a northern paper; she'd had a four-hour sunbath on a towel on the cement outside Anybody's, an entrance we rarely used, while I was anxiously washing spinach; and while collecting her pay she had a shot at *us* replacing the shoes.

23

"What Ho, Cimarron!"

CIMARRON rose above the horizon again in the form of an invitation. They wrote and wanted Ran and me to attend the world premiere in Oklahoma City, November 29 through December 1, on the cushion of MGM's fat purse.

I still felt puny. I also needed to see Red Krohn and to find out how to prevent another such debacle if medically possible. Actually, Ran had business to discuss in Honolulu and was willing to take the razzle-dazzle of a premiere for my sake. We both longed to see family and friends around the holidays. I would have a windfall visit with Mother and Dad. And Quilty and Katrina could fly up and meet us in Honolulu before Christmas. I especially wanted Katrina to renew her brief acquaintanceship with Dawn's children. It'd be like watering a plant to give her children to play with. Perfect. Everybody happy for the price of one and a half.

I had to admit that Quilty's bilious attacks were an increasing puzzlement to us. I suspect we really didn't want to know the answer. We would have put up with a great deal to maintain Katrina's educational routine, such as it was. At least she was with us and learning something.

I can't even remember where we stayed in Los Angeles. It doesn't matter. Red Krohn and I put our heads together over any eventuality. He gave me several vials of clear liquid to be injected weekly if I found myself pregnant again. Delalutin, he called it. He also emphatically explained that when nature aborts a pregnancy there's almost always an excellent reason—and to for heaven's sake stop whipping myself.

Ran chose an impossibly expensive, surprisingly tarty French satin for my Oklahoma premiere dress. My ever-staunch friend, Edith Head, made a stunning sketch; Western Costume charged an arm, a collarbone, and two legs to make it up and off we flew on what was revoltingly called a junket.

Judas Priest, as Ran would say, what a cacophony was old-style MGM'S *Cimarron* premiere in Oklahoma!

After exhausting breakfast interviews and an endless parade with strutting high school bands, that pimple of a day came to a head with barbecued buffalo at the huge Kerr-McGee Ranch, swarming with press and public. No time to eat under the frantic crush of taped and televised chitchat.

Ice had formed between Glenn Ford and Maria Schell for ugly private reasons, which didn't help. During shooting, they'd scrambled together like eggs. I understood she'd even begun divorce proceedings in Germany. It was obviously premature of her. Now, he scarcely glanced or spoke in her direction, and she looked as if she were in shock. Ran found some ranchers and held forth about Australia between beans and buffalo. He left early with a busful of merrymakers.

Two and one half hours later I was a grinning cliché from being mauled and pestered by photos, questions, quips, and onlookers. They drove me back to the hotel in the very last car, to put another layer on my aching face. Oh, well, I thought, pressing a steaming washcloth over gritty, clogged-up pores, nothing is for nothing. As I rushed into the shower I wondered why it was so quiet. No sign of Ran. He was probably still chewing the rag somewhere with his hearty Oklahoma ranchers. Hope he realized the time—there wasn't much.

I'd hardly thrown on a robe when the studio hairdresser knocked sharply.

"Coming," I yelled. Oh, boy, have to do my face while she's using the hot curlers.

Twenty-five minutes later the door closed on the puffing hairdresser; poor thing had been on call for everybody for thirteen hours. All I had to do was climb into my gorgeous gown.

196

Where was Ran? The suite felt empty. I wandered through it looking for him—the huge bedroom beyond the living room was dark. I pushed the half-open door. He was pistachio and prone on the middle of the bed.

"Darling, what is it?" I cried, alarmed.

"Dunno. Barbecued buffalo maybe. You go without me." He groaned.

"Have you got a fever?" I said, worried.

"No! *No!* It's nothing. You just go."

"Here, wait a minute." I rushed back across the living room to the far bath and grabbed a thermometer out of my cosmetic case. I took his temperature under protest. Oh, God, 102.

MGM's Bill Darnwell, from publicity, rang the doorbell. He was all smiles as I opened the door. "Are we ready, hon?"

"No, but don't worry, I will be. Look, Bill, Mr. Galt's very ill—ptomaine, I think."

"Really?" His face fell into instant concern. "Let me get a doctor!"

"And Bill," I said as I trotted after him to the phone, "we'll just have to forget the Governor's Ball."

The governor's doctor saw Ran as I swooped into the theater in orange and pink overdress. That damned fabric wore me, *why* did he choose it? When the lights dimmed I crept up the aisle head low; I never did see the picture. The press said I'd left in a huff, unhappy with the final cut. How could I explain barbecued buffalo. Or was it Cimarronitis?

Christmas was attractive in Honolulu. A catherine wheel of parties. Much is made of Christmas in Hawaii. Perhaps because it's tropical and the old families had brought along strong New England traditions. They even pretend winter, wearing dark colors for a month or so. Anyone not island born is automatically an outlander, at least until he's been well established for thirty years or so. I felt outlandish. I couldn't even hula. All the young matrons did, charmingly too, covered in perfect tans and perfectly nice clothes. By young, I mean younger than I. Ran's and Dawn's and Bill's friends all knew Hawaiian expressions and songs from childhood. I barely mastered "*Mele Kali-*

197

kimaka" (Merry Christmas), *"Humuhumunukunukuapuaa"* (a tropical fish), and *"pau,"* meaning finished. Not to mention seventy or so new names. It all made me feel out of it.

In Los Angeles I'd already lost touch with who was doing what where. Hollywood's mythical kingdom didn't brook those who dared to turn their backs on that dog-eat-Dogpatch of quicksand. Even if you cut loose to brave Broadway, 3,000 miles was an abyss. You just disappeared into "whatever-happened-to?" I had cut myself adrift with a wicked cleaver and desperately hoped a steady wind would always cast me on Ran's shore.

Ran bloomed. He shifted colors like a chameleon of grand design. Smoothly green on the velvet rocks of Hawaii, homespun sandy on the vast rough slab of Australia. I'd brought my rainbows with me and never blended into anything. Katrina was a round peg too. Just too old for Dawn's and Bill's happy brood; too little time to scout for others. At least she learned to hula and make a skirt of ti leaves and string some lovely leis.

As I was packing us up and feeling my oats enough to wrestle Giro once again, we got an anxious phone call from Hazel Sujiyama, my mother-in-law's housekeeper at the Galt's Kahala beach house where we'd had our wedding breakfast. As there wasn't room for Quilty at the big house, she'd been staying there. Katrina and Wayne Sujiyama were pals. He was about her age and taught her to fish near the lagoon. Hazel loved Katrina, sewed things for her, and cooked Katrina's favorite sukiyaki.

Bill's mother and father had a house with a pool right next door. Katrina and the Aull children liked to swim there, playing Marco Polo and screaming down the water slide. We'd dropped Katrina off that morning to swim at the Aulls'. "Miss Flostquirt is acting funny," said Hazel in an agitated voice. "I think you better come, Mrs. Galt."

"Just a minute, Hazel." I held the phone away from me and called to Ran to come in from the terrace with his mother.

"I'm on the phone with Hazel. Something's gone wrong out there with Quilty."

"What do you mean?"

198

"I'm not sure." I lowered my voice. "Hazel's all upset. We ought to go and check out what's going on."

He gave me a penetrating look. "Tell her we're on our way. Where's Katrina?" I put the phone to my ear. "Hazel, where's Katrina?"

"She's swimming next door."

"Fine—we'll be right there," I said crisply.

We leaped into a car and sped out to Kahala. The house looked so serene, perhaps nothing too serious was wrong. Katrina was with Hazel in the kitchen, looking a little scared and a lot excited.

"Hi, dear! You go back to the pool. We'll come over in a few minutes. Hazel, why don't you go with Katrina?" I said gaily.

"But I just swam."

"I can see that because you're dripping all over Hazel's nice kitchen!" I began to hear awful sounds coming from Quilty's room. I chattered even more cheerfully. "Say, is Aunt Dawn over there?"

"Yes."

I glanced at Ran. He nodded. "OK, fine. You tell Aunt Dawn your Daddy says you can have lunch with them. OK?"

I turned to Hazel. "Would you take Katrina back? Maybe you can help Mrs. Aull with the children."

Hazel unstuck her stare from the direction of the awful sounds and took Katrina's hand. "We'll be back a little later."

Katrina craned her neck at me. "Is Quilty sick?"

"I don't think so. Have a good lunch, we'll see you in a little while." I waved and blew her a kiss. As they disappeared we heard another long, low howl followed by an ominous thump.

Ran and I looked long and hard at each other. She'd either gone mad or was literally roaring drunk. Drunken people always frighten me, they are so shockingly exposed.

"Ran," I murmured, "I'm afraid to go in. Maybe she's crazy. And what if we can't handle her?"

"Yes," he replied pensively. She *was* large. "I'd better call a friend of mine, a doctor. He might come by, the family's known him for years."

He came. By then the sounds had been replaced by rattling

snores. The doctor went into Quilty's room and reappeared after a minute or two, confirming quantities of alcohol, and suggested we let her sleep it off.

Quilty was one of those women brought up in a Victorian cage fifty years ago, and life had teased her through the bars. Alcohol must have been a blessed anesthetic for the blighted being locked inside. I hoped Katrina didn't know, but I'm afraid she did.

We walked away and I prayed to God it wouldn't mean boarding school so soon. Katrina was too young for it and had accepted a lion's share of adjustments for one small girl.

We left Quilty there for three days to recuperate enough for confrontation.

When we faced her she looked so drawn and ill I wanted to gather her in my arm. She haltingly explained about the bilious attacks she suffered now and again, unable to look us in the eye.

We couldn't steel ourselves enough to shake the truth in her pathetic face and we were to leave for Giro in two days.

When Ran and I were alone, I spoke the thoughts we were both thinking. "If one or the other of us is at Giro at all times, what do you think?"

"I don't know. I just don't know." He lit his cigar and stood up.

"I sense she knows we know."

"Probably." He paced rhythmically in soundless bare feet.

"I absolutely cannot bear the thought of Katrina away in a strange school, Ran."

"I can't either."

"Should we chance it?"

"How do *you* feel?"

"The alternative stinks as much." I sighed, unutterably depressed.

"I agree. Why don't we try it and hope?" he suggested, choosing the lesser evil. I studied the lonely kiave tree rattling in the trade winds and he nursed his cigar.

So the three of us went back to Giro, bringing a chastened Quilty with mendicant eyes. She could hold out for two or three weeks at a time and then it would start: only in two- or three-day spasms, weekenders. We'd find several "cordials" on the bill from Town. She'd been a governess a long time. It's a bleak life loving other people's children. She always called them her bilious attacks, and judging from the intermittent weepings, and quavering songs along the riverbank, she must have suffered tortures. She was the loneliest woman I've ever known.

Miss Frostquilt lived with her nose against our pane; it punishes me now that I was not generous enough to open it. Perhaps because my own nose was flattened on the bush's tight-shut window.

24

Home Again, Home Again, Jiggety

ONE of the reasons I'd felt easy about leaving Giro that December was that another of our constant cries for help had recently been answered.

Rory and Pegeen were newly ensconced when we left. They were young and seemed competent and eager. She was soft and attractive, and a no-nonsense worker. He'd been a juvenile delinquent and had learned to butcher and bake while on leave from society. Ran and I mentally rubbed our hands and felt we might have found lasting 3-in-1 Oil for Giro's grating cogs and wheels.

I did notice that Rory had an exuberant hand with the fancier cuts of our beeves. He distributed steaks and roasts as his personal largesse until I found a way to stanch the flow by removing some to a lower shelf with a sign, MRS GALT: WALK AWAY AND LEAVE IT, printed in big letters. It worked. Pegeen was most impressed with my household decor. She oh'd and ah'd over my proudly displayed Hawaiian quilts. Never seen anything like them, she said. Used to sew, too. I brightened further to think I might pass on my hopeless mending. She even enjoyed cleaning silver.

Rory cheerfully came in a day or two before we left and gave me a pro's lesson in pie crust, while he lauded the fresh country air and how they'd made quick station friends. The heavens had opened. I've always suspected Paradise is for fools.

Walking in through filthy doors, January 3, 1961, I greeted

desolation. Speechless with dismay, I looked back out the veranda. Ran was still near the plane, deep in conversation with the manager. He looked unhappy. I turned back. It was evident Rory and Pegeen were long gone, and had gone to pot beforehand. Rats had nested in the curved linen couch, doors hung open, and leaves were scattered everywhere. The floors and rugs were tramped with muddy footprints—even our bed had been slept in. I'll forgo describing how we knew. I wanted to cry, but anger won, and I stomped back and forth spewing rage.

That was inside. Outside was worse. One of Giro's strangest gifts rose out of the fairy tale weeds that greeted us that January. The rain had begun in December and the vegetable garden had totally disappeared in a sodden jungle of monumental weeds. Even the orchard of struggling apples, pears, and almonds was nowhere to be seen. Nothing but a roiling tidal wave of amazing growth. In final shock we looked in vain for seven-foot-tall corn. Some of the weed trunks were ten inches in diameter, Jack's bean stalk was there, and nightmarish broccoli-looking things, all choked and chained with a crazy tangle of melon and cucumber vines. Rousseau would have grabbed his brushes in inspiration, and I immediately picturd his unique zoo peeking out in cross-eyed splendor.

The tour of the wrack and ruin lasted one short hour. Just long enough to follow my instincts and check the silver and the quilts. Several spoons and the green and white quilt were missing; the prettiest one, with breadfruit leaves. And one of my new down pillows. They had feathered their future Celtic love nest tastefully. Two weeks later I was still sitting in mud, legs akimbo, invisible save my peaked straw hat, rhythmically and savagely pulling weeds. I used an ax and a short shovel on fifty or so. Size alone did not indicate power, the deceptively short ones could be veritable wisdom teeth, and I am ashamed to say I withered my vocabulary.

But I learned from it. One of Giro's better lessons. I learned what it was like to have salty sweat blind your eyes, roll off your nose tip in stinging drops, course down your back and legs, and creep from behind breasts and between fingers. I never knew we humans were so liberally endowed with sweat glands. Day by

203

day I reveled in the nether regions of understanding; steve-
dores from everywhere, coolies, rice paddy women, the pickers
of the world, galley slaves, on down the list of worlds I've never
touched with anything but my mind.

I also discovered I was pregnant again, and called it Weedy. I
figured if it could hang on through all that, God meant me to
have it, and relaxed. Another lesson. Safe in my handbag were
the six vials of Red Krohn's magic potion for use at the first sign
of pregnancy. I was to be given a shot every week by Dr. Burke
for the first four months. Red felt confident that amount of
time would put me out of danger. He and I were determined
the four-poster would remain a fallow guestroom, not a charnel
house.

The January sun woke up early and went to bed late. Ran
bought killer sheep for the larder and I learned about curry.
Mexican spices were foreign to Barnard's Emporium but curry
wasn't; India again. Lamb was consumed more quickly, and a
good thing too; meat stank in a hurry in that heat. I never
thought it would be that hot. We ran the engine an hour or so
during the day to hold back decay. The bright side was being
able to use my American washing machine if I planned it right.
You had to watch for snakes, though. We had two kinds, black
and brown, both venomous. The brown was cousin to the co-
bra, and deadly. They'd make for cool spots like a freshly
mopped laundry floor or a dark cement outhouse. I began to
carry my snakebite kit in my summer smock pocket and bored
Katrina silly making her carry hers.

Brown snakes were especially treacherous because they
looked like everything else. They'd protude pug-nosed cables
from under the house, and if you didn't catch the gleam of
darting tongue you'd reach for what you thought was a hose
someone had left in a corner. I'd see Ran stop dead on the veranda, hand up for quiet, whisk in for his gun, then tiptoe back,
very careful not to let the screen slap. He'd aim quickly,
efficiently, and shots and snake leaped in the soundless air.
Right sporty!

I began to make tall jars of gazpacho with my herbs and we
often dined on cold soup, cold lamb, and cold beer. Anything
to avoid big Bertha's hot body.

My days of weeding were long, but often flowered into priceless moments.

I'd slog mechanically into the laundry at sundown, peel off mud-caked boots and clothes acid with sweat, wrap up in a dirty towel from the ever-present pile, and tiptoe down the passages to my bath. Cold supper for Quilty and Katrina had been planned and cooked by eight A.M. Where was Ran? I stopped breathing to listen. Faint rushing of water. He was in the shower, which meant a tepid one for me—there was never enough hot water. Who cared in that heat? I bungled my way across the living room to stand outside his shower curtain.

"Ran? When would you like supper?"

"How about later? It's hot."

"Okay. That's what I thought." Back to my bathroom, tripping over the clutched towel. Climbing out of the shower I thought, you have to get that dirty to feel that clean.

Nine thirty at night and it was still hot, but a cool hand on a fevered brow compared to noonday. Everything stuck in the fast-rising humidity—doors, window, clothes, sheets, and floors. Feet had been near bare all day and were splayed and swollen. Hair seemed to clot on one's head.

But with the night came a fine-sieved breeze, or was it a zephyr? In other words, sitting still you felt it.

Especially on the veranda by candlelight in rumpled shorts. The veranda faced almost due east and was a catbird seat for risings of moons. Already I could sense a pallor in the sky behind those round mountains of big gums opposite us.

"Hey, darling, you got a fresh lemon?" Ran sloshing around in El Bar.

"Coming up!"

Steaks off the fire. A handful of plates, cutlery, and paper napkins; then peace. And behold: Giro at its best.

There's never been anything before or since like stretching hot and weary legs onto our veranda railing on a sultry January night while sticking a nose into wild-lemon-scented gin and tonic clanking with ice, awaiting the greatest show on earth for an audience of two.

Ran's big toe silhouetted against a crescent of that golden disk didn't hurt a bit. And nobody had to talk.

Giro full moons rose with such swift, inexorable orderliness. First a huge melting copper coin bonfiring the sky, up, up, cooler and cooler; then from eighteen billion carats of raw gold to acres of silver gilt and finally to a monocle of frostbitten platinum.

"Rain!"

A thunderclap like God Himself applauding over our heads smacked its hands for attention and a loose lion of wind galloped straight through the house. Big drops of rain hurled themselves at Giro's crumpled helmet.

Galvanized, we ran through sleeping porches, six banks of louvers to yank shut in each; then the bathroom ones, slamming doors and screens gone mad.

Drenched, we collided in the parlor only to turn and stare, bewildered by the moon still eyeing us with serenity.

The storm had risen behind our backs. That black, puffed African chief of a cloud had appeared like the bogeyman from the west and gone *Brrrrrraaaaahhhhgh* all over us.

We laughed ourselves hot again and watched the rest of the unruffled moonrise in the dripping wake of Australia's best spent storm.

Like some people, Giro's moods had an explosive quality. You were never really prepared for anything. Winter dryness cracked your lips; laundry crisped like crackers as you'd hang it. Old Will would drag out ominous stories about the river reduced to festering pools draped with dying cows, incorporating visions of dingos and snakes arriving by night in furtive legions to nestle under water tanks. And just as you settled down to Giro as a budding desert, the heat came and Sadie Thompson's own rain poured down like an upended pail. Inside of two days, lushness would be everywhere.

After a week of solid rain we'd stir at night, uneasy, and greet a different sound from the pelt of endless rain on our tin armor—a sonorous roar. The river was up. Meaning: Can we get out? Meaning: No mail, no food from town, no doctor in emergency. Meaning: Will the mist open for the plane if necessary? A whole new set of obstacles to confront. Mildew and mold, and our fine green friends, the frogs. And, O gentle creeping Jehosophat, the laundry again. It took days to dry. True, there sat

206

my dryer from America. But what the dryer asked of our generator pulled every light in the place down to banana yellow, and if the engine went we'd had it. No repairmen from Sydney could make the river.

I ran it a few times in desperation, but only after wet trampings down to the MacKendricks in squelching boots to check that nothing electric was on and to dispatch stern directives in all directions that everything must be turned off. If one electric heater had been left on that dryer could have blown the engine—an expensive disaster for us all. Drama. Not always welcome at breakfast, lunch, and dinner, but a guest I couldn't seem to oust.

I almost hated the rain. I was grateful from the standpoint of cows, but I simply didn't enjoy living in green gloom day and night. The bread is green, the air and one's skin glows green. One looks for mushrooms in between one's toes as well as in the pastures. Mud is everywhere; spreading lakes appear. I walked with sucking sounds down to watch the lettuces climb to leathery seed in jig time. Sheets were soundless with damp. Giro's world was encased in a sweating green membrane or drowned in gray water. Patrick White writes of rain in *Voss* as no one can, and I would feel like that.

The fleas arrived with the wet and fell in love with me. What hell they could dispense. They hatched in grass, my fur and wool rugs, and sucked me unmercifully. Long kite-tail bites ringed my waist, ankles, and buttocks. If I dared the disgusting luxury of a groaning scratch, beware. Trembling water blisters would appear, tear, break, ooze, flatten, scab, and scar. Like Job's boils, they plagued me, and I carried shiny, mauve scars in memoriam.

The river became a milk chocolate torrent with teeth. Carrying tough branches and offal and animals, it roared past at ten miles an hour. What had been dry gravel beds became feeder streams and tributaries. Brooks and waterfalls welled from the hillsides. The road from Giro nineteen miles up to the Myall became impassible.

The rain stopped as suddenly as it came, leaving us in a steaming tropical land in which Ran felt at home, coming from Hawaii. But about which I knew nothing, coming from lots of

207

places, but mostly California. If I'd known I'd be living in the tropics, I'd have found out things about weevily flour and moldy shoe bottoms and sweating fur rugs. Australia was *dry*. It *had* to be. The dead heart and all that sort of thing. Actually a generous slice of the country is very tropical, and we were in a civil war between two climates. Frost but no snow; high humidity, except sometimes, meaning those searing west winds, when the air becomes a crushed Saltine. Six hundred feet above sea level gave no relief when the wet hot summer descended. You just hoped it out.

At the end of the rain, Giro steamed in the sun like a locomotive. But the river raced on for days, a witch at a wedding. Until, finally spent, it shrank slowly down to its littered home banks, a bad kid crawling home from a spree without a dime. Sun made the earth a soggy blanket, veils of mosquitoes rose furrily from stagnance everywhere, and armies of flies descended. Blowflies planted maggots on our meat before it could be corned, and the garbage actually moved. I often thought that instead of carting and burying it, why not just nail up a sign, with an arrow pointing to the right direction? The garbage would have traveled to the dump wriggling in unison.

25

Pour le Sport

IT'S tough to work a trowel in among meadow muffins and leaky gravel. So one stolen afternoon I picked some flat-ironed rocks beyond Giro Creek, which joins the river a half mile upstream, for a sunbath.

I wore boots, and a jacket over my bikini because I needed pockets for snake bite kit, cigarettes, a book of John Donne's poems, Skol, and an apple. Boots looked terrible, but snakes were everywhere, and wrote Arabic in the grass on the way. A leftover Palm Springs hat, with velvet and rhinestone bees on it, a red beach towel, and I was equipped.

It was a lovely walk with the willows brushing me out of their hair. I followed the river which curved and creamed shallowly, all green and silver between the hills. Vermont! Yes, without farms and stone walls. What about the bald grass-country ahead and across? Wyoming? Yes, an evocative duet. The Prussian-blue ranges high up stopped me. Not craggy, but rugged, and steep enough from our low vantage point. Colorado? There came Giro Creek as I softly sang to the tune of "All of Me," "ala meee, why not Koala meeee—" *Cheese it.* I froze. A bull the size of a barn stood knee-deep in Giro Creek, watching me like a snake charmer. Outside of a cape buffalo, no horned animal is more forbidding than a full-grown Hereford range bull—a behemoth. I'm deathly afraid of bulls. It disgusted Ran, but I am, I am. He said, "All you have to do is say *shoo.*" I tried, but they always dropped their ton of head and horns and pawed the ground when *I* did it.

I creaked forward two feet, cursing the red towel and hearing faint "Ole's" and "La Virgen de la Macarena" on a cornet. God, he'd stopped chewing! We stared at each other for four stanzas of the Donne poem I wasn't going to get to read on that warm rock. A hypnotic deadlock.

He stepped toward me and I threw myself into reverse. Walks are healthier anyway. Who wants to lie around in the sun? It wasn't worth it.

A few days later, we planned a picnic. I was to head Rover over the hills on a faint track to meet Ran at a far fence. He looked so ornamental on his fat white charger, Johnny Walker, I forgot to watch the track and ran Rover's belly onto a hostile boulder, wheels spinning ignominiously. Ran had to push us off. It's a good thing the food was good: white wine, roquefort hand-flown from Sydney, watercress salad, skillet potatoes and onions, spicy chops, and rich brownies.

Katrina joined us on—alas and alack—a mare, and as delectable aromas assuaged Ran's crippled humor, there came the Station stallion, Casanova the Cad, sprinting down the hill with rape in his eye, kicking dust all over my nice picnic lunch. I fed Katrina from the ground while Ran threw pebbles at Casanova's derrière until the mare could make a run for it. Still, it was great fun.

There were games to play and fun to be had. But not enough. I knew I didn't laugh enough. What seemed to curdle my spirits? Perhaps it was because the few hours Ran was home he spent at his heaped-up desk or asleep. On rare nights we'd pace the strip together, thunderstruck by unfamiliar stars and the gossamer scarf of the Milky Way, as bright as full-moonlight. We'd hang together and listen to the earth turn.

But many nights I'd walk by myself, and loneliness was bitter medicine that tied my tongue and dried me up and blew me away.

If gloom settled on my shoulders like a cape and I raged against the flypaper of the scullery, I could often walk them off, but not always. On nights so black you might as well be blind,

210

I'd jump in fright at disembodied munches by my ear. Sometimes I swam them off. But river swimming made me uneasy. I was me at age seven again, standing miserably in the ooze of yellow mud in West Virginia, screaming to be removed. To me, rivers are full of Nameless Horrors, and a few eye-poaching stories about leeches, river eels, water snakes, and occasional dead cows simply made me more certain I was right. All that, plus a dilly of a current, unbelievably painful rocks, stones, pebbles, gravel, etc. (even Intrepid Randolph wore whole tennis shoes) and the unmistakable smell of animal urine on hot days, definitely turned a swim into adventure.

I had brought lots of bathing suits like oversize postage stamps, jackets, hats, clogs, etc. What I should have brought was a frogman's outfit. Oh, well. The "beach" was ankle-deep gravel and the cows had always recently left. You could tell. The current was worth your life to swim against, but fortunately there were low, strong branches on the far side, usually free of lizards, that were great for clinging. The trick was to stagger in, face contorted from submerged terrain, and go like hell for one of those branches. If you missed, you could always let the current carry you down to a wide-curving shallow area. However, that shallow place was turgid, warm, and slithering with Nameless Horrors. It was nip and tuck, but once hanging onto those branches with cool, swift water churning like nature's Jacuzzi bath—celestial. Your whole body waggled free in S shapes. Head back, looking up hundred-foot willows, I'd think, in those timeless moments, of people hunched over steering wheels, breathing gas fumes from the cars ahead and be lost in gratitude that I wasn't one of them anymore.

Ran had been brought up on more dangerous games. Surfing on Hawaiian beaches for a start. He was a powerful swimmer. I fancied I had style, but power and speed were not my bag.

When the river rampaged in flood that summer, Ran eyed it hungrily and decided he'd try it in an inner tube. He finally did, and limped to shore at the Biddefords' three hours later. Ten miles in three hours doesn't sound fast, considering the speed of the maniac water. I wondered what went on during that trip.

211

Ran never said much, but wore Tom's clothes home and never suggested another try.

When the river was up just enough, Ran used to shoot the rapids on the seat of his shorts. I got talked into it that February, rather ill-equipped with my two-month pregnancy, rubber thong sandals, and bathing suit Number 13. We went down in tandem. He sat and I sat behind, straddling him, his back against my front and my arms around his woolly chest. It was a dismal idea. After a few yards of blood-curdling "Look out's," "My god's," "Ran's," and a handful of chest hair, Ran plunged after my sandals, wedging me between two boulders, with the rabid current dislodging me by inches.

Not even Ran could have battled upstream in that water, and it was a tedious walk. I got to shore somehow, in possession of what I supposed to be at least three broken toes.

There came Ran in the distance, waving one sandal, yelling, "Wait! Wait! Wait!" I said to myself, "Wait?" With the walk back through stinging nettles and rocks, that sandal was like a Band-Aid on a leper.

I got carried, which was sexy.

26

Jam

THE station was preparing to brand. All the calves would be VIP's (our brand) whether they liked it or not. The males and females would be shunted away from their mothers and sent through varieties of necessary hell. Hell *assortis*. Old Will would cut the baby bulls down to steers; Ran would brand each flank in smoking iron letters. The new yards weren't ready yet at Corroborree; the old ones were being readied half a mile up toward Giro Creek.

Katrina was behaving like a jackeroo one moment and an hysterical child the next because she was to be let off lessons to help muster.

Since Honolulu, Quilty had become more formal and hesitant with Ran and me, and increasingly testy with Katrina who, in turn, grew more insubordinate by the day. There was an edge of insolence in Katrina's manner toward her that told me absolutely that Katrina had ferreted out Quilty's secret. And that pathetic Quilty was trying to protect her inadmissible weak spot by biting first. I did my best to referee, but that's all I was.

The three of us had just wrangled through another breakfast and Quilty had gone off to the schoolroom in a huff.

"Katrina, please clear the table," I said tartly. "You were very rude to Quilty and I won't have it. Do you understand?"

"I don't care!" she replied hotly. "She's just as rude. And, besides, she gets mad all the time."

"Katrina." I stopped scraping plates into the chickens' bucket. "Quilty's very lonely out here. We have to be kind."

"Well, I don't have anybody to play with either!"

"That's true, but that doesn't mean you can hurt other people's feelings."

"Can I go now?" Katrina ran to the kitchen door. "She'll be crabby if I'm late."

"Wash your hands first, please," I retorted, "or I'll be crabby."

"OK," came an impatient sigh as she whirled around and ran to the third bathroom kitty-corner from Ran's office.

I called after her, "How about reading *The Arabian Nights* tonight?"

"Sure, that'd be very fun, Mom." She had come back with wet hands. She never dried them. Then why were her towels always so grubby?

"What do you say we see if you could go to the Biddefords this weekend? You'll be busy with the branding next weekend. It's been a while since Dan's been over here."

Her face shone. "Gee, that'd be great. Wait'll I show Dan how high Bluebottle can jump now! I bet he can even beat Lady!" Lady was Dan's pony.

"I'll talk to Mrs. Biddeford. Hurry up, now! Get a move on. Quilty'll bark at me if we're not careful." I winked. She grinned, hugged me around my thickening waist, and bounded out.

"Oh, Katrina!" I'd forgotten to ask her. I ran to the door and shouted after her pumping legs. "Katrina!" She slowed down but kept running.

"Yes?"

"If you see Errol ask him to help me pick plums. I'm going to try making jam."

"OK." And she cantered out of earshot.

The plums weren't really ripe, but if I waited any longer the fruit flies and flying foxes'd get them. The batlike foxes were already screeching after dark in the huge Moreton Bay fig. Also, never having attempted jam, if it turned out to be lousy I could always blame it on the plums.

The jam was not only not lousy, it was just delicious. All lumpy with lemon and orange rind. Perhaps that was an answer to

214

Christmas presents—fancy labels—use the GIRO stencil. How about Wild Lemon Marmalade from Anne Baxter Galt's Country Kitchen? No wonder countrywomen liked to put up (or was it put down?) fruit and jams for the fairs. It was the one thing they could cook that didn't get eaten as fast as they made it.

As I labored to clean the sticky jam kettle and sticky rims and rings, I vowed to parcel more of myself out to Katrina. Ran would often come home around her bedtime, and reading would be cut short by his evening meal. Speaking of parcels, what about sending Quilty to Sydney for a respite? With Katrina off to the Biddefords, Ran and I could have a quiet weekend before branding.

The phone *crank-crank-cranked* in the office. I lifted my head. Ran was back. That's funny, I hadn't heard him come in. I checked the clock. Three. He'd raised his voice and had forgotten to shut the door. I couldn't help overhearing parts of a long, serious conversation with his solicitor, Martin Worthington. Something about another overdraft at the bank and an extension of some note or other. Then I heard, "I'll see if I can make it—if I leave in an hour. Right. My best to Sylvia. See you then."

He hung up and came to the kitchen screen door.

"Sweetheart."

"Hi! You're home early."

"Had to make a call. Smells interesting. What're you concocting?"

"Jam. Taste?"

He checked his big flyer's watch. "Afraid I can't. I have to fly to Sydney."

"Oh!" I moved to the screen.

"I have to see Martin Worthington. They asked me to dinner. He and I can talk before we meet some people tomorrow. The bank is being ridiculous about this and that."

"Oh. Katrina's off to the Biddefords' early tomorrow."

"Is she? Good idea. Tell her not to wear Bluebottle out, he's got to be in fine fettle next week. Listen, darling, I've got to throw some things together and get going."

"Ran." A thought suddenly occurred to me. "Quilty's getting nervy—could you fly her in with you? She could have a few days on her own since Katrina will be away." He knew what I meant.

He looked at his watch again with distaste.

"I guess so, but she'll have to hurry."

"When will you be back?"

"Sometime Saturday, maybe even tomorrow night, depending on when I can see whom I have to."

"Everything all right?" I asked, hopeful for some direct scrap of information.

"Oh, sure, just a bunch of red tape. You'd better tell Quilty," he said hurriedly as he turned and strode down the hall to get his things.

"I will," I said as I watched his tall back move away from me.

Katrina and I read *The Fisherman and the Genie* that night. Halfway through, her eyes folded shut like little fans. I closed the book and rose to go. Grandfather loved that story too and had it painted in his six children's Oak Park playroom as the symbol of imagination given rein. I turned off the lamp carefully and peeked back at my child. She really was a talented sleeper. I knew she'd be up at dawn getting ready to ride ten miles cross-country to the Biddefords'. Dan would meet her halfway, as always. The river was up enough for fine swims. Even irascible Bluebottle liked his dip. I stepped away and lit a cigarette. It was too easy to smoke when you knew it wasn't irritating anybody. I heard footsteps out the side door.

"You there, Mrs. Galt?" It was the manager.

"Yes," I called. "Be right there!" and came to the door. It was unusual. I hardly ever had contact with him. He and his young blond bride had dined at Giro once or twice. He was not at all talkative and carefully formal.

"Just letting you know I'll turn off the engine in about half an hour," he stated coolly and went briskly off.

No pleasantries from that one. He was as friendly as a well-trained cop about to give you a ticket.

Should I have a nightcap? What did I mean, should I? Why not? I walked in to El Bar, barely seeable in the light sneaking from Ran's office. Nuts. No ice. Oh, well, I'll have it English style. I poured myself a warm gin and tonic. Tasted peculiar—

216

must be that new cheap gin. It was too dark in there to see the label.

I walked out on the veranda sipping my drink, kicked off my shoes, and flopped in a chair. The stars were ganging up on the sky. It was Friday night. Party night—or used to be. What a lot of glamorous fuss I'd been to. Behind my eyes grew a parade of parties. The huge, milling studio bashes after premieres or Academy Awards. Tents and flashbulbs and sexy dresses cut down to there on newcomers hoping to flag down a producer's eye. Thousands of perfectly capped teeth set in waxy crescents. Noisy with boredom.

Elegant medium-sized ones at Clifton Webb's with Ethel Merman singing every single word in every show tune you'd ever heard in that clarion clarinet voice of hers. Obliging Howard Dietz at the piano—as you listened you'd studied fabled Marion Davies, sunk in a chintz couch, hung with sapphires the color of her enormous eyes. I crushed my cigarette in an ashtray on the floor. I'd given a few parties myself. Mostly arms-around-the-neck-I-love-you-too parties. Music, good food, good drink, good friends, and lots of flowers. I mused on. That was a handsome coming-out party for Dundeen Bostwick. Her delightful grandmother had given it at the St. Regis Roof in New York. I'd bought my one and only Mainbocher for that. Azalea pink bias-cut French crepe. Most expensive dress I'd ever had before or since—$1,000. My dear friend Watson Webb, who was Dundeen's uncle, had taken me. It was a traditional confection frosted with red, white, and blue corpuscles.

I drained my gin and tonic English style. A coming-out party, English style. That was a party to remember. The Douglas Fairbanks, Jr.'s party at Cliveden for their eighteen-year-old Daphne. The engine died in agony and the veranda glowed in the dark with star shine. I clasped my empty glass, leaned back, and closed my eyes, reliving that extraordinary night.

Douglas was producing a picture in London in 1957 called *Chase a Crooked Shadow.* They were loaned a great and famous country house belonging to the Astor family, called Cliveden. Cliveden was first built in Buckinghamshire in 1666. It burned down twice and was rebuilt for the third time in 1851. The

Thames flowed by its lawns and gardens, which were designed by the legendary Capability Brown. It was open to the public at certain times, but only a few reception rooms. Doug and Mary Lee were given carte blanche by their good friends, the Astors, for Daphne's coming-out ball.

It was arranged that I'd be escorted by Billy Wallace, then one of Princess Margaret's beaux. She was to be there, as well as the Queen and Prince Philip. There were many festive dinners beforehand; Billy and I went to one at Lord and Lady Lambton's. Doug explained that Tony Lambton was a stormy petrel in the House of Lords. The Fairbanks had kindly briefed me about some of the guests I'd meet at dinner and I was light-headed with anticipation. No one I knew would be there. But everyone sounded intriguing.

Unfortunately, I had spent the entire day crying. We'd been shooting the hysterical collapse of the neurotic character I was playing. No amount of ice had retrieved my swollen eyes. My evening gown was specially made for the occasion. It looked as perfect as I did not.

As we entered the downstairs foyer at the Lambtons', Billy excused himself to go park his car. I was ushered up the narrow town house stairs by a parlormaid and left to myself in a sitting room. There was not a sound. Were we early? I hadn't thought so. There was a charming terrace at the end of the room and I strolled out. Great clay pots of shrubs and massed small ones of white geraniums banked its sides. I went to the far balustrade and leaned over, enjoying the neat rectangles of other town house gardens and terraces, much like some of the New York ones I'd known. I heard a rustle and turned expectantly. A very tall lady was regarding me coldly. She was dressed to the teeth in white. Raising her long slim arm, she pointed a long slim finger.

"Would you move that pot over there?"

Dumbstruck, I looked vaguely around at various shrubs and geraniums and asked, "Pot?"

"*That* one," she insisted in a tone of annoyance, flicking her finger. I tentatively stretched out my hands toward one to my right and looked at her inquiringly.

218

"Just put it over there," she ordered, pointing to the top of the balustrade behind me.

"Certainly," I said, and moved the pot. The arm fell to her side; she turned abruptly and left.

For a guest, I thought, she certainly seems to know her way around. I never did meet her. In fact I never met anyone but Lord Lambton, and he introduced himself. Later I deduced she was my hostess from Doug's conversation.

There was a man called David seated next to me at dinner. He was perfectly charming. Billy Wallace was on my left.

Stavros Niarchos and his wife were there, among others. Just as Doug had described, he wore his decorations and a wide yellow ribbon across his stomach. That fact and his accent helped me place him. She wore no makeup and an oddly fireless diamond, the size and shape of a codpiece, on a fine platinum chain. At nine thirty or so, as we were gathering to leave for the drive to Buckinghamshire, I sensed a commotion in the marble vestibule of the elegant skinny house. There were stern-looking black-uniformed guards filing in, ladies were shouldering politely forward, twittering with excitement. Through the opened front door I glimpsed an armored truck with BANK OF ENGLAND on it in golden letters. It was tiara time. Hat-sized black suede and velvet boxes opened again and again, revealing glittering headgear of all descriptions. Lady Lambton, my mystery hostess, owned the tallest and thinnest, and rightly so. Hers was a veritable cliff, a palisade of intricate stones rising straight up from an already high forehead. Not becoming but damned impressive.

Billy Wallace held the door as I gathered my taffeta, stuffed it and myself into his low-slung Jaguar and we joined the procession of Rolls-Royces to Cliveden. To see that magnificent house blaze alive again, with music floating out of twenty-foot-high French windows down sweeping lawns to the Thames was a thrilling sight. I'd practiced my curtsy. Mary Lee Fairbanks had warned, "For pete's sake, don't go down too far. The Queen is awfully sick of hauling up American ladies."

The ball began at ten. At ten thirty Billy and I walked into a giant marble rotunda and ran straight into Princess Margaret, standing with three young men under an enormous chandelier. I was so startled I barely bobbed. "How d'you do, ma'am?" She stared back icily over a shatteringly beautiful turquoise and diamond necklace as Billy greeted her rather uncomfortably. Her three escorts looked like Max Beerbohm drawings. She never spoke. It was a rude moment, all of us jellied in discomfiture. I was told she apologized three days later to someone I knew well, saying, "I was very rude to Anne Baxter. She was with Billy Wallace. Escorts are hard to come by."

What a party! Cinderella's very own ball. Prince Philip slew the ladies. He whirled around the polished parquet with them all. They stood in luscious bejeweled groups, melting like ice cream cones as he danced by. Merle Oberon looked ravishing in hot pink chiffon and brooklets and rivers of diamonds. My friend Lady Elizabeth Clyde, whose husband was Doug's executive producer, said the Queen wanted to meet me. Eliza and Tommy were staying at Windsor Castle that Ascot Week. She was the Duke of Wellington's daughter and a beautiful, slightly wicked Peter Pan.

The Queen was as charming as her sister had not been. Her husband's two hands could have spanned her waist, though her bosom was deep. Creamy skin and lively eyes. Easy as pie and far prettier than I'd ever seen her photographed.

"Daphne" was spelled out in sparkling fireworks across the river at midnight. Even the venerable Thames looked made of champagne in the moonlight.

I leaned forward, wishing I were gowned and coiffed and perfumed again, or did I? I looked at my grubby feet. Be a long way from those to that. A flea bite started to itch. It was one I couldn't get at with clothes on. I showered in a starlit bathroom and traipsed off to bed.

220

27

My Adjustment

EARLY the next morning Katrina waved at me one more time before she vanished behind a hill. I walked around the outside of the house to start chores.

Loneliness was a prescription at Giro. You took it every morning, like vitamins. I've never minded being alone; enjoyed, even craved it many times, and have talked to myself since I can remember: an only child pinching a chance to suck its thumb in broad daylight. But being alone in Australia was like living with a dead presence; there but not there. It was a crafty, senile presence and I was emotionally at odds with it.

The morning was fresh-minted. I looked south at the waving acres of emerald and amethyst lucerne Ran and the men had so laboriously planted. They were bordered by my long-haired willows. I resolved to be quick at chores and stride out to breathe the lucerne's perfume. Especially nice after distributing slops.

Alone as I was that day, I managed to break out for a half-hour's walk and spotted a women's club of cows, some of whom had brought the kids.

I stopped, contemplated them long and hard, and opened fire. "You tired old bitches, you slobs, you damned smug-bellied fatheads! There you chew year after year, standing around while some hot bull does his job, giving calf after calf to the abattoirs. For what? If you don't bleed to death or fall apart or,

221

God forbid, refuse to breed—a bullet in the head and a butcher knife!"

I shouted expletives and abuse in a torrent of release. Most of them held their cuds and gazed at me in mild wonderment, but one old bag took umbrage. I swear she really heard me. She had a twisted, drunken-looking pair of horns and her ump-teenth calf nosing around for lunch. There seemed to be a sudden swift connection between her watery orbs and me and I let her have it. "And *you,* you ugly madam, *look* at that sagging bag! Those *corny horns!* You, you, you damned *cow,* you aimless junkheap, you spineless numbskull. *Sale vache* —you *Dummkopf* of a *Kuh!*"

German did it. She charged! Slowly at first, then faster and faster. My legs started pumping like pistons. She chased me straight at a tough-looking barbed wire fence, which I dived through, leaving a flapping piece of jeans. My heart pounded and my knees shook and I rolled around in the lucerne roaring with laughter. I was so deliciously relaxed I could have slept in the sun and the wind for hours. That august lady had taken my psyche by the scruff of its neck and shaken it into a horse laugh.

Lucerne is such a grandiose word for alfalfa, one wants to pronounce it in French. What a boon it is. One decent planting and you can reap six to eight times a year for years, with luck and rain. Nutritious and delicious. I ate it more than once. The flowers are like mop-headed lavender clover and taste exactly like fresh string beans. I don't blame cows. So much fun and beauty at Giro if you could get to it. Even alone.

I stretched luxuriously and felt for the hole in the backside of my jeans. I checked the barbed wire fence for the torn piece. There it was, a faded flag. Mending again, damn it. Have to, though, only one other pair left. I plucked it free and saun-tered back to the house.

I really was alone today. Even the manager and his wife had gone on a short trip. Ron might be back, I thought hopefully. Oh, well, I'd have the mail to myself. Wonder what was going on in Sydney and what the meeting was about?

I also wondered whether most Australian countrywomen's lives were predicated upon the Overheard. Mine was. I literally overheard my life; at least its patterns, boundaries, and the core

222

of it. Did they, too, pilfer shreds of conversation on a veranda as they poured tea before making themselves scarce? Or glean clues from raised voices on bad phones, or shouted plans over throbbing machines at dawn? Or, and I blush, treat themselves to the humiliating business of reading the scraps and bits of paper on the desk as they tidied up after their masters? I hope not. Eavesdropping is so repulsive.

But I felt shut out from so much that governed my life, and my voice was unpopular unless it spoke of food, flowers, furbelows, and fetuses. So, I fell prey to the sneak thievery of the Overheard. I became a flap-eared poacher in Ran's male preserves.

One of my cherished beliefs is that we are first human beings, second, male or female. I hear an Australian male guffaw and a creak as Simone de Beauvoir swivels in her chair. It irks me to be lumped into a wad like yesterday's chewing gum. Women can, or Women don't, or Women are, or Woman is. That customs condition us to a maze of acceptable reactions in different countries and situations is true of both men and women. Or should I say *man*. That's a lump we're all in willy-nilly.

The women I'd heard about and observed in the Australian bush catapulted me into admiration. What was asked of them, and what they gave with only a cursory gripe, was a revelation to an American female.

The American pioneer woman would also have left my jaw ajar. But this was *not* 1849 or 1880, or even 1910 or 1940. It was 1961. The hardest lesson for me to swallow was my own inadequacy compared to those stalwart ladies. The changes I wrought at Giro were not impressive. They didn't see why I bothered with candles in the dining room or atmospheric "decor." A chair was to sit in. A bed was for sleep. What I wore at Giro flabbergasted them. They preferred flowered frocks, and a gas fire to a fireplace—cleaner, you see.

I was at best a curiosity, the actress myth came into play. What did seem to impress them was my being there at all. Their starved imaginations ran riots around Hollywood and the theater. Nor did I disillusion them. After all, what else did I have but their concept of glamour? That blessed mote in the spectator's eye.

223

They could do anything. Split kindling and keep a wood or a coal stove going twenty-four hours a day. At all the right heats. Produce from that black beast the tenderest of meringues, "Pavlovas" they called them. Feed ravenous families year after year with their own jams, pickles, vegetables, and fruits. Cultivate picture-book vegetable gardens as a matter of course, refinish floors with beeswax and turpentine, a killing job. Wield a mop and bucket with better result than a vacuum cleaner, which needs both parts *and* electricity. I'll always remember explaining that vacuum cleaner to Pegeen. What an ass I must have looked, down on my knees, sucking in huge breaths so she'd get the idea. She awakened my latent missionary complex.

They raised chickens, they sewed, they knitted, they crocheted, they carried the water and built the fires under copper basins to boil laundry. And what laundry. Blood-encrusted, manured, creosoted, and muddy. Lugged meals to far-off men, visited the sick, attended funerals, weddings, choirs, and ACWA meetings, children in tow—and that's a feat in itself, over rotten roads.

They milked, mustered in a pinch, and educated their children well enough by correspondence to place them in the right grade at the right time in town or city schools. That really floored me.

Medical help was either unavailable or sketchy, and though some of their remedies were hair-raising, they survived in general, as did their children and husbands. Even Kath Biddeford refused to use thermometers, and she'd raised three healthy children. They entertained. They not only did it, but managed to spend time with their guests, something I was never able to do, to Ran's embarrassment. He was always trying to cover for my frantic twenty-five-minute sojourns in the kitchen. Although to his joy I learned to cook, nothing I made looked pretty the way theirs did. Once I made angel pie and stuck geraniums on it and Ran flushed with pride. We ate many a desiccated roast in Australia, but the queen was in the parlor with her guests. Better to shut the oven door on culinary triumph than to stagger in hot and bothered like me, late for cocktails and conversation!

224

No, I don't know how they do it. But they do. Maybe they don't look like ads for soap, but there's a dignity embedded in their bones you couldn't buy with money.

I did chores by rote and was out bucketing my baby pine trees by one o'clock. And here came the mail. I could hear the sound of crunching wheels speeding down the strip. She was always in a tearing hurry on Saturdays. A hello and a good-bye and I dragged the leather sack down through the house. The groceries could wait! I felt for the key where it was hidden in the office and opened the padlock. Selfishly I rooted through for mine. Four. Three from home and one from—Parramatta. Parramatta. Who did I know in Parramatta? It was the oldest suburb of Sydney, quite far out. The city had grown in other directions. Originally it was the first convict settlement of any permanence.

The name on the back was hard to read. I made out P. White. My God, it couldn't be! What a strange and wonderful man he was. I'd shared that Japanese dinner with him during the filming of *Summer of the Seventeenth Doll.* Sir John and Mary Mills knew him from London. We four had sat curled up on the floor, had eaten sukiyaki, and had talked and talked. God, it was fun. I tore the letter open. It was indeed from Patrick White, asking me to lunch with a writer called Thea Astley. She'd written a book he thought might make a good film—*Descant for Gossips.* A week from tomorrow. If only I could. No. Branding would still be on. Hell, I could take the train if I could just get someone to drive me in. They'd need to have the vehicle back. Please, God. I need a lunch like that. I really do. I squeezed my eyes and clenched my teeth in fervent prayer and ran for a nervous cigarette. He was sending a copy of the book and remembered our dinner. I tramped around the kitchen with excitement, puffing madly. Somehow I'd do it. Somehow I would *do* it. How about a cold, cold beer to celebrate? Only costs a few more cents to go first class, as Ran would say. I went to the coldroom for imported Victorian beer, just the best, and wished I had guts enough to turn the engine on. I needed music, too. I wandered through the house, reading the letters from home, gulping beer, and living in other lives with other people, mashing out one cigarette and lighting another. During

225

the next two hours my thoughts continued to bandy me about, accompanied by another nice cold beer and an angry broom.

Ran pursued Giro's man's world outside. I was pursued by the woman's world inside. Giro could be unregenerate inside and out. Sex-mad colonies of rabbits consumed feed like bushfire; broken fences, broken gates, erosion to fight, cattle to move, cattle sick, horses sick, machinery sick, on and on and on. He thrived in a world of bold strokes, and if he ever felt ill-prepared by his Yale degree in History of Art, he could fly off to Sydney's marketplace, or to a cattle sale, or over to Worcester for a three-hour chat about a bigger tractor. He could labor as long as it retained the flavor of fun. Or so it seemed to me, although stuffing creosote into recently dehorned cows' horn holes shimmering with maggots didn't seem much fun to me.

The role of drudge filled me with savage resentment and I railed inwardly against the murdering ennui. Like being forced to submit to periodic hypodermics of anesthetic. Whenever you'd rise above the morass of mops and slops, it all had to be done again. Above all it was deflating to realize any one of millions of simpletons could have bested me like a snapped finger.

I couldn't talk to anybody about it. Women there took it all for granted and perhaps enjoyed believing they'd escaped the larger responsibility. But I'd been free, and struggle or no, I despised my shackles. They'd have been angry and shocked if they'd known. So I never mentioned my predicament. If I had I might have been rejected by my own sex as well as by the men. That silenced my tongue but it hid a tarantella of frustration. I was always thinking 150-proof rum and talking buttermilk.

I'll admit I hit bottom many times, always to do with my Adjustment.

Most people asked about my Adjustment, that chimera. What could I say? Tell them my plates were too big for the sink? Or never to wash sheets when the river's up? Or that I missed being coddled like an egg by American anything? Or that I was horror-stricken at maggoty garbage? Or that I was singularly inept at floor mopping? Or that I was often desperate for a dial phone with a friend at the other end. That I wasn't up to much of any of it and secretly despaired at all my professional training going to waste.

226

Reporters tried to pry out details about my Adjustment. "Must be quite an adjustment, Miss Baxter," I'd hear again and again. I felt like saying, "It's right here in this big jar. Isn't it cute?" They asked identical questions, Americans and Australians, and played the same broken record.

"How does it feel to be way out there; must be quite an adjustment. Must be quite a change from your glamorous life in Hollywood. What do you think of Australia? How is it living in the outback?" "Sorry," I'd reply. "I don't live in the outback. We live in the bush." I'd try to explain that in the outback even the government worried about you; in the bush they couldn't care less. The reporters would look bored and ask me for a funny anecdote.

Those anecdotes they always plumped for. I'd want to say, "I fell in love and got married *therefore* I am having one blast of an adjustment to a twenty-three-room tin-hatted shack called Giro in the Australian bush. Period." But I never did and would drag out a knock-kneed "anecdote" calculated to be harmless and, consequently, dishwater in print.

Chunks of what I thought of as "living" were disintegrating in Giro's harsh routine, and more and more I'd begun to grasp at a civilized raft called the cocktail hour, or bathed, changed, beaker and chat.

What time was it? Quarter of four? Was he or was he not coming home? I'd planned roast lamb, but canceled that when he left for Sydney. Could always do soup and salad. There was a bit of lettuce and a couple of tomatoes left in the wreck of garden. And orange cake from yesterday's lunch.

By five I was sure he wouldn't make it and was thoroughly depressed. It was the witching hour, when people went to cocktail parties. All dressed up. Why don't I have a bath at least? Why don't I make myself a dressing drink? Why not, indeed? replied the phantom of that elusive hour, laughing hollowly. No husband around. Carrying a tray of ice, I walked dejectedly into El Bar and peered at a new bottle of gin. It wore an unfamiliar Australian label. I'll call it "Dixon's." I filled a glass from a pitcher stiff with ice and trickled fiery snow water into a stomach that had greeted beer instead of lunch. It was clear not even French vermouth had helped the ineffable flavor of kerosene run through a loaf of bread. Possibly the worst gin ever invented. Elixir of fence nails! A sorry mist to swallow a state of mind.

Sneers and sarcasm entered and sat with me in my bath. Swaddled in a towel, I thought of all the nice napkins I'd placed that nobody ever picked up; cigar ashes in my nice brass lamp; the sticky wigwams of dirty dishes as I listened to the faraway laughter in a guest-infested living room; being herded with the females to talk gardens I couldn't grow, or people I didn't know.

I sang, voice dripping with venom:

> Austrylia, Austrylia
> They do strange things and they SYE
>   strange things
> In Austrylia, Austraylia!
> I'll neverrrr go therrrr any moooore!

The room bulged with silence. Silence covered me like a pall. I leaned my head back and through half-shut eyes noticed my noble much-traveled Kwan Yin watching me. "Don't you change for 'tea,' Mrs. Galt?" she whispered with a derisive smile.

"Yes," I mused. "I change for 'tea' like a mad-dog Englishman in the tropics." No matter how tired, Ran and I made that small effort at yanking ourselves together, hot or cold. A brass ring of sanity.

I rose out of mounting lethargy and opened a wardrobe, noticing the floor had developed a pronounced slope. Tenderly I leafed through pistachio silk, azure organza, black lace (for the third anniversary), white net; until I felt the sleek ivory satin and long chiffon of the pièce de résistance. Hangers dropping by the dozens, I hauled it out, skidded into a wall, and slipped it on. It felt like scented water, and the sheer coat floated along its tiny foamy edges of coffee-colored lace. I located my glass in the gloom and, leaning heavily on the door frame, growled a spate of purple prose.

"Oh, Giro, thou palace of ineptitude, what a whippersnapper am I to wrest a silken reticule out of yon Freeda's hairy ear," and an arm slid hammily down the jamb.

228

It was lighter and cooler out of doors. *Where* was the engine tonight? I mused drunkenly, fumbling for the gangplank of cement. Wading in the poisonous Salton Sea of self-pity, I swerved to avoid the grass and found myself seated under a shrub, like some bandicoot measuring the evening's pickings. Satin freckled with a leaky faucet of tears, my fingers twiddled with a crush of muddy chiffon, and my poor stomach told me in a soundless shout that the Dixon's gin I had swallowed disliked me as heartily as I disliked it, and the enemy Australian tundra came up and punched me in the beezer.

A while later I crept down the halls and climbed into Anybody's narrow bed, a cocoon of misery; as the springs creaked, Ran's heavy tread clumped down the hall. He swung back the door and peered at me with alarm. "My God, where have you been? I've looked everywhere! Are you all right?"

"You're home," I creaked, hoping I wouldn't be sick again.

Tears splashed his blue cotton chest as he carried me to bed. He'd flown out of Sydney at five forty. They almost wouldn't let him go. I'd been too smashed and ill to hear the plane.

Breakfast was early and hushed. I was starved and contrite and very grateful Quilty didn't know I was hung over. Ran fiddled at his piled-up desk. I stood in the door to the office.

"More coffee?"

"Sure." He smiled.

I don't think he wanted any really. As the mug filled I watched it, saying, "Terribly sorry about getting schnockered on 'Dixon's.' Ghastly stuff."

He took the cup and circled my shoulders with a familiar arm. "Don't give it a thought. Maybe we can fly up to Loch Glen tomorrow to try the new saddle I ordered for you. Only a short day's trip."

"Be fine," I mumbled, leaning on him.

"See you later," he said.

"See you later," I said. And he was gone.

28

How to Trip over a Small Plane

SMALL planes landed in my life along with Ran. Giro made them as usual as morning toast. He'd learned to fly jets in the Air National Guard, and when we'd known each other two months, I remember his dickering over a used Mustang. Very fast, and passenger-proof, which I found interesting. Single-engine planes always remind me of large, hazardous toys. But since I had to fly quite a lot, why not learn away my fear?

"Darling, couldn't I learn to fly?"

"You don't have the personality for it," he replied.

"What does *that* mean?" I bristled.

"Never mind."

"But I don't mean to tootle around. Just enough to bring it down or up in an emergency!"

He never really explained it, but whatever he meant he was right, especially in the bush. The trip to Loch Glen taught me.

Ran and the manager had disagreed over a long period of time about buying a larger caterpillar for Giro. The manager maintained the D-4 was perfectly adequate, and besides the station couldn't afford a D-6. Ran felt strongly a D-6 was imperative and the Station would eventually be able to pay for it. I had often heard snatches of the argument rumbling out of the office door as it opened and shut.

Loch Glen, where my saddle was being made, was northwest on the high plateau above us, beyond Armidale. There was a comprehensive farm machinery show in Taree, due east on the coast. Ran had invited the manager to Taree and me to Loch Glen. A neat parlay. In other words we all went to everything.

It was a nice day and a real privilege to be with Ran and the manager in the world of men and machines.

The sun beat down on brightly painted iron at Taree. Some of the machines might have been designed by Rube Goldberg. All of them bore spines or teeth or huge blades—I could never help thinking what power and ferocity they tendered ordinary men. Turn you into a bloody giant sitting up there, I thought while looking at a D-9.

I made myself scarce. That had become a kind of art: scarce, but not so scarce you couldn't be found when it was time to be introduced or time to go.

By noon, the day was a scorcher and the sun flared off metal and glass. Ran waved at me over a knot of men. I waved back. He beckoned. I joined them and said, "How do you do?" to two or three sunburned salesmen. Ran looked elated and took me aside.

"Sorry it took so long. You OK?"

"Sure, fine. How about lunch? I get hungry right on time these days." Actually I was starved.

"Well—uh—that's a bit of a problem. I think we'd better get going up to Loch Glen. It's seventy more miles from here than it is from Giro."

"Oh, well, I guess we can get something at Loch Glen." Damn. I knew I should have brought sandwiches.

The manager appeared and we cadged a ride to the airport from one of the salesmen. He was much too obliging—I bet Ran had made some sort of deal on his own. I watched the manager; he looked scrupulously blank.

It was a remarkably long flight. The country below looked lovely—lush and craggy. That Scottish-sounding name had an obvious reason.

The saddlemaker was out and had to be phoned. He was a true artisan and kept his own hours in that dozing, distant town.

Fitting the saddle was an experience, almost like intimate apparel. Every curve of mine was attentively pushed and settled into place. I felt like saying, "I dress left." Best saddle in the

231

world, though. With a squeeze of your thighs it would hold you safely—at full speed or straight up or down a steep grade. The pigskin was as meticulously worked and tanned as the old cobbler's intent face. The Australian saddle is nowhere as flat as an English one and much lighter and less a rocking chair than the Western ones I'd learned to use in films. My stomach was unmistakably grumbling and I felt a little faint. I'd been empty since six thirty A.M.

Ran looked at his watch, then at the sky, then apologetically at me. I knew what that meant. No time to eat. Too bad. God, I was hungry. The saddlemaker was extremely pleased at my interest and sincere praise and drove us out to the town's dirt airstrip in his ancient pickup.

As we climbed into the plane, I finally admitted I was starved, whereupon the manager produced a small carton of candy mints, which helped.

I gave myself up to the beauty of the sky. The sunset was glorious; like snorkeling in scarlet water. Lights had begun to twinkle in Armidale as we flew over, and the sun was going down as fast as the mints. I noted Ran uneasily rubbing the hairs on his fingers over his upper lip—a bad sign. He peered below with a slight smile, the very worst sign. Why? The motor sounded fine; I never took my ears off it.

What was wrong? Something dreadful. It was getting really dark. We were over dense gum forest. The plane dipped a wing; Ran searched the ground below, smiling faintly. This is it, I thought, feeling ill. My insides chinked with broken glass. We were terrifyingly low now, over solid treetops. Please, dear God, protect Katrina. I made myself look down and saw a rough, short strip cutting through the thick trees. It was crawling with dirty sheep. We were much lower now, I could see their dirty tails! *Alley oop!* We were buzzing the sheep and they were scattering helter-skelter.

Down we thundered again with a roar, and I desperately hoped the wings would hold. *Alley oop!* An aerial roller coaster, oboyoboyoboyoboyoboyoboyoboyoboy. I opened my dizzy eyes and dared to look again. Ran was actually bringing us down this time. *Please, God, keep the sheep out of our path!* They baaed in an uproar at the edges as we hit down hard through the thickening night and skidded over stones to a screeching stop, just short of the wall of trees. The engine surged, reverberated, and died. I breathed a prayer of thanks and looked at Ran. He switched off the engine and said casually, "Thought I might have had to land on the forest track. This was a breeze." He glanced at me. "You OK?"

I wanted to throw myself in his arms and bawl. "Fine," I answered. "How'd you ever find the strip?" I stared in amazement and admiration.

"They have a lot of these up here. I thought we'd run into one, they use them for supering" (spreading superphosphate by air).

We unbuckled ourselves and crawled out. I was grateful he couldn't see my knees twitch.

It was absolutely dark on the ground. We could see and feel nothing but stars and empty cold. It was much colder up there. I wondered where we were, other than on earth, which was a triumph. A gravel road ran near the trees. Ran and the manager had gotten out; I could hear them talking in undertones. I heard Ran saying it had been impossible to distinguish Giro's valley from the other valleys dropping off the high plateau. We couldn't go back to Armidale. Ran would lose his license if we landed on a public field. I began to relax and now ached again with hunger.

Fifteen minutes later we saw headlights moving on the road. It turned out to be a shiny pickup truck with a young boy at the wheel. Ran and the manager hailed him and after a disconcertingly long conversation they motioned to me. We all climbed into the pickup and I heard them say that we were eighteen miles outside of Yuldee. Wherever that was. Another fifteen minutes later the young fellow pulled into a dark farmyard. He and the manager went into the homestead, apparently to use the phone. It was pitch black and getting colder and I was now dreadfully hungry. I promised myself it was the last time I'd ever go in the plane without sandwiches, even to Worcester. Just stupid of me not to have thought about it. I tried to throttle a belch.

233

Half an hour passed and the manager hadn't returned. "Ran, do you think they murdered him and stuffed him in a trunk? The place looks like Wuthering Heights."

No answer. After forty-five creeping minutes, the manager emerged looking harassed. He said the boy would drive us to Yuldee. It had taken him all that time to convince his tough old dad it was the thing to do.

Why was the farm so dark? The young fellow's dad allowed one lone 32-volt bulb at the phone. The wife knitted by firelight. Dear old dad had just sold cattle for £35,000 (about $90,000) and the pickup was brand, spanking new. Wuthering Heights, my foot.

We were dropped off at the one grizzled hotel and had a beer in the ladies' icy linoleum alcove, as women were not allowed in the pub. The pub sounded warm and cheery through its closed door. I felt like a real spoilsport. I was so hungry I was not hungry. At nine forty-seven we ate in an empty, steamy cafe down the street: a skinny steak one foot across. Even the gristle seemed succulent.

The hotel towels were so thin you could see through them as well as the slivers of soap in the bathroom across the creaking hall. Looking like a bag of laundry with feet, no makeup left, and wearing a large scarf, I was recognized. I don't know how, but they did. They always did.

We went back and forth to our room from the bath accompanied by tiptoes, whispers, giggles, and oglings.

Next morning at seven an AML&F man drove us back to the forest strip. Ran was right, it was used for aerial drops of superphosphate. We took off for Giro, shaking dew off our wings. The manager's bride was still frantic as we landed. She had tearfully lighted bonfires all over Giro strip the night before.

29

Lost Battles

NOT that the trip did it, but the manager was leaving. Ran wasn't surprised. He'd had a fine offer of a gentler, richer property down south near his candy-pretty bride's family and had decided to take it. That the new station had an absentee owner made the offer irresistible. No matter how many pairs of kid gloves they wear, there are bound to be clashes between owner and manager when both occupy the same territory. I'd heard Ran making urgent inquiries into someone new, and approached him with a fragrant loaf of fresh-baked bread and a cherished idea.

"Ran, darling, why don't you take over? We'll glue ourselves here twenty-four hours a day for one year. Getting help looks hopeless, and when the baby arrives, I won't be able to leave at all. Why not *try?* Even if we only swing it for a year, you'll have proved something to yourself." He knew I was dead serious.

"You'd go crazy."

"I go crazy as it is. At least it would give me a goal. This donkey craves a carrot. Please, Ran, can't we try?"

"Branding's coming up."

"I'll bring you iced tea! Ran, the men like you. They'd respect a tough decision. I'll bet even George Peckett would agree with me." My voice mounted in intensity. He hated me to be emotional but sometimes I couldn't help it.

"We wouldn't be free."

"Hell, I'm not free anyway. See picturesque Australia through mop and broom!"

"I should go to Western Australia. Haven't seen my place out there in too long."

"Can't it wait? It would mean the earth to know we'd bitten off the same-sized chunk together. Even if it doesn't work, we'll have really stuck our necks out and tried."

"I'll think about it." But my bones knew the subject was closed, as he cut himself another aromatic slice of oatmeal bread.

Some people need goals. I did. He didn't. I can't seem to live at random. And probably shouldn't have tampered with someone who could.

Ran did things only if and when it suited him. Appeared and disappeared like a jinn, unplanned, unannounced, unpredictable as Giro's weather. I could suffer tortures, and often have in my profession, as long as I could go toward some accomplishment, some end result. My donkey had to sniff her carrot as it dangled. He had a pit-bull's grip on a most precious freedom—choice. As owner he could do as he chose. Work with the men, if he chose; fly off, if he chose; tear down the shearing shed, if he chose; ride, if he chose; plow, if he chose. As owner-manager he'd have relinquished choice and chose not to do so. Perhaps I was just jealous. My choices were apocryphal, like when did you stop beating your wife? Chores had to be done; the sole variance was the order of their doing.

Everything came to a halt when the manager left. Branding was postponed for a week. I mourned my lunch with Patrick White. I knew it would have to wait so I didn't even bring it up. One morning, after Groceries, I called and told him how glad I was to hear from him. Could we make it later on? I asked. I'd write or phone. I told him I'd look forward to Thea Astley's book.

At the end of a rather terse three days, Ran flew Tom Biddeford and me to Queensland to meet Hugh Aildred, who was to be our new manager. My cherished goal was a losing battle. Thank God, Hugh was a prize. His initiation into small planes as a sport was immediate. The four of us met a wind with fangs.

I liked wind, which may have annoyed bush dwellers, but then I was a foreigner and they put up with such vagaries. Wind made an essentially passive land active and superalive. Australians hated it. Wind gave you oranges you couldn't reach and kindling on the ground; it whipped your cheeks to strawberry; sun shines in it. Sheets are at war with it and you hoist them like schooner sails, feeling buffeted but gay withal.

But Australia's undisciplined winds can be suicidal in the air. Coming down from Brisbane, we were flying around nine thousand feet as Ran started his long descent to Giro. When we reached seven thousand feet the plane was jerked into the stall-warning three times, a sound to drain your blood and clench your teeth until they ache. He wisely gave up and veered away to land on the coast at Taree. With a half-hour of daylight he took a chance on flying up the valley seventy miles to Giro. My body grew frilly with fear as we climbed back into the plane. What one endures under one's husband's gaze. It was a corking trip. Wind like that in a light plane makes you feel as if St. Anthony's devils were trying to slap you out of the sky. The willows' long branches were horizontal. We were whipped insanely up and down and nauseatingly zigzagged sideways, cracking our skulls on the roof of the plane. Giro was heaven on earth that twilight and I calmed my knees, wrists, and elbows with beer and additional prayers. By the way, Alexander Calder, your mobile is at home in a Giro wind. With paint clanked off, it looks diseased but remains a high-class wind chime.

So Hugh and Joan Aildred came to Giro with small John and Janie in time for branding.

The Aildreds commanded instant respect from all hands. Joan's father was English, which gave her Old World polish along with country-bred resilience. Joan the Good I dubbed her privately, and was her ardent admirer. She was everything I felt I should have been.

Hugh was a crackerjack fellow who boosted Giro's spirits upstairs in no time flat. Ran and he were on excellent terms from the start. Outside of a few stiff-necked meals, I'd known our former manager and his wife curiously little. A taciturn fellow was Jean Taggart's nemesis. Hugh was an open door and you felt he could spit straight into a hurricane. Ran and he were gone a good deal; in 36,000 acres there's a lot to see.

Bless Joan the Good, with her round brown eyes full of everything an eye should be. She was such a prize, I hardly saw her for fear of burdening her with all I needed—friendship, book's worth of how to do anything at all, and the bush indoors and out from A to Z.

Even Giro's frabjous chickens succumbed to her blandishments. When she'd march to those wayward birds, wearing a beribboned straw hat, they'd drop their peccadillos and bustle around practically handing her eggs in a basket, mincing, and *puck-puck-pucking* with delight at her smile.

Even after thunderstorms, they'd gather their scattered wits and come through with their usual "Come on, girls! Hell, it's for Joan!" they'd *puddawk,* dropping eggs all over the weeds. She never forgot to let them out to scratch about for a salad. But *I* did. They only put up with me if I stood in her place. In her hat. I used to steal it the few times she and Hugh went to visit her family in Queensland.

Hugh had already begun to fence their cottage neatly, and in what seemed a trice, I watched an English postcard garden spring up to flower it—delphinium and roses and their pals. A proud beacon among Australia's shining ranks of country-women was Joan. Her batteries were always charged with equable energy and a prodigal spirit.

February was finally cooling off. My waistbands were tightening, a good sign. I was overpoweringly sleepy, another fair, omen although that may have been due to the birds.

I got used to the bigheaded kookaburra birds *hoo-haha-hooing* at three A.M. and, thank God, they only appeared when snakes were plentiful. They ate them. And, of course, the roosters started at four forty-five, but the birds at four fifteen did me in. They shanghaied sleep and reduced me to earplugs that second year. Earplugs in the bush. Ran shook his head. I emphatically dropped a notch. Well, damnit, when you're pregnant you wee all night anyway and sleep can be lost in the shuffle.

The air was hobnailed with an initial thousand chirps, but one pernicious birdsong rose above the rest: the leatherhead.

238

Predawn after predawn I'd hope it would switch to another tree, but it never did. You couldn't call it a song. A loud ditty? Again and again the same damned sequence of piercing sounds until five, when Freeda, the pig, took over.

Freeda and I worked out a few primitive setting-up exercises. They were inspired by trees. I'd wanted to hide the house in trees, and had slaved over baby deodars, Norfolk Island pines, sundry other evergreens, and even three redwoods. But the horses chewed them, the cows kicked them, and pigs are hell on anything. I'd hear scrapings and the unmistakable crashes of Freeda and her vaudeville act: Freeda and her Nine Little Missiles. Leaping out of bed in fury, I'd steal down the hall, hoping to catch her red-snouted. If possible. She kept a wily ear cocked.

I'd burst out the back hall door, shouting, *"Hhaaaagh—Get out! Get out!"* And like a bunch of chorus girls startled naked in the dressing room, they'd squeal and jump in a body, heels striking tattoos on the cement as they scattered. Blowsy Madam trotted ahead, an insulted blimp, her nine missiles racing behind. And me after them, hair in my eyes, bosoms bumping and jouncing in a furor of sheer nylon. I'd chase them until they disappeared in the lucerne, then, breathing hard, dash another fifty yards to check my precious trees and find the tips broken or wounded. You only have to do that once to a pine and it just limps along through life, a forever injured party.

Discouraged into reality, I'd remember my near-nude state and make another hundred-yard dash back to be greeted by what I'd been too mad to see: five garbage cans nosed over in charming disarray.

Back to bed with dirty feet. No, why bother? Nothing like early coffee after a brisk morning trot.

"Good morning, darling," I'd say, dashing toward my bath past Ran, who'd be sleepily walking down the hall.

"Did you catch her?"

"Too late," I'd call back over my bare shoulder.

"I'm going to sell that bloody sow," he'd say balefully, starting to sneeze. He often started the day with an attack of sneezing, a Galt family scourge.

239

The Aildreds blended into Giro like sugar in a cuppa. Everything smoothed and sweetened in their capable hands. Regret still stung me here and there. We could've tried to run Giro ourselves. But appealing that case to Ran would've been like fighting City Hall.

Joan the Good gave Quilty someone new to talk to about India. Katrina played older sister to little Janie, and Ran flew us to his far-flung property called Maikurra, in Western Australia, 2,500 miles away. He said I could read him the air maps. I called Patrick White again and we planned lunch the first week in March, if all went well.

30

Torumbarry Revisited

THE D-6 was delivered among much male excitement. As a matter of fact, it didn't seem to me Ran much minded driving the D-4 to Worcester. A beer at Tom Biddeford's and a chat, grinding through river crossings like parting a private Red Sea, trucks moving over for *you*. If the former manager balked at the D-6 caterpillar, he'd have choked at our new plane. The 182 gave way to a powerful 210, the most powerful single-engined plane Cessna made.

We certainly had a nice selection over a period of time. The 210 had a retractable landing gear and an intractable fuel injection engine. When very cold or very hot it wouldn't start. Stark terror for me because I'd have to sit in the pilot's seat, a shaking hand on the stick, and watch Ran leap, grasp the prop, and yank it down and around, again and again. At the slightest cough I was to pull the stick; just enough to keep it coughing but not enough to take off and/or hack Ran into hamburger. Nothing has ever scared me as much.

Still, it was a comfort to know we'd be flying to Western Australia in a powerhouse. It cruised at 200. The most fun would be spending a night at the Baillieus' on the way. We'd have to fly south to Melbourne first, and then west to the Riverina and Peter and Edwina's Torumbarry.

How strange it would be to see them there again. How much had changed since I lay stretched out in the sun beside the

Murray River a thousand years ago. I wondered if Edwina still had that pink parasol.

Melbourne was soaking in fine gray rain. We were just able to land through low clouds. At least it was cool enough not to make the starter fractious. I didn't fancy me at the stick and Ran doing the ballet of the propellers in that wet.

We took off at noon, although it looked more like dusk. Barely in the air, Ran rubbed his upper lip on his fingers. Oh, God! Now what? I realized we'd started to dip down and up. I checked the altimeter—wow! Five hundred feet. Ran was literally following the rolling contours of the land beneath. Four hundred feet. Needles of rain pelted and melted on the windshield. It was like flying through blowing milk. Three hundred and fifty feet. I felt sick.

"Ran," I said in a faint voice, "aren't we awfully low?"

"Only way I can see," he replied evenly. The plane seemed to strain to maintain power. I began to perspire and wiped my upper lip with a shaking forefinger. On and on we rolled, like a boat in swells.

"I wish I knew where in hell we were," he said dreamily to himself.

I stopped breathing for a second. For the first time since I'd known him, Ran admitted he was lost. I went limp with fright.

"Damn it, I can't get up enough to see my landmarks," he murmured, deep in concentration. He looked down at the road, silver with wet. I suddenly pictured us neatly landing on the road, splashing into a driveway, hopping out, knocking on a farmhouse door, and asking some slack-jawed, popeyed farmer, "Where are we?" I later learned that was exactly what Ran had been planning.

"I'll just keep going west—this has got to break—just hope we don't overshoot the lake I use as a signpost to find Torumbarry." He smiled vaguely. It was as if I weren't there. If I kept quiet enough, maybe I wouldn't be. Ran kept ducking his head and searching the white mist above us. I watched the ground and prayed we wouldn't scrape those two trees on the hill coming up.

We started to circle, Ran scrutinizing the sky in all directions.

"I'm going to try it," he said. "This is for the birds." And up we climbed. I thought we'd never come to the end of smothering vapor. We climbed and circled and climbed and circled. I stared at the altimeter—500, 1000, 1500, 2000, 3000, 4000, 5000, 6000, 7000, 8000. A piece tore off a wad of cloud. Ran went for it full speed, like a charging cheetah. The plane responded with a reassuring burst of power. So much faster than the 182. It was a real kick.

"That's what I want!" He pointed through fast-shredding cloud at a flash of lake miles beyond us in the sun.

"That's my guide. Torumbarry's right over there. I almost missed it." I giggled stupidly with relief and fell madly in love all over again. Minutes later, Ran dipped his wings at the tiny figures on the ground and we came down on the country airport strip a few miles from Torumbarry. Edwina, Pete, and the children waved at us wildly in sunshine, blue sky, and lamb's wool clouds. I was exhausted.

We fell all over one another. Ran and Pete beat each other on the back, Ran singing the praises of the mighty 210. Pete thought he might buy one for the station. Also, he'd become involved with the King Ranch in Australia, which now owned several far-flung properties, making a fast plane a necessity.

"Banana!" I lifted my head from a busy conversation with Edwina about our charming trip from Melbourne.

"Yes, darling?"

"I'm going to take Pete up for a ride, let him see how the plane handles."

"Sure, fine."

"We'll see you back at the house," interjected Edwina. "Pete, I'll take the station wagon, you and Ran keep the Land Rover."

A while later, I stood once again in the spacious grace of that lovely old stone house and knew that no matter what I did to Giro it would never approach this. Maybe we could build a big stone house someday, I dreamed to myself. Edwina came swiftly in, her flowered silk shirt billowing.

"Where do you suppose they are? It's been an hour and a half."

"They are having a ball." I bent over a bowlful of roses for a sniff.

243

"Well, I'm going to tell Dora to serve tea. The children are filching cookies right and left."

She trotted off to the kitchen.

The dial phone rang melodiously. How different from Giro's aggravating clang-bangs. It kept ringing. I supposed Edwina wouldn't mind if I put the phone out of its misery. I walked over and picked up the receiver.

"Hello, Baillieu residence. Who's calling, please?" I heard sterterous breathing and pricked up my ears.

"Who's *calling*, please?" I repeated more clearly.

"Hel–hel–hello." It was a man's dreadfully quavering and agitated voice, obviously verging on hysteria.

He blurted out, "There's been a–a–a–terrible accident out here—pilot's very badly hurt–is–is–there—a Mrs. Galt there, please?"

"Jesus," I screamed. *"Edwina!"* I dropped the receiver in instant shock. *"Edwina!"* I screamed again.

She rushed in, saw I was in a terrible state, tears pouring down my white face, and grabbed the receiver off the floor. She rattled into the mouthpiece.

"Mrs. Baillieu here. What's happened?"

I staggered to the couch, trembling and swallowing uncontrollably.

"Oh, my God!" she cried. "Wait a minute." She turned quickly from the phone.

"Anne, darling. Anne! It's all right! It's all right! It's not Ranny or Pete. Ranny's just asked the man to call and warn us they'll be late. A local pilot's crashed and they're helping out."

That finished me. I now sobbed helplessly in relief.

"Right!" I heard her say. "Right. Anything I can do? Right, I will. Thank God it wasn't. Yes, not to worry, I will." She hung up and ministered to what was left of her mess of a guest.

"You poor darling. Here, let me get you a brandy."

"No," I sobbed, "I'm fine. I'm fine," and I burst into tears all over again. What a long, long day. And all I had to do tomorrow morning was to fly to Western Australia. And that's exactly what I did.

Australia's interior is a reducing machine for egos. Its hugeness conquers and reconquers one with an endless splendid emptiness. And so inconceivably old, a billion-year-old earth, caught in a mammoth yawn. The land that belongs to nobody.

Adelaide was appealingly situated overlooking the Indian Ocean. Its dry look, the surrounding wheatfields, eucalyptus, and vineyards made me think of California. Lots of new buildings, a restaurant on top of the newest and highest. The place-names never failed to intrigue me as we flew from the Riverina: Echuca, Yanac, Meningie. And on beyond Adelaide toward the Nullarbor Plain.

31

The Land That Belongs to Nobody

WHYALLA. Pimba. Woomera. Ceduna. Tarcoola. Ooldea. Ooldea used to be Uldil Gabbi, the last aborigine watering place before the parched plain.

Roughly between Pimba and Ceduna I was poring over the air maps, my special job. We were supposed to be somewhere near an enormous lake called Lake Gardner.

"Is that it, Ran?" I shouted, pointing ahead at a bluish-white streak.

"That's it." We flew closer.

"It's bone dry," I commented in a loud voice and studied it in amazement.

"They all are," he called back, looking down.

Lake Gardner was a forbidding sight. It looked like an ice rink for titans. Ugly ragged trees were etched blackly along the—what—shore? No, basin rim. They knifed brilliant blue shadows into glistening salt.

What fortitude the Australian pioneers must have had. From the coast westward they greeted similar starkness. You wondered how they had the guts to go on. In America we were lured west by thousands of miles of rich country.

"Imagine coming onto that as you're expiring from thirst!" I shouted, again struck by the desolation below. Nothing moved. Nothing lived. Burned white.

Mesmerized by the astringence of that final negative, I instinctively hunted the positive, and began to remember the wettest I'd ever been. Germany. Munich in July, 1953. We shot at night for three solid weeks during *Carnival Story* and it rained through every one. We all but slept in tents. Everything was under canvas, like real carny people. My dressing room was a large tent with straw strewn on the damp dirt underfoot through which mushrooms peeped when you weren't looking.

A naked bulb swung from the tent peak, and the wooden dressing table mirror was framed in bulbs. The rain came straight from the Alps and literally drummed on us. One of the German crew members (only our cameraman was American) was detailed to poke a broom handle into the dangerously sagging canvas over us and the camera. He'd poke up hard and rainwater would sheet down in shining walls around us. I loved every minute. I loved my part—Willi, the vagrant German girl who becomes a carny high diver. I loved the freaks and real carnival people, most from Austria and without a word of English. The dialogue director was Hungarian and had been a German teacher in Budapest. He gave me *Das Erste Buch* and I became an insatiable pupil. Which helped, because my Berliner make-up woman, Jette, and Bavarian wardrobe girl, Emmy, spoke no English. Our two assistant directors had been Nazi war aces, our director, Kurt Neuman, and producers, the King brothers, were Jewish.

Steve Cochran was our problem child. One minute I was Mother Cabrini, helping him with his complicated love life, the next kicking him out of my tiny penthouse for attempted rape. He was a handsome, talented, undisciplined bastard. Lyle Bettger was a square like me and loathed his carnival bathing costume encrusted with bicycle light rubies.

One stormy night around ten, he burst into my tent where I was telling fortunes in between shots.

"Don't have to work. They won't get to our diving scene!" he exulted, tearing off his hated white lamé helmet.

"Lyle, no kidding!" I looked up from my greasy pack of cards.

"Positive! Anyway, it's the eve of the Fourth of July. I'm going over to the commissary and celebrate with cheese and wine!"

Lyle didn't drink much, in contrast to Cochran, who was usually crocked by one thirty in the morning. We could only shoot until three since the sun came up at three thirty.

I used to be driven back from Geiselgasteig to Munich, half-dead tired, and drink two icy beers stuck in a champagne bucket, put my earplugs in, my sleepshade on, and fall asleep. Not even the streetcars donged me awake.

"You're sure you're sure?" I kidded him.

"Absolutely. See you!" And he charged out through the rain.

The storm abated. Our American soldier crowd returned. The King brothers had cleverly avoided paying extras. They'd cleverly avoided paying a lot of things. The only expensive luxury Frank King allowed was his cigars. They had to be good. Every time I asked for another take he ate one, grinding cigar chunks in torture.

The King brothers had simply advertised: SEE THE DAREDEVIL DEATH DEFYING HIGH DIVE. JOIN CARNIVAL FUN. BRING YOUR WIVES AND SWEETHEARTS BOYS AND JOIN THE FUN FUN FUN.

I admit Solly Solomon's 150-foot dive was sensational, but he didn't do it that often. Most of the time the crowd of servicemen and girls moseyed around drinking beer and eating sausages and nudging one another as a soggy actor went by. The King brothers owned the food concessions, of couse.

Just before midnight the sky actually cleared, and I was informed we were indeed to shoot the preliminary to the diving scene, after all. Where, oh where, was Lyle? He was in his comfortable dry slacks and shirt guzzling Mosel wine. They got him. I heard his irate and surprisingly drunken protests all the way in my tent where Jette was trying to freshen my makeup. *"Meine arme Dame, meine arme Dame,"* she crooned. (My poor lady, my poor lady.)

An assistant batted at my tent flap: *"Ja, was gibts, Georg?"* I practiced my German whenever possible.

"Miss Bexter. Mr. Bettger is not happy but we will shoot anyway," he announced with a bow and a grin.

"Thank you." Oh, Lord, would he remember his lines? Just having to climb back into his fancy wet suit would be a hassle. Poor Lyle, caught out in his one foray into Cochranesque dissolution.

The Bavarian band played; the crowd surged with expectant

248

excitement. Lyle stood and swayed his eyes wide and unblink-
ing.

"I'm not going to wear that effing hat!" he said as they shoved
it on and tried to buckle the chin strap. "I *hate* this goddamn
effing *hat.*"

I walked over to him, adjusted his long, lamé cape, and spoke
out of the corner of my mouth: "Now, Lyle, dear, I know it's
Fourth of July at midnight, but that's why they'll have to quit
right after this shot. Now just let's get it over with!"

Blindly he stared at me. The camera rolled. The band
played. Lyle and I loped up to the platform somehow and
bowed. As he unbent from an abnormally deep bow, he looked
out over the gaping crowd and said very deliberately:

"I'll fuck any dame in the crowd!"

I heard Ran say, "What is it?" and realized I'd been chuckling
to myself.

"Nothing, darling," I shouted. "Something just struck me
funny."

Lyle didn't think it was funny. The next morning he looked
like a whipped hound and cringed for a week. Steve Cochran
gloated behind the wheel of his dervish of a Porsche.
Steve . . . Peck's Bad Boy should've grown up in a hurry
when nobody would hire him anymore. Years later they found
him on the deck of a cabin cruiser that had run out of gas, drift-
ing aimlessly off the Gulf Coast of Mexico. Two terrified sixteen-year-old Mexican girls cowered inside to avoid his three-
day-old corpse. Heart, they said.

"Anne?" called Ran.
"Yes?"
"See if you can locate Mundi Rock."
"Righto," I called back, feeling official. Air maps were fun
and had to be scanned constantly for sacred landmarks; even a
dark rock was marked largely and carefully, so few are the
bumps on inner Australia's bland face.

I will never forget Forrest. Not a tree for a thousand miles,
but Forrest was. It was a buoy in the ocean of the Nullarbor

Plain, 400 miles from the nearest town of Kalgoorlie. Supplies arrived by the one railroad once a week. The railroad was Forrest's original reason for being, and during the war a landing strip became another. There was one railroad and one dirt road across the continent, and we'd followed both closely, our shadow flying along those crude child's pencil lines mile after mile to Forrest.

The great Nullarbor (I always felt like saying Nulland Void) Plain is dull red, pocked with colorless huddles—I suppose you could list them as scrub—they were flatter than sage, and all of it hopped with millions of rabbits.

Sterile wooden houses and barracks sat quietly, blinking their dirty windows against the wind under a warm gray sky as we taxied down the strip. I climbed painfully out, feet feeling stumpy from disuse. Not a sound. No signs of life. Just a warm wind tugging insistently.

A building just off the strip caught my eyes, and a mirage of steaming tea drew me to it.

I went up to the door and walked in. A muffled radio voice droned and a clock ticked loudly. A couple of wicker chairs and tables, wrinkled magazines, the large console radio, and *two* pictures of the Queen furnished the nearly empty room. I heard a woman's voice and the sound of dishes clattering down a hall to the left. The kitchen. Wandering down the hall in its direction, I saw a washroom with cubicles and rust-stained basins obviously large enough to accommodate an occasional onslaught of train passengers. The whole place had the look of a station waiting room, very ugly and used to crowds.

Tentatively opening a frosted door, I met the two ample ladies who ran the show. The taller and younger version stood near the big black stove. I hesitantly brought up the subject of tea and was promptly handed my mirage in a pot, with dainty cup and saucer in attendance, and store cookies and homemade fruitcake for good measure.

Not knowing what else to do, I took my treasures back into the first big room to chew by the radio, which still emitted that bumbling voice. Lord, it was cheerless. I ate and drank everything, understanding only too well why the kind ladies were ample; food is such a comfort.

I braved the washroom, which echoed woodenly. I picked up a six-month-old *Women's Weekly* and thought of fiddling with the radio but didn't dare, perhaps they liked that human mumble, perhaps they left it like that all day. Company. Picking up the tray as an excuse, I went to join the party.

They were delighted to talk and I reveled in listening. Two sisters and one daughter. They'd been there quite a few years. Liked it. It was peaceful, they said. They enjoyed cooking for the people coming through—railroad men, maintenance crews, some of whom lived in Forrest with their families. Like a pleasant soap opera they gossiped about them kindly and complained about the supplies every week. They sent any old thing, half of it not what you ordered, knowing you couldn't send it back 400 miles and do without. You sensed the running squabble with the shops, and especially the butcher, in Kalgoorlie.

They'd tried to grow grass on an oval plot in front and had come out one morning to find forty-nine rabbits and not a blade.

"Tsk, tsk," I commiserated, rooted to the chair at their bravado. Grass on the Nullarbor, a sitting duck in a sea of rabbits and red dust.

We all had more tea and cake, and I basked in the beating heart of that barren place. A kitchen transfused with nourishing food and gossip, presided over by two contented cows and a heifer.

They got out to relatives every two years or so, but were always glad to get back. Christmas for the children of Forrest was much planned for and discussed. This being February, memories were fresh and I heard all about it. Very few storebought gifts; most were homemade, and a lovely rash of parties.

It was time to go. Our ETA (Estimated Time of Arrival) and SAR (Air Rescue) were logged, the plane was filled with gas, and the weather reports were discussed. Shaking hands warmly, we parted. They insisted they had only served me refreshments, meaning tea and such. I left with a full meal under my belt, meaning that I'd sampled an abundance of charity, hardihood, and cheer.

We were now on the last lap to Esperance. Geographically, Esperance sits alone on the far western corner of the Great

Australian Bight, with its boot licked by the waters of the Indian Ocean. Maikurra's 17,000 acres lay about forty miles east of the town, and its rough strip was our goal.

Forrest had rolled over the horizon behind us and we were still magnetized to the fine tracery of dirt road and railroad far below. Ran said we'd turn south now and would be on our own, no special landmarks. High-octane emotion rose in me at that remark, along with fear; a lowering ceiling was suspended to the southwest and we were flying into it. It was small comfort to know that any serious delay in our arrival would eventually bring an air search.

The sun disappeared in the cloudbank. Ran pushed the plane hard. We had to make Maikurra before dark.

More lakes. Lafroy. Cowan. Dundas. The dry lakes were chalk dust in the now somber light in a darkling land of titanic nothing and no one. On and on we droned. I dwelled in a purgatory of mute anxiety until, through Ran's practiced eye, after what seemed a year of hours later, I made out an angular smudge underlined in lead pencil: Maikurra and its strip. We came down.

Maikurra was my only contact with the true outback and as such was stimulating and absorbing. To live by radio with three time periods each day allotted to dire emergency was a revelation. I sat perched in the dark little box of a breakfast room staring at that omnipresent radio.

We stayed in a prefab house Ran had had put up, a poor copy of an American design. Naked floor-to-ceiling glass rattled incessantly in the February winds. A small fireplace gaped in the corner of a bare room. No one had ever stayed in the house except itinerant shearers. From the kitchen galley wall out across the wooden floor were dotted paths and butterflies of grease. The laundry tubs rose in full view on a platform of clammy cement, which continued to a partition where I found a toilet, a basin, and a shower head. A shower drain was sunk in the cement to the left of the toilet.

Gracious living reigned again as I shoved a dented trunk and a mattress near the fire's hole. We ate off the trunk. Not a tree or a shrub to screen us from anything.

But, as I had begun to realize more and more, indoors didn't count. The people who dwelt therein were the plainest punctuation in Australian country living. Outdoors dominated their whole world from roots to soil to hooves to boots to eyes crooked at sky after sky after sky. I sensed the compelling urge in men down there to tame the passive, leeched-out monster of Australia. Tame? No, I don't believe that word is possible. Teach, cage, fetter, force to temporary submission, yes. But like turning one's back on a jungle, I always felt the place would have rediscovered its own blank destiny in moments, left to itself.

What they didn't do to land out there was nobody's business. I studied a handful of virgin (more like ancient prostitute) soil, gray, puffy stuff, supporting the toughest of tropical deserts, lowly but densely grown. "Black boys," their palmetto trunks topped by black spiny things; damp sumps growing groves of paper barks, the only wood available for fenceposts, and growing so far down in their odd sinkholes that you saw only the tops like a closetful of dusters; and a stunning variety of rough carnelian and verdigris-colored shrubs, some flowering in chromes and all tenaciously hanging onto that treacherous gray powder.

First they chained it—anchor chains pulled between D-6's or D-9's. Then they burned it and day and night the place choked and glowed with miles of spreading fire. Then they tore out stumps like abscessed mastodonic teeth. Then they harrowed it over and over again. Then they seeded it, adding a trace of vital zinc. And inside of a year, clover so rich it bloated sheep. Miraculous.

Water was a pitched battle. They'd hit it, but many times it carried too much salt for the animals. Sheep can take the most—200 grains per centimeter. Cattle die on that much. We lost two cows while we were there when they broke down a fence near the sheep's water tank. Giro's land seemed luscious compared to Esperance.

Maikurra was fourteen miles from the Duc of Orleans Bay, named for the man who had discovered that whole coast in the eighteenth century. The exquisite bay was a scalloped necklace of granite coves and pure sand that met water the exact color of melted aquamarines. Five hundred resorts wouldn't have made a nick in that coast. Wild, empty, sparkling with trillions of shells pounded to sand in the relentless mortar of the Indian Ocean. We got stuck deep in that sand for hours, allowing me a leisurely look at placid granite boulders like a giant's beads flung out into the sea, chaperoning cove after cove. Between the granite boulders, miles of beach would run along the shining water, then more shimmering alcoves, and on it went, without a footprint. It made you long to pitch a tent.

We flew to Perth, 350 miles northwest up the coast, taking the Maikurra manager and his wife, whose children were there in school. I thought Perth far and away the prettiest city in Australia. It lies in the warm coils of the Swan River and embraces a large, free-style, hilly park smack in the middle. Western Australia is as big as all America west of the Mississippi, if you leave out California. Ninety-five percent of the population of Western Australia lives in Perth, population 525,000. A clumsy way of letting you know how empty are parts of Australia.

As we left Perth, we got a call from the airport tower, which wondered whether we'd fly due east first to Kalgoorlie before going to Esperance. A child was desperately ill and needed antibiotics. We took the package, of course, but it came too late. We were terribly saddened by the child's death. If only someone could have flown the medicine a day sooner. Odd to have your homebody plane thrust into such frantic importance, but not at all unusual out there.

The man who managed Maikurra was named Fergus Whittlesby. He was lanky and weatherbeaten and could easily have been a West Texas cowpuncher instead of a Western Australia sheep and cattleman. His wife, Fiona, was the opposite, as white and pudgy as he was ruddy and lean. She indolent with loneliness now that the last of the children had gone off to boarding school. She talked incessantly, sounding like a harmonica sucked in and blown out. It wore me out to listen, but I felt too sorry for her not to. She was sympathetic regarding my miscarriage, about which she'd read far too much, and launched into a shocking account of her own. As I listened reluctantly, I knew I'd never escape my inadvertent membership in Fiona's all-female club. She explained how when she was three months "gone" (interesting word), she had miscarried, but kept having

254

morning sickness. She'd hounded the doctor week after week by radio. He'd pooh-poohed her constant stream of complaints but six months later she gave birth to the remaining twin. As if that weren't enough to entertain me, she went on to describe her next pregnancy, which resulted in the twins she'd just seen in Perth. I glanced out the window at some soft white petunias flattened by the howling wind and wondered at them and her. I never mentioned my currently "gone" state.

Ran flew to Kalgoorlie where we picked up the railroad tracks as a guide and followed them eastward. At one solitary fueling stop the starter balked maddeningly. We waited while the plane cooled. Another stop was unattended and necessitated phone calls and another hour's wait for a truck bringing 100-octane fuel from the sleepy settlement nearby. All in all there was a lot of waiting around in buzzing silence.

The second night we stopped in the famous mining town of Broken Hill. It reminded me of a shoot-'em-up movie set that had been taken over by Five and Tens and dingbat tract homes. By then I had become a muddle of double-exposed film.

Our room was big, ugly, and had a bed I suspected had been rented by the hour. A light bulb swung from the ceiling as in my tent dressing room in Munich. I was grateful for the impenetrable sunglasses protecting my sagging self. Ran found an acquaintance in the usual all-male pub and disappeared after a supper of mutton. The next day I stood aside draped with bulging flight bags as he paid our bill. No, he didn't. He came toward my corner and muttered, "Can you take off your dark glasses? I want to cash a check." Why didn't he ask me to strip? Just as easy. I fought with myself.

"Okay." The cashier simpered at me with recognition and the check was cashed.

From Broken Hill we went east again past Condobolin then north to Dubbo, where we'd bought my pine trees in cans, northeast to Muswellbrook and over the mountains to our valley.

It was the first time Giro gave me an inkling of homecoming, and well worth the trip.

255

32

Crown of Gold

IT was unbelievably good to unpack and wash dusty hair in my own shower. Giro looked idyllic after the outback. It was nice to walk around outside without a compass.

The situation between Quilty and Katrina was worsening steadily. I saw the glint of drawn daggers the moment we got back. Boarding school was the only answer. I had discussed the possibility with Edwina that afternoon at Torumbarry. She mentioned one in Bowral, not too far south of Sydney. And also said that Peter and she might have to move to Milton Park, the new King Ranch Australia headquarters in Bowral. At least they'd be there to keep an eye on Katrina.

I was distraught at the thought of her going. But guilt about her lack of a real education nicked away at me. I was mother and friend, but no companion. She never mentioned being lonely, but she must have been. That ever-present fact disturbed me terribly; that and knowing I was at the exact point in time when I'd miscarried and lost the other baby made me nervous and preoccupied. I was the only buffer between Quilty and Katrina, Ran and Katrina, and Katrina and isolation—and it was slowly tearing me apart.

As I was mulling this over, I bit into a hardened, leftover crust of toast and felt a filling lift out of its tooth and drop in my mouth. I reached a finger in and scooped out a large gold crown. I put it in my palm and looked. It was small for a disaster. My tongue searched the exposed cavity of a back lower left molar. The edge next to the inside of my cheek had a jagged point and was guaranteed to start jabbing at the first chew. Eyelash glue! Why not? It was liquid rubber and worth a try. I let the latex adhesive get good and tacky, dried the sharp-edged hole with toilet paper soaked in rubbing alcohol, fit the crown back in, and bit down hard. Katrina came to the door of my bath. She looked at my skeleton grin, the alcohol and glue, and asked, "Are you all right, Mommy?"

"Nnnn." I said through my clamped-together teeth.

"What's the matter?"

"Nnnnuhing," I grunted. Nothing—nothing at all, I thought. All I have to do is call Dr. Christenson in Beverly Hills and make an emergency appointment. Hell. I let go. It held. I sighed and smiled at her.

"Don't look so worried. I just lost a filling and I'm trying to glue it back."

"Oh," she replied, relaxing into interest. "Is that stuff going to work?"

"Probably not," I said, "but it's worth a try. How was school?"

"Oh, dumb. Quilty's always bugging me about my handwriting," she said with disgust.

"Well, it's important. Look at mine; nobody can read it including me."

"Nobody bugs *you* about it."

Oh, dear. "Well *I* do. It's a mess—all my friends tell me."

"Grammy's is a mess, too."

"Yes, it certainly is. That's why she learned to type."

"Why don't you learn to type?"

"Well, now, I just might." She brightened.

"Maybe I could learn to type, then she wouldn't bug me."

"We'll see." I wondered if they had typing for ten-year-olds at Gib Gate Boarding School in Bowral.

The gold inlay held only until the middle of dinner. It fell under my tongue. I fished for it and whisked it out and down into a fold of my napkin until the meal was over. Nobody noticed. I was afraid to leave it in at night for fear I'd swallow it.

"Ran?" He turned his head on the pillow.

"I hate to tell you this, but I need a dentist."

"Why, what happened?"

257

I gave him a swift outline. "And the inside of my cheek is getting sore."

"Well, I don't know anybody. You'd better call Bill Sweetapple in the morning."

"Good idea." He never seemed to know any members of the medical profession.

"Darling?"

"Mmmm."

"Patrick White asked me to lunch next Saturday. Can I go? Maybe I could go Friday and see a dentist?"

There was a pause. He turned and lay on his back.

"I can't fly you in. Hugh and I are scouting a new road to the Myall. Also," he added reproachfully, "the Two-Ten uses a lot more gas, and hundred-octane. Pretty expensive for short trips."

"Couldn't I take the train? I could have my shot at Dr. Burke's Friday morning," I suggested hopefully.

"That's no good. The train leaves at noon—you wouldn't get in to Sydney until seven."

"Oh. What about Thursday? Could somebody drive me in Thursday?"

"Maybe. I'll see. Who's Patrick White?" he added curiously.

"He's the terrific Australian writer I told you about."

He turned back over on his left side. "I'll see who might be going in." He yawned and prepared to sleep.

"Great," I whispered, "And I'll call Bill about a dentist." My tongue cautiously searched the cavity again, and gently kneaded the throbbing cuts inside my check.

Hugh Aildred drove me in to Worcester early enough Thursday for him to get back in time to ride up and meet Ran on his way to the Myall in the D-6.

I bared my bottom for the weekly shot at Dr. Burke's home cum office. His wife looked forward to my visits and scraps of station news. She offered fresh cookies or a slice of pound cake and good strong tea while I waited my turn. His waiting room was always full.

I climbed aboard the one and only train at twelve and was jerked and rattled down to Sydney by seven P.M. Out at the apartment I joyfully picked up the phone to call Ross Sweetapple. It was dead. Frustrating. Maybe Ran had forgotten to pay the bill again. It had happened once before. I could check tomorrow from the dentist's office. I warmed a can of soup, occasionally holding a mouthful against my tender cheek, and went to bed.

The phone had indeed been disconnected. It would have to wait. I had no account in Australia and couldn't write a check in anything but dollars.

At the dentist's I produced my gold crown from a plastic eyelash box and it was summarily pasted back in.

Well repaired, I eagerly awaited a soul-refreshing dinner with Ross and Bill and the long-awaited lunch with Patrick White.

It was hell deciding what to wear. I can't remember what I did pick. Patrick would. His memory is disturbingly keen.

I'd arranged a Hughes Hire car from the Sweetapples' phone and was driven to Parramatta.

The old-fashioned house was all but obscured by a remarkable tangle of growth. Vines and roses and nasturtiums fought the tiny weathered gate as I pushed it open and hesitantly searched for a path and a door. The place reminded me of Miss Hare's Xanadu in Patrick White's latest novel, *Riders in the Chariot*. His ascetic countenance appeared suddenly, its body hidden by the disheveled garden.

"Here you are," said his dreamy, haunting voice.

"Yes!" I cried breathless with excitement. "Here I am!"

He was even taller and a bit younger than I remembered, and I was even more in awe of him. He leaned halfway out from behind the shrubs. "Come in. It's this way." What was there about him that made me robe him in a monk's habit as he moved soundlessly away? I wound my way, picking away the twigs and rose thorns as they plucked at my skirt. I looked up. He was standing in the doorway, smiling slightly with amusement. His almost colorless eyes bored through me like augers, without meaning to. They just did.

A dark-eyed, vibrant young woman rose from the couch as I entered.

"Hello," she said intensely, stretching out her hand. "I'm Thea Astley."

Ah, I thought, here's another eager beaver like myself.

259

"How nice to meet you," I replied, answering her nervous warmth. "I loved your book," I enthused.

"Good!" She laughed. "I want to hear!"

A foreign voice sounded richly from the next room. "You must have needed a cane knife—the garden is so wildly overgrown from summer."

And a handsome young man walked in with the lithest of steps. He must be the Greek friend Thea had described to me in the letter that came with her book. Small-boned, graceful as a dancer, with skin the color of olive oil.

I do not have the temerity to report our luncheon conversation. I do not have Patrick White's elephantine accuracy. We drank cold, rather too sweet, white wine; and ate some delicious cold eggplant dish and salad which the beautiful Greek had made. Two things I do remember vividly: first that our conversation was rife with theatrical possibilities. A film of *Descant for Gossips,* Patrick's new short plays, a trip to Greece, Patrick's novel in progress, Thea's novel in progress, exotic food, London, and my Adjustment. As for the last-mentioned, I not only didn't mind it being discussed, we found it worth a laugh. Which is a lot.

The second thing I remember is as alive in time as if he'd just spoken. I was about to leave. I haltingly tried to voice some of my vague apprehensions about the hostile presence of the Australian bush. Patrick looked down at me, his eyes the same opalescent augers that first dismayed me, and spoke in his peculiar, faintly acrid voice. "But didn't you know? Australia doesn't like people."

I left in the wake of that remark and roused my driver who was cooking in the car, and went back to Sydney in a daze.

I stopped to pick up some fresh calves' liver, which we were seldom able to get in Worcester, and some beautiful new crayons, a drawing pad and "How to Draw Horses" for Katrina. *Never on Sunday* was playing at a small theatre in Kings Cross. A Greek movie would prolong the glow of the lunch in Parramatta. Four o'clock. I ran back to the butcher and asked if he'd keep the liver until six o'clock. I turned in the car and crept into the movie and lost myself in Piraeus.

The alarm woke me at five-thirty Sunday morning and I

made the seven A.M. train clutching my packages. Ran was meeting me. On the long, rough train ride I kept hearing Patrick's last remark. "Australia doesn't like people." It was good to know that it wasn't just me who felt the presence of the Australian bush. The stubborn mental picture reappeared: messy picnickers swarming like flies over a colossus sprawled in half-sleep, too bored and old to swat.

To me there was pathos and effrontery in the extraordinary efforts expended on much of that worn-down land. The land, the land, the "man on the land." They said it in pubs, in political harangues, in newspapers and in magazines. I'd begun to think that one lived *in* America, *in* Europe, or *in* Afghanistan but *on* Australia.

33

Nocturne in A Minor

YOU can turn in a king-size bed but you mustn't toss—it wakes him up. I turned carefully and went on thinking. It wasn't impossible. Was it? The idea of making a film in Australia. Thea Astley's book was based on so much truth that she'd had to move away from the small town in Queensland where it all happened. A chance at re-creating truth. Especially on film. Film was so fluid, so free; it could creep unnoticed into the vulnerable realities like a good actor's imagination. That was it. Film was invisible truth made visible.

How would Ran feel if I attempted the project? Would it be worse for him because it would be on the doorstep of his bailiwick? Would it embarrass or shame him? Our brushes with the press and public had done both. I loved him passionately, partly because he was unsullied by the blatant egotism and greed I'd been used to. I squeezed my eyes and flexed my knees.

Actors were not people in my business; they were commodities. The public fixed the price on your head; the producers bought you, sold you, or dumped you back on the market. The agents either fed off the crumbs or picked the carcass, even if they liked you. Very few directors were any different anymore. They'd become commodities themselves. Writers suffered the same fate. They spoke of high-priced, medium-priced and low-priced writers. Just like actors and directors. Nor did the price-tag denote quality.

I searched the pillow with my cheek for a smooth patch. They always had you, though. Like a girl at a dance, you had to be asked. They knew it. You knew it. Ran was his own man. He'd never had to knuckle under the way I had. It did something to you if all you wanted to do was act. There were actors who thrived in peripheral and social manure. I had avoided it; often to my cost. I'd avoided it all the way to Giro with a fresh-souled man. But something gnawed at me. Not ambition, not lack of luxury, but that I was not using myself—that I was stultified by routine that took all and gave nothing.

I'd thought seriously of taking over Katrina's education. But in my heart I not only knew my patience was innately limited but that she was wavering on the brink of adolescent introversion. As a mother I should expand her world not contract it. The Latin root of educate, *ēducāre*, to lead out. I must let her go forth. Perhaps if Ran had taken my hand and said, "Let's grapple with Giro together," I could have learned. Perhaps that would have used me. At least I would have felt more useful than a Jean Taggart, who could cook.

It was no good. I wasn't sleepy. I'd try my familiar trick of getting cool. Slowly I uncoiled like a torpid snake and inch by inch eased out of my side of the bed. Bracing myself with my hands on the floor, I slithered silently out of bed onto the floor. I lay listening to his breathing. Ran hadn't even felt the bed move. Good.

I rose and slunk silently out of the dark bedroom. It was absolutely still. You could smell the night dew. I crept across to my bath and got a cotton robe. Where in hell were my cigarettes? I patted my hands along the long chest in the four-poster, found them, and lit one. I could just see the smoke; my pupils were opening up. Be careful he doesn't smell that smoke. I needed to think. The lunch at Parramatta echoed through my mind and made me ponder excellence.

I padded out onto the veranda and went to the far right end, as far away as I could get from our bedroom windows, and sat cross-legged on the couch. That position warmed the now chilly soles of my feet.

Excellence. That was the perfect experience, wasn't it? *All About Eve.* I was good, I was respected, I had a great part, the script was superb; the actors were perfect and perfectly cast. Even me, and I wasn't always. Funny. It had been perfect for Bette Davis, too. She'd thought she was through at forty-one.

263

Now suddenly she had Margo Channing to play. She was in love, too, though God knows she and Gary Merrill were hardly domesticated. Neither were the big martinis they shared after work. He was a permanently undomesticated animal. Later she told me he thought he'd married Margo Channing and she thought she'd married Bill Sampson and thereby hung their marriage. None of us, Marilyn Monroe included, *none* of us could wait to get to work. And Joe—Joe the Mank. Joseph L. Mankiewicz, the wonder man. Two large plastic kewpie dolls were glued to his script lectern—representing the Oscars he'd just won. *All About Eve* was to give him two more. Joe was at flood crest, a controlled manic. None of us knew we were making a film classic. Every day was like a glorious relay race.

John Hodiak and I were happily married then, but I had a secret crush on Joseph L. Mankiewicz. His wit, his modest perspicacity, and my latent father complex drew me to him like a magnet. In fact, all the ladies on the set melted and gravitated to him as I did. Another completely effortless lady slayer was Walter Huston. He had one innocent ploy: a bowl of dried fruit on the table in his portable dressing room (for energy, you understand), thus allowing females from six to sixty-six a valid excuse to drop by and step through the always open door into his charmed domain. My grandfather cast the same spell. I think it was simply that all three *liked* women and transmitted that rare attar of empathy like a sixth scent.

Censorship blighted one of Joe's best lines. Eve crouches humbly in Margo's dressing room and unreels her pathetic story. Sniffles and silence. Thelma Ritter, as tough old Berdie, Margo's dresser, says, "What a story—everything but the bloodhounds snappin' at her ass." Under considerable pressure, Zanuck sent a last-minute directive and the line was changed, over our disgusted groans, to ". . . everything but the bloodhounds snappin' at her rear end." How prissy, particularly in the light of future license.

George Sanders did not in the least resemble Sleepy, the Disney dwarf. However, they shared a penchant for shuteye. George slept soundly in his portable dressing room between shots. It bothered me only once. Eve's climactic scene, when Addison DeWitt confronts her with her real self and lays down their private ground rules, was a formidable challenge. It required a gamut of emotions, building to and culminating in hysteria and ending in acrid defeat.

I am a starting gate actress. From the moment I climb into the makeup chair my mind is prancing around the track, eyeing that gate—the first take. Many actors are the opposite. They start to really move in the stretch—in the fifth or sixth take. By then actor A is losing ground if he or she isn't careful. George yawned his way through rehearsals. I was spiraling through them. That first take was an opening night. Joe took me aside.

"Take it easy, Annie," he cautioned gently.

"Godalmighty, Joe, I don't know *how*. Can't we stick a pin in George?"

"He'll warm up," said Joe in a near whisper. "Just be damned sure you don't exhaust yourself. *Save* yourself the first few takes."

I tried, but by take five I was a rag. Understanding Joe called a short break and took George aside. Bending his heavy, handsome head, he talked with a hand on George's elegantly tailored shoulder.

I walked around, taking deep breaths and trying to relax and yet maintain my emotional juices.

Take six. Take seven—and George went off like a rocket. You know how you hold smoking punk to a firework? And just as you think it's a dud, it explodes into action. I felt like that punk.

Joe winked at me, which meant a lot of things, including that I'd been able to withstand George's kind of race and win my own.

We were all a little nervous to begin with, Joe included. Such a roster of highly charged personalities could have quickly degenerated into a lineup of randomly set time bombs. Only one went off, with good reason, on the day we began. We were to start shooting on Stage 9, definitely one of the smaller stages on the lot. Our assistant, Stan Hough, didn't want to crowd the sets, and after pushing and fitting five portable dressing rooms here, there and everywhere, he left Celeste Holm's outside. Out in the cold was more to the point. Celeste took one look, aimed, and fired at everyone in sight and tearfully flounced back to her permanent dressing room.

Joe was horrified and furious. He knew all too well how vital it was that we work easily together. All we needed was a sour note right off the bat. I never saw anyone get that mad. He all but foamed at the mouth.

Everything stopped for two solid hours while Joe, all three assistants, Celeste's agent, and several emissaries from the front office made elaborate apologies. She came back on the set chin high, wet eyes shining resolutely—we couldn't help wondering if she'd toured in Saint Joan. Nothing like that ever happened again. And nothing as perfect as *All About Eve* did, either.

A long ash fell off my cigarette. I crept out the screen door, buried the butt in the dirt beside the wooden steps and went back to my couch. Damn that lunch at Parramatta. It had thrown me into relief. I'd sat there at lunch like a dolt; a country bumpkin basking in sophistication and creative possibility with nothing to add but a hayseed's tale of daily battles with chores.

Oh, boy, I'm in a mess. A real mess. No. I'm the mess. I began to beat the couch with my fists. God Almighty, I needed to expend myself at something I did well, something worth doing, something with depth, something that would expand my soul, not constrict it. Perspiration bathed me. I breathed faster and faster, but without a sound. Mustn't wake him. I folded my arms and began to rock myself. Soon, if God willed it, I'd be rocking some small new body. That would use me without grinding me down the way Giro did. Forgive me, Lord, for forgetting the miracle going on inside me. I cried a very little, without sound, my face contorted like a tired child's. I was cooler now. My body was chilled by night air on damp skin. I'd sleep now. I went back to my bath and rinsed my mouth of cigarette stench.

"Anne?" Oh, no. I rushed out of the bath and picked my way through the living room furniture.

"Ran?" I came into the bedroom. He was halfway up on one elbow.

"What's the matter, dearest?" he whispered.

"Nothing, sweetheart, I'm so sorry I woke you."

He smiled. "You didn't—I just missed you!"

I tore off my robe, crawled into his arms, and kissed him with overwhelming love as we curled into blessed sleep together.

34

"Walk on the Wild Side"

AS April came, the sun went earlier and earlier. The decision to turn on the engine became increasingly vital. The men were out and around and caught the last rays, but down near the river we tumbled into night suddenly. The engine was a generator, but was never anything to me but the engine—Giro's and my bête noire. It was tethered in a wooden room with a resounding cement floor and iron roof. If you turned it on, life had juice and light; if you didn't, it didn't.

More often than not, we'd be fumbling and fuming in the dark by the time Ran or Hugh rode in to the rescue. So I said it's spinach and the hell with it, and learned to turn it on. Neither Joan nor Mrs. Mac would touch it.

The engine had a collapse peak of 7,500 watts. I lived in constant fear too many things had been left on when it went off the night before. Heaters, or a frying pan, or lights; it not only serviced Giro homestead but the three cottages, the shearers' quarters, and the welder as well. One heater alone pulls 2,500. Everytime I pulled the "On" lever I half expected a shattering explosion.

Think of hearing a New Year's Eve noisemaker the size of an American post office flag, slowly building up speed and noise. *Racketa-flap-racketa-flap-racketa-racketa: racketa! racketa! Bunk gettah bongetta bracketta bongetta racketa bongetta bongetta*, etc. In full voice it developed a nasal whine like a kid imitating an airplane, and seemed to know that any serious ailment had to be doctored from Sydney, plunging us into guttering candlelight and spoiling meat for at least three days. I cooked many a meal and made many a bed in the half-dark, waiting for and waiting *on* engine doctors. A damned good thing none of us got sick as much as the engine. Once in a while it flatly refused its wall lever, and you had to reach into its pulsating abdomen to flip a tiny—*what?*—hooklike thing? which absolutely terrified me.

Several times, with Ran and the men gone mustering overnight, I had to turn it on the hard way. I'd take my courage by the ear, a flashlight, and mush blindly through the inky grass, not dwelling on what could be running around in *that,* and stand palpitating before the door. The noise was bad enough outside, but as that door opened I walked into Hades. Black with grease, leaping and slavering like a mad dog on a chain, it charged me with furious sound and motion, and to have to reach deep into that belly was torture. Each time I did it I said good-bye to the hand. It never just stopped; it ran down, reluctantly, in vicious snarls and evil sighs. Icy with relief, I'd walk out to stand in a night thick with new silence, and wonder how I had gotten so terribly far away from the things I knew how to do.

Weedy was a fact. My bottom had been punctured weekly with Red Krohn's magic liquid. I'd hoodwinked Dr. Burke by telling him I was hoping said potions would boost fecundity. Our baby remained a fact.

One morning àt three we were ousted yet again from precious slumber by the phone's piercing jangle; looong–short–looong–short. Ran banged down the hall in righteous indignation. After the usual muffled "What's?" he lurched into the bedroom doorway.

"It's overseas. For you."

"Oh, my God. Why can't they understand our time difference? Jerks!" I railed impatiently.

"You want them to call back?"

"No, they'll only get caught in Groceries, I'll go. You go back to bed." I found my robe and slippers and scuffled down to the phone, furry with sleep. As usual, it was my agent, Arthur, in sunny California. There were two offers: a live television special in New York and a movie called, longwindedly, *Walk on the Wild Side.* Arthur and I batted around our code for various salary figures designed to confuse any of the nine parties listening in and I said I'd call back. What a crazy way to transact business. Shivering and yawning, I stumped back to bed.

"Ran."

"Hmm?"

"He's sending the scripts."

As I slid back into bed I couldn't help thinking about doctor's visits and bills. Arthur said my part in the film should only take three weeks. I could probably get away with it. I hadn't even felt life yet. Only my bosom was outsized at that point, and nobody objected to that in Hollywood.

A week later Ran came home late, and he and I were supping alone, watching cheese, onion, and green chili sandwiches turn a tantalizing bronze. I'd put them in crackling butter in a small French chafing dish called a Grillon. It was fun drinking a cold beer and watching them brown melt in front of us on the kitchen table.

"It's impossible, darling," I went on in exasperation. "And, furthermore, the scripts aren't that good. Arthur says Charlie Feldman wants to take a look at me before they decide. Not for the television show, I mean the movie." How humiliating, I burned inwardly. What the hell did they think—that I'd turned into a cow? God, all they ever cared about was what you *looked* like. "And what about Katrina?" I put out the flame under the chafing dish and lifted our sandwiches onto plates with a pancake turner. "I mean, you know the situation with Quilty. We have to watch that like hawks. Gib Gate School isn't possible until next September."

"I don't know, darling," said Ran. "I'd feel a lot easier if you saw Red. I'll make a point of being here. Katrina can ride out with me sometimes. She can visit the Biddefords, and Joan's here now."

"Joan's got her hands full," I commented flatly.

He smiled at me and bit into another juicy corner of buttery crust, melted cheese, and green chili.

"Stay loose. It's not the end of the world either way."

"Yes, but Arthur has to know. It kills me to decide something that affects all the people I care about!"

"Don't sweat it so hard, sweetheart."

269

I sighed disconsolately and frowned at the kitchen fire as it tumbled into embers. Suddenly I burst into laughter.

He grinned in surprise. "What?"

"Oh, Lord, I meant to tell you. Katrina got her marks in the mail from London. They're really quite good, especially in English, but wait'll you hear the best!" I slapped the table in delight.

"What?" He laughed in anticipation.

"She got—hold your hat—she got A plus in handwriting!" I guffawed again.

"Unbelievable!" Ran remarked, tipping his chair back and reaching for a wooden match in the tin cup on Big Bertha the stove's black edge.

"And, Ran, you know Katrina was miffed as the dickens because Quilty's bugged her unmercifully about it. And now Quilty's won!"

"Listen, dearest," he began again, lighting up his after-dinner cigar, "the scripts are your department, but in principle I think you should go. By the way, what's happened with the house at Brooktree Road?"

"Oh, brother, that's a real hassle. Paying every month and there it sits. Lots of people have looked, but it's a very specific house, not just for anybody. There's a veterinarian with five kids who's interested. Eric wrote and said I might have to put on a new roof; the water's been standing in spots."

Ran was silent, happily digesting a delicious supper and savoring his cigar. Sometimes this kitchen was really attractive, I thought idly. Decision hung in the air about us. Ran's attitude was, "Why not?"

The scripts were only adequate. But there were good reasons for going and, truthfully, to my everlasting chagrin, this formerly spoiled child was devilishly tempted once again by the prime spoiler of the universe, America.

After a seesaw of indecision and more than a twinge of guilt at my inner hunger for many things, I left. Ran flew me to Sydney with his blessing. Katrina's small brown arm waved as long as she could see us far below.

"It won't be that long," he said in a voice like a caress as I stared longingly at him, about to board my plane.

270

"I hope so, dearest. With luck I could be home in five weeks."

I flew straight through to Los Angeles, but tired as I was, I passed muster and was hired. Red checked me and all was well. I flew on to New York to make the *U. S. Steel Hour* special.

April 10 I wired Ran from New York in the beatitude of a Pierre Hotel suite: GOOD MORNING, SIR. IT'S 7:15. (It was a wake-up call I'd had on tour once—I have a deep voice—and our code name for the child awake and stirring.)

I got back to the hotel from rehearsal the next day and found a message from Charles Laughton. He was in New York and wanted me to lunch. He'd directed me in *John Brown's Body* with Raymond Massey and Tyrone Power. We had all toured for five long months together in 1956. I hadn't seen him since London in 1958, when we'd been on stage next door to each other. He was playing in Harold Pinter's *The Birthday Party;* I was struggling with a mediocre play called *The Joshua Tree* at the Duke of York's Theatre. The best thing about that play was that theater. It was like inhabiting a royal jewel box. I was deeply fond of Charles and deeply admiring of his extraordinary talents. Grandfather had loved him, too. He'd been to Taliesen many times giving his unique readings for mutual fun.

We had an unforgettable lunch at Pavillon. Marvelous Pouilly Fumé and sole with shallots, tomatoes, and mushrooms. His ego stretched and flexed its considerable muscle to an eager audience of one. Then he turned his hooded headlights onto me. What was *I* doing? Oh, God, where did I start?

"Well, Charles, I'm learning to cook." He stared at me with mild disgust. But what was I *doing?* I quailed, playing for time, and took another bite of my sole. "I read a lot," I fibbed weakly.

He stared right through my face. "You'd better work," he said imperiously, "or you'll dry up." I shuddered inwardly. To an actor the expression "to dry up" means a mind that slips its bonds. You "dry" on stage and even your own name escapes. I defended myself, but he just kept eyeing me all too knowingly.

When we embraced good-bye, he said again with thunderous finality, "*Work!* Anne, you must work!" I smiled in distress. "I will, Charles," I replied meekly. The tiny creature inside me stirred as I watched him wedge himself into a cab and be driven away into the traffic.

Back in Hollywood it was touch and go with the insurance doctor who came to check me during a hurried fitting at Western Costume. Dr. Gorson was an old friend; his company insured many independent productions.

Lying is not my forte. "Are you pregnant?" He asked offhandedly, pencil poised.

"No," was my bald-faced answer as my babe booted me in a kidney. Please, Lord, don't let him notice my blush.

Luckily I was playing a Spanish-American lady with full skirts and Mexican blouse, but I dearly hoped the picture would start soon, as I planned on wearing a twenty-two-inch belt. It not only didn't start, but once it did, I thought it would never end. A swarm of nasty situations developed. Charles Feldman, our producer, was determined to launch Capucine into stardom. It never works that way, not since Sam Goldwyn and Anna Sten, but nobody ever believes it.

Laurence Harvey was backed (or was if fronted?) by Harry Cohn's widow, Joan, who then owned the studio. He, very rudely and in graphic terms, said Capucine couldn't act and walked off the set. She wept for a week. Barbara Stanwyck blew her top at Laurence Harvey daring to be an hour late on the set. For which I did not blame her. Mrs. Cohn gave Laurence Harvey a mauve Rolls-Royce. Jane Fonda fought our director and rewrote dialogue, egged on by her current Greek mentor. Walking on that set, you needed a hatchet to cut through high tension. The director quit. And my babe grew and grew but the twenty-two-inch belt didn't. I made frantic phone calls to Edith Head. She suggested avoiding profiles of my stomach and strategic Mexican rebosos. Red Krohn repeatedly reassured me the child would not be squeezed out of shape, only me. I starved on a dish of berries, a carton of yogurt, two glasses of skimmed milk, and a slice of meat per day.

Just before things got so bad on the set that no one was speaking to anyone, Mrs. Harry Cohn gave a dinner party for us. I munched my lip and wondered what I could wear that wouldn't reveal my secret, which was growing bigger and kicking harder each day. I'd brought my sleeveless black wool Norell, which ordinarily loosely skimmed the body. I tried it on. It no longer skimmed, it sat, but was so shapeless and black it effectively hid my tattletale curve.

272

Her house was extravagantly pastel, as was she. She wore delicately printed chiffon and looked and moved like a Laurencin watercolor. Larry Harvey was the last to arrive—just late enought to make a chic entrance. Capucine's face was as impossibly lovely as a marble by Houdon. Charlie Feldman consumed her elegant bones with every look. Jane Fonda didn't come.

Larry disdained the butler and said he'd make his own martini, thank you. Joan Cohn consumed *his* elegant Lithuanian bones with *her* every look. He returned from the bar with a beaded soap bubble of a glass atop a foot-high stem and toasted her; wherewith she allowed the ghost of an intimate smile. We waited while he made himself another, his long cigarette holder clenched at an impertinent angle, his wily eyes slitted against curling smoke.

The dining room was aglow with candles and tinkled with dangling Baccarat crystal. Every bit of crystal was either heavily leaded Steuben or featherweight Baccarat. I sat between Joe Vogel, then MGM's lion of production, and Larry. As I gratefully spread damask over my jumping bay window I enjoyed the beautiful paintings. I wondered if she'd chosen them with the decorator and an investment counselor. Probably. After all, I'd heard only red-bound books were allowed in the library, anything else would have clashed.

The paintings were mostly Impressionist and extremely valuable. Obviously the room was done up around them, as was she. Our first course was a water-lily-sized artichoke hollowed out and filled with fresh crab ravigote. To hell with my starvation diet. I didn't have to work the next day. It was gastronomic heaven. Champagne flowed. Larry had them all in stitches telling tales about a weekend party at Mrs. Cohn's Palm Springs villa at which everyone had vaulted into her swimming pool fully dressed. I made myself slightly unpopular by candidly asking Joe Vogel why the studio had been foolish enough to take the entire company for the remake of *Mutiny on the Bounty* down to Tahiti in October during the rainy season. He gave me a dirty look and retaliated curtly, "Had to shoot when *actors*"—he swiped at that word—"were available."

Rare beef bouquetiere followed, then a fantasy of imported cheeses and crackers attending Bibb lettuce salad, then some

273

ice cream dessert I don't recall and couldn't eat. I was too dizzy from rich food by then. Before dessert, as the Baccarat finger bowls arrived with tiny gardenias afloat, Larry drained yet another glass of champagne. Looking sidelong at me, he said in an undertone, "I know it's all a bunch of crrrap—but I love it!" And crinkled the corners of his mouth with a near-smile. I looked at his narrowed eyes and suddenly saw Ned Beale, who squinted not from oversophistication but from shyness. There was a remarkable resemblance. A lean, slant-eyed, wolf look. The polar difference between the two—Larry casually encased in silk, cashmere, and cologne at that lazily glittering table, and Ned Beale hacking at cows' tails in a yardful of fresh dung thousands of miles away from this insulated, suffocating world, made me feel oddly buoyant. I was so genuinely glad I didn't live here. That I didn't depend on these jaded people for human need, and resolved to bring Ned Beale a Countess Mara tie just for the hell of it.

On and on the picture dragged. My phone and hotel bills were staggering. I was staying at the Bel Air Hotel, in the tower room, number 240. It was a small bed-sitting room in an old bell tower and Phil Landon had given me a theatrical rate. Meaning I paid a little less. Even so the cost was astronomical. I'd only stayed there because I thought it would be for such a short time. Oh, dear.

By June's end I was expiring of longing for Ran and Katrina and expiring, period, from that damned belt. Ran gave up and flew to Los Angeles where we eked out the picture's end with a new director. I walked out of the studio into a maternity dress July 3, almost seven months pregnant and lighter from my original weight by eight pounds. Red Krohn took a disgusted look at hangdog me and said "*Eat*" the way Charles Laughton had said "Work!"

35

$\mathcal{D}$iscombobulation '61

THIS wasn't funny. This wasn't funny at all. I stood up in my new, pretty, divinely comforable maternity dress, and my new, ugly, horribly uncomfortable maternity girdle and walked over to look out the window. I was too upset to say anything. Red Krohn's office was in a high-up corner of a slick medical building at the junction of Linden and Wilshire Boulevard in slickest Beverly Hills. Red was still talking, and Ran and I were listening.

"You both have to face the total risk. At Annie's point in pregnancy a miscarriage would be extremely dangerous to mother and child. No trips in the small plane. No Land Rover. Obviously no horseback riding. All ranch activities would have to be severely curtailed." My God, I thought, sinking into quick despair, I won't even bother to describe that rattletrap of a train trip between Worcester and Sydney. That's right, why bother? Rover had just been banned from Giro to the train.

I stared at the endless traffic flowing up and down Wilshire Boulevard. Like a mad multiplication of an assembly line, flaring its hot chromium in smoggy sun.

Ran spoke now. "I see." His voice was subdued. There was a long pause. "Well, what would you suggest we do?"

I shut my eyes for a second and wrung my hands in acute distress. Dear, gentle heaven, what a problem I had become.

Red answered with his usual vigor. "I'll tell you what I think you should do, Randy." Damnit, Red, *don't* call him Randy, he *hates* it.

"I think you should go to Honolulu, have a pleasant vacation and then you go on back to whatchamacallit—"

"Giro," Ran interjected quietly.

"OK, Giro, and let Annie come back here, rent a house for a few weeks, and have the baby here. When's that due date again?" I heard cardboard snap and papers whisper. "Yeah," said Red. I could hear him shuffling my records and thinking aloud. "Here we are. Probably around September sixteenth, if the baby's on time." I roused myself and beamed a slim ray of sunshine into a black conference.

"I was right on the nose with Katrina. Two A.M. on July the ninth. Remember, Red?" I said, still facing the window.

"I certainly do." I looked around at him contritely, remembering what a rough time I'd given him. Katrina was alive only because of his incomparable expertise. His saucer-sized blue eyes twinkled.

Ran was deep in thought. I came over to him, put an arm around his shoulders, and asked blandly, "Shall I commit hara-kiri or would a nice divorce do the trick?" Ran glanced up, not entirely amused.

"Like I've said before," he commented lightly, "as a comedian you'd starve."

"Sorry, " I apologized swiftly. "Bum joke. It's just that I feel so miserably responsible for this whole mess," I replied, removing my arm.

"Now look, darling," he protested in an exasperated tone, "that's just stupid. How can you possibly help it?"

"Not *now* I can't, but I never should have made the bloody movie," I cried, starting to pace the floor. Red swung back and forth in his swivel chair and twiddled with his ball-point pen as he watched us warily.

"Never, never should have done it. The whole situation couldn't be worse. So *damned mad* at myself I can't *see* straight, " I barked. I paced, getting more and more worked up.

"Now wait a minute." Ran raised his voice to halt me and went on vehemently and deliberately. "I agree it's not ideal, but it's not all bad either. In any case I'd want you to have the baby here. And you running around upbraiding yourself is of no use whatsoever. Now sit down, calm down, and let's try to work something out."

I sat. Shamefaced, I looked at Red. He had swung discreetly around to face the window. All I saw now was his roseate bald head, fringed at its base with fine orange hair and freckles. I drooped on the arm of the leather settee, drowning in remorse and discouragement.

Ran looked at his flyer's watch. "Its one thirty. Let's go into the logistics over lunch. There's no point in wasting our good doctor's time." He stood up, turned to Red, and asked very tentatively if there was any possibility of my going back to Giro, if he made sure I was extremely cautious, then returning in time to have the baby. Red replied with a sympathetic but emphatic "No."

We bade him good-bye and left, in what you might call low dudgeon. What we really needed was a quartermaster general. My house was out. It was in escrow and being rerooofed. The veterinarian with five children had finally bought it. Some dear friends of mine, Whit and Ebi Cook, were going to their farm in New Hampshire until October. We rented their house in Bel Air. Katrina would meet us in Honolulu and come back to Los Angeles with me as Ran left for Giro. Australian school would be out for their winter holidays anyway, and I very much wanted the three of us to be together when the baby arrived. Also, Katrina could have a long visit with her fond grandmother and grandfather in Portola Valley. They'd missed her sorely.

Using our unbelievably complex change of plans, we let Quilty go. Feeling like the Snow Queen, I wrote her good-bye; and cringe now to think of her bilious attacks in other people's lives or in cheerless hotels. Bad cess to a life denied, and to my own woeful poverty of soul.

My mother suggested Katrina enter school up with them for a month in September. Since I didn't know when or how long I might be in the hospital, I agreed. I flew up with her the first of September and stayed a few days. I shudder to think of the first days in new schools that child has mastered, to say nothing of Miss Frostquilt. I consoled myself with the hope that her mastery of them, which was extraordinary, would stand her in strong stead the rest of her life.

Ran, Katrina, and I shared three sun-drenched happy weeks

277

with the Galts in Hawaii after which Ran and I said good-bye for what seemed like the hundredth time. How I loathe airports. Minideaths on terrazzo bathed in morgue light.

Ran flew up again the first of September to be on time to greet the new baby. It was three weeks late. Delays seemed to dog us the way they had dogged the ill-fated movie.

By that time I was so big with child I found myself all but worshiping my formerly disdained maternity corset. It was a cumbersome, complicated contraption, complete with steel bones, three sets of lacings, various large hooks, and an inner sling under the baby's weight. It extended from my shoulder blades to well below my bottom. All I needed was pink bloomers to look like my Victorian grandmother. Never mind. I used to wash it and lie flat until it dried.

Knowing Ran was quietly going crazy sitting around, I appealed to Red Krohn. Please, couldn't we medically get the show on the road? Again his answer was an emphatic no. In desperation one day I flippantly suggested Disneyland. Ran thought that was a capital idea and off we drove. I inched through the turnstile of Flight to the Moon in Tomorrowland. We sincerely hoped the considerable vibrations during the blast-off would be efficacious. What next? Oh, yes, Autopia. Hurray! Ran planned to get in the car behind and gently but firmly back-end me; couldn't hurt, might help. Two very callow youths were taking tickets. They threw me a few surreptitious looks, had a whispered confab, and called Ran aside. Blushing, they asked was the lady expecting. What an understatement. I didn't have a belly, I had a prow.

Ran laughed and came back to me saying, "No go—and I guess that lets out the Matterhorn." Damn. We tried the Tea Cups and Mr. Toad's Wild Ride to no avail. It was fun, anyway.

A week later, at seven A.M., I felt something definite. But, afraid of a false alarm after all Ran had been through, I shut up. Though faint at first, the pains were measurable as the day wore on. Ran must've wondered why I kept asking the time. At seven P.M. we'd ordered steaks and martinis in a gloomy leather-covered restaurant called the Intrepid Fox when an unmistakable labor pain backed me up against the banquette with a beaut of a spasm. As the martinis arrived, Ran was in a phone booth calling Red Krohn. After an arduous trip the baby ar-

278

rived at five A.M. October 4, a roly-poly girl with three double chins. No wonder. She'd been curled up in there getting fatter and fatter. Joanne Woodward sent me a message before she left the hospital with her Melissa the day I came in. But Melissa was the favorite on our list, so at the risk of being called a copycat, Melissa it was. It means honey bee in Greek.

The heat was unbearable that October. A desert wind pushed temperatures to 106 and dried the elegantly manicured suburb of Bel Air into rustling tinder.

The house cooked us upstairs. Ran carried me down since I wasn't allowed stairs yet, and the three of us slept on couches in the living room. Finally we had to bring Melissa downstairs, too, in the seventy-year-old Wright-family spool bed that was traditionally shipped to its newest member. Katrina had been back since October 1 and had entered Bellagio School. School for her by now had become a kind of progressive dinner. More like sojourns in summer camp. She took it all in her short stride. I suppose that in her mind anything from Quilty on was up. She'd enter Gib Gate School in January. At least she'd be ten and one-half years old instead of nine. They kept horses at the school and that would help her bear her separation from Bluebottle. She missed other children more than we knew. Giro's ragtag and bobtail world was a poor substitute.

Red had recommended a baby care nurse for the recuperative weeks. As I started to move around I understood why. Dr. Krohn's famous needlepoint certainly put you back together again but you took a time to heal.

My agent, the handsome Arthur Park, who'd never learned to tell Australian time, and his delightful wife, Merril, asked the Paul Newmans and ourselves to dinner at their home to celebrate Joanne's and my first night out. Joanne and I both arrived carrying our rubber doughnuts behind our backs. We knew why. She and I both shared newborn Melissas and Dr. Krohn's fancy stitchery. Paul wore an orange cotton jumpsuit which he'd borrowed from a test pilot at Edwards Air Force Base. He'd just enjoyed a wild ride in a new jet plane. Ran and he shared a passion for flying and speed in general. The Newmans had an enviably excellent marriage. Never easy, but especially admirable considering the magnitude of two highly talented egos in a polarizing profession. It was a great evening and Ran had finally met actors who could talk about other subjects.

As soon as I could properly sit on my wicked stitches, we made a visit to the King Ranch in south Texas. Mary-Lewis and Dick Kleberg, Jr., were exceptional friends. They were the ones through whom I'd met the Baillieus when I first went to Australia to make *Summer of the Seventeenth Doll*. The convolutions of one's life. If I hadn't known the Klebergs, I wouldn't have met Ran. I knew it would be much-needed stimulus to him to see the biggest cattle ranch in America and hoped it would alleviate some of the tensions and frustrations of the last months. Small reward for large forbearance. My Los Angeles friends were apt to talk ballet, films, theater, music, and art. He could now talk cattle, horseflesh, feed, seed, and bloodlines. Thank God all his travels to the States would finally bear his particular fruit. Luckily it hadn't cost him anything but irritation; I'd insisted that *Walk on the Wild Side* pay the mounting bills. And Mother and Dad had come down the day before we left to see the baby and take Katrina to Disneyland. In the end, Melissa's complicated arrival had made everyone happy.

The third noon at the King Ranch the Klebergs and ourselves were joking and laughing over beers and wild turkey when the phone rang. It was my father. I wondered why on earth he'd called and immediately worried. Melissa? Katrina? What?

"Anne?"

"Yes, Dad. What's wrong?"

"Now, I don't want you to worry. You'll probably see it on television—"

I broke in. "What do you mean? What?"

"The fire. Bel Air is in flames."

"Oh, my God. Dad! No. What about—"

"Please. Now don't get upset. Katrina's been evacuated from her school to us. We managed to break through the police cordon at nine thirty this morning and get the baby and the nurse. It was just lucky we were here. Your mother noticed the smoke as we sat at breakfast and we rushed to the house. Anyway, all's well."

"Thank you, Dad. Thank you so much. I—ah—we'll be right home!"

Ran was standing beside me. "Oh, darling. You can't believe it," I cried, grabbing his arms in distress. "Bel Air is in flames! Worst possible time—the whole area's a tinderbox."

"Thank God your mother and father were there," he said. "Is everything all right?"

"Yes, they've got Katrina, the nurse, and the baby."

We rushed to turn on television and there it was. Firestorms with spiraling winds up to 150 miles an hour. Cars and delivery trucks melted to the street. It looked like a war. We were stunned.

"I'll make a reservation on the first plane out of Corpus Christi. You'd better go pack," Ran said hurriedly as he stepped to the phone. This was definitely not our year. And yet we had a most adorable child named Melissa.

Of course my friends the Cooks were long since back from New Hampshire. I'd apologized profusely. Melissa'd been so late—could we stay on? They were wonderfully understanding and bunked with a friend. Whit Cook was away for a couple of days when the fire happened. Ebi Cook and a mutual actor friend, Max Showalter, got through to the house despite stubborn police. They defied the flames and stayed on the roof all that holocaust of a night, yelling for firemen everytime it caught fire from blazing debris.

We couldn't get a plane out until the next morning. Dick Kleberg flew us into San Antonio in the ranch plane and back we went to a scene of fantastic devastation. The house we'd been in was the only one standing on that street.

Melissa was safe again in her spool bed. Katrina was safe in school, excited and awed by the immensity of so close a disaster. The house next to ours was a pile of ashes. Ran and I drove around Bel Air in silent shock. The ruins were still faintly smoking in some areas. The high ridges like Linda Flora Drive had been engulfed by voracious firestorms. Nothing was left of expensive homes but mailboxes and chimneys. Insurance men were standing grim-faced, holding clipboards, like patient carrion crows. Owners pathetically gesticulated at them and pointed at what remained of prideful, joyful homes. We stopped to talk with one of the policemen standing guard in one of the more ravaged districts. "I'll tell you something," he said with disgust. "Do you know that people have been trying to sneak in

281

here at night and steal the few lousy plants that escaped the blaze? Honest to God," he spat, "a bunch of ghouls."

We were further appalled to learn that Arthur and Merril Park, our charming hosts that night with the Newmans, had lost everything. They'd been away in Mexico. Their house had burned to the ground along with both cars in the garage. Merril said the only thing they had left was a pair of andirons. What irony. She also remarked that the thing she really missed after fifteen years in the house were family photographs. I never forgot her saying that.

Tons of precious belongings and one of the most magnificent suburbs in America totally demolished in a few hours. It made me remember some of Europe in 1953.

Melissa had been so late the nurse had to leave for another new baby and as soon as we could pack up, we left for Honolulu and home. Giro at long last had become home.

How I wished I could have had Melissa at home. Or rather in Sydney. Such a terrible lot of hoo-ha over simply having a child. It had been a grueling time for Ran. I looked into his eyes and saw a man in a cage. A free soul behind the bars of a predominantly female world. His California aunts and cousins cooed and billed over Melissa, who was quite pretty for a newborn baby. The American and Australian press demanded pictures of us all. He even put up with that, too. The man who hated exposure had been exposed for my sake. Had he even enjoyed Chasen's Restaurant's gala gift of cold champagne and steaming Beef Stroganoff with a liveried waiter outside the hospital room door? Happy birthday to Melissa's original chromosomes and genes from Dave Chasen? He'd loved the time in Texas talking ranching with Dick Kleberg, but that had been cut short.

Guilt assailed me. All wrong, but I felt helpless. At least he adored Melissa—that was something. If we could just get back to Giro and lick our psychic wounds.

36

Sister Isabella-Mac

HONOLULU was not a howling success. Melissa was cherubic on the trip, but the sticky heat of the Islands, plus the two-hour time change, made her as crabby as a Model A; meaning me up and down all night and fresh as a lead daisy for clan gatherings at breakfasts, lunches, and dinners.

Ran's mother and father adored Melissa too. Ran's first child. The morning after we landed in Hawaii, I crept down at the crack of flower-scented dawn to play Dr. Kildare-makes-a-formula only to find a different brand of canned milk. Now what four-and-a-half-week-old baby could possibly know the difference? I kept telling myself. An hour later I took one of the mathematically measured treasures to soothe an empty stomach with big blue eyes. She hardly rolled a droplet on her tongue before she exploded. We were to have stayed ten days for a happy tropical rest, but after three I looked and felt like a reheated zombie. We decided to push on to Giro as soon as possible. A temporary nurse named Sister MacDonald was champing at the bit in Sydney.

The plane was to have left at one A.M. but left at three and got us to Australia around two P.M. the next day, our time. But your time is never their time. Their time was eleven A.M. I guess. I never really knew. We had hoped to fly from the airport to Giro in our small plane, which Ran had left at the airport in readiness. But Sydney was in the throes of serious storms and floods, and so, blearily, we hauled up the four flights to the musty shadows of Ran's apartment.

A near hurricane flung torrents of water at the leaden harbor below. Every window smeared a slate-colored tossing world. Everything for the baby had been sent to Giro. No crib, no nothing for Melissa. We found repulsive dirty linen in piles from a recent loan of the place. Our muddy suitcases filled corners and the sneaking damp was oddly augmented by the one hissing gas fire.

My supply of formula was fair—six ahead—and I had brought two cans of the right milk, just in case. Australia taught me to travel just in case, and children tattooed the lesson. I could hold out on diapers until the next day.

Katrina curled in a corner and drew horses with fiery manes. I sat down hard to think, and winced, reminded of my surgeon's skillful shirring. I'd optimistically left my repugnant rubber doughnut in Hawaii. Ran had gone in a cab for chops and coffee. Melissa wailed like a DP in her carry-all on the floor and the sky poured its heart out too. I dragged a spare mattress into our room and barricaded it for the baby that night. I think she felt as if she'd been abandoned on a football field. It was a busy night. By two A.M., or whenever it was, I could hardly find her mouth with the bottle. Up and down and out, upsy daisy made-of-lead.

The nurse's name was Sister Isabella MacDonald, and she arrived at nine twenty-nine and one-half A.M., wearing a veil. A nurse's veil, that is, like an unreligious coif, starched and crisp. I was not quite glued together in a rather vibrantly pink robe with chiffon sleeves.

"Good morning, Sister," I lied. She stood there, tiny, resolute, taking in everything like a pint-sized computer. As she looked and listened, her neatly gloved hand moved up to the neatly pressed veil and neatly removed it. She told me later, with a refreshing giggle, her only worry had been would she have to wear the damned thing *all* the time? An actress, etc. I never saw it again, although I think she wore it to Mascot Airport four days later to impress the lounging mechanics.

Sister marched into our lives that morning with the lightest of steps. Her name was a perfect fit. Her smallness, all over, rather dainty feet even in nurse's shoes that snort "sensible" at you. And hands, carefully kept no matter what they'd been do-

284

ing, and always feminine and smartly turned out. But along with the curlicues of Isabella there was a stiff shot of Mac. Some people called her that. She was long ago wise to people, the Australian bush far and wide, and babies and more babies inside out and backward. A walking book of harrowing tales and priceless experience in what to do when you had no one and nothing to help you do it. But the Isabella in her gave her fiendish ulcers which the Mac in her ignored (until my tongue-tweaking curry woke them up).

As Sister nipped off her gloves, she asked what I was doing about the "nappies." I looked blank. Diapers, she explained. "In here," I said and showed her three rooms draped and upholstered in drying diapers. I had the oven door open and going and the electric heater in the bathroom on to no avail. She commandeered the small kitchen table and put it in the shower for a changing table for Melissa. I phoned and ordered a crib and sheets. It turned out she'd worked for a lady in the neighborhood with a well and truly working dryer, and in an hour I found myself in euphoria, and slept and slept and thank you, dear Isabella-Mac.

Four liquid days later the gray curtains parted and Ran came off the tiny cement balcony where he'd been scanning the sky with blood in his eye.

"Let's go. I can make it to Giro if we hurry."

Things leaped into bags wet or dry. Because of Sister and Melissa, I stuffed the bursting closet with a few more clothes and other junk to lighten our load and we jammed the rest of us into a cab.

Mascot Airport was a long way out. Fifteen minutes later, at three P.M. sharp, the cab pulled to the curb.

"Sorry, I'm going off duty."

Ran paled before iron-clad Aussie routine. Out we piled to stand in a ragged island of luggage as the cabbie radioed for another fellow for the rest of the way. Sister's language was held together only by her coif, which she'd worn for the airport only. We finally took off to the private tune of my prayers. The storm's tail switched with erratic winds. Halfway to Giro Ran literally wove a dance pattern between massive thunderheads whose puffed edges spat rain at us. I only dared one glance back. There sat Sister with a face of stone, clutching her tea rose-colored bundle of joy. Katrina's green eyes were wide; all I saw of Sister's was the icy flash of spectacles as the plane sank and bucked. Ran flew like an escaped convict. Anywhere ahead beat anything behind. Paul Newman would've loved it. Worcester appeared at last. Moments later there were our willows' wisps; there was the river, foaming like cappucino; there was Giro's accordioned head, and down the strip we rumbled home. Melissa had slept through it all.

Then came a low blow. All of Melissa's things, screened crib, bathinette, clothing for months ahead, the works, that I thought awaited us, had been shipped on a slow boat, and various furnishings I'd bought (against Ran's wishes I might add), with which to jazz up the sullen apartment, had gone on a fast one. There I was in hot water yet again. I had sent American diapers and plastic pants because they use terry toweling in Australia and I had visions of bowlegs and a dragging behind on Melissa. Even Sister was impressed with our light, soft, pre-folded nappies. (Dreadful word. How I despised that euphemism, along with "bubbies" (babies), "walkies" (walks), "bickies" (biscuits or cookies), "dinkies" (water), and "bottl-ees" (milk), and all the other horridly cute nomenclature employed by "nannies" (nurses).

Although we were solidly fond of and respectful to Sister Mac, I can remember Ran standing in the dining room doorway a week after we'd arrived at Giro and announcing through bared teeth, "She's not her bubbie and her name is Melissa!"

Nothing arrived. Nothing. That crib we'd bought sat in Sydney, and if the washbasins overflowed with three pairs of my nylon panties, and the kitchen sink wouldn't take a twelve-inch plate, what would we do with a twenty-two-inch, fourteen-pound baby? Borrow. Joan the Good had a plastic tub saved and Jane's and David's well-worn crib, which we hammered together. That first night Melissa slept in a towel-padded bureau drawer.

Sister's only deep-rooted demand was a baby carriage. She recommended an old-fashioned wicker one because of the growing November heat. Her routine for the baby was beyond compare. Up, fed, out and kicking in the morning sun by seven thirty. Short nap and food; mosquito-netted nap under various trees, then what Sister called "out on the bed for a kick and a grin," sans pants. I mean, wouldn't you like your bottom aired without all those wads of wet diapers? Then bath, food, and straight into bed. *No toys.* Toys all day, never at night, and for babies up to a year at least, bed after meals morning, noon, and night. Stomach full, siesta time; and bed at night is for sleep, not play. Both worked like white magic. She taught me always to undress Melissa, and in a sieve of a house with no heat, she had one three-day sniffle in a year and a half.

Sister only used occasional canned stuff. It wasn't always available and when it was, not in variety. She taught me how to use a small French food mill properly called a moulin. I used it on fresh vegetables, meats, and fruit, and I must say Melissa's food tasted terrific. Since I followed Sister's pattern religiously after she left, Melissa ate any and everything put in front of her and thrived, thanks to Sister's jet start. Sister MacDonald's bete noire was a fly, any fly. "Death to Flies" was our motto. One fly can mean gastroenteritis and sudden death to a baby on a station. It's no cinch anywhere.

Sister stayed five weeks and took home awakened ulcers from my imaginative cooking. Two fiercely glared warnings in stentorian tones (her voice was unusually soft and wavy for an Australian) were her last bequest. *Death to flies,* and at the first sign of "it," *Boil the nappies.* I followed every if, and, or but with pounding heart, never having taken care of a baby before, completely on my own, and certainly not in the bush. As she climbed into the plane she gave me a sharp look. "Don't forget to feed her," she said and winked.

37

Little Jack Horner Sat in a Corner, Eating His Christmas Crow

THE day Sister left was a lovely one. Warming up fast, but dry and windless. Even so, I admired her firm step up into that plane after her rocketing arrival. Good-bye to our Mary Poppins in mufti. Good-bye to a lively live-in friend. Katrina and I waved as far as Sister could see us. As I squinted up at the circling plane I couldn't help thinking that pretty soon it would be good-bye Katrina, away to Gib Gate Boarding School after summer holidays in January. Mother would then be grounded for a good long time. Not only grounded but house-boundaried by a small wonder named Melissa. Maybe we could have another go at finding help. Ran was game. Perhaps after Christmas. Our first Christmas at Giro was coming up. Damn it, holidays always catch me napping. You turn around and here comes another one. America's terrible that way, all those busy merchants pushing. Buy, buy, buy.

Depressed and unaccountably lonely, I put my arm around Katrina as we walked back from the empty strip. Sister and the plane had become a faint snarl in the still blue sky.

Katrina's life had been a potpourri of mixed blessings of late. Freedom but no friends. Melissa's advent and its surrounding flurry had set her to one side, no matter how hard we tried to pull her close.

"Would you like to feed Melissa, darling?"

"That's OK. I have to catch Bluebottle."

"Right. See you later, alligator." I squeezed her hard and off

288

she went. She needed other children. Not babies. Not grown-ups. Ten-year-old people.

It followed some strange pattern. I had been exactly ten years older than my little brother, Toby. For the three and one half years of his cruelly short life, I had been reprieved from being an only child. I'd adored him to such an extent it created serious problems. I literally competed with my mother for his care and love; to the drastic point of making him cry in order to comfort him in the role of pseudomother. My poor mother. Katrina had reacted the opposite way. She pretended not to notice Melissa or the amount of time it took me to care for her. Also, ten-year-olds made mistakes. Babies didn't. Ten-year-olds were nagged about picking up their rooms and brushing their teeth and hanging up saddles and putting things *back where they found them*. Babies weren't. If she'd had a more populated life of her own, things might have been very different. As it was, I was painfully conscious of her unspoken resentment. It didn't help that Melissa swiftly became a picture-book baby inside and out. Before her bedtime Katrina and I would read Bible stories or fairy tales or Dr. Doolittle. I put down a book one night and smoothed her hair.

"Katrina, dear," I asked very gently. "Are you jealous of Melissa? It's quite normal if you are, you know," I added lightly.

After the tiniest hesitation she answered nonchalantly,

"No."

"What I mean," I went on, trying as casually as I could to open her mind, "there's always a tremendous fuss about a new baby. There was even more fuss when *you* were born. And you must understand that Melissa can't do anything for herself yet. She's absolutely helpless and needs a great deal of care."

She assiduously avoided my searching gaze. "Sure, I guess so." Again she tossed the subject off as if I'd explained why she needed a hair cut, which annoyed her.

"You'll have a lot more fun with her when she's older. Babies are kind of boring at this age." What a white lie. Mine were always fascinating to me. It was clear everything I'd said had made it worse for her. This time she shrugged without a word.

I smiled, trying to hide some of the aching tenderness I felt and kissed her goodnight.

289

"Sleep well, dear," I murmured. "See you in the morning." I wanted to cradle her the way I used to do a few years before, but she'd grown too big. I stroked her hair again as she wordlessly turned on her side ready for sleep. I saw that her eyes were staring into the wall as I snapped off the light. Someday I might reach her, but not now.

I walked down the hall and sat in the living room hunched over a freshly lit cigarette. Not that it was right, but the endless intrusions of complex car driving in American home life tended to muffle the cries for help beneath human surfaces. At Giro they were as arresting as sirens: simple to answer if one could admit to them, impossible if one couldn't. Katrina couldn't. I knew all too well what Katrina missed.

One heard so much about something or other being a "delicacy," always pertaining to food. Our delicacy was people. We were owners. A tacit barrier, the hidden "no trespassing sign" I'd discovered early. It was a fact that pricked like a cleaning tag one forgets to remove.

People to talk to were so few we instinctively handled one another with tongs. You couldn't afford a social spat or even a slight gaffe. There weren't any new recruits, so you avoided merest skirmishes and never encroached on privacy. Easy friendships were reined in by constant editing of every word. In short, we weren't alone on 36,000 acres, but we weren't one big jolly family and we did all stew in our own lives.

Certain of us exchanged meals at formal intervals, particularly on birthdays or holidays. People need other people to celebrate things.

Our first Christmas at Giro was a rare example. Christmas, 1961, we'd been married a year and ten months, Melissa was two and one-half months old, Katrina ten and some. Everything in the last two months had harried me and all I had done was order a small pine tree growing in a tub from Sydney. My holiday trees had always been expansive; sometimes I'd even put two together. Giro's Christmas trees were the casuarinas, or false pines, with long, needlelike leaves, too floppy to decorate heavily. I like to load up a tree. They used balloons, which were fine, but I was homesick. *We* were homesick. I was alone so much I always had to remember to think "we."

It was hot and wet and dismal. Only Melissa didn't care. Everyone but me had baked Christmas cake (fruitcake) weeks before which depressed me, and the station lay under a shocking pall from the sudden death of one of Mrs. Mac's visiting grandchildren, a little girl two and one half. She died of pneumonia four hours after Ran flew her in to Worcester. They thought she had a cold. Since they didn't believe in thermometers, how could they know her fever reached 107°? We never knew she was sick until too late.

Joan the Good had asked us to dinner Christmas night with Kath and Tom Biddeford, Byron and Gladys Stroud, who lived twenty-two miles away near Worcester on their hilly station, Tigrah, and another couple, relations visiting Joan.

We all nibbled at gin and tonic on the Aildreds' veranda in the sticky evening, making pussyfooted jokes and oh, reallys. Joan excused herself to create a groaning board she'd cooked for days and in twenty minutes produced a buffet like a photo in *Women's Weekly*. We drifted in to find eating spots in the living end of the room, and as I was about to go for a plate I noticed the men were filling theirs. Uh-oh, I thought, the gentlemen are supplying the ladies tonight. When in Rome, etc. I'll wait. I sat down where I was. Tom Biddeford heaped a plate at the buffet and, shoving a platter or two aside, pulled a chair up to it and *sat down*. My eyes widened. Another male plate was calmly filled among a buzz of talk. Another platter shoved to the center and Byron Stroud *sat down*. Ran looked hesitant, but noting the drill, picked up his cutlery and goodies and *sat down*. The buffet was a burgeoning Elks Club banquet. As the last two bottoms were poised in descent, I rose in shock and Dutch courage and said, "*What is the matter with us? Do we have halitosis? Can't we all eat together? Do we smell? It's Christmas!*" A jumbo pause, which I broke by dragging my chair across the room and calling over my shoulder, "Come on, ladies!"

The men froze, then shoved their chairs away to make room for us. Joan laughed breathlessly and hurriedly sat where she'd been serving the men. In between the scrapings of chairs I heard Tom grate in a voice like sifting gravel, "I wouldn't let my wife push me around like that." A bull's-eye. I crumbled inside. Oh, God, I'd embarrassed Ran and Joan, and the whole

291

shooting match was now a soaked bomb because my big foot was up to here. Merry Yuletide, my big foot.

We had a very good time after the conversation closed over the wound. A fine time. Very friendly. But walking home the 100 yards or so was not. Ran was even more upset than I'd imagined about what he explained was a violent breach of etiquette, and that he himself had only followed the others in an effort to fit into local custom.

"I just didn't realize what I did would create such strong reaction, Ran. I am so terribly sorry. Of course I'll apologize to Joan. Should I call Tom or talk to Kath Biddeford? What about the Strouds?"

"Definitely call Joan. I'll talk to Tom. You can call Kath later if you like." His face hardened and I was in a misery of remorse. Why couldn't I keep quiet, read the signs, and fit in, no matter how it seemed to go against my instincts?

As my Adjustment whirled in its formaldehyde I apologized abjectly to Joan first thing in the morning by phone. She protested warmly, "Please don't feel that way at all. Glad you did it! Goodness! I couldn't have!" But communications with Ran were down for quite a while. The specter of parallel lines haunted me and loomed like a repeat sign in terribly hard-to-play music.

The next afternoon at two I sat alone with a second cup of coffee. Out of nowhere rage began to rise in me like a fever. My hands shook with it. Why, why had Ran been so harsh with me? Why hadn't he understood that I didn't understand? We'd both been rehearsed hundreds of times in similar social behavior. Wasn't it normal that I'd think husbands and wives would want to share Christmas dinner? It must be more than protocol. I examined last night's debacle. For me it'd been the classic actor's nightmare: there you are onstage, but you never heard of the play or the other actors and you don't know a line and the audience boos. No. There had to be more to it than mere convention. I heard Tom's insinuating voice, "I wouldn't let my wife push me around like that." It had left a whip's scar of disgrace on me. I gripped my cup, hunting the truth. Had Tom and the rest of the men been subtly digging at Ran flying back and forth to Los Angeles; all that upheaval over nothing more than hav-

292

ing a child? Especially since they knew nothing of the difficulties involved. Had they hinted, as Tom had just done, that Ran was a sort of milquetoast? That I'd put a ring in his nose, that he was dancing attendance on a spoiled American woman?

And had Ran finally erupted out of all proportion at last night's final straw, in front of his daily male audience? How ironic—to have been made to feel castrated in the midst of ultimate manhood—the fathering of a child.

I began to see what hell it must have cost Ran to be a loving husband. And I resolved, with this sudden insight into his lacerated pride, to write a note of apology to Biddefords, Strouds, and Aildreds. If what I'd unearthed through Tom's caustic remark was true, nothing would be too much.

Bertha, the stove, twanged the bottom of an oven for attention. I looked over at her wearily.

"When will you ever learn your place?" she hissed.

"I'm an old dog, Bertha," I answered.

"Well, you'd better learn yourself a few new tricks. You're at Giro now!"

Resting my head in my hands, I sighed, "Old Girl, I've suffered yet another Pyrrhic victory, among many."

"What?" she complained.

"I mean I won but I lost. Oh, never mind."

"Humbug!" she retorted through a monstrous yawn.

Bertha always had the last word.

I rose, measured Melissa's milk for the next day, and put it on the stove to pasteurize. As I watched it heat I wanted to weep, but went to change Melissa instead.

38

Lunch

THE needle rammed an already perforated fingertip. I sighed in aggravation and sucked it dry of blood. Even socks had to have name tapes; KATRINA GALT was sewn on every stitch of underwear or uniform. It was a nice name. Ran had adopted her formally at Honolulu in July. While Sister Mac still stood guard over Melissa, Katrina and I had bumped down to Sydney on the train to outfit her for Gib Gate at the famous David Jones department store. All I remember about the uniforms is lots of dark green, voluminous bloomers, and yards and yards of those blasted name tapes.

At the apartment there was a note from the shippers that the things I'd sent to redecorate our city nest were due to arrive, which meant that, hopefully, the shipment of Melissa's necessaries was only a month away, the calculated difference between a fast boat and a slow boat.

Ran was completely out of patience with my wanting to make the apartment attractive. Number one: I felt we'd be using the apartment more now that Katrina would be in boarding school. Perhaps she'd have friends she'd want to bring and there might be her friends' parents to be entertained. Number two: Dreaming up color schemes and how to make the apartment comfortable helped retain my sanity during the weeks in California before Melissa came. Funnily enough, things like that were far easier to do from the States than if I'd had to shuttle back and forth from Giro. None of which reasons convinced Ran an iota. He displayed active disinterest.

After the fitting at David Jones, Katrina and I went to the beauty salon. I was our barber and had kept Ran's and her hair interestingly trimmed if not cut; lopsided and pinked edges were more the style. We walked out admiring our proper haircuts in every store window on the way to lunch. How I'd looked forward to a pleasant restaurant lunch alone with Katrina. She had, too. We felt like a couple of just-lit sparklers and strolled hand in hand into what I hoped was Sydney's version of the fancy Fifth Avenue Schrafft's I remembered from my childhood. Mother and I used to go there after outfitting me for school at Best & Co. or Lord & Taylor. The hostesses were always beautiful and fruity-voiced. Tantalizing jars of my favorite sourballs were stacked on counters, and glamorous bed dolls in starchy ruffles draped over the bronze stair rail, waiting expectantly to belong to you.

This place was much more sedate, but smelled the same. A combination of fresh pastry, hot rolls, furniture polish, and clean women. We were led to our table, threading our way between busily gabbling lady lunchers. I grew suspicious the second the hostess beamed much too broadly at us.

"*Such* a *pleasure* to have you *here*, Miss Baxter! Is this your kiddie?"

I smiled stiffly, trying to sit as quickly as possible. "That's right." Oh, please, dear, kind lady, do not spoil our badly needed private lunch.

"Getting ready for school, eh?"

Katrina looked at me and sat down. I looked at the hostess bending over us like a Jewish mother with her first male grandchild and said, "That's right" again, very crisply.

"Well, isn't that nice! We're honored to have you with us, Miss Baxter," she purred, "and what's our little girl's name?"

I glanced furtively at the next table. A lady was staring at us—elbowing her companion and whispering. Oh, no.

"Ahhh . . ." I hedged, then replied in staccato, "Katrina–and–could–we–have–a–menu–please?"

"Certainly! We really are thrilled to have you with us. Would

295

it bother you to sign this menu for my dear little niece? She'll be really *thrilled* to know you were in," she burbled on, handing me three menus.

"Of course," I whispered, snatching my paper napkin and wishing to goodness she'd keep her voice down and not daring to look at Katrina.

"Do you have a pen?" I murmured under my breath.

"Oh, goodness, hang on! I'll just run and get one." And she bustled back through the tables. Everyone was craning around and nudging now. We'd had it.

"Sorry, sweetheart." I faced Katrina, who looked embarrassed and puzzled. Not that she hadn't experienced all this before, but I think she was confused to discover her new Giro-type mother's other life had traveled this far. "It's just one of those things—I can't be rude to her."

"That's okay," she answered in a small voice. No. I couldn't be rude to all seven waitresses either. Or the pastry chef or the ladies at the other tables. Everytime we started to enjoy each other, here would come somebody else. Always polite, always prefaced by, "I hope this isn't disturbing your lunch," or, "Isn't this terrible. I hope you don't mind my bothering you at lunch." What can you do? All kind people. All polite but they had, in fact, stolen our lunch.

"Come on, darling, let's go to the zoo. I'm beginning to feel like one." I grinned ruefully; she smiled back. We were suddenly close again.

Taronga Park Zoo was a pictorial ferry ride across one of the loveliest harbors in the world. We both loved zoos, although I always deplored cages. Some zoos had abolished them as such, and they were the best ones.

Free of Giro and chores, I leaned over the rail with an arm draped around Katrina and dreamed.

Our zoo of a lunch had reminded me of something I remembered to the point of mentally inhaling a certain, high-altitude air, and even feeling its crystal against my cheeks.

In 1950, while I was at Twentieth Century-Fox, I'd made a movie called *Ticket to Tomahawk*. My dear friends Richard Sale and his wife (Mary Loos Sale, Anita Loos' niece), wrote the script; Richard directed it. Dan Dailey played a traveling salesman, or drummer, as they were called in 1890. I played a gun-slinging, knife-throwing sheriff's daughter in a town called Epitaph. Chief Yowlatchee (Yakima tribe, I think) played the head Indian; Rory Calhoun was the villain. I could never fathom why he'd changed his name from Smokey MacGowan to Rory Calhoun. I could better have imagined the reverse. Oh well. Hollywood believed in hokum. Sassy-eyed Walter Brennan was the train engineer and Marilyn Monroe played one of a trio of the required dancehall girls. The whole nutsy shebang was a spoof on Westerns, a form of high camp far ahead of its time. We shot on location 9,000 feet up in the Rockies, driving laboriously up from Durango to a tiny, old shoot-'em-up silver mining town appropriately named Silverton. We were thereabouts for eight long weeks. All of us lived in Durango at the Royal Motel, a euphemism, and ate at the local greasy spoon called the Chief Diner. Marilyn Monroe came in with a different crew member every night, wearing the same sweater. She was eminently braless and I particularly remember the pink V-necked angora sweater. It was said she slept in it. We never saw hide nor hair of her, or of her two roommates, outside of dinnertime or during their occasional days of shooting. They slept whenever possible and all day Sunday. Or were closeted in the only phone booth, calling Hollywood.

I felt about my sitting room in the Royal Motel the way I did right now about Ran's dog-eared apartment. After five weeks I couldn't stand it. I bought yards of cheap turquoise cotton and redecorated it. Since I couldn't sew, I simply used 3-inch wig pins to reupholster chairs and sofa. They of course jumped out every time anybody sat down, but I politely asked my guests to push them back in. Which they did. I may say with pardonable pride I was known as the Elsa Maxwell of Durango, Colorado.

Rory Calhoun and Lita, his hot-blooded Latin wife, had many engrossing altercations at the top of their voices. I learned a lot of Spanish with my ear glued to the Royal's cardboard wall. I entertained lavishly at cocktails, featuring fresh butter-fried almonds and walnuts. Which woke up Richard Sale's ulcer as I'd awakened Sister Mac's.

The team of twenty Missouri mules pulling our little steam engine, named the Emma Sweeney, over the Rockies (the gist of the story) were unused to altitude and contracted distemper, which the horses got. Before every take my patient horse's nose had to be wiped. We had a ball.

The Silverton train station was a set we used for several days' shooting. A narrow-gauge steam train carried tourists from Durango to Silverton through the precipitous gorge of the wild Animas River.

The mountain air was distilled sanity. Lunch was madness. People jabbered and grabbed at us for photos; shoving and clutching so avidly we never ate a peaceful bite. The town constables roped us off, but still they catcalled and gaped as if we'd been in cages.

Dan Dailey loathed it even more than I did and was explicitly profane, carefully within earshot of any and all tourists.

After three days of it, Dan was looking dyspeptically at the little joyride train getting ready to chug back to Durango. Tourists were hanging out the windows like bunches of grapes, staring hungrily and pointing as if we were indeed zoo inmates. Suddenly Dan danced up to a cluster, shoved his face viciously forward like a striking snake, and hissed, "They feed us at four!"

Taronga Park Zoo was fun if tiring. Every step was up or down winding ramps on a steep hillside above the harbor. I was particularly intrigued by a cassowary bird that looked eerily like Estelle Winwood. It should've been in costume for *The Madwoman of Chaillot*. In fact, it was.

Instead of going back to Sydney from the zoo, we took a different ferry and got off at the Amusement Park.

During *Summer of the Seventeenth Doll* we'd shot a long sequence there. It was as tawdry as ever, with the same grotesque entrance. A gigantic fat woman's head through whose open mouth one walked to the recorded din of cackling, whooping laughter. Somehow walking into that phony grin with Katrina sent my spirits below zero.

What a contrast, I thought, fingering my tight-shut ego like an old gold watch. Was it a comedown or a comeuppance? Staring at the garbage in the waters of the Tunnel of Love, I conjured up the four of us: Ernest Borgnine, John Mills, Angela

298

Lansbury, and I, riding and squealing with fake excitement, toward camera and blazing lights through take after take on a muggy midnight. Might as well have happened on the moon, although the garbage remained the same. Katrina and I had blended into the candy-smeared country gawkers seeking the sights.

My mind wandered as we did. Just recognized enough to ruin lunch. But not enough to be asked to work at something good, said an inner voice. There you go again—isn't your family good enough? My family was far better than good enough, but I missed my work. Charles Laughton's "Work!" There were things inside me that wouldn't come out any other way. And if they did, they were deformed and dangerous like cornered rats are dangerous. Katrina had stopped and was watching me. I must have been scowling.

"Are you mad at something, Mom?"

I laughed a short laugh. "No, did I look like that?"

She smiled cautiously.

"My feet hurt. I guess I have zooitis. Come on, sweetheart, let's go have some fried John Dory in Rose Bay, they won't bug us there. I'm just plain Mrs. Galt at the fried fish place. Besides, it's six o'clock. We have to get to bed early; that overgrown streetcar of a train leaves at seven A.M."

Watching the countryside go by the next morning, I thought about Katrina's "exposure" to opera or music or ballet. Or theater. They were occasionally available at certain seasons, but how could we get to them? She'd be an hour or so south of Sydney; I was five hours north, after I made it to Worcester. Ran increasingly skipped Sydney's allure, and it was now clear the plane was too expensive to be used for anything but business or emergency. There was the usual nasty twinge about Katrina going away at all. A good Australian country mother could have taught her at home. I had wondered sometimes about living in Sydney and going to Giro for a month or so at a time. My mother had often presented that to me as the only salvation. Ran would've hated it and, in a way, so would Katrina. Giro's uninhibited outdoors fed them both; the only fences were the ones you built yourself.

Katrina left at the end of January just as branding was about to start. To free me to see her off, Ran took over Melissa for the weekend, armed with a pile of heavily underlined yellow sheets of instructions to rival Dr. Spock. Hugh Aildred drove us to the train.

Tears welled as I hugged her good-bye in Sydney's Union Station and watched her sturdy dark green back disappear into a bobbing throng of other green-clad backs, small, medium, and large. The youngest was six. Katrina was ten and a half. I felt like a cow watching her first calf trucked off to market. The train slipped away and as I turned to walk back down the platform I realized Angela Lansbury and I had played our first scene in the film in that exact spot three years before. What a flip-flop my life had performed. Perhaps that explained the somersault in my chest.

At cattle sales they always described calves weaned from their mothers as weaners. Suckling calves were deemed to be "at foot." I always thought it should have been "at teat." But they'd announce, "Heifer with first calf *at foot!*" Come on, I scolded myself, your weaner's gone; back to the calf at foot.

As Ran had promised, he'd searched again for help in the house. We awaited a Mrs. Bundy. Like Miss P of the shoes, Mrs. Bundy wasn't used to "this kind of work" either.

It's a puzzle to understand the basic Aussie attitude toward working *for* anyone; there's a chip like a national badge. Sam Pugh had it. Australia was the most powerfully unionized country in the world; I suppose you'd call that a bigger, more organized chip. National epaulets? It's the only country where I've had tips refused in quick temper. They wanted to do a favor. The tip made it seem like a service. Dirty word.

I wondered about its origin. A throwback of two hundred years to a tight-knit British society sending them packing to the ends of the earth and devil take the hindmost? The feeling of being so far removed from their roots that nobody gave a tinker's dam and Bob's your uncle to you, too?

There's a feeling for Americans because we've made it on our own, but they feel too, I think, that we're so filthy rich now that we may be straddling the enemy Establishment fence. So they are disposed, but leery. The Second World War helped both sentiments. We were a thumping help, but our boys were loaded with cash, breeding hearty ambivalence and busted marriages. Mrs. Bundy carefully explained she'd been forced to work for us through misfortune. She'd been divorced and ends had to be met. And, there was Grant. Grant was four; wiry and dirty. We gave them the cottage, but unhappily, in order for her to work, he had to come with her. He never did figure out the labyrinth of Giro and was a perpetual lost chord in room after room hunting Mum. "Mum! *Mum!* MUM." He wore a faded bikini and avoided me like the plague, been given the word.

Mrs. B had a nice face. Eyes, nose, mouth, ears, and hair, but nothing in particular. Like a seven-year-old's drawing of a person.

Every morning she'd sit across from Grant at the round wooden table in the kitchen, a cigarette in one hand and a two-foot plastic strap in the other. Fortunately her aim was bad.

Mrs. B: (slap) Eat your cereal.

Grant: No.

Mrs. B: (slap) Did you hear me, Grant?

Grant: I want a banana.

Mrs. B: (slap) Eat your cereal. You had a banana.

Grant: I want a banana.

Mrs. B: (slap) Did you hear me, Grant?

Ad nauseam. The drops of water on our morning brains.

Grant would eat two things, cheese and bananas. He drank orange juice and bottles and bottles of sticky sweet drinks in violent colors and, occasionally, milk. He ate nine bananas one day, and since Melissa's only fruits then were applesauce and bananas, which came with the mail twice a week, I hid them in a drawer. His cries then alternated between "Mum!" and "I want a banana! "

Where the tuna things started I don't know. Mrs. Bundy made a fantastic variety of tuna things: tuna loaf, cold or hot; tuna jellied; tuna creamed; tuna soufflé; tuna sandwiches; tuna mince; tuna salad, garni. I never asked her to; she just did. We never ate them and it took ingenuity to throw them out for Freeda without visible signs and hurt feelings. One day I was cooking chicken paprika and flew to the sink to rinse a dish. Sitting in two inches of water was a saucepan half-filled with yellowish stuff. Thinking she'd left it to soak, I sloshed it with fast

301

water, dumped it, emptied the sink, and ran back to my skillet. A loud cry of dismay whirled me around.

"My tuna soufflé," she wailed. The funny thing was she never ate any of it either.

Our first breakfast I'd planned very simply: seven fifteen (late for Ran, but he'd been out and had come back), orange juice, scrambled eggs, and toast. I'd made early coffee and had given Melissa her bottle. At eight we all sat, staring at one another listening to unfathomable chopping noises and to Grant prattling on and on. Melissa was entranced by Grant. I went out finally to discover Mrs. Bundy lovingly mincing a sizable pile of parsley.

"Mrs. Bundy," I said, "Mr. Galt has to go. Could he have his eggs, please?"

She smiled patiently and stated patronizingly that you couldn't have scrambled eggs without chopped parsley, could you? I said yes, we really could. At eight thirty we were brought nice dry mounds of yellow, sporting flecks of green, which Melissa instantly spanked and squeezed through clenched fingers.

I remained cook.

The end came when Grant's eternal frustrations drove him outside to shadow Ran. Ran and his grubby disciple. Poor Grant became a living question mark with a whole male all to himself, to Ran's sympathetic exasperation.

And so Mrs. Bundy and Co. wended their way into the sunset.

302

39

Blue Jeans and Sunday School

OLD WILL's triumphant new yards at Corroborree, nine miles up, were ready for action. Something about the Aildreds made branding a family affair. Mrs. Mac, her daughter Sheila Blackburn, and Joan the Good all brought lunch, and sometimes tea and cakes, to their men—children packed in next to the baskets. Mrs. Bundy had stayed just long enough for me to leave Melissa for a couple of hours here and there, and I went up, too. I'd use up our last sliver of ice in lemony clove-spiced tea. Ran loved it. The men disdained it—"A nice drink. But tea, never!"

Manpower was in short supply in the Australian bush. Our branding and yearly muster of approximately 2,700 cows and calves was well handled at Giro with five or six men. They rope not, neither did they throw. They use dogs and yards; especially the fine new ones at Corroborree, whose logs were magnificently hand-felled, hauled, cut and let-in by Old Will. And narrow cattle races, and rough, tough "cradles," cushioned by discarded tires, for the actual branding and castrating. Old Will was surgeon with a trusty pocket knife. Females were branded and dehorned if they were judged good enough to join the herd. Ran disliked horns and Giro couldn't afford a polled herd. Polled meaning bred hornless.

Ran chose the job of burning the brand, VIP, and stoking and fanning the ferocious branding fire, a sickeningly hot job in late January heat. I'd pull up the long, steep hill in Rover to see him waxen with heat and fatigue and would try to sluice his blistering neck over the fence until he could break away from his human rotisserie.

With our owner's tag, Ran indicated it behooved us to lunch on our own. At baking noon we'd lurch in Rover down to the river where Ran walked slowly in, clothes and all, his eyes half-shut in wordless bliss. I'd watch him stretch out flat to lie in water coursing over him to the lips, gulping it as it flowed.

If they were nearing the last calves of the day and if it wasn't time to get back to Melissa, I'd stay to hear the big shout, "Right! Mother 'em up!" The last bloody and bawling calf would be freed from his iron maiden of a cradle and skitter, each leg pointing furiously in a different direction, tongue blathering in panic, on the hunt for mother. She'd be looking for it too, *maw maaowing* like a battered trombone. They always came together. A miracle. Scent, I was told. A computer would have broken down in that deafening animal mass boiling with dust, but cows find their own unerringly.

Old Will would carefully wipe his knife on his trousers and over raunchy jokes, they'd roast testicles over the tag end of the branding fire. Roast stones, they called them. Bush wives wouldn't allow roast stones over the threshold. Ran brought me a cartonful which, after a little head-scratching, I sautéed. Quenelles of sweetbreads? Kind of. Melissa enjoyed them too.

Branding was over.

The shipment of apartment things had been deposited there and left in cartons. Ran couldn't have cared less. It was a topic to be avoided. I'd planned to tackle the situation on my first trip down to see Katrina.

We'd had a first glowing letter from her saying she'd been assigned a horse and that she'd comforted a younger child who'd been very homesick. So far so good.

Melissa's American screened crib, feeding chair (actually a seat surrounded by a formica table on wheels), and clothes were finally being delivered with the mail. What a relief. She was growing out of everything except diapers, which is all she'd been wearing much of the time.

Ran had just flown back from Sydney from a conference with

304

George Peckett, planning on how many wieners and when they'd be sold, I supposed. I hoped the large cartons sitting in the apartment hadn't annoyed Ran too much, and wondered how soon I could visit Katrina without hovering. Perhaps Sister Isabella could come for a long weekend, or some local girl, to help with Melissa once in a while.

After supper Ran suggested for the next day a drive up to the ghost gum forest high above Giro's valley. I'd never been, and accepted with enthusiasm, provided, of course, Joan or possibly Mrs. Mac could watch Melissa.

"How long would we be gone, Ran?" I asked eagerly.

"Oh, maybe three hours or so."

I knew him. I'd better make that four. With half an hour's grace like a parking ticket. I wanted to go badly.

"The forestry people are extending the forest track up there. I'd like to take a look," he added. "Early?"

"Sure, early as you like!" I thought a minute. "It's only eight thirty, let me go across and talk to Joan," I said intensely, figuring how much time I could beg.

"Want the flashlight?"

"No," I shouted over my shoulder as I charged out the side door. "Moonlight's terrific!"

"OK." He grinned as he watched me leaping over the hundred yards of grass and weeds toward the Aildreds. As usual she was her generous self and said she had laundry and gardening enough to be housebound until noon. I'd bring Melissa over in her carriage at seven A.M. with everything necessary for her until eleven. Since I didn't impose often, Joan seemed genuinely delighted. Watching David and Janie put Melissa in a trance broken only by shrieks of exultation.

The next morning I literally threw breakfast dishes in and out of the sink. Melissa was changed in thirty seconds, in her carriage, and over at Joan's by six fifty-five. Her painted wooden mobile clacked in the breeze above the mosquito netting and she smiled me good-bye with a fat foot in one fist.

Ran was in Rover and waiting in front as I slammed out the veranda and down the steps. Halfway to the vehicle he called, "Better grab a jacket, it's colder up there."

"Right." Oh, damn, I forgot the thermos. I slammed back up

through the veranda to the kitchen, got the waiting thermos of coffee, ran to my closet, pulled a jacket down, ran out the door, down the steps, and out again to Rover, heaving with exertion.

"Relax," he said lazily. "We're not going on safari."

"*You're* not," I remarked through lessening huffs, "but *I* am!"

Ghost gums. What would they be like? I'd heard they were as gigantic as their native continent.

"I'll get it!" I cried and jumped out of the still-rolling Rover as we came down to Giro gate. Not because I liked to open gates, always a crashing bore, but because if Ran did it he'd leave the vehicle in gear and there you sat, rolling on down the hill, nervously ready to scramble over knobs and levers to the wheel just short of runaway disaster. Another quirk of his I'd learned to cope with by simply cheerfully saying, "I'll get it!" and jumping out. Girl Scout credit was a dividend.

"Look!" he exclaimed. "Mountain larries." And I followed his tilted chin with my eyes. There they were. A chittering bunch of them perched on the crags of a wild lemon tree.

"Aren't they something!" I said breathlessly, watching their ravishingly feathered brilliance flicker in the sun. God, what a day! What a magical day. All to ourselves with a new sight ahead.

I climbed back into Rover, feeling as if we weren't married yet and I was meeting Giro again for the first time. Same blue jeans, looser now. I'd been quite slim without effort since Melissa.

Those blue jeans. I really had stolen them from *Yellow Sky*. Excellent picture. They'd had to buy me boy's jeans size 29—you wore them slung low on your hips. No one knew then what a fashionable explosion Levi's would become. These had old-style copper rivets and were early chic: blue-gray boiled suede.

Yellow Sky was another picture I wasn't supposed to do. Somebody else was cast—Zanuck had a tiff with her or some such tangle—and they called me. After all, I was under contract. Would I be flown in Twentieth Century-Fox's Beechcraft Bonanza to Death Valley for a test? Yes, I would indeed.

It was 122° at high noon on the salt flats. They sat me on the salt in these very jeans. The photographer, Joe MacDonald, all encrusted with peeling sunburn and melted Noczema, looked through his black filter monocle. William Wellman, "Wild Bill" they called him, said, "All right, now, let's get this!" Almost no makeup. Hair kind of nothing, no time. They were shooting in infrared film for high contrast and had put a smidgin of brown lipstick on my mouth. Reds didn't show up. My character's name was Mike. I got the part.

Bill, as he rapidly became to me, was in a lather because Zanuck wanted the horses in the same state.

"Jesus Christ! He wants the goddamned horses with foam on 'em. Jesus Christ! Doesn't he know the goddamned horses can't sweat in this fucking dry heat! Send him a goddamned wire and tell him to stuff his fucking soapsuds!" He fumed, stalking up and down on the salt, shock of white hair whipping in the fierce, ovenlike wind over his Indian-dark furrowed brow. Sharp blue eyes squinted with honest fury. "Shit," he growled. "We're gonna do it right. We're gonna do it like we've *been* doin' it!"

He cupped a strong, bony hand over the "elbow" of the leather brace on his right arm. He'd broken it so many times that arthritis had had its way with the joint.

It was love at first sight between Bill Wellman and me. He knew I was game for damned near anything, and tough enough physically to do just that. I knew he only asked people he liked, or hated, to put out that much. With Bill it was easy to tell the difference. Did we work like hell and did we have fun! No wonder I stole those pants. Had to have something close to remember an experience that good.

I was married to John Hodiak then. He came up to Lone Pine, at the foot of towering Mt. Whitney, where the company had moved from Death Valley. We stayed in the motel everybody else was in. Our room turned out to be on the highway. All the huge trucks from up and down the state of California revved their engines and shifted three gears as they negotiated the curve outside our window. Sleep was catch as catch can.

Those jeans. I had several pairs; possible attrition had to be planned for. Halfway through a sequence I'd be sent to the one-holer to change into nice, newly boiled ones. Gad. I needed a shoehorn. The new ones always developed kidney fat where there really wasn't any. I'd walk out sucking in my belly and

307

hoping nobody would notice the bulge riding out just over the belt behind. It wouldn't've matched the shot before.

Nobody would've believed the lips on Gregory Peck. The makeup man had laboriously made them out of collodion and tissue paper. They were hanging in disgusting tatters as he tried to hold me down and kiss me while I fought lying on my back in the shredded donkey dung of the corral, during our madly ambivalent love scene. Always a gentleman, he apologized as we panted between takes. I said, "Nothing to it, Greg. If I eat some, I'll just spit it out and they'll think I'm being sexy, OK?" He laughed and on we went.

One afternoon there was a drowning. It was in the script. Somebody had to try to drown somebody, and I was supposed to come to save them. To my peril of course. It was rough. No doubles. Bill had sent them packing. He was right, they were anemic. What he wanted were actors who could lose themselves. He got them. The two actors were submerged back and forth and finally the water was still. One of them almost drowned. The horrid feel of stiff, wet jeans is still clear in my memory.

William Wellman was vastly interesting to me because he represented "Hollywood," quote unquote. He had been there early. He was imbued with all the early razz-ma-tazz and still had, in his unique way, as much talent at making film as anybody I'd ever worked with. Thirty-five setups; meaning camera, lights, actors, crew, and horses—the lot; and five car-driven moves in one day. All well directed, all beautifully chosen, all well acted. Try that for size. Over dread terrain—and hot.

He made no bones about having once been a periodic alcoholic. After three or four marriages (even *he* wasn't sure) he'd married an Irish beauty, twenty-five years or so younger. She immediately proceeded to have one child right after the other. She had great faith in her way of fighting his propensity for an occasional three-week bender. She turned out to be right.

When there were three on their feet, one in a crib, and one to come (I think the oldest was seven) the seven-year-old and two younger ones got their father out by an oleander bush:

"Daddy, at school they say you're a drunk. Are you?"

"No," replied Wild Bill. And that blew the whistle on the benders. What a man! What a woman!

Bill taught me how to throw a punch. Greg Peck was pretty tall. The first go I missed him. The second time I missed him again and ended up on the ground. ("Put your *back* into it, Annie!") The third time around I got him, and though it must have felt like a fleabite, old-school-tie Greg went down like a nice actor.

"What?" I said dreamily.

Ran raised his voice. "I said, *we're going up* ." I glanced at him. He was looking sidelong at me.

"You mean up to the gums, the ghost gums?" I asked.

"Yes, the next turn we climb toward the trees. This is Peachtree Cutting."

I looked. Still Australia's bland palette. Slightly deeper green up ahead. Australia's basic palette is jejune; overexposed color film on a sun-shy day. Sallow ochers, etiolated greens, blues, and chromes, making man-grown greens bright as jewelry, the eye-smarting lime of Giro's mandarin willows, and the birds, even more gorgeous than they are. Birds are Australia's most boisterous pigment and win a natural victory over dust-tinted land.

Flocks of scarlet and blue-violet parrotlike mountain larries, in a pale tree knocked your eye out; or four and twenty budgerigars perched on a weathered fence, turquoise, aquamarine, citric-yellow, and cobalt. Even audacious crazy quilts of black and white magpies are brassier than usual. And clouds of two-inch redheaded finches polka-dot hedges and mangy grass with crimson.

The remote Giros themselves are curved out of heavy French satin. Purple-black. I saw them only once; eight or nine swooping in quintessential grace through young gums; and heard low discreet whistles as they passed. The imperial signature caught my breath.

As we entered the forest I thought I heard them. Startled, I began to listen hard, mouth open in concentration. The mountain gums were alive with bell-birds pricking the atmosphere with tuning forks. They hid their tiny, mossy-green bodies like hundreds of Tinkerbells, until the scimitar of vermilion slashing across their eyes caught yours. I'd heard and seen Willie Wagtails ride the cows, frosted gingersnaps, their tails wagging impudence; and the surprise parties of wild parrots in bawdy cerise, gold, puce, and paris green were a flagrant paradox. This was different. Knowing all of it made me again conscious that Giro was a place in the world I'd never truly share with anybody but Ran, or Katrina or Melissa.

The dirt road grew soft and dark from moist forest floor. I shrugged deeper into my jacket. The air was cool and dark from the amazing columns of gums. They were aptly named ghosts. Smooth and pale-skinned, they rose in silent splendor hundreds of feet into the mountain air to branch in the far-up sun. No underbrush. Only the brown furred stalks of thirty-foot tree ferns, slim Gothic pillars among the thick columnar trunks.

"Ran, could we stop a second? I want to walk in it," I pleaded, lost in contemplation.

"Sure," he answered placidly, obviously calmed by the refreshment of that extraordinary forest. He rolled to a stop and turned the engine key. It was a shame to break that waiting silence with the smallest word. Fern mold made one's feet absolutely soundless. It was a cathedral. The bell-birds could have been boy sopranos in a distant choir stall. It had been too long since I'd been in a church. This was a church, and satisfied my soul. After an awed moment, I shut my eyes, folded my hands, and thanked God for the quality of my life, my husband and my children, and the ability to sense that very quality. I opened my eyes and leaned my head back, trying to penetrate that dizzying living roof.

"Sweetheart?" Ran spoke without effort; sound carried in God's auditorium.

"Yes?" My voice sounded funny coming out of a throat bent back.

"We should go."

"I know." I brought my head back to normal, looking for him. He was yards away by Rover, watching me. I came to him without a word. We got in the vehicle and sat for a second, staring at nothing.

"It's like some undiscovered planet," I said quietly.

"Yes." He turned the engine key but didn't start it. He was as loath as I was to destroy that majestic peace. "I've often thought of having a cabin up here, for when it's broiling down below," he said.

"Maybe we could, The girls should see this—what a place for Sunday school." He started the engine and we rolled down the primitive track.

That's another something to be confronted, I thought. Sunday school. If my piano ever came down, I could learn to play hymns, and Bible stories were already at hand. What was I, anyway? I smiled to myself. Part Presbyterian; part Druid. I'd attended many types of churches, even mosques and temples. I suppose I tried to be plain everyday Christian, the most difficult to live, but the most replenishing.

40

Maintenance

RELIGIOUS education at Giro was not the only contretemps to be faced head-on. Something else to be faced was my face.

Slobovia always threatened women who lived in the bush, and I was no exception. Ran was used to spruce ladies, and between Giro and motherhood I had certainly lost gloss. Mirrors were frequently painful, expecially since I'd been crushingly conditioned by that Hollywoodsy theme: "How does she look?" Talent was down the line.

Marilyn Monroe instinctively knew that. I heard she wore her braless pink angora sweater into the Twentieth Century-Fox commissary for lunch one day. Ben Lyon, who was then head of casting, saw her and came over, waggling his finger. "Now, Marilyn, honey," he admonished severely, "now don't wear things like that. After all, honey, you want to be thought of as a *serious* actress!" She'd evidently looked crestfallen and, as he left, commented in a voiceful of feathers, "I guess he doesn't like pink!" Marilyn knew what she was about.

Like a cracked record it went on and on—"You look marvelous, darling," "Looking great, sweetheart," or, "What's she look like *now*?" Makeup men and hairdressers had clucked and shrugged for years over my obviously mediocre material. Baby-fine mouse-brown hair, upturned knob at short nose's end, small mouth ("We'll have to build up that upper lip, hon"). I'd done the best I could with all of it, but had had plentiful expert help. Giro offered zero, except for a superannuated hair dryer

Ran had flown up at my earnest request when we first came.

Alfred Hitchcock had turned me blond for *I Confess,* and I'd stayed that way, at considerable cost in time and money and effort, until *The Ten Commandments* three years later. At which point, Cecil B. De Mille turned me auburn. The use of henna was prevalent in Egypt, and I was to play Egyptian Nefertiti's granddaughter Nefertiri. Actually I wore several wigs, but the picture went on so long I got used to myself reddish.

I took a cut in salary to work for De Mille; a lot of actors did; he seemed to expect it as a kind of due. There was only one De Mille and there wasn't an actor in the world who didn't want to work for him just once, however short the salary or tall the corn. I could still picture Angela Lansbury coyly running around in chiffon skivvies, letting arrows fly at the back end of a lion skin tacked on a patio wall in *Samson and Delilah.* I always thought that looked like good fun.

Edith Head and I really got to know each other during *The Ten Commandments.* We had fittings on the unbelievably extravagant costumes for over a period of eight *months.* I made two other pictures in between fittings. Our most serious problem regarding the costumes was what to wear underneath. Egyptians wore nothing. I was too full-breasted to go without a brassiere, so we settled for a skin-dyed bra and a skin-dyed G-string. Both Edith and De Mille were sticklers for authenticity. Even the toothbrush I was to use in my opening scene was a frayed stick. I remember how worried Edith and I were at the preliminary showing of the first finished costume.

De Mille always insisted on a private showing in Edith's inner sanctum flanked by aides-de-camp—meaning Henry Wilcoxon in thick crepe soles, a secretary, and a studio photographer. We were justifiably worried because I was damned near naked under knife-pleated chiffon; body makeup or no body makeup. It was well known that De Mille had a foot fetish and I had artistically rouged my bare feet (not my best feature) in their handcrafted jeweled sandals.

Not much was said in front of me. They adjusted spectacles and peered a lot. They made one truly memorable wardrobe still. It was taken from behind, as I self-consciously posed

313

against the fitting room door and looked coquettishly back through a foot and a half of dark red wig. Subsequently that shot, in which everything was visible *except* the G-string, was surreptitiously reprinted and widely circulated through the studio, to my embarassment.

Edith and I were sent back to the old drawing board and firmly counseled regarding modesty versus authenticity.

I can still see Sir Cedric Hardwicke sweating copiously in what he bitterly called his plastic beanie, which was two feet tall. He played the old Pharaoh Seti. And Yul Brynner, expressionlessly arrogant, thrusting out his arm with first and second fingers open in a victory sign, into which his trembling body servant slid a lighted cigarette. Regal Yul never, ever looked around. That used to really impress De Mille. There was always a kind of hush on the set no matter how crowded or huge.

The first day we shot together, Charlton Heston and I had a passionate love scene. It was very quiet. I knelt by the right side of his bared chest as he reclined on an Egyptian version of a Récamier couch. The camera shot across his pectorals at my adoring, upturned face. He had an admirable amount of chest hair, I noted. We rehearsed for about half an hour. Mr. De Mille helped me up off my cramped knees and Heston mysteriously disappeared.

An hour later he returned to the hush of the set—without a chest hair. Nothing whatever was said. I learned later all you could see was my nose peeking over the curly mass, like the moon coming over the mountain. Goodness, the elaborate care given a De Mille player; the meticulous attention to the thousandth detail. Early in the morning the wardrobe girl even warmed my deep, flat enameled collars before reverentially clasping them in place. She was so right. My bosom ran to gooseflesh if she didn't. And gooseflesh was all wrong for Cecil B. De Mille's very own Egypt. "Oh, Lord," I said with a laugh as I faced Giro's nicked, grayish mirror. "Nobody knows. Nobody really knows what it's like unless they've been there."

I let Katrina come on the set one day. She was about five and a half years old and I thought it might be fun for her. It was a scene fraught with melodrama. I was the villainess of the piece, in pleated silver lamé, purple cape, and authentic horsehair whip. At first she admired Mommy's beautiful costume. We shot the scene in which Queen Nefertiti, jealous me, tries to steal Moses' son from Moses' wife by pretending to take him to safety. Yvonne de Carlo, the wife, is understandably furious, clasps her child-actor in horror and shows me the door of the hut. Cut. I searched for Katrina. I could see her face, a pale egg of distress. I came over to her beyond the camera. She looked up at me, hurt and confused. "Why doesn't that lady *like* you?" she whispered. "She's not supposed to," I whispered back. "It's just part of the story, dear." She looked anxious, unconvinced, unhappy, and never asked to come again. The gulf between real and unreal, mother and actress, always upset her.

During *Cimarron* , a hairdresser at MGM had offered step-by-step instructions on how to apply henna every six weeks—couldn't hurt, might help mouse brown.

Hair coloring was planned carefully. Before Melissa, afternoons were choice; warmer and quieter. Melissa's routine eliminated daytimes. So it wasn't until a Wednesday night in early February that I got to my hair. It was about time. And it was already six fifteen P.M. Dark descended on the heels of six thirty, but Ran or Hugh Aildred would turn on the engine when they rode in around seven and candles were atmospheric for a while.

I had been saving newspapers from mail days, leftover Dirty Annie (Resch's Dinner Ale) was secretly stored in an empty jam jar for hair set. As soon as Melissa's screened crib was snapped shut (too cold for mosquitoes but not for rats), I ran and held a match to my bathroom's gas heater.

Balancing the ale, the newspapers, a chipped enamel pot, and a kettle of boiling water, I closeted myself. Newspapers and the precious flat beer both deposited on the toilet seat cover, I set the kettle and pot in the bathtub, and began.

First, the sky blue rug was rolled up, revealing ancient and embarrassingly gritty lino, splotched with thick white paint left over from Projects X, Y, and Z, and covered it with newspapers like lining a cake tin.

Just when I wanted them to be late, the engine racketed, telling me the men were back. I ran out to the record machine and piled on a stack of buttery music to strip to. Back in the bathroom I took off all my clothes, retrieved the kettle from the tub, and stirred a viscous mess of pulverized henna and steaming water in the cracked pot with a rescued paintbrush, feeling like a rapt witch whose bosoms bobbled unheeded.

Thick enough? Too thick? Directions scramble me. More water. Damn. Too much. It'll crawl. More henna. Looks good. Looks like— Oh, well, never mind what it looks like. Applying it is a nearsighted, frowning job.

Next, remove jar of Dirty Annie from seat cover to washbasin and choose a random sheet of Sydney's *Morning Herald* from the floor and sit reading until the glutinous sauce crusts. Fifteen minutes later I poked a somewhat wizened scalp under the shower and switched the water off five minutes after that.

Two minutes to stir, five minutes to paste on, ten or fifteen minutes of henna, five minutes to shower, and sixteen minutes to clean it all up.

A discreet knock halted the cleanup squad of one rustling among the newspapers. The newspapers crunched as I stepped to the door.

"Darling? You're back!"

"Yes," he called through the door. "Would you like a dressing drink?"

Dressing? I surveyed skin and boiled pumpkin hands and wet reddish hair on a drowned rat. "Sounds divine!" And as sleek jazz seeped under the bathroom door, I paraded gleefully, two feet in each direction, feeling like a single spot in a girlie show. Too many times that purple mood would ignominiously meet sudden death in a skid and a pratfall on gummed-up newspapers. Cursing, I wildly wadded them into a clump, which was cravenly shoved onto the adjacent frigid sleeping porch, and tugged and fitted the jelly roll of rug once again.

Another discreet knock. "Madame! Your potion awaits without."

A blue towel was swathed instantly with careless artistry around a gorgeous, luscious, irresistible body and I opened the door; just a little. Ran looked approving and inquisitive and set a beaded glass in an outstretched hand.

"Randolph, you are a gentleman and a scholar. Thank you."

316

"Think nothing of it." He smiled. An agreeably cheeky smile. "What are you doing?"

"Oh, nothing much. I won't be long."

He checked the dripping walls and tub, luckily clean by that time. "I think I'll have a shower too."

God! I wondered if there was any hot water left. "Wonderful, love. See you anon!" And inched the door closed.

Quickly, before he comes back, toenails. After a hurried sip of the tinkling drink, I put it carefully on the toilet seat cover and located the surgeon's kit of implements to be dumped on the rug. Contorting in all the neck-creaking positions necessary to toenails, I clipped and they flew. Every wicked little tool bit and scooped and dug, smoothed and rasped, very professional. Last came hasty slathers of iridescence on the toenails and haggard fingernails, and what ladies' magazines call a hint of cologne. Only I drenched in it; from a necklace of scent to slaps and swipes along bare arms and thighs. Good thing I picked cologne, perfume would have asphyxiated me in there.

Seated tailor-fashion, I sipped the drink, delighting in the music, while the lacquer dried. I soaked in the warmth of the heater, drowsy with well-being, to say nothing of relief at hearing no injured shouts from across the house. The water had held out. I was without stain, save the henna.

A third discreet knock. "Anne?"

"Yes. How was your shower?"

The door swung open. "Sensational."

"Come on in, I'm just drying my polish. And please shut the door—it's freezing out there."

He closed the door and lounged against it while I looked up and he looked down.

"You smell very nice."

"Black Narcissus. Thank you for it again!"

And there we'd be, chatting idly, his blue sweater glowing in quivering patches and slices of orange gaslight.

What was it about Giro? There were times when insanity became indestructible. Perhaps to fully roll a droplet of luxury under the tongue, one must needs have experienced its absence.

As the Red Queen chides Alice, you have to run hard to stay where you are, and twice that fast to get anywhere else. I

317

pumped and puffed after all forms of maintenance at Giro, but finishing off the gadflies of Projects K, Q, and W were beyond me. I can hammer a nail back in, but I'm no carpenter.

Big Bertha had replaced a wood stove that had formerly been next to the kitchen fireplace, leaving a broken, gaping hole six by five by three feet. Ran saved five or six different magazines, from the *Yale Review* to *Cattle Breeding*. I can't resist pocket editions of Tacitus or *Quick Swahili,* poetry, plays, or anything fun to read. I love books. We were almost without shelves and cupboards. Quilty had ruined a precious Mexican chair to add to a vexing accumulation of postponed repairs, including a roof and gutters that looked increasingly like the rims of my crudely crimped pies. Hugh Aildred promised rescue in a name, Prosper Bowdoin, if we could get him. After five months of last-minute sorry-can't-make-its, he appeared out of Queensland. Houdini in the bush.

Have you ever had a French-Canadian draft horse in your kitchen? Prosper Bowdoin was inordinately proud of his stock and resonant about it. He occupied Quilty's old room and I fed him lunch and "tea," meaning supper. Joan the Good shouldered breakfast, and got a whole new veranda.

Mr. Bowdoin unwittingly inveigled me into cooking Australian. He ate such prodigious amounts and I had so much else to do, I boiled and fried pounds of potatoes and pieces of meat the size of table tops. It was simply a question of filling a void. One night I eyed the pile of steak Ran had cut for both of Prosper's feeds the next day and cooked it all for "tea." He ate every scrap; six slices of town bread, seven potatoes, and a slab of pie with cheese, all the while regaling me with tales of his Norman forebears. It was a privilege to watch a man eat like that.

Mr. Bowdoin's ingenuity was spellbinding. I'd outline some impossible wish, off he'd go, back in a flash with just the thing. Niches, shelves, magazine racks, gun cases, or wig stands were created out of the hoarded packing case pine rescued from my sea shipments. Even Quilty's crashed chair came in handy. He sawed shelves and fitted them in the gaping stove hole, and we used the bright Mexican chair rungs as bars in a double door.

The spectacle of Mr. Bowdoin put me to work on project W. The louvers. There were 246 I wanted to switch to clear glass in

318

four of the sleeping porches, the kitchen, and laundry. I was determined to look out of my house.

All you had to do was measure them and order the amounts and sizes from Yates & Twomey. Watch that ring at the end of a steel tape. It means an additional inch, I found to my dismay. Every bank of six were a different size: 2'⅜" or 2'⅓", or 23¼", or 25". The day they came, Prosper helped me scratch out the old ones. O misery; O breathed four-letter words—I'd missed that inch on every one. Couldn't send them back, take weeks. A call to Yates & Twomey. They kindly suggested a glass cutter and Prosper said he'd show me. Ashamed before his ingenious self, I agreed. I cut all 246 louvers, only fracturing ten beyond recall and fitted them everywhere.

He showed me how to thump a stencil, too. You just wad a soft cloth over cotton batting, dip in very little paint, and thump. GIRO got thumped on anything flat. In red.

His pièce de résistance was a twenty-four-foot book and cupboard thing under the hall windows in oiled sassafras wood; and plastering in a black marble mantel we'd discovered in a junk shop in Sydney the year before. Ran had flown it up piece by piece on business trips. Now the sleeping porches were so blinding bright you needed a welder's mask. Sewing curtains was beyond me so I decided to plant trees. The forestry nurseries were a short flight, and as Ran needed shade trees for the Corroboree Yards, we could use the plane. I ordered all types of wattles and gums. They came in cigar-sized tubes, two or three leaves per tube. It'd be years before one of those tubes even chinned itself on a bottom louver. I planted them close against the porches.

You wouldn't credit it, as the Aussie says. They were above the roof in eight months—needed a machete. Plumbing was in dire straits from roots. I'd met a gum tree in action. They were bossier than curtains, but it was a nice view just the same.

Maintenance brought unexpected entertainments in which I always chose the role of a tearoomy waitress, all tiptoes and chopped-off smiles and anxious eyebrows. "Won't you have another? A little more?" Usually these were in the kitchen with bright-colored mats, wild flowers, and my absence whenever possible, so the *men could talk.*

The Plumber's Feast was representative. One hasty day a toilet snatched a diaper into Giro's snake pit of plumbing. I confessed it not and hoped against the worst. A week later everything still flushed and my lips remained sealed. Because I was feeling particularly groggy one morning, Ran got Melissa up at five thirty and came back from her bathroom with the news of what he didn't realize was diaper mishap no. 2. I sheepishly confessed my similar crime and we hoped together.

That afternoon an evil miasma fogged *my* bath (the pipes shook hands with one another along the line), and Ran telephoned Yates & Twomey. They were hardware, plumbing, machinery parts et al, in Worcester. To save time Ran flew in that Saturday morning and picked them up. It was an unspeakable job to even locate Giro's cesspool, much less the horrid diapers. The men dug noisome trenches and bucket after reeking bucket was unearthed.

It was pushing noon and the least I could offer in reparation for such a frightful morning was a decent lunch. We were at the scraps end of a carcass. Meat was out. What? Rooster soup! (With the strings out. Rooster was like cotton twine.) Plus a casserole—bubbling cheese, noodles, tomatoes, and onions—a big salad, cornbread, hot peach pie with Mrs. Mac's cream, and Ran could start them off with cold beer.

I got everything hot or cold and waited. In my best tearoom-waitress style I peeked out at those miserable, stinking guys.

"How much longer do you think, Ran?"

"Oh, about twenty minutes, I guess." He didn't sound hungry.

I was still keeping things hot or cold an hour and a half later. I knew they'd go home and tell their wives what I'd cooked; curiosity about Ran and me was still at fever pitch. That cheese *had* to bubble. I buttered the cornbread, hoping it wouldn't dry to crumbs. Good old cornbread, it was always a smash. They thought it was cake. Ran's sister sent cornmeal from Honolulu once in a while. They had only cornstarch in Australia.

At last there they came, dragging up from the stench. I beat it to a lipstick, cologne, and a comb. I couldn't have taken over four minutes.

Scurrying down the long hall, I flung open the kitchen door and viewed lunch. They were all leaning around chewing

320

mouthfuls of folded-over bread and what was left of the hunk of cheese. A pot of jam was open with a knife in it. Everything was being washed down with strong tea.

The tearoom waitress went down in flames. They turned in embarrassment as I turned to stone.

"Sorry to bother you, Mrs. Galt," said Yates.

"We'll be out of here in a second, darling," mumbled Ran through a thick mouthful of cheese and jam.

"Surry we're late, Mrs. Galt," said Twomey.

I swiveled my eyes to Ran. "There's a few things in the—"

"Oh, don't bother, sweetheart. We'll just scrounge something."

Flooded with unreasoning anger, I slammed the door, tore off my cute little apron, and beat a retreat toward the river, in tears of unsporting rage.

What was the matter with me? I sobbed to myself, tripping over Freeda's spurned orange rinds on the way to the path along the river. Those poor men slaving over a filthy job, what did they care about a fancy lunch? What were you supposedly suffering from? I berated myself. Did you want to grab a spade and join them? *No.* But couldn't I have been included in a reheated casserole at least? ran the inner argument. The instant picture of a former actress emerging from noodles and onions like a stripper from a pie began to straighten me out. I slowed down, hopping cowpats and rocks. The afternoon had been too hot for that kind of lunch anyway and rooster soup was hardly a treat.

The river was still bubbling and fast from the last of the summer rain and I wondered if we'd have a dry winter. Your face must be a mess, I thought, and found a willow tunnel to the water. Sinking ankle deep in gravel, I bent to pat water at swollen eyes. You know what's the matter with you, Mrs. G? You won't accept the dawn of unimportance. The nightingale is gone to bed. It is Giro's lark thou hearest. Shaking drops of water off my hands and running them through the hair at my temples, I turned back up from the shore through the willows to the narrow cattle path.

Refreshed by tree shade, I walked along quietly and whispered out loud, "How could those men have known you'd cast

321

them as audience for your absurd playlet?" The idea of the three of them innocently stepping into the stark drama of "The Luncheon," directed by A. B. Galt, struck me funny enough to laugh out loud. No grammar school play could have been more ridiculous. God, it was good to laugh. Slightly hysterical, I leaned against a great branch beside the path. The branch wriggled. In panic I jumped away and saw an enormous lizard, a goanna, running up the tree. It matched the branch magnificently and would stop in flight to blend instantly into scenery. Now that, I said to myself as I watched, that goanna knows what it's doing. It's not important, it just belongs where it is. The sunlight looked yellower. Melissa would be up, said the sensible part of me as I headed back. Freeda was rooting in the grass a few yards away.

"Freeda!" I yelled, feeling as light as she was not, "wait'll you wade into those slops tonight, old girl! Rooster soup!"

As I got near enough I saw Ran leaning out of the kitchen door with Melissa in his arms. I hurried toward them.

"She just woke up," he called. "Where were you?"

"Took a quick walk. Sorry."

"I didn't change her." He looked at me curiously.

"Here, I'll take her." I smiled and came puffing up to take my rosy-cheeked baby, who was wet but happy.

"I've got to fly the men back to Worcester."

"Right," I answered, taking Melissa from him. "What time do you want dinner?"

"Oh." He paused. "Not too early. Just had lunch, remember? Anything you need in town?"

"The Sydney papers?" I asked. "Mail doesn't come till day after tomorrow."

"I'll see if there's one left," he called back as he went off to the plane.

Freeda ate the feast and the toilets flushed, musical background to lesson # 7-99-F-300-J.

41

Disaster '62

LONG-DISTANCE decisions, half asleep, in cold bare feet, are a bad idea. My agent, Arthur Park, never did get it into his head we were tomorrow and seven hours earlier. As usual he just picked up a handy Beverly Hills phone and said "Get me Anne Baxter—" He'd get me: at two or four or twelve fifteen in the morning, with a headful of boiled macaroni instead of brains.

I'd been offered a film called *Mix Me a Person*. The picture was thoroughly English and to be made in London. I'd already refused it twice and had dismissed the idea. The script was fair and I felt it was parochially English to the point of not being of the slightest interest to American audiences. The part was interesting: a well-bred woman psychiatrist working with tough juveniles. The studio was amazingly insistent. Their offers grew and grew, so much so I was forced to reconsider it. Myriads of questions floated in my mind. Had the plane been paid for yet, or even the D-6? The weaned calves wouldn't be sold for a good while. Could I help if and when needed? I'd spied Cessna brochures on Ran's desk again, these for smaller, less expensive planes, using 80-octane gas. He'd carped at grocery bills and chafed at my request for slipcovers made from the material I'd sent down for the apartment. Thank goodness the curtains had been made in Los Angeles and were ready to hang. Funny. Why was I so tongue-tied about Giro's finances? I suppose because all discussions regarding that subject were assiduously, almost absurdly, concealed. Any reference to money on my part elicited the same response: a curtain was jerked across an inner window. As a subject it was like living with a fully scented pet skunk; friendly if left alone.

My house had finally sold, but after all sorts of fees, real estate taxes, new roofing, and the many months of running expenses, little was left. Withholding taxes, especially as a nonresident, had slashed at my salary checks, and the cost of having Melissa, with expensive monthly bills and trips back and forth for all of us, had cut them to ribbons. Arthur had called just after midnight this morning with a titillating thought. "Why should we care about its Englishness?" he asked very directly and quite sensibly.

"But, Arthur," I argued, "nobody will even release it in America. I just know they won't," I shouted into the phone.

"What difference does it make? Take the money and run. And why don't you and Ran have a holiday in Europe after the picture? Take a break from the ranch and the cows?"

His voice implied, "Doesn't everybody take a nice European vacation?"

"It's not a ranch, it's a station," I said with an impatient snort.

"All right, station," he answered good-humoredly. "Why don't you think it over again and I'll call you back tomorrow?"

"Whose?" I replied dryly. "Yours or ours?"

"Sorry, the time thing always messes me up," said Arthur with an unruffled laugh.

"It messes *us* up, you mean," I retorted tartly.

"OK, I apologize. I'll try to remember. We'll have to let them know within twenty-four hours. And either way I'll have to call London. They're getting antsy."

"Right, Arthur, I'll give it one last, long think."

"Bye Annie, talk to you later." And he clicked off.

I thought I heard another suspicious click on the line and wondered who was listening in. There was a large selection. I hung up, hugged my robe around me, and walked slowly back to bed. Ran was awake and looked at me inquisitively.

"What's up?"

"They're crazy. They've upped the offer again—certainly not six figures, but it's a healthy amount. Arthur says they're really anxious to have me. Maybe Les Norman wants me because he directed *Summer of the Seventeenth Doll.*"

"Not a bad position." He smiled briefly. I strained to read his face in the dark. Why didn't I ever know what he was thinking behind those hooded hazel eyes? I shucked my robe, sank into bed, and pulled the covers up.

"Oh, Ran, it's just out of the question. Just imagine: I'd have to take Melissa with me; get a nanny in London; get an apartment and help, etcetera etcetera."

"How long would you be there?"

I laughed shortly. "The schedule's only thirty days, but we know about schedules, don't we."

"Maybe they'd be more precise in London," he suggested in a sleepy voice.

I let out a scornful "Ha! Are you joking? The crew stops for several tea breaks as I remember, and can quit in the middle of a shot if it's quitting time unless they *vote* not to."

"When do you have to decide?"

"By tomorrow."

"Then why decide tonight? Go to sleep and stop worrying."

I turned my head to him on the pillow. "I'll try, darling." I said, consciously straightening a puckered forehead. He turned over and went back to sleep. I didn't.

Like telephotos from Hades, in flooded my accursed mental pictures. A holiday together. As closely as we were living, we needed to be together. With me cut loose from Giro's daily grind and looking and feeling attractive. Through half-shut eyes I saw peacock-hued Venice, a mirage of unknown Dolomites, Salzburg, Chartres, Paris, Avallon, Florence, Ravenna. Infinite possibilities, infinite irresponsibility, with the one I loved. Places to revisit, with him. Places to discover, with him. Who knew, perhaps Ran and I would be able to share more things away than we did at home. None of this had anything to do with the film. The film, hard work, and separation would be the price. But what didn't have its price? Giro did. Love did. Children did. Everything. And there'd be enough money left, if I were extra careful, to bolster Giro if need be. Deep inside I longed for Ran to want to be with me the way he had before Giro.

The next morning at four A.M. we made a compound mistake. Still in a swivet of indecision and drugged with sleep, I somehow managed to get to the phone.

"What do you say, Annie?" came Arthur's cheerful voice.

"It's four o'clock in the morning." I groaned.

"Sorry, but I have to call them in London."

"Arthur, I still feel it's just too English to mean anything in America—"

He broke in. "Remember what I said? Why should you care about its Englishness?" Then Arthur took a cue from Mephistopheles.

"It's a pretty good part, don't you think?"

"Yes." Oh, God. I rubbed my eyes hard. How I detested big decisions. I even hated little ones. "Hang on, I'll talk to Ran."

He stood swaying groggily in the murky bedroom door.

Would he like us to have that kind of trip together? To places we'd been separately years before, and strange ones, too?

He said, "Why not?"—I'd take Melissa with me, there would be friends and family on the way. He'd be here at Giro for Katrina while I shot the picture, whose schedule was only thirty days. We'd have three weeks together in Europe. Twelve thousand miles would be the sugarcoated pill.

"Ran, what on earth do you think we should do?"

"How do *you* feel?"

I couldn't resist it. Satan prompted the actress buried in me and the line was: "Would you like to ride a gondola with me?"

He smiled hesitantly. "Sure."

And a warning bell was silenced as I ran barefoot to the still-swinging receiver.

"OK, Arthur, tell them yes and ask how soon I'll have to be in London."

Ran hadn't said no. Was he waiting for me to?

I called Gib Gate and arranged a special weekend off for Katrina. The only way to have a real visit was to meet in Sydney and stay at the apartment. After she'd been there just a month, I had ridden two trains down to Bowral for a Sunday visit.

She was in high gear and seemed to have taken to dormitory living with gusto. It was charming countryside and she had plenty of time to ride. She was thrilled to have friends her age and took pride in comforting the younger homesick ones. I was glad I went, but there were no facilities for visits together at school. Since I had no car, we finally ended up sitting on a grassy slope along a street on the outskirts of the small town of Bowral. Not ideal. But I left at the end of that meager Sunday together feeling she was happy and busy.

Ran and Melissa spent a third weekend together and I met Katrina at Union Station in Sydney. I'd taken the train the afternoon before so we'd have half of Friday, all of Saturday, and Sunday until four together. Then she would have to go back to school. After explaining my plans her one question was, "Do I get to go to the Sydney Show?" Meaning the famous Royal Easter Show. It was a stupendous happening once a year. Every conceivable breed of animal from all over Australia, and New Zealand as well, competed for medals and ribbons. There were polo matches, jumping contests, horse races, and lavish displays of everything from everywhere. A high and mighty animal fair.

When I had gone for the first time with Ran, I decided to dress casually and wear walking shoes. To my amazement the wives of breeders, owners, dignitaries, and their guests wore rhinestones, feathers, silk, and spike heels dyed to match. It was rather like an Australian version of Ascot Week in London. The hotels were bursting with people and parties. Ran had taken me our first year and taken Katrina the next. She'd adored it. Especially the unforgettable climax of the afternoon's competitions. What seemed like hundreds of white-coated grooms led the four-footed winners in a coiling parade. From the great gates they circled around and around until the huge arena was teeming with concentric rings of magnificent animals. The throng in the stands had been cautioned to salute them with silence, for fear of touching off the already excited creatures like short-fused dynamite. It was a breathtaking sight; pulsating wheels of ring-nosed prize bulls, cows, rams, ewes, boars, sows, snorting stallions, and mares.

Despite the comparative stillness, the intent crowd was keyed up for the chaos of stampede. When the lead animal turned at last into the center core, they all halted, paused, and switched carefully back around. The only sounds were the low grunts and cajoling of the grooms. And the living serpentine uncoiled back out the same great gates to acres of stalls beyond. The last animal disappeared, the gates swung shut, and the place went

327

mad. The band blared in a frenzy, the crowd thundered with shouts and stamping applause. The prizewinners hadn't stampeded but the humans had. It was thrilling.

"You'll go, sweetheart. Daddy'll take you, of course."

"Could I bring my new friend?"

How good that sounded. My new friend. Two little girls in tow would bore Ran, but this was important.

"I don't see why not. We'll ask her family. Doesn't she come from around Sydney?"

"I think so." Children never seem to ask pertinent questions like last names or home addresses.

We had a great time opening cartons and planning where to put things. I'd made an appointment with an electrician to re-wire the lamps for Australian voltage. He arrived early Saturday morning as Katrina and I were staggering over a crumpled sea of bright-red carpet. Because of Ran's jaundiced attitude toward apartment décor, I planned to lay the carpet myself. (I'd ripped up and thrown out the old one the morning before.) The rug was unbelievably unwieldy. As the electrician whistled at his rewiring, he looked up to see Katrina and me jumping up and down on a particularly stubborn heave of carpet. Treating the whole farcical situation like a game, he joined us kangaroos and between the three of us we pushed the carpet into corners on our knees, as red in the face as the rug, the electrician twinkling all the while. He knew my other name and was greatly amused.

Later I took Katrina to a Disney movie after which we had steaks and revoltingly sweet desserts.

Sunday we lunched with the Sweetapples. Ross had just had her first child, and they were full of plans for a house they wanted to build in Woollahra. We kissed a thousand subjects good-bye. There was never enough time. They thought Ran was marvelous to take over Melissa and I agreed. Ross mentioned a charming girl, from up around Scone, who might take over for long weekends so Ran and I could get away. She had a beautiful name—Moira Brown. We basked in their warmth until time to take Katrina to the train. She hoped she'd be back in time to feed her horse.

"Good-bye, darling," I said into her shiny brown hair as I held her firmly in my arms. "I'll bring you a new kilt from London." She looked up wistfully. "I wish you could take me to the Sydney Show."

"I know, sweetheart." My heart tightened. "So do I. We'll go next year, OK?"

"OK. 'Bye, Mommy, and have a nice time."

"I'll try. Work hard now. Mind your p's and q's." When upset, the Middle West of my birth peppered my speech. She boarded the train, turned, and waved. I blew a last kiss and the coach pulled away with a crump and a screech. I stood rooted to the platform until the tracks gleamed emptily, and walked stiffly back through the echoing station to a cab. I wished I hadn't chosen a red that bright for the carpet; every ineptly sawed edge showed. It was too late now. So were a lot of other things.

On the long trip back to Worcester I wondered if other mothers who worked felt like jugglers juggling hand grenades.

Ran hated my going. Not that he'd lied. He'd just left out the truth and I was falling headlong into the gaping trap. He punished me with silence. With what he did not do or say. I'd hear him on the phone to Worcester, shouting with camaraderie and guffaws, then he'd stroll by me without a word.

It had happened before, but this time the tide went well and truly out. This time the sand dried up and I was positive my mind's eye saw a tiny cactus poke its head up. Instant desert. He barely touched me before I left.

He flew Melissa and me to Sydney just in time to make the flight and watched with a set mouth as I walked to the plane lugging diapers, bottles, and the baby, who was a leaden wad of sunshine. I looked back at his still figure and knew beyond all doubt I was walking full speed ahead into disaster. "Disastrophe," he used to say in lighter moments. But the contracts had been signed.

Melissa was an ad man's angel baby for 12,000 miles. From the brief halt in Honolulu with the senior Galts to our visit to our Los Angeles pediatrician, who pretended to inspect her for a possible beard when I told him she'd had a meal of roast stones. Had I realized the amount of testosterone in calves' testicles? No, I hadn't. Her wings fell off upon our arrival in London, midnight our time, eight A.M. theirs. She roared, and rightly so, as cameras flashed. I covered up her carry-all and begged the jostling welcoming committee from the studio to drive us immediately to the apartment in Sloane Street. My miracle of an English friend, Lady Elizabeth Clyde, had arranged an apartment and a nurse.

The nurse quickly brought a parrot to mind. Crimson beak dusted with flour, glassy-green eyes rimmed with red. Her voice was an officious, irritating squawk. Nasty combination. I suspected Melissa and I were stuck with a classic basilisk of a nanny.

But I couldn't work without her. There was no time to make a change, and she knew it. She ran Melissa like a typical sergeant major and the baby writhed but thrived physically in healthy clockwork.

She used to watch the mail, pinning me with a plastic eye, like the bird of prey she was. "Any news of Mr. Galt? Everything all right, I hope?"

"Of course. Everything's fine," I'd lie. Snuffling around the mail the way she did, she knew damned well nothing had arrived from Australia save Katrina's highly decorated scrawls, which I devoured.

Six weeks without a word from Ran. I wrote and wrote and wrote until I felt as if I were standing tight against a refrigerator door, talking gibberish. Phone calls were hopeless. All of England seemed to do business with Australia when I could call. I'd book three or four days ahead, only to find circuits down or clogged or something dire. It was slowly hanging us.

The picture's long days leafed away like a frostbitten artichoke. It wasn't very good, or very bad. Just another nonentity. Worry ate at my innards. I felt as if I were being poisoned very carefully so no one would notice. Even the weather sickened. Not once did I see the sun that spring.

Nothing worked. Nothing. One Friday, in desperation, I fled to Paris, only to run smack into an impending general strike. Frantically I boarded the last plane back to London Saturday noon. The night before, drinking champagne alone at one A.M. in a velvet hotel room, was wretchedness. Blooming chestnuts

330

blew kisses in off my balcony but Paris that spring smiled like a Santa Claus with alum on his gums.

Saturday's mail bore fruit. Not news from Ran but from his mother and father, who would stop by London on the way to a Scandinavian cruise.

They came as I started two weeks' night shooting. Melissa was a joy to them as always, and to their delight had developed scarlet English cheeks. I couched my own dismal lack of information in asking if they knew exactly when (I should have added "if") Ran planned to come. Reservations had to be made in Venice and so on. They weren't sure.

A Honolulu girl the Galts knew well, Bobbie Atkin, was married to an American living in England. She and her husband wanted to give a party for us. Meaning the four of us. When would Ran arrive? I hedged and said I'd let them know. Finally we picked a date the weekend before filming was to finish and I prayed my jinn would materialize.

The party came and went without him.

I was reduced to sleeping pills during the long nights of work. I'm a bad day sleeper. As I padded woozily out of my cave at ten A.M. the day before the picture's end, there he was. He stood looking at me with the look of a hunter who suddenly doesn't want to shoot the deer. I let out a strangled "No!" and ran into my bath across the hall to gather my trembling wits. My shaking hands grasped the cold white china washbasin. I whirled on the tap and splashed water on my hot, salty face. After five endless minutes my bare feet turned almost by themselves and stole toward the door. I made myself open it, and stared. He was still standing in the same spot.

"Ran?" I said, choking.

He held me to him, water-spattered nylon and all. We quaked with a battalion of emotions. We'd hung separately, but not together.

Late that afternoon we were sprawled in my bedroom, the door locked against Nanny the Parrot, engrossed in watching Melissa alternately exploring and attacking a large paper bag. Moments had been so bad; this one was so good. I suppose the valleys in a marriage match the peaks. Neither of us wanted bland, if safer, terrain. The babe's utter fascination with so

331

mundane and cheap a toy was a lesson. My mother was a whiz with children, she always believed in giving them cartons to climb into or pot lids to clash or plain old paper bags. What wisdom. Melissa learned every nuance of that exhausted paper bag before she conquered it. Love and weather are peculiarly exquisite after a storm.

Ran's mother and father canceled their cruise and stayed near Melissa while we took the ill-omened trip. Venice was a saving grace. Our tapestry-draped suite was called The Museum and had belonged to a doge. We ate like pigs and drowned in pasta, olive oil, wine, and local music.

In Florence I suspected I was pregnant. In Cortina d'Ampezzo I knew. In Munich I sensed Ran was increasingly restless, half his mind out the door and back at Giro. I realized that in truth he'd never even wanted our trip. In Paris my early pregnant gorge rose at rich French menus; I can remember wildly sniffing smelling salts below the table as a brace of kidneys flambée went by. In Paris I also saw signs that could mean I'd lose the child. I knew if I kept running around I would.

We were staying in a tiny two-story penthouse made from servants' rooms at the small old-fashioned St. Regis Hotel. I went down the stairs from our bohemian bedroom to lie on the couch of the little study, and surveyed the roofs of Paris out the window near my head. It was very early morning, and there I pondered mightily. Ran was asleep. Should I just let it happen? Deliberately having a child to plug the cracks in a marriage is the ultimate mistake, though God knows this hadn't been a calculated one. Or had it? I honestly didn't know.

Unlike Ran, I was discouragingly transparent to everyone but myself. I'd seen it happen to other people. In terror or backsliding into strangers, subconsciously a child becomes a desperately tempting foothold. A factual shrub of love for me to grab. At least, please God, don't let me make it one more calamity. I crept back to bed, whose warmth closed my eyes.

The phone rang at eight thirty. I heard Ran say, "When did it happen?" Melissa sprang into my numb skull. I sat up in alarm as he came in.

"Guess what?" He looked grim. "Nanny what's-her-name has

332

fired Miss Hoff, the relief nurse. Miss Hoff was worried and just called."

We were both furious at the Parrot's incredible effrontery. I said I felt bum anyway, explained why, and we went back to London on the quickest plane. Nanny went packing, a doctor came, and I was put to bed. Ran paced the apartment cage and bought a ticket to Giro. I didn't blame him. He'd suffered quite enough. Marking time in London was more than he could bear after all the rest of a poor bargain. I'd gambled at dangerously high stakes and had ignominiously lost. Katrina was bringing her new young friend for winter holidays. As it was, I'd get home just in time. At least he'd be there in case there were further problems.

Melissa and I would come when it was safe for me to do so. I sneaked a call to Red Krohn and the magic liquid that helped bring Melissa to us was prescribed through proper English channels. All I needed was the usual shot of it each week and Dr. Burke could do that again in Worcester. It had worked before, why not this time?

I finally decided that if it is meant to be, it will be and, more important, whoever it might be was conceived in passion.

42

The Edge of the Razor

BEACHED again, I mused wryly, lying in bed hanging for dear life onto the creature within. My mind cast into a swiftly coursing future. Katrina would be at Giro for her winter holidays. She'd missed me a lot and Ran had said she was catching Aussie parlance like a slight cold. Melissa would be crawling soon, heaven forfend, and this new child would be bigger and busier every day if all went well. Every department was poised awaiting me. How was I going to do any of it? Even the 12,000-mile trip home with Melissa seemed more than I could tackle, to say nothing of Ran's needs. At least I supposed he needed me. The bald truth was that he needed me to be fun, to toss life over my shoulder like a pinch of salt, not a 109-pound pack of nerves. Our marriage was already black and blue with rash decisions. Suppose I didn't go back, would that be the worst one yet? Or a relief to us both? That idea put me in a state of shock. My thoughts ran on and on. Where would I go? My mother and father couldn't possibly have coped, nor would I have asked them to. Melissa was only months young. Transplanting Katrina again might have finished off whatever tentative roots she'd struggled to put down.

It was like—wait a minute—yes, like the aftermath of a traumatic dream I'd had in 1946. I was seated in some dark restaurant surrounded by hostile strangers. Yet, somehow, I knew them. They deliberately behaved as if I weren't there. The dream had left me singularly depressed. Not because of any childish fears, but because I couldn't shake the ugly feeling of premonition that pervaded the dream. I never told anyone about it. It seemed so nebulous, so innocuous. Most memorable bad dreams are gory, or at least bizarre. This one was quite normal on the surface but disturbed me for days with a sense of foreboding.

Nineteen hundred forty-six had been quite a year. I had married John Hodiak and, through a ridiculous Hollywood series of flukes, got the coveted part of Sophie in *The Razor's Edge*. I knew about the film—they'd tested thirteen girls on and off the Twentieth Century-Fox lot. It never occurred to me they'd even consider me for the part. I'd been sidetracked into sweet-ingenue roles, and from what I'd heard about Sophie, I didn't have a prayer.

Gregory Ratoff told me five years later why I had suddenly been considered for Sophie. Gregory, or Grisha, as we affectionately called him, was a close friend of Darryl and Virginia Zanuck's, a sort of court jester. He spent most weekends with them at their Palm Springs home. This Sunday, so Grisha described, Darryl was pacing around the pool in his bikini, swinging his polo mallet and cursing the problem of casting Sophie. Grisha spoke up: "Darryl, darling, what about Anne Baxter?" he suggested in his thick Russian English.

"Nah!" Zanuck is reported to have snarled disgustedly. "She's a cold potato."

With that, my pal Grisha went into action. "Darryl," he growled with an evil leer, "please, darling. I have had it—it's marvelous!"

Zanuck evidently pulled out his foot-long cigar and grinned in astonishment.

"You're kidding, Grisha!"

"That's right, Darryl. Marvelous!"

Monday morning my agent got a call. Could I dine with Edmund Goulding, the man who would direct *The Razor's Edge*, and test Tuesday? Yes. Oh, yes. I rushed out and bought Maugham's book and swallowed it whole.

That evening Eddie and I dined in his handsome penthouse on Wilshire Boulevard in Westwood. We ate oxtails (which I'd never had), made and served by an excellent manservant. After dinner we repaired to his library where he tried, out of copious experience, to shock me with all the terrible things Sophie had sunk to in Paris. I ended by shocking him. All he got out of me was "Of course," or, "Naturally, and no doubt she . . ." And I'd add some even juicier morsel picked up from Hitchcock's tales of Hamburg in the twenties or Orson Welles' stories of anywhere, anytime. We both ran the gamut. Poor Sophie—she wouldn't have lived long enough!

I treated the fact of the test like a secret lark. Not that I didn't concentrate, just that I knew I'd do better if I cared less. I knew I wouldn't get the part and treated the test like an improvisation. I got it. My agent was ecstatic. I was pleased, but not apart at the seams, and went to work on Sophie, whose background I understood without effort. A nice Chicago girl. Country-club dances. I was born fifty miles from Chicago and went to the same kind of dances. Who could forget a country club named The Pottawattomi?

The schedule was long and strange. I had three weeks off in the middle of the picture. I returned to work in Sophie's café scene. While I was gone, many interesting situations had developed. Tyrone Power and Gene Tierney were head over heels in infatuation; Clifton Webb was giving gorgeous parties for them. Herbert Marshall was included in all "family" jokes and here I came for rehearsal. The interloper, left out of high-powered international and internecine gossip.

The first few shots I was too concerned about the scene itself to notice much. But when the camera moved in on the round, wooden café table and I had to wander drunkenly up to join the chatting group, it hit me. God Almighty, my dream. It was exact. Total déjà vu. The dark restaurant. I knew them, but they ignored me like a stranger. Sophie and I felt perfectly, weirdly rejected. I walked away from that scene awed by a premonition so accurately come true.

I still don't know what it meant. I got an Academy Award for Sophie, proving perhaps that the worst and the best were often simultaneous in my life.

A marriage in serious trouble, two beautiful healthy children, or was it three? A life far from the junkheaps and madding crowd, sometimes poisoned by loneliness. Superb health, but not so hot at having babies. A respected professional career, and couldn't mop a decent floor without swearing.

Where was my perspective? Or my sense of humor? I studied the yards of limp gray satin hanging at the windows of my rented bedroom. What fool had decorated a London bedroom in the usual color of a London sky? It was raining again; the whole afternoon seemed covered with a film of gray grease. Giro would be dry and blue now. I felt a surge of passionate longing for my husband, which promptly crumpled my face into silent tears. Damn the perverse streak in human nature that drives away what it loves, then feels deserted.

I'd insisted he go back because I knew he'd go mad marking time; and yet felt abandoned that he'd gone. Ran had done that too; he'd said yes to a ride in a Venetian gondola and then had punished me for making it possible.

Out of irritation with myself, a peculiar energy returned. I climbed out of the clammy bed, crossed the hall to the bathroom, and bathed a blotched face. That had become a habit. Like the proverbial cold shower, it served a certain purpose. Oh, Lord, was it time for my pill? That brought me up short. I decided I was simply the victim of disgruntled hormones. Think ahead. What was it Grandfather often said in answer to "How are you?" "Battered, but still in the ring," he'd reply with a seasoned glint. Wasn't that about right for me?

Wow, what an idea! Dottie Edwards. She was my darling Cockney friend and dresser during Carson McCullers' *Square Root of Wonderful* in New York and Alec Coppel's *The Joshua Tree* in London. She was due back from the States any day now with Margaret Leighton. The third actress she dressed was Eva Gabor. A wide-ranging triumvirate, with musical comedy stars interspersed. Dottie was a prize. Would she come to Australia? She would be perfect at Giro.

I walked to the window, lost in meditation. The crazy thought of Dot's twinkle toes, earthy streets-of-London humor, and sympathetic heart enlivening Giro lifted my spirits. A smile grew behind my eyes—Dottie Edwards in the Australian bush. Nothing was impossible. Worse mistakes in casting were made every day.

Grandfather was also reported to have said, "Doctors bury

337

their mistakes. Architects plant vines." Far better to plant my kind of vines all over Giro before it planted me; to love my children, born and unborn; to love my husband, there or not there; and try, try again at the most difficult part I'd ever taken on: Australian country wife. A far cry from Wycherley's country confection.

I went back to bed, rolled over, and tried to doze. Melissa would wake in a short while and I owed Katrina a letter. Though Giro had both despoiled and unspoiled me, the peculiar bond that can form between captor and captive still tugged hard at me. However painful, Giro was teaching me what I could and could not do without, the lesson of a lifetime. Fortunately, I was just wise enough to recognize its value, and that made me feel strong.

The traffic on Sloane Street sizzled in fine rain. I closed my eyes and was beside Ran as we droned across the faceless Nullarbor Plain. I remembered he'd let a wing tank run out to test it and we'd stalled in mid air. He'd noticed me blanch as we lost altitude and had hustled to switch to the left tank. Fear shuffled me like a pack of cards before that engine coughed on. He had laughed at my obvious fright and had blithely quoted his favorite flight instructor. "Whenever you're in trouble in the air, go back to neutral." I was certainly up in the air at this moment. What was *my* neutral? Wrong word. My "neutral" was still violently partisan; it was love. To think ahead from that fact might rescue me.

As a small child, I used to try to organize my normally scattered brain with purposeful lists. Things To Do Today: 1. Get up. 2. Get dressed. 3. Brush teeth. 4. Have breakfast. Perhaps a nice list would dig me out of chaos. 1. Learn to split kindling, so can stoke fire under water heater. 2. Learn five easy casseroles so can be with guests. (Guests?) 3. Learn how to teach school by mail. 4. To sew. 5. To grow vegetables. 6. Make it all look easy.

Gather thy wits, O Baxter, the best is yet to come. This mouse would turn again to face Giro, that hefty Cheshire cat.

Ran's mother had sent me a gift after they left. A tiny gold stork holding a tiny gold diaper perched on a little gold box, which when pushed underneath lit up a sign saying, "Bet it's a boy."

338

On the way back, my father and mother took one look at Melissa and almost forgave Australia. It boggles the mind to think of the amount of traveling that child had under her belt by the age of eight months. I can still see her sucking on smoked salmon hors d'oeuvres, gazing benignly at a planeful of martini-sipping strangers. I sipped one myself. It was a long trip. At least I'd learned to nap when she did.

Melissa and I had a brief twenty-four hours' rest in Honolulu, and Ran managed to get through by phone to say he'd fly down to meet us. I was greatly relieved we could go directly up to Katrina and Giro.

As I looked down over the red roofs of Sydney, I felt nervous and shy; almost as if this were another first arrival. So much had happened; how much had changed? How would it be for us? Was he dreading the responsibility of a rapidly growing family? To say nothing of an actress whose moods could swing from A to Zero, however hard she tried to quell them. Mustn't try too hard at any of it, I warned myself. Life, at Giro, must not be allowed to bury itself in mere existence. One thing I would try to do was garner friendly visitors. Perhaps my friends the Sweetapples could manage a visit. And Ran's mother and father might join us for Christmas.

We were coming down. I gathered Melissa in my arms and strapped us in my seat. Down we settled with a jolt. They knew us well at Customs and were most helpful. There stood Ran, taut with anticipation, his eyes dancing. I began inanely rattling on about the trip to cover my awkwardness. He took Melissa from me. We walked along at a quick pace. My chatter ran down like a cheap clock. He looked at me past Melissa's glowing English cheeks.

"It's great to have you home," he said softly.

"It's wonderful to be home," I answered. Nothing else seemed necessary.

43

Melissa

GIRO was brisk and fine; the willows combed the breeze with leafless limbs, and the frogs had gone away for the winter. Katrina galloped up on trusty Bluebottle as the plane threw dusty plumes behind it down the strip. She seemed taller and browner and altogether more assured: less child, more young person. You turn away and they're gone; you turn around and they're grown, if not grown up, whatever that might be.

Her friend's name was Margaret. She was a quiet child, shy as a parsnip with me. Katrina usually chose a combination of friend and audience. They shared Bluebottle and giggled insanely at absolutely nothing. After ten days, I'd run out of desserts I knew. Food was of great importance after boiled boarding school fare. Without the discipline and Gib Gates' book of rules to worry about, the mess in the bathroom and Katrina's bedroom were monumental. Ten days later Margaret's family came to pick her up in a mad hurry to get to another station before nightfall.

She left minus a sweater, seven unmatched socks, three undershirts, two pair of bloomers, and a blouse. No name tapes. She also threw up quite frequently. I sincerely hoped it wasn't my cooking, but Katrina assured me she did it at school, too. It seems to me she had only one nosebleed. She just traveled badly—like certain light, sweet wines.

Routine clicked its heels and ushered me into each new day. Folding mammoth sheets one morning, I heard a new sound. *Slap, shush, thump—slap, shush, thump.* Dropping the sheet, I ran to look where I'd left Melissa playing with Katrina's old stuffed koalas. She crawled methodically toward me; one hand spanked the floor, a corduroy knee slid forward, thumped, and the other hand reached out to spank again. She was smug with the triumph of moving by herself. Now I'd never know where she was and ransacked Giro for a bell. All I would have to do was bend an ear and assess the speed and direction of the tinkle. The poisons, mousetraps, and medicine went a long reach up.

Katrina had heard me talk about the Druids' circle, and I'd told her how to go, but Bluebottle always managed to sidetrack her. Joan Aildred kept watch over Melissa so we could share it with a picnic one day before she left for school again. I walked, she rode. It was absurdly important to me, that secret place. Perhaps because I extricated moments there so seldom.

The Druids' circle must have been used for sacred purposes by the Aborigines. To get there one walked along the river for about half a mile to Giro Creek. The creek corkscrewed narrowly out of the Eastern range that faced our homestead, and was rich with watercress as it joined the Barnard, our river.

Directly across the creek the ground swept up to form a round green bluff crowned with the feathers of a spreading white cedar tree. Large, flat rocks, flanked and spurred two sides of the small bluff, seductively planted with a natural variety of shrubs and grasses. The animals had cut a rocky path up the bluff from the creek as you faced it, and behind it swelled a steep hill.

The place was always orchestrated with water music, and down from the cedar's lookout was a veritable bowling lawn, broken by more slabs of saffron-lichened rock which jutted into the rustling water to form a natural dock. Willows lackadaisically trailed mandarin fingers in the current; the whole effect was one of cunning asymmetry. Artful, but without artifice; a caprice nature had let fly with consummate skill.

Across the river the land climbed, wave after wave of steepness, first sparsely grassed, then sprouting ruddy-tipped gums to the rock-strewn top of Giro's Western range. A stern backdrop for that arrogantly beautiful place.

How I longed to build a wooden room around that cedar's trunk, to collar it with a round platform holding to the tree; a place for a piano and books and a mess of paint and paper and pencils, all the tools of fun and imagination and music.

We lay on our backs, she and I, and planned it, drowsy with pleasure in the winter sun. The roof could have been a corrugated umbrella with wedges cut out allowing a look up through leaf embroidery, supported from a central pole with windows all around. The fireplace, we thought, should back up to the hill, in the only stone wall. We had a mock tiff over how the kitchen faced and paced it off complete with cornerstone. A gift house for guests from Sydney or home, or her friends from school as the years went on. Through a mouthful of cookie Katrina decided a high, curved bridge over Giro Creek. I thought of flags raised for various signals: "Stay away. In lousy mood," or, "Weather clear, track fast," or "Cold beer and eats." Oh, well, we built it all in our heads. So much cheaper, especially in the bush.

Lavender-black wraiths of Aborigine chiefs still inhabit the night there, I'm sure of it, and dance corroborees while the cows munch in the dark beyond.

Katrina went back to school, a new Scottish kilt in her suitcase for best and a heather-green sweater with knee socks to match. Margaret's left-behinds were in a separate package, heavily marked. I prayed it wouldn't end up on the train seat. It did. Ran flew her in on the way to a conference about the weaners, which had been sold, and put her on the train. She'd made a crayon picture of Giro for me as a present. It was clearly a gesture toward her new home.

There were days when Melissa, the magpies, and I were Giro's only occupants. They chattered at us, I chattered at her, and she babbled back. Everybody was off and gone. There were the million things to do, but Melissa was the reason for being. I had a hunch Ran felt the same. He adored her, and why not? Her needs were plain as daylight and fulfilled. She required nothing more than his timbre of voice and his presence when he chose. Something in him gagged at having to be anywhere, and now with Hugh Aildred's easy grasp on Giro, he didn't have to be anywhere—and certainly could avoid Home and Mother. To woman's work I had added Mother in bold type.

Grandfather quoted Aristotle in brass on the threshold of the Guggenheim Museum: "Every man must exercise the art he

342

knows." I was blindly exercising the "arts" I was beginning to know, doggedly heaping molehills into mountains. Even diapers became a kind of ballet.

Flawless is not a used-up word. I shall use it for Melissa. She has a freckle on the bottom of her right foot. Flawless. Hair like buttered silk, long aqua-quiescent eyes by Giotto, body by Botticelli, cheeks by McIntosh, and a disposition like a shaft of sunlight in the Black Forest.

In the dry weather, her toys were bugs, wind, fallen oranges, flowers, birds, and leaves. In the heat, I washed her three or four times a day and she never wore anything much. In wet weather, she played in crates of onions, carrots, and potatoes with pots and pans, egg beaters, whisks, and nuts in their shells. The deafening frogs never *wrawck-wrawcked* her awake. Hugh Aildred has assured us it'd be her first word, but how would we have heard it?

She thought life was the nicest accident that could ever happen to anybody and fondled every second, every drop, every sound. She loved to wake up, she loved to go to sleep; she loved to eat, she loved people, animals, trees, songs, and she loved us back. In sparse rages her mighty bellow rang the roof, always because lunch wasn't quite ready, bad timing on my part.

We were dim with wonder at her astounding quota of joy and beauty. Her health and temperament were so superb it made me uneasy; so much on one side of the scale shot me full of fear at what the balancers might be, and a part of me never closed an eye or ear.

The morning was at her feet from seven thirty until eleven. Not only the morning was at her feet. Her father would have allowed her to snatch him baldheaded—and she certainly tried. His hair was crisp enough to get a really good hold, which she did to their mutual delight. He literally let her crawl all over him. It was divinely satisfying to watch a big bear of a man try halfheartedly to protect himself from a curly, fat, ferociously feminine baby. Both pink in the face with laughter. I often didn't have time for anything but a loving shout and a wave, or a drink of water or change of pants. It made her independent and taught her to discover constantly widening circles of world by herself.

As she grew, we'd trundle over rugged ground late after-

343

noons to meet chickens, cows, horses, and the river. And Ran and I could give her books and music, too, and warm, clean clothes and Bertha and I boiled her river water and pasteurized her milk. Melissa became a full-blown rose, with the roots of stamina and protective thorns that only Giro and Sister Isabel-la-Mac made possible.

As careful as I was, a fly finally got her.

The bottles I'd brought from America had large white plastic covers for the exposed rubber nipples. I swore to myself I'd never failed to put one on or cover her food. But I must have. Sister's warnings about gastroenteritis had been all too well founded and the battle to save Melissa was on. Thank God the telephone was working and I reported every other day to a doctor in Taree, eighty road miles away. Bill Sweetapple had researched him and his efficient clinic, through a colleague. The plane was there just in case, but I was determined not to let it get to that point. I envisioned Sister's stern visage and boiled the nappies in the jam kettles.

She ate nothing for three long weeks. Nothing but painstaking measured water, sugar, and salt. It destroyed me to watch ribs begin to show and bracelets of chub disappear, but three weeks later she was out of danger, if pounds thinner. So was I, from nervous wreckage. We'd simply starved the germ away and her naturally strong body had done the rest. I also prayed a lot.

The fact that I couldn't leave the house now was debilitating, as I began to look for projects within earshot outdoors. Ran had spasmodically expanded the area around the house. Meaning he took down fences. Our marching row of ragamuffin shrubs were now without backup fence. Lines of odd-sized recruits standing at attention in a field of weeds. I tried transplanting them into groups or massing them against a further fence as my gardener mother had often done. Then that fence would come down and nothing made any sense yet again. The farther away things grew the longer the job to bucket them. There was never enough hose. The bottlebrush grew in profusion down by the river. I tried digging a dozen or so during Melissa's naps but they had six-foot roots like corkscrews and I'd end up thrown on my backside in the wet gravel after mighty tugs. Three of them lived. Not exactly what you'd call mass planting.

One day Ran came back unexpectedly and said, "Luxor's just foaled. I hear it's a colt. Grab Melissa and we'll drive up to see them!" She was just up from her afternoon snooze. I thrust a cookie in her fist, grabbed a bottle of water, and off we drove. Luxor was a retired racehorse and beautiful; bay with gold leaf.

"There she is!" We saw her on the rocky hillside in a patch of growth, head down, licking a colt with still-folded legs, the afterbirth gleaming wetly on the ground.

"Could we go closer?" I asked, entranced.

"I think so, if we're quiet. What about Melissa?"

I looked at a calm stretch of clover across the road. "I could sit her there. She'll be fine for a few minutes," I said in a stage whisper.

He ran Rover off the road near the clover and cut the engine. Luxor studied us warily and the colt tried hard to untangle his knobby legs. I sat Melissa in the clover with her legs wide for balance and we stole slowly closer to the mare and her foal. We watched her mother him with low gurgling noises in answer to his creaking whinnies. I clasped Ran's arm in excitement. It was the richest of moments together. The colt finally tottered to its feet and wavered toward her bag of milk, guided by gentle nosings. Lost in natural miracles, I completely forgot Melissa. We smiled in shared pleasure and both remembered her at once. We looked down across the road. She was leaning over, bent almost double, dipping a finger deep into a large cow-pat dotted with mushrooms.

"My God," I gasped, stumbling down the hill as she poked the finger in a waiting mouth. She was regarding the finger with a puzzled look as I wiped her tongue off as best I could. The flavor was not one that matched her experience. I gathered her up onto a hip, laughing back at Ran. What could one do but laugh? Luxor had frozen at the sudden movement. We drove back curiously refreshed and closer than we'd been in too long.

The other side of the coin was a broken-necked bottle of kerosene Ran had left on the pantry floor in front of the fridge. I didn't laugh at that. I pictured the headlines: BABY POISONED

345

ACCIDENTALLY, or, TODDLER DIES WHILE PLAYING WITH SNAKE, or, THREE-YEAR-OLD DROWNS IN RIVER—MOTHER UNABLE TO SAVE HER AGAINST CURRENT or EIGHTEEN-MONTH-OLD ELECTROCUTED BY 200 VOLT ENGINE TURNED ON UNEXPECTEDLY

It had never occurred to me that Ran wouldn't know a doctor or two in Sydney. He proudly said he healed like a wolf. Well, I'm as far from a hypochondriac as you can get but even wolves don't always heal if they're bleeding or mangled. Slowly but surely life had forced us to acquaint ourselves with medicos. Melissa would certainly need vaccines, polio included. Polio vaccine was distributed by the government in Sydney at prescribed times, difficult for us to meet. The local shire could have had the serum, but wouldn't spend the money on a refrigerator. Tetanus shots would be a must. Ran was allergic to horse serum, the only antidote for dreaded tetanus, and had a tag to wear saying so.

Early education was just as serious a situation. Again I'd assumed he knew the score, having been down under for four years before I met him. The Biddefords had explained that usually if there were seven or more childen on a station the government would send a teacher. Not that I could have had that many in time for Melissa's schooling, but I seriously began totting up possible candidates. David and Jane Aildred, Melissa Galt, Daisy and Gordon Blackburn, and eventually their little sister, Lana. Six. The child inside me made the seventh but we'd have to wait awhile. Truly a do-it-yourself one-room school. I discussed my concern with Ran, who thought I was ludicrously previous. One evening I was anxiously perched on the red office chair.

"Judas Priest!" he commented with familiar exasperation. "Melissa's only eleven months old. There's plenty of time to work something out!"

"That's what *you* think," I remonstrated. "I know how fast time can run away. You just hate to plan ahead, always have."

"That has nothing to do with it—as usual you're anticipating trouble before the problem arises."

"Ran, the problem won't *arise*—it's *here*. This is one thing we're going to plan for whether you think I'm lamebrained or not!" I stated in steely tones. "Look what we went through, or rather what Katrina went through, with Quilty!"

346

He threw a cold look in my direction. "She was your idea."

"Well, what ideas did *you* have?" Silence. Thick, pulsating, angry silence. Say it, I told myself, say it.

"You probably thought I'd be able to do what Kath Biddeford did with Mary, Kip, and Dan."

He slammed one pile of papers onto another on his desk.

"Well, I can't! Not unless I train for it. And how am I going to do that? It would be haphazard at best, and Melissa's worth a better start!" More silence.

"Do you mind if we continue this hysterical discussion at some later date? Hugh's coming by to go over accounts," he said, turning away as if I were an unlikely job applicant.

"I do mind, but station business always comes first," I retorted with what I thought was the last word in sarcasm and left the room, seething.

I stalked outdoors. The light was still lingering at the horizon, but not like high summer. I'd grabbed my cigarettes and stamped through the weeds up onto the strip. The strip was good for concentration. Nothing much would lurk in hard-packed sand and pebbles. I lit a cigarette as I started down the strip.

America had obviously brainwashed me out of confidence. Education had such enormous importance in the States; teachers needed five years of college training to qualify. And the fact that the early grades were damned important had been solidly inculcated in me. Somehow college wasn't so important. Perhaps Australian countrywomen had learned at home and therefore could teach at home. I just didn't feel qualified because of my long indoctrination into America's sacrosanct educational mythology.

How readily Ran dismissed time. I knew too much about it. It was an item I was always out of. I smiled quizzically to myself as I walked, remembering the look he'd darted at some nineteen-year-old in Hawaii who'd called him "Sir." He'd been piqued and surprised and had immediately urged the boy to call him "Ranny." I stopped, threw my head back, and took a last puff of my cigarette. All I'd have to do tonight was to smoke anywhere near my lord and master and *he'd* ignite. Damn it, this time I was right. A plan of action must be made.

44

The Tap Dancer on an Island of Sweetapples

THE child in me had awakened to put my heart at ease. It was gradually developing into a tap dancer, not exactly Fred Astaire, more old time soft-shoe. Balancing a teacup and saucer on my stomach when stretched out for the night became a comic strip. That cup's antic gyrations needed "Way Down Upon the Swanee River" as accompaniment. Melissa had floated serenely: this new person jigged and jogged on its way to birth.

Ran had finally finished tearing down the enormous old two-story shearing shed. I believe I would have salvaged it, but then I was a sucker for salvage, and the year before he'd bought the bigger tractor. You couldn't have a pet rhinoceros and not ride it, could you? God, how he loved that tractor. His newest project had used it to the hilt. A new road up the Myall. The old one followed the river and twisted like a wounded snake, scenic on a horse but a series of booby traps for any vehicle. The new road needed the D-6 and the fillip of dynamite: an ambitious cut into the hillside's haunches. It was dangerous, innovative, and a new wrinkle on stale station work: Ran's perfect fit. Privately I wondered if mustering wouldn't be simpler via the old way, but I never voiced my doubts. After all, they'd always have the low road, and the view was striking from the high one. Besides, it was none of my damned business.

There were some supreme vistas and "beauty spots," as Dubliners call them, on Giro. Lucky Louie was more of a blemish. Giro's ineradicable birthmark, I called the hill because its heaped rocks and whispering bladygrass rose to the left of the homestead's outlook and effectively eclipsed the grand views of our upper valley. Those rocks, pushed in the middle of Giro's face, annoyed me beyond words. How I craved the majesty they hide.

It took an hour to scale the hill, half that on a puffing horse. But what a treat to stand on Lucky Louie's head. On either hand you watched deep sweeps of earth wheel into distance, like pods of tawny whales arcing through billowing, bruise-colored earth, the river trailing like their spume.

Ran crawled the D-6 over Louie and we dreamed about a home up there. A fine stone house to capture every possible aspect. Grandfather had taught me never to place a house on top of a hill. He said it should hug its flank. I wanted the site abutting a cliff, with a view of looping river and willows. Too tame for Ran, I gathered. On Sundays he'd climb on the rhino's back and clank across the river up the perpendicular rise opposite the Druids' circle for a look-see. Wheeling Melissa, I'd watch him from the strip, the tractor grumbling in the distance, and cover man and beast-machine with my raised thumb. How swiftly physical power was reduced by perspective.

As November arrived, I was busting out all over and Ran looked for help once again. He'd flown to Sydney on station business and came back optimistic about Miss Hart: English, in Australia eleven years, taken care of half-sister's five children, sick of it, divorced, loved the country, had never worked, wanted to save money and be on her own. Promising!

She was quick, dark, and would have been pretty without the network of anxious lines on her face. She preferred the cottage and brought one small suitcase. This was, I prayed, someone I could leave Melissa with for an afternoon or a weekend. After all, she had taken care of her half-sister's five children.

She'd be oddly depressed and uncommunicative for two or three days, then, like turning on a roomful of electric lights, she'd sparkle and chatter and laugh with wild abandon. On those days I heard all about men (mostly bad), what a bad mother her half-sister was, how jealous of Miss Hart's place in the five children's hearts was the sister; her own sad inability to have children (here came details of her hysterectomy). In short,

349

verbal diarrhea. On those manic days, I'd work hard for a peaceful beaker together with Ran on the veranda, and there she'd be, poised in the doorway, gushing uncontrollable, nervous conversation. At which we'd nod politely, wondering if there wasn't some other thing to do. Politesse is its own reward.

It was two weeks before we got the bombshell letter from her husband. The five children were hers. They missed her so terribly. The oldest, a fourteen-year-old girl, was taking care of them all, but he didn't know how long she could carry on as her schoolwork was suffering badly. He said his wife got into money trouble at the races and went off like this every so often to pay back her debts. Nor was her name Miss Hart. Much love to Mrs. W. Sincerely, Mr. W.

Her obvious instability had stopped me from leaving Melissa with her, and now should we or should we not risk a confrontation? Perhaps she'd go to pieces and tear the curtains. Her husband had written that the coming Saturday was their wedding anniversary. She sank into profound depression by Thursday.

We offered her that weekend off in Sydney. She seemed pleased and, looking me in the eye as she lied, said she would get some nice nylon uniforms while she was there.

"Yes, good idea," I said, lying just as quietly, never taking my eyes off hers.

I knew she knew we knew in that illumined globe of a moment.

And we never saw her again.

It didn't matter. I was manic those days myself. Besides, the Sweetapples were finally coming to visit. They'd fly to Taree in a lumbering DC-3 and Ran would wing them to Giro from there. Only a weekend because Bill had to be at the hospital early Monday. Anesthesiology (wouldn't you hate to try that word after Dixon's gin?) was a vital, separate art in Australia, too. I'd have to twit Bill about the lady doctor who'd almost done me in with morphia. What fun to have friends to joke with and be able to throw a banana peel in front of Giro's shortcomings.

It's impossible to describe the excitement engendered by the prospect of friends in the bush. Robinson Crusoe sighting a rollicking cruise ship full of his favorite foods.

350

Warming November weather boded well for a picnic and I planned a feast and a half. It wasn't hot enough yet for lamb killers so I ordered fine chops from town, and pored over menus to tease the palate but free the cook. I sprinted through the days, imagining six repasts to parade before my precious friends, and broke out our fanciest sheets for the four-poster.

The firewheel tree was in bloom and I cut flaming carousels for the living room and bouquets of wild flowers for their bedroom. I blush to say I was starved for an audience, not that Melissa wasn't one, but she applauded unpeeled onions with equal glee.

Where to picnic? I knew Ran would want to show them his road. What was wanted was a "beauty spot" adjacent. The two beauty spots I nursed like lovely children were first, Katrina's and my Druids' circle, and second, the Islands.

The Islands were formed by the confluence of the Barnard, which flowed by the homestead, and the Myall, which poured out of the mountains above Giro and through the station's rugged upper valley.

Both rivers ran amuck in flood and the Island disappeared; but most of the time they were a bucolic paradise in miniature. The two rivers laced fingers in an ecstasy of meeting, creating a diminutive archipelago, punctuated by pygmy waterfalls, rapids, and a myriad of tiny rivers. The gum trees and she-oaks trembled tall on the heavy banks surrounding the Islands, and young willows flourished on the Islands themselves. It was an enchanting place for picnics, although I always wished everyone would shut up and listen to the water music; an undercurrent of Brahms flowing beneath the more explicit grace of Vivaldi. Surrendering to that delectable counterpoint, you became a human cello, strings running taut from throat to knees, the music drawing a humming bow across one's solar plexus.

Saturday at sunup I organized Melissa, then breakfast, then the picnic: wine and beer, playpen and diapers and bottles; hoarded ice, parboiled potatoes ready for fancy-fry with bacon, herbs, and onions; skillets and cutlery; an army-sized salad with dressing; stuffed eggs; fruit compote; teasugarbread-cheesejamcake; and not least, a large pink baby. Rover was a smorgasbord and there was barely room for people, especially

351

considering the room I took up. My lap was disappearing into the tap dancer.

Why was I always so *encumbered?* After jolting excursions up mountainsides for views, during which I was sure the stuffed eggs were copulating in their dish, all was deployed around the Islands, the fire alight and, blessed Jesus, the chops! Not true! O dullest of thuds, no bloody, bloody chops. They all howled with laughter but I thought even the dogs looked crestfallen. Damn. All that fuss and Ran would have been totally happy with just the chops and billy tea. My picnic had suffered from the usual overkill and instead of a fuse I'd become a fusser. After our vegetarian feast, Melissa lay in her pen under the trees, Ran took the Sweetapples up to the road, and I collapsed.

I flopped on the left side of a swollen stomach and scrutinized the stones beneath the waters' trembling aspic. I couldn't resist one, and plucked it dripping from its bed and watched it dry in the sun and air. There was nothing for a moment but it and me.

What about stones? echoed in my head—the emotion-packed stones that fall into the quiet reaches of one's life and send ring on ring of inexorable happenings wider and wider. I fished for another. If I had known Giro as I knew it now, would I have married Randolph Galt? Probably. I would not fall that far in love that fast, again. The baby in me jumped, I smiled and put my hand on the spot. Elbow? Big toe? Knee? Quite right, little one, I mentally addressed my unborn babe. Your mother has just asked herself the $64,000 Question. You rightly reminded me that it was also a rhetorical one. I dozed a minute or two.

Melissa was up. I hauled myself to my feet and grabbed a diaper and a bottle. The tap dancer did a buck and wing as I teetered across a rivulet to Melissa. A new baby just might be your bush headstone, Mrs. G. Well, I laughed to myself, you always got a kick out of hats.

Here they came, Ran beaming with justifiable pride. The road was an extraordinary feat anywhere, but done piecemeal by Ran with nobody but Old Will and Ned Beale to help, it was a miracle.

"Annie!" called Ross. "Really gorgeous. What a job! And the views are just superb!"

352

I looked up from kneeling with a mouthful of diaper pins, "Great, isn't it? They even used dynamite." I took out the second pin and finished off pinning up my child, who was straining to crawl away. "Ran had a ball, and he picked every inch of the route, too."

"My word!" exclaimed Bill, coming along behind Ross and sincerely impressed. "Beautifully engineered! Ranny, did you study engineering?"

Ran hooted. "No!" God, he was pleased. "Nothing like it, but you don't need that kind of expertise if you know the land you're dealing with. Did you see how Old Will shored up some of those hairpin curves with logs? He's terrific."

I'd sat back off my knees, one hand holding onto Melissa's corduroys as she struggled to reach a waterfall just her size. Ran needed people just as much as I did. I was more determined than ever to get more and more friends to Giro in the future. It would cure many a fissure in our marriage. Friendships were indispensable first aid to any human relationship and, above all, to lovers. Perhaps that was why isolated honeymoons often shriveled.

The road was complete. What would Ran's next project be? Like me, Giro didn't seem to be enough for him; but unlike me, his chores were not the same every twenty-four hours. Choice again. But too much choice carried its own stress, as does too much freedom. My tap dancer did sudden acrobatics and made me gasp at what I divined was a foot landed in my bladder. An "Oooo boy!" escaped. Ross grinned sympathetically and plopped down beside me.

"Poor Annie! Don't I know. I thought Antony was taking skiing lessons in there."

Woman talk—but different with a sweet friend who could also spout about new-fledged artists in Sydney, or architecture, or newfangled ideas about anything.

"Ran," I asked, "should we go?"

He was deep in conversation with Bill, who'd just lit a fresh pipe. He hadn't heard me. I was glad he was that involved with a friend of mine and someone who wasn't solely an adjunct of the animal business. I overheard the words "artificial insemination" and "pregnancy testing." Both procedures were very useful on a ranch or a station. If you definitely knew that a cow had conceived, you could count on her progeny. If she hadn't, and you knew in time, you could breed her again. If she failed to make the grade two years in a row, you could eat her.

Ran saw no reason why he should pay pregnancy testing fees to the vet if he could do it himself. The vet had shown him how a few times. The difference between Ran and the vet was a rubber glove. The vet always wore one—Ran didn't bother. That bothered the heck out of me for several reasons, and he knew it. He was nettled by my unhappy complaints and impatiently explained, as to an idiot, that a bare hand was more instructive. It had become a running aggravation between us. I saw a rare opportunity to plead my case.

"Bill?"

He looked over his pipe kindly; I'd interrupted them. Ran watched me incuriously.

"Yes, Annie?"

"Aren't vets supposed to use gloves when they pregnancy test?"

"It's the better idea, yes," Bill answered innocently, all doctor. Ran gave me a dirty look. Bill moved toward me a couple of steps.

"I suppose one excellent reason is because the animals are scared and lose sphincter control. It's easier and safer, of course, for veterinarian and animal to avoid infection, when rubber gloves are used."

Ran stared at a nearby tree and glanced at his watch.

"Shall we go? The sun's almost gone," he remarked crisply, covering growing annoyance at my underhanded ploy.

Ross was helping Melissa out of a session with some really good mud and I started to pack picnic gear without a word.

They say the female is more devious than the male. That may be, but sometimes it's the only way a flyweight can throw a winning punch against a Joe Palooka.

The Sweetapples' weekend was an energetic delight of conversation, fresh gossip, current goings-on, and explorations.

I fed them as well as I knew how and they fed Ran and me with friendship. What was needed was more of the same.

354

45

Onions and Shoofly Pie

I WAS feeling marvelous. A motor purring with vitamins and hormones. Perhaps that's why that spring was particularly beautiful at Giro; fresh but not cold, blue and white skies arching a thousand shades of green. It had been the kind of winter that Jane Fyfe would have loved. Only six frosts.

At night Melissa slept in her screened crib on the veranda, zipped into a wooly pink blanket with sleeves. We'd be up at five thirty with the sun and she'd greet me with wriggling joy and flailing fists. It warmed my heart to know I'd given birth to a friend.

The Cessna 210 had gone. We now had a 175. Ran had flown off in it to Western Australia, which I now strongly suspected interested him almost more than Giro. Hugh Aildred ran the Station so capably there really wasn't that much left for Ran to do. The Western property was truly the outback, and a challenge more to his taste. I never told him, but it bothered me he might want to move out there. The thought of pulling up our rickety stakes was more than I could bear. With all its faults, Giro was home; I was coping with tasks and even savored isolation.

I wondered if solo flying lit the fires of imagination the way Giro's solitariness lit mine. I'd always had the impertinence to believe I had unlimited inner resources. I was wrong. I'd met my limitations all at once but I was learning to expand and restore myself with the scraps at hand: a passing tender look, a newly blooming tree, early morning air, a wave, Melissa's growing perceptions, letters from home, letters from Katrina, a meal with the Biddefords, thoughts of the baby growing inside me, and prayers of thanksgiving on the veranda floor in the starlight or anywhere I felt like it.

Giro's gift was a strength that would never leave me. I could make do with less and do without more than most of the people I'd ever known. That hard-earned fact remains a psychic ace-in-the-hole.

The bad experience in London had embossed my daily country life in sharp relief. Giro resembled an artichoke. Thorny, yes, but as I pulled the leaves away, carved out the choke, there sat the nourishing heart. I'd bloodied fingers on those thorns, but had been nourished, and had begun to know it.

Hollywood's world had passed on like a carnival. I'd said a last good-bye—not that anyone heard. And that reminded me of Clark Gable's devastating good-bye to MGM. He sat in his spacious dressing room, which had been stripped, from eight thirty till one, waiting for someone to say good-bye. Not a phone call. Not a knock. All those years, all the millions he'd earned for the studio, all the days of the King, as they'd dubbed him, and not a word. He drove out the gate and vowed never to come back. Nor did he, until he died running after a truck in the broiling desert at the urging of his director.

That brought to mind another classic good-bye: a caustic joke we actors used to quote acidly: "The SOB up and died on us!"

SOB. One of the few times I heard De Mille laugh included that antique epithet. It was one or one fifteen on the day we were shooting a scene at Pharaoh's Court with hundreds of plumed and bedecked extras. Into the hush came audible mumblings in a far-back clump. De Mille's eyes squinted dangerously as he motioned for his mike.

"*You!*" he boomed. It was utterly silent. "You over there in the red hat, what were you saying that was more fascinating than this scene we're trying to shoot? I suggest," he went on witheringly, "that you kindly share your earth-shaking remarks with the rest of the company." He finished grandly and waited, aware of the poison on his dart. The extra was a good-looking woman in a red-feathered headdress. She straightened up, cleared her throat, and projected a voice that had been on the stage.

"I was saying, I wonder when the old SOB is going to call lunch?"

De Mille squinted harder and burst into laughter, switching to the role of Great Kind White Father in a trice. "All right, lunch!" he announced and walked away, his shoulders jumping with mirth. What a funny, terrible business it was.

LOOOOONG–short, LOOOOONG–short!
Damn that phone. Sometimes it rang right through me.
LOOOOOOONG–short!
OK. OK. I'm coming!

I was in the laundry, ready to march out the back door with a steaming white pile of diapers. I set down my load and went back through two screen doors to check Melissa, who was sitting in a drift of papery onion skins in the pantry and had just bitten into a huge, carefully peeled onion as though it were an apple. I ran through the kitchen door, the hall, and the office to the phone.

"Hello?"

"Who'm I speaking to?" said an unmistakably city voice.

"Look, if you want Mr. Galt, he's not here."

"Am I speaking to Miss Baxter?"

"Who's calling, please?" I shouted, crackling with annoyance.

"I'm from the press. We understand you expect a new baby."

Caught out. Had to happen.

"That is correct," I barked, barely polite.

"Are you going to have it in Australia?" he mewed.

"Actually we're not sure."

"What's wrong with Australian doctors?"

That finished it.

"Did it ever occur to you there might be something wrong with *me*?" I replied curtly. "Nor, I might add, is it any of your

357

affair." I crashed the receiver into its innocent black hook. Infuriated, I stormed through the kitchen to the pantry. Melissa was sitting quietly, her eyes swimming with onion tears, studying the onion still clutched in two juicy fists.

"Here we go, sweetheart, let's go out in the nice fresh air." I settled her in her pen for a morning snooze and went back to my steamy basket of laundry.

Tramping through the grass lush from summer's first rains, I had a tug-of-war with myself. Why didn't I have the baby here? Or, rather, in Sydney? I hated that hospital but, for heaven's sake, thousands of people flew from all over Oceania and Asia to avail themselves of fine Australian care. Why not me? It'd only have been seventeen months between babes; my body must still remember its ABC's. Perhaps I could convince Ran. It was worth a try.

Later I brought Melissa in, rosy from her nap, and sat her in her feeding chair. She jounced it unmercifully in anticipation, pounding her chubby palms on the table. Henrietta VIII before a banquet. I finished preparing her lunch, feeling grateful Ran had valiantly said he'd try again for help in the city on the way home from Western Australia. I couldn't leave the house now, and soon there'd be two babies. Melissa'd been a placid, easy baby; this one might run me ragged. The tap dancer kicked on cue as I focused my attention on it. Never mind, I told myself, you'll have two small friends.

You'll have to teach them music, Mrs. G. "I will," I answered myself out loud. Melissa threw me a sparkling glance as she heard me and proceeded to attack the eagerly awaited lunch I'd just set before her. Music might be fun, I thought happily.

My small Steinway had come to Giro months after the furniture. When it arrived it took weeks for the men to find time to unpack and move it to the room next to the one Quilty had been in. As the men let it drop onto its last leg, a string twanged and snapped. Twenty-eight years and 8,680 miles those strings had stayed strung, but Giro was the last straw.

Ran was tracking down a repairman in Taree, but in the meantime the game was to transpose what you knew how to play away from the busted note. And I wasn't that good. Even Beethoven sounded like "The Little Organ Grinder," but Me-

358

lissa liked it. "Didn't you, sweetheart?" I said over my shoulder from the kitchen sink. Melissa was spooning up her lunch and looked across at me. We smiled cheerfully. We were instantly responsive to each other. Katrina had had a nurse. I was sorry.

Come to think of it, I was a cinch candidate for a homemade kindergarten. My mother'd taught it. I even had her old songbooks. Her mother, my beloved grandmother, had created one for the neighborhood in grandfather's Oak Park playroom, and my great-grandmother, Anna Lloyd-Jones Wright, had presented her son Frank with the inspirational blocks, colored papers, and other creative materials from Germany when the word "kindergarten" meant the last word in progressive education. Teaching the three R's might be out of my ken, but a kindergarten could be a rewarding project for everybody.

Ran was due home in a few days. I wondered what he'd say about Freeda. He'd thrown in the pig business towel, but the day before the truck arrived to cart them all to market, Freeda died. No one knew why. A snake? A tick? I knew. A severe case of spite. She was damned if she'd give us the satisfaction. A nonsensical poem unreeled in my head as I lifted lunch-covered Melissa into my arms. She grinned a magenta grin. Beets were always a mess.

The day Ran was to come home I wrote down my silly ode to Freeda and laid it on his desk.

> We're stuffing Freeda on the hoof
> Now that'll be the day!
> She up and died
> Of wounded pride;
> They carted her away.
>
> The boar under a willow roof
> Peeked out, a tear astray.
> He looked and cried,
> "Though she be wide—
> She was wonderful in the hay!"

Since I wasn't ever sure what time he'd arrive, I planned an easy last-minute supper and toward four o'clock began the usual vigil. Every so often I'd halt, walk outside, and listen with complete concentration. Sometimes I'd hear a phenomenal high-pitched whine long before I could spot the plane. The ghost of the plane's vibration would fly ahead to pluck the phone wire eerily, and I'd know he was almost home. All that remained was to minutely guard the landing with my eyes. Mexican sandwiches were a toothsome Giro invention and there were still some onions left over from Melissa.

It was a favorite supper of Ran's and as we sat together sharing bits and pieces of outside world I broached a tender subject.

"Ran, why can't I have the baby here?"

There was a pause as he tipped his chair forward onto its two front legs.

"It's not a good idea."

"Why? I'm sure I could. I know we'd hate the hospital and nosy newspapers, but which is worse? The whole agony and expense of going up home is, in its way, just as bad." Should I tell him about the phone call? Not now, I thought.

"No," he said quietly.

"Why?"

He rose and reached for one of Bertha's matches in the red tin cup. "I just don't think it's a good idea."

What did he know that I didn't? I only knew that, when his feet were planted for or against anything, give up.

He pulled a letter out of his shirt pocket. "Mother and Dad hope they can come for Christmas."

"How terrific!" I beamed, thrilled that we'd have a genuinely familial holiday. I'd given up on mine making a visit; for the time being. Perhaps next year.

"Sydney's full of new Australians. I think I could get a family up here," Ran said as he relit his cigar. New Australians meant any genre of fresh immigrant from a host of European countries except Sicily.

"You're sure we could communicate?" I demurred. "I can get along in French and Spanish, but my German is paraplegic."

"Don't worry about it. I'd trust your sign language any day." He laughed. "I think I've got a good lead on a family that might work. They're Dutch. The guy's perfect for the station," Ran enthused. "Even knows how to weld. They have five children, so she should be really good with Melissa."

360

If she has time, I said to myself. "That sounds really encouraging, darling. Let's hope they settle in!"—and prayed they understood some English.

"Ran, do me a favor?"

"Yes, sweetheart?"

"Think a little more about what I said. About my having the baby in Sydney?"

His smile faded slightly. "All right, I will."

But I knew the subject was closed.

"Could you manage another beer?" he queried.

"Why not? This is a celebration. You're home and Freeda no longer chews my pine trees!"

He got up with a laugh, kissed me, and went to the coldroom for the beer.

A week later Mr. and Mrs. Dierk Voort arrived with five children, ranging from eight months to sixteen years.

Mrs. Voort was like the figurehead of a sailing vessel, crowned with masses of curly carrot hair. She docked in the middle of the kitchen each morning and in slow but trumpeting English asked what I wanted her to do today. That laboriously spoken sentence backed her English into a corner. Smiling radiantly, she listened as I'd outline the orders for the day. "Yah!" she'd shout, and surge off leaving a pungent trail of honest sweat in every room. It was easy to check on her movements and whether or not she'd understood orders, that rich odor was her personal log.

Dierk was another matter. Gutzon Borglum could have carved his strong Dutch face and body. He had been trained in practically everything. A Clydesdale pulling a pony cart, he churned at Giro's unskilled chores, and at the bush way of repairing things. Ran pointed to a pile of broken cement one day and asked him to make a path. He tore it out three times and it took three days, but it was the finest path at Giro, a work of art, signed mightily in cement, DIERK VOORT. No date, like a master.

Our men and their families avoided him and never included the Voorts in station doings. That and his ego, bruised every day, ended it. The oldest boy sided with his father and deliberately broke two new brooms as a curse on the house the day they left. I was sorry about it all, and it gave me a clue to the ancient attitude toward foreigners in any society, however friendly or in need of clever hands.

I'd heard that central Europeans had turned Sydney on its ear by working earlier, later, and longer weeks in their new shops. They were ordered by local petitioners to close when everyone else did. Unfair competition. That sort of resentment was understandable, if not commendable. But the resistance to the Voorts at Giro seemed to be simply a reaction against "differentness." But then, what about me? I'd had to cure myself from correcting Katrina saying "frock" for "dress" or using her knife and fork English style.

The French ate frogs' legs; that was different, call them "frogs." English sailors were different and ate limes to fend off scurvy, call them "limeys." Many Swedes had distinctive wide faces and brows, call them "square heads." The Germans were different and ate sauerkraut, call them "krauts." Name-call the differences; poke fun at them.

As a woman I was automatically attuned to difference. I grew up hearing "women are *different*." I heard it from both men and women. It took me a long time to find out whether that was good or bad. Nor did the picture of a French *boulevardier* twirling a waxed mustache as he lifted a tall silk hat saying, *"Vive la différence!"* make it any clearer. It was just a basic female state you were stuck with. Fortunately I was brought up to believe being different was equated with individuality. I was taught to respect it, not only as being good, but as essential.

The holiness of the individual creates a passel of problems, but it made America explode into its spot in the sun. Without it, my grandfather wouldn't have been able to keep growing against impossible opposition; or my mother against rigid bridge-party suffocation; or my father, to retain and maintain his lofty ethics in a business world as undermined with greedy compromise as roquefort cheese is veined with rich, green mold.

The Voorts could have given the station ballast, new color, and rich experience if given half a chance. As an owner's wife I was held back, as I was with the others at Giro. I'd learned that the hard way. So I stood aside and hoped the clannish barbed wire against differentness would eventually be clipped away.

362

My husband had handled his Yankee differentness almost too well. From the time Ran first bought the station, he never meant to lick the Australian bush world. Quite the opposite. He badly wanted to join it. Day by day, through Giro itself, he'd won a victory so complete it frequently petrified me. At times I'd feel he literally was Australian. Whenever this happened I'd feel cut off and shut away from him. Strange that Ran's victorious Australian self should have reared and panicked me.

Ran may not have been aware of it. Or of the degradation eavesdropping wrought, or of the size of my cancerous hatred of confinement, anymore than he noticed the broken blood vessels, like violet daddy long legs appearing on the insides of my knees. What he did see were the general effects of my battles with Giro. He just didn't know what to do about them.

On doctor's orders I avoided salt when carrying a child and was extremely chary of rich goodies. But, oh how I craved both! One afternoon I gave in and picked up June Platt on pies. Every description of pie. I thumbed through, humming tunelessly. I decided to wow the Laird with shoofly pie. Uncooked, the pie looked awful. It didn't look much better coming out. It smelled unbelievably delicious. I dug out a lusty hunk and dropped a dab of cream on what resembled custardy-gingerbread. There are other entrances to heaven; I'll take shoofly pie. Unparalleled ambrosia of spice and texture, particularly to dietetic me.

We wowed the Laird.

Later, Ran and I sat at the round kitchen table in a pool of yellow light and gorged. Between bits he seemed to be watching me; something was afoot. I could see it in those clear but waiting eyes, behind which he was studying me.

He'd been doing that often of late. His gaze would have made me uncomfortable if it had been less gentle.

I tried to think when he'd started studying me in that preoccupied way, but I couldn't remember. Glances are ephemeral and difficult to box in time. We just sat there, tipping back in our gay Mexican chairs, in the warm galley of what could have been a tramp steamer named Giro, going anywhere at all. I eyed the pie again and cut myself a third slice. Ran couldn't believe it.

"Ah, darling," I said with a sigh as I chewed. "It's such terrific fun to be spineless and greedy once in a while."

He smiled and nodded. "Couldn't agree with you more." He stood up and leaned against the sink on the rim of the disk of light and casually asked me what I'd think about us having a small property, or rather ranch, in America. One foot in America, in other words. It took a moment for me to understand what he'd said.

"You mean divide our time between Giro and the States?" I asked, confused but intrigued.

"That would be the idea."

"You mean just a small place, to give us a business reason to go back sometimes?" I paused and took a sip of fragrant coffee.

"That'd be about right," he confirmed, subtly amused at my obvious bafflement.

"Wow! Where? Have you thought?"

"I'm not sure. I'll have to look around." He paused and searched my bewildered eyes like an actor hunting a cue.

"I took a quick look at a place outside of Albuquerque in the Ponderosa country, on my way back from London."

"You did?" So that's why he was so anxious to leave—it hadn't just been Giro. "New Mexico's magnificent!" I agreed warmly. "Is it anywhere near Santa Fe?"

"Not really, farther west."

"Let's get the atlas," I suggested, my interest whetted by his.

With mounting enthusiasm we began to wander the Western states in our minds. Both ardent map fans, we pored over maps and talked around and about. Both of us knew Arizona. California was very expensive. Nevada, a really desert place. Colorado was handsome. And New Mexico, of course. Ran knew I'd spent the loveliest summer of my first fourteen years there, in Santa Fe, so we examined it more carefully than the rest. Such an absorbing subject to explore. And what it could mean to our lives, I thought, my mind leaving Giro far below as my balloon soared once again. This way the children would know their own country and this amazing second one, friends everywhere, shared family rituals, the fullest kind of life experience—up I wafted into the land of what-might-be.

Late that night, lying wide-eyed in the dark beside my sleeping husband, I couldn't remember ever having been happier. I'd begun to conquer Giro. Katrina was busily content in her school; Melissa was safe asleep in her beautiful skin; the unborn child of the man I loved was growing and stirring; my stomach was full of shoofly pie and thick cream; and Ran and I shared a tantalizing idea. My adjustment snored daintily.

He mentioned it only once again fleetingly, and I supposed we'd talk about it after Christmas. Look out. Here came Christmas—bringing sheets of rain and blankets of heat.

46

The Pageant

"MOTHER and Dad are definitely coming down," said Ran with great satisfaction. I heard him folding a letter as he emerged from his office.

"That's wonderful news!" I called from the kitchen.

He walked in the door and looked at me seriously. "Only one thing," he went on, "they're worried about the extra work for you."

"Please tell them to relax, it's no trouble in any way, and it'll mean the earth to have them here," I replied firmly.

"The agency in Sydney has a line on a new couple. He's English. Only two children."

"Well, fine." I shrugged resignedly. "But I'm not exactly counting on them after what we've seen. Maybe they'll work, maybe not. In any case it shouldn't affect your parents' decision. I know I can cope."

He raised a warning eyebrow.

"No, honestly, Ran. Nothing but casseroles." I grinned.

He smiled broadly, knowing I truly longed to see them, and went back to his office.

I'd begun to have to reach over my stomach for the water taps. What was that corny old ditty my mother used to recite? "Fatty, fatty, boom-a-latty, this is the way she goes; she is so fat around her waist she cannot see her toes!" Not that they were worth a look. I smiled to myself. Or that I minded being pregnant; it was a pleasure to do something so constructive even when you were asleep. From six A.M. to six P.M. my feet grew sticky from the flypaper of the scullery. When the wood floors got too dirty I revarnished them dark oak. When wool clothes spotted I washed them; sometimes it worked. It had to; no cleaner in Town. Spreads were a bathtub job, frightfully heavy to handle. Rugs were beaten, hand-shampooed, and hosed, hanging over the passion-fruit trellis.

The fleas bit and I doctored oozing sores. The mossies got to Melissa and I fought them in a tiger's rage. My hands puffed and scarred, and some days I hardly dared face myself in the mirror: hair like cat fur, mouth a crack in a sidewalk. I'd turn away abruptly and say to myself, "Christmas is coming and Katrina will be home. Celebration is in order."

Ran and I had a fight standing in the kitchen one night. I'd flatly stated I could be A, a drudge, or B, the curry-combed, laughing creature from outer space he'd married, but I could not be both. Please to make up his mind. He'd answered with arresting intensity, "I never wanted the drudge."

Ran walked out in his boots to turn off the engine and I lay waiting for the dark to collapse like a night-colored tent. The sound of his feet came back. Through a half-open mind I heard myself mumble, "Sorry I blew my top. I just get to feeling ugly. I'm the one who makes me a drudge."

The feet stopped in the dark. Maybe he hadn't heard me and maybe he had. Never mind, it wasn't important. Yes, it was.

Most times you'd learned to shut up, to your credit. When his best horse died because he couldn't locate the penicillin when Hugh had gone off somewhere, or when diesel fuel went into the plane by mistake, or during forced landings, or when Rover got hopelessly stuck in the mud while I held a rapidly starving baby, or when snakes were being bashed to death with sticks or kangaroos were *not* shot, or you were *not* flung to the grass in sudden lust. But who wanted to live with a volcano sealed with Scotch tape? Ran simply backed away in self-preservation. How I longed for a dispassionate referee to our soundless shadow-boxing. Please God, let me sleep. I can't keep looking tired.

My sense of humor threatened to jingle out of sight. If anyone in us needs a pep pill it is our clown, I thought as my eyes closed. Shake the lead out of his baggy pants, we need him more than we know. He is hope in cap and bells and I loped after him into sleep.

But there was joy in Giro. Katrina came home and was my eager friend; and Ran helped every possible step and loved me—drudge, actress and mother. A large pear with busy feet.

Bertha and I made pound after pound of Christmas cake meekly drowning in 150-proof Queensland rum and the kitchen seethed with jams and marmalades, marbling the air with molten sugar and fruit.

Ran's mother and father were about to arrive, and the summer rains had come in torrents. I was determined Christmas would be better than last year and my imagination went to work. A pageant, that's what we'd have. A Christmas pageant, outdoors, with fruitcake and sandwiches and beer and every station soul and Biddefords and Cookes.

Ran was lukewarm. Nothing had ever been done like it and he wasn't at all sure local protocol listed a Christmas pageant. Neither was I, but it's important to give protocol a razzberry once in a while.

He was adamant about having the party outdoors. "I just can't see you having everybody in here. They won't feel comfortable. It'll be a mess and invade our privacy."

"But, Ran," I assured him, "they won't be anywhere near the house really. I can rig up trestle tables with boards and saw horses and turn the music up full blast. Maybe we could get a long extension cord for the phonograph from Yates and Twomey? Please, darling, I really think it'll be fun for everyone, especially the children."

"What if it rains?. It could, you know," he demurred.

"Well—" I paused, casting about for supportive argument. "It's almost rained out by now. There's always the veranda in case."

After three days he accepted the idea and stood back.

I'd nurtured two young deodars at a far corner of the place. They'd escaped horses, cows, and Freeda, and were perfect sentinels to a crèche.

Katrina was to be Mary, holding Baby Jesus: Melissa. I figured she could shush Baby Jesus in a solemn moment without Baby Jesus going off like a rocket. Wonderful Dan for Joseph, if he'd stand still for the costume; Janie Aildred and Lana Blackburn for angels; Gordon Blackburn, David Aildred, and Daisy for Wise Men; and the two little boys belonging to our current try at help for shepherds.

No rehearsals were possible. Everybody was too far and roads were a mess. Joan the Good brought me the angels' cheesecloth and buckram from Worcester, as Rover and the tap dancer weren't speaking. I planned to create the rest of the costumes out of Katrina's gaudy dress-up box on the spur of the performance.

Afraid it would be a dud without dialogue, I compiled the story of Christmas from the Bible, to narrate as the tableau jelled. I had lovely Christmas records of all kinds of background music and alternately worried and grinned with anticipation.

It rained and rained and slopped and dripped; the river's voice swelled into bass fiddles.

The Galts were helplessly stuck in a hotel in Sydney and Ran alternately paced and scanned a thick wet sky. Our road was impassable, thereby making anything other than a plane flight impossible. Two short days before Christmas the clouds parted for a few hours and Ran took off after hurried calls to alert his mother and father in Sydney. The patchy skies held just long enough for him to fly down and back.

Katrina and I waved like human semaphores as we saw them circling through fast-lowering clouds. I waved Melissa's hand for her. In utter absorption I watched Mrs. Galt step gracefully down onto the puddled strip from the plane. She was totally unfazed by a rather dramatic arrival, and looked "bandbox fresh" as my mother would have said. It poured again as Ran drove her and Mr. Galt and their bags up to the veranda from the strip.

"Isn't this dreadful!" she chimed, smiling with mischief. The filthy weather only tickled her, like getting the Old Maid in a children's card game.

We embraced. She eyed my girth, partially hidden by Melissa's squirming bulk, and ordered me to sit down.

"Certainly not," I replied emphatically, shifting Melissa to the other hip. "You have to have the Class A tour. Katrina?" I looked over at her expectantly. "Would you be sweet and take your sister for her orange juice and a biscuit?" I sounded like Isabella-Mac, Jr. Katrina turned from fondly greeting Mr. Galt and smiled a lilting "Sure!" That situation had noticeably improved since Katrina had gone away to school. We transferred Melissa and they waltzed away to the kitchen.

Mrs. Galt was poised in the living room, turning slowly around.

"Anne," she breathed in characteristic italics, "I don't believe *any* of it."

I grinned and flushed with pleasure. "Slightly different from our first tour, isn't it?"

"Show me *more!"* she demanded, tilting her head at one thing after another.

"Voila!" I exclaimed, backing toward our bedroom with a flourish, "the master bedroom, madame!"

She laughed musically and shook her head. "I can't *believe* what you've done."

"It's old hat to us now. Be careful, you're in danger of becoming a captive audience!"

Katrina loved the growing commotion surrounding Christmas. The Galts had brought mysterious packages; all of Giro seemed effervescent with suspense, and she was elated by her costume and starring role as Virgin Mary. To say nothing of Dan attending her big moment as Joseph. It made her very beautiful and very much in charge.

The morning of the pageant glowered and rained, a day that sat on you like a green glass paperweight. At four P.M. I gave up outdoors.

"Ran, you were right about the weather. I'm so terribly sorry," I said, sincerely contrite. He was very understanding and knew we couldn't halt all the plans at that late date. Besides, his mother and father were looking forward to their first Christmas party at Giro, although they were upset at my size and the way I still sailed into chores.

Where thirty-four people, nine of them children, would fit in Giro homestead I didn't know, but it was too late now. One end of the veranda became the crèche; rustic benches, straw and things, and a huge gold paper star.

Our new groom's wife had baked miniature mince pies, Joan

had done lemon cheese tarts, and we had all made 191 sandwiches and cut slices of aromatic cake. I dragged out my silver punchbowl and clouted saved-up ice to stick the beer in. The firewheel tree was still in bloom and I hacked off two magnificent branches for corners. Time flew. The engine *racketa-bonggetad-bunketed* on, and I rushed to put on records. Nothing. Not a sound—only a kind of rhythmic scratch. O profanity, O epithet, no Christmas music. Much hopeless tinkering. No. No. No. Besides, there they all came; just-married Ned Beale resplendent in a clean shirt with his very pregnant sixteen-year-old wife; Mrs. Mac in a nimbus of brand-new permanent; Old Will in a tie and young Willie in a tie and brand-new pimples. Ran had flown Errol, our jackeroo, from the hospital in Taree for the occasion; he'd fallen off a telephone pole and had been under observation. They arrived, Errol pale and blushing; Joan the Good with her Hugh, looking slick; the Biddefords, splashing mud and gaiety; huge beetle-browed Corey Blackburn, all neighing laughter, red cheeks, and curly wet hair; Sheila Blackburn in a flowered frock; our new English groom and his pathetic little Missus; Byron Cooke, dandified and full of quips; and his Gladys in frills and furbelows.

And the silent bush country children. Katrina and Wonderful Dan were fine, but the others stood and clung to things and family with scared faces.

The whole thing was a paralyzing, irrevocable mistake. I shook with nerves and incipient shame, and smiled at everybody over my belly.

Melissa was getting sleepy, I noticed. Please, O Lord, let her hold out until that halo is on. The party stiffly shifted from one foot to the other like a parked horse. Ran came striding to the rescue. He thawed into a rousing host, dispensing beer and jokes and easy camaraderie with a prodigal hand.

Now, I said to myself, now, while they're all wreathed in Christmas smiles and lemon cheese. I raised my eyebrows and ducked my chin at Joan and Sheila and, motioning to Katrina, out we all trooped, the children giggling and bewildered but game. Each child's array had been roughly planned and lay in heaps in the forgotten room where the piano had landed. Torn pieces of paper with penciled names lay on top.

Joan and Sheila got Lana and Jane into their wings, cheesecloth and old sheets cut up, and I went to work. Satin flew, sequins whirled, sashes knotted, plumes erupted out of velvet turbans fixed with ten-cent-store jewels, beads writhed and hung, veils foamed, colors whipped and bound, rayon slithered into capes and trains, bracelets clanked and eyes grew wider and wider, sparkling with ecstatic delight. Those country children's eyes were worth two twenty-three-room Giros. Bright wool cords and Mexican stripes fell in folds over two skinny shepherds; Katrina grew graceful in cascades of tulle and blues. Dan was a long-suffering Joseph in rebozos and nightshirt. The women gaped. I only used two safety pins. They couldn't believe it.

Wise Man David's mosquito punk was smoldering in its brass pot as I gave them firm instructions, not many, but *firm,* and shuffle-trotted out to swaddle Baby Jesus and warn the buzzing audience. Melissa was so bewitched by all the excitement she forgot it was time to be tired and lay smiling as I bundled her to her armpits and tied on her plate-sized halo.

"OK, Katrina," I whispered hoarsely, "here!" Baby Jesus was handed over and the show was on.

The Holy Family filed in to sotto voce "Ohs." Next the solemn angels with teetering halos, next the two small shepherds with homemade crooks, still as bookends. I lit all the candles and began to read: "And it came to pass . . . a great star in the East . . . Bethlehem in Judea." Sharp hand motion to waiting Wise Men in dimmed living room—"Gold and frankincense and myrrh!" Gordon and his towering plume knelt directly before the Holy group, effectively covering the works. The children were enthralled, hypnotized, an exotic whiff of theater had caught them in its ageless spell. I knew all about it.

The story ended in silence. There they glittered and glowed, incandescent with enchantment. These seconds demanded music and I dived headfirst into "Silent Night." It was the only one I was sure we'd all know, and of course, we did. Even after beaming applause, the children moved not, nor did they want to take off those cherished disguises. What uncanny magic theater is if only from a dress-up box in the Australian bush. And I wish you could have heard their voices telling how it was.

The gorgeousness of the Orient trod that veranda and, all in all, Christmas Eve, 1963, was an unabashed smasheroo.

Christmas Day was drenched with sun, for a welcome change. I was making cornbread to accompany salad and a pot of onion soup for a late lunch. Melissa was already fed and down for her nap. Ran came into the kitchen and cuffed a hand around my shoulder.

"Yes, darling?" I inquired, happily grinding away at the eggbeater.

"Listen, Anne, please don't be upset. Mother and Dad are leaving."

My fingers froze on the beater handle. I jerked my head around and stared at him.

"You're joking!" I cried. He couldn't be serious. "What's happened?"

"Nothing," he declared stoutly. "They've loved it all. They just feel it's too much for you."

I dropped the eggbeater, incensed. "But, Ran, they're not a bit of trouble. My Lord, can't you tell them I do this all the time? I'm used to it!" I cried in exasperation. "I love having them here. Where's your mother? Let me—"

"No. Now, calm down," he said, putting his other hand on my rigid neck.

"Yes, but they've only—"

"Mother'd rather come back after you've gone up to have the baby. She feels she could be a help then, not a guest to fuss over."

I could see he was extremely serious. "But, Ran, I'm *not fussing,*" I pleaded. "The place is a bit of a mess yet from last night, but Joan and the groom's wife came and gave me a hand early this morning. I'll have things back to normal by this afternoon. Please tell them not to feel—"

"I've tried to explain," he interrupted, dropping his hands and moving around uncomfortably, "but they won't hear of it. I'm flying them back to Sydney while the weather holds."

I was speechless. I didn't know what to feel or say.

"Aren't they even going to stay for lunch?" I asked incredulously. He looked at his watch unhappily.

"Well, I guess so. Sure. Is it about ready?"

My God. They hadn't planned to. I stared at the bowlful of precious cornbread mix from America. "Twenty minutes."

"All right. Go ahead. I'll talk to them."

373

His father was as genuinely distressed as his mother was. Nothing I could say, no sort of protests or urging, moved them. Ran acted oddly subdued. Something I didn't understand was in the air, but I knew something of consequence had gone on among the three. I was mortified to know I hadn't been able to make it all look easy enough. Thousands of miles for a two-and-a-half-day visit. Madness.

We hugged good-byes, pretending everything was lovely, and off they flew.

Katrina was greatly perplexed. I told her the truth, or at least as much as I understood. There must have been more, but I could only guess at it. As she walked through the paddock to catch Bluebottle, I thought a little bitterly, there it was again: the best and the worst right next door. A once-in-a-lifetime Christmas Eve, a Christmas Day gone straight to hell.

Katrina left for Gib Gate eager for her friends.

Sister Macdonald came toward the end of January to help with Melissa until she and Ran would fly up to greet the new baby. Sister had always thought I was funny but never really trusted me. There sat her baby, a fugitive from a Franz Hals painting, shoveling in more food than Sister Mac ate in three days. She gave me a grin like a medal.

Though Hugh Aildred stayed to help with branding, Ran had generously freed him for a further opportunity up north in Queensland. Giro echoed forlornly as he and Joan the Good drove away.

I left January 29 to have the tap dancer, who was due the first week in March. The airlines would have refused me if they'd known, but they didn't.

47

Maginel

I LEANED in as far as my belly would allow to what was left of my plate of excellent cold poached salmon and cucumber salad. The restaurant was politely buzzing with well-dressed ladies and gentlemen and I was having a sinfully carefree lady's lunch with a cousin of Ran's. I didn't know her awfully well but I wanted to. She had an insouciant surface that charmed, but lots of character underneath. She hunched forward, her expressive face alight with impish interest.

"What do you think of going to New Mexico?"

"Oh, well," I replied idly, crunching a paper-thin cucumber. "Sounds interesting, but so do a lot of other places."

She studied me curiously. "What do you mean?"

"Well, I mean Ran and I've just started to discuss the idea. A small place in Arizona might work, or even Colorado."

She lifted an eyebrow.

"Of course," I rattled on, full of enthusiasm, "he's seen one somewhere west of Albuquerque that sort of interests him, but he'll have to look around."

She looked at me strangely. "You mean you don't know?"

"Know what?" I asked, surprised at her startled tone of voice.

"That he's bought it?"

My fork hung in midair. I must've looked like an imbecile. I certainly felt like one.

"I'm sorry, Anne," she apologized guiltily. "I think I've let a large cat out of the bag."

I swallowed hard, aghast at the implications in what she'd

inadvertently revealed. The waiter rescued us from silence.

"May I offer you ladies something from the pastry cart?"

I smiled tightly and shook my head.

"Coffee, Anne?" she asked solicitously. I nodded.

"Just coffee, Frederick."

"Yes, madam, thank you. Right away." He bowed pleasantly and left. I moistened my lips.

"You're sure?" I said in a low voice, staring at the white carnations on the table.

"He's borrowed the sizable down payment. Would he do that if he hadn't meant to buy it? Anne?" She stretched a sympathetic hand toward mine, which was gripping my water glass.

"I'm really terribly sorry. I had no idea you didn't know all about it."

I tried not to look at her. The tap dancer kicked at my lunch. Be careful, be careful, don't let her see too much. I took a sip of water.

"Well, you know Ran. He loves being mysterious. Maybe he wanted to surprise me." And I forced what I thought was a nonchalant grin.

"For heaven's sake don't tell him I told you. It'll send him up the wall. It'd be a family *crise.*"

"Goodness, no, I wouldn't think of it." I felt slightly ill and emotions welled, badly disturbing that last slice of cucumber. We parted twenty minutes later, having changed the subject to more harmless plateaus and, in a state of shock, I drove my rented Chevy back to the bungalow at the Chateau Marmont in West Hollywood.

No, I would never divulge what she'd let slip. But I wanted the truth from him as soon as possible. He and Melissa were flying to San Francisco first, as I had done, in order to let Melissa visit my mother and father. He'd leave her there while the baby was born. Mother and Dad would bring her down as soon as possible afterward. Please, dear God, don't let the tap dancer be as tardy as Melissa was!

She arrived a week late, on March 11; my parents' forty-fourth wedding anniversary. We named her Maginel after grandfather's youngest sister, a great artist and my favorite relative. Elfin Maginel of the thatched, dark crown and almond eyes; I swear I felt her funloving soul the moment I held her in my arms. As newborns, Katrina had been the strongest and most vibrant; Melissa had been exquisitely feminine; Maginel was utterly winning and cuddly. Three miraculous fruits and flowers of a full life, I mused as I lay at rest in my hospital bed.

There hadn't been much time to talk before the baby came. Ran's cousins entertained us. We had a dinner rife with reminiscence with my friend Watson Webb. Ran was full of stories about Melissa's latest antics. Both of us were slightly worried that she hadn't walked as yet. Somehow you didn't actually fret about Melissa, though. You knew that when she felt she could walk perfectly, she would, and not before. Which is exactly what she did at eighteen months old—just as deliberately as she'd crawled. An altogether amazing child. Nor had she said a coherent sentence. But I felt she'd talk the same way she'd done everything else—when it would come out right she'd speak and not fumble a word. After all, Winston Churchill didn't say a word until he was three.

Ran effusively praised his mother's cooking, which made me jealous. I wondered meanly if Bertha the stove would have simmered for her, too while she was at Giro. The Galts had come back down shortly after I left. I listened and listened and reacted and reacted and waited and waited. Finally he brought it up.

"As soon as you're feeling well enough I want us to go to New Mexico and look at that place I saw."

"How big is it?" I queried casually.

"About eleven thousand acres."

My God, it's even worse than I thought. "Eleven thousand acres?" I commented very lightly. "Isn't that a lot more land than you want?" I asked, careful to treat the entire subject in an offhand way.

"Well, out there you need forty to sixty acres a cow. It's nowhere near as rich grazing land as Giro."

I felt like cold lard. What should I say? Whatever you say, do not confront him. The truth must come from him. I shrugged imperceptibly.

"I would have thought you'd want a much smaller, easier operation. Something that would almost run itself. Wouldn't eleven thousand acres be hard to handle long distance, even with adequate help, assuming you could find some? By the way, darling, have you done anything about replacing Hugh Aildred?"

He looked away. "Not yet."

I plunged in headfirst. "Ran, why don't we forget about the extra burden of a place up here and you take over at Giro and manage it yourself?" I looked at him steadily. He walked around like someone looking for an exit sign.

"We discussed that at great length some time ago. It wouldn't work!" he retorted in impatient dismissal. I let the conversation lag. I felt suddenly exhausted and began to realize the child in me was unusually still. Perhaps it was resting up for the trip. I prayed so. I'd better do the same just in case.

"Ran, dear."

"Yes." He looked away from the window where he'd been standing, lost in thought.

"I think I'll have a nap."

"Good idea," he agreed, giving me a gentle smile. How I loved my Chinese puzzle of a husband. "I'll walk down to Schwab's and get the evening paper," he said with what sounded like relief.

Maginel arrived at five o'clock the next morning.

We came home from the hospital to a nurse named Georgie, who made delicious salad dressing. She was as white as a sliced turnip, only went outdoors when absolutely necessary, and kept the baby's room so hot it made her fussy. Maginel was far more volatile than Melissa and somehow more fragile. I couldn't wait to have her on my own. And it eased my mind to know that Giro would bring her small self into bloom.

My stitches were as miserable and slow to heal as ever. I all but cursed my expert, kindly doctor.

I was propped on the couch one morning, just having reluctantly relinquished Maginel to clucking Georgie, when the mail came. Mail would never lose the importance Giro had given it. And I was right.

"Ran!" I shouted as I read the familiar wiggling script that distinctively belonged to Lieutenant Dorothy Evelyn Edwards, ex-Girl Guide, otherwise known backstage on two continents as Dot or Dottie. "Dottie's coming to Australia with us!"

He came into the bungalow living room with measured tread. The waiting around for me to get well drove him nuts, too.

"Wonderful," he said guardedly.

378

I glanced quickly up from the letter. "You knew I'd asked her?" I remarked, uneasy at his lack of reaction. "I mean, it's at my expense. I made that clear when we talked it over, didn't I?"

"Yes, sure. I'm— It's great she can make it."

"She's such a unique little person, you'll be crazy about her! And she can do anything—and tells outrageous stories about theatrical people. She's a book with feet—she's—oh, well, you'll—" I paused, noticing his eyes darting in discomfiture.

"Ran, what's the matter? Would you rather she didn't come down? Please tell me. You look so funny," I begged, increasingly alarmed at his nervous pallor.

"Where's the nurse?"

"What? Oh, she's in with Maginel. It's bathtime."

"Can we talk?" He looked a bit the way he did just before takeoff.

"Sure!" I put down Dottie's letter and looked at him a trifle apprehensively.

He took a deep breath and dropped his voice an octave. "We're not going back to Giro."

"What do you mean we're not going back?" I didn't say it, I heard it as it fell out.

"I mean we're not going back to Australia."

Not now. "I see." No, I didn't. I'd been very poorly rehearsed for this scene. "When will we?"

"When will we what?" He looked confused.

"When *are* we going back?"

He frowned and raised his voice as though I'd gone a bit deaf. "We're *not!*"

It took a long moment to grasp exactly what he was saying. I heard the water running behind the closed door to the bathroom. Vainly trying to clear away the husk in my voice, I tried once more to understand. "We—we're not going back to Australia"—I halted a moment—"ever?"

"I wouldn't say that."

I stared up at him like a retarded person. "What would you say?"

"Western Australia looks very interesting and frankly more possible economically than Giro ever could be."

The water stopped. I pictured thin white fingers sponging a tiny rose-veined body.

379

Eleven thousand five hundred miles away. I cleared my throat again. "When did you decide this?"

"It's been on my mind for quite a while." He stood up and pulled down his blue sweater.

"Are you going to sell Giro?" I hardly believed this conversation.

"Possibly. In time." He got up abruptly and went to his favorite spot at the window.

"What about—" I swallowed inadvertently. "What about our things? All our things?" I mumbled dazedly half to myself.

"We'll use them here. Send them up." His back was to me but his voice was very clear.

"Where?" I now looked away from him and scrutinized the boring print speckling my couch.

"New Mexico is a possibility," he answered coolly.

"I see." *God! Ran, don't lie to me. You've already left out enough to bomb me like an air raid, don't lie to me too.*

"It's unusual country," he went on. "A few ice caves, even lava beds, like parts of the big island of Hawaii. And ponderosa pine shows up halfway to the ranch as you drive south from Grants."

"Grants?" I echoed tonelessly.

"Grants, New Mexico. The ranch begins twenty-six miles south of Grants."

I remembered a glimpse I'd had of Grants years ago: a nondescript truck stop between Gallup and Albuquerque.

"What's the house like?" I asked, now frozen in concentration on the ceiling. I felt him look back at me.

"Well—there really isn't one. There was a fluorspar mine on the place ten years ago. The shaft's still there. As a matter of fact, the guy who currently leases it to run three hundred head of steers drinks the water from the mine instead of bothering with a well. Great water. Ten years ago there were one hundred and fifty Mexican-American miners working the mine. The mining company built a lot of cabins for them and their families. They're still there. But there's no house as such. We'd have to build one. The Starkeys live in a trailer."

I sat up gingerly, avoiding my stitches, feeling as if I'd aged twenty years.

"You've bought it, haven't you," I stated in a colorless voice.

We were motionless. An angry cab blatted on Sunset Boulevard.

"More or less."

I looked at him, searching his face for the man I loved. I might as well have studied a safe whose combination I didn't know.

"Have you bought this place?" I asked again slowly and deliberately, never taking my eyes off his.

"Not quite," he maintained stubbornly. "I suppose I could still look around," he added defensively while the lie turned his eyes into agates.

My hands felt sticky and cold. I reached for a cigarette as if I were drugged, and had trouble fitting the flame to its tip.

He smiled crookedly. "Don't look so stricken, sweetheart. Let's go over and look at it. I think you'll like the area."

What difference would that make now? answered my mind. I smoked in silence, my fingers almost pinching the smelly little white tube in half. I began to direct my actress self: This scene was not about a ranch, this scene is about a marriage. Make it real, I told myself, prodding like a demanding director; a six-day-old baby; a seventeen-month-old child; an eleven-and-one-half-year-old girl; one in the next room, one visiting her grandparents, and one in Australia. Everything we needed to bolster living was almost 9,000 miles away and we were now to build some sort of house and life somewhere south of Grants, New Mexico. And if I refused? I crushed my cigarette and folded my hands to hold them still. I watched the coal die in a dirty mess of ashes.

"Ran," I pleaded desperately in a strained voice. "Couldn't we go back to Giro and try just once more?" My voice sounded like sandpaper.

He threw up his hands and sat down. "What's the point?" he said in exasperation. "It's hopeless. It wouldn't work. Besides, as I said before, Western Australia's got more future and makes more sense economically than Giro!"

How could I refute that last? I had never known any of the details. "Esperance is eleven thousand, five hundred miles away," I muttered in disbelief, daunted by the enormity of that removal.

"We could go down for several months at a time."

381

Unlike me, he seemed very sure of his lines. Evidently there was no aspect he hadn't rehearsed mentally except me. I saw the flimsy, prefabricated, three-room house at Maikurra, its windows chattering like teeth in the wind. And then tried to imagine an abandoned mining camp complete with ice caves and lava beds; then myself alone with a moribund occupation and three children to raise. I asked it once more.

"Then we're not going back to Giro at all?"

"No point."

What hearing that again did to me I can't describe. I saw him in the months before we were married, speaking of Giro with the burnished eyes I could never resist. His place. His place in all the world; and stung with shame and defeat, like an actress reading the closing notice on her play, I heard the muffled drum of failure.

He went on to mention the impossibility of help. I silently answered, other women could do it. Then he spoke of schools and that there were now not one, but three, to educate, awaken, and instruct. Australian women did it, answered the drum as I wheeled at last to face my accusing mob of limitations.

Ran, I ranted inwardly, Ran, why couldn't you have married some strapping, simple girl who drops babies in windrows like dumplings in a pot with the same amount of hooha? A girl of twenty-three or so? Instead of a charlatan-hooligan like me who prefers faking ballet in the pale moonshine to pavanes with daily spoonfuls of cold daylight, and who never had anything to recommend her but an abiding love of life and a most individual man.

Through my inner fog I heard him say, "Have to put up a house in a hurry—seventy-two hundred feet high on the edge of the Continental Divide—below-zero winters—should consider a prefabricated—pretty attractive models available—fairly inexpensive, too—"

The lie lay between us like a dead body. I was revolted and fascinated by it. As he rambled on with growing enthusiasm, it was as if something inside me got up and left the room, never to return. I didn't want to think anymore and I didn't want to talk anymore.

"Excuse me," I said.

382

He looked surprised. "Are you all right?" He cocked his head and peered at me. It made him look foolish.

"I'm fine," I answered quickly, managing to turn up the corners of a numb mouth. I rose and walked awkwardly in to look at Maginel, who had been put down for her nap in the stuffy half-dark room. She was barely a hump and a bump under thin blankets. Her hair looked like damp feathers. A noose tightened on my throat to think she'd never bruise her knees chasing oranges all over Giro's rackabones lawn, or play with Mrs. Dare's onions, or Mrs. Mac's bent birds, or bellow as she burned a finger on Bertha's knee, and prayed I could replace that kind of wild and shaggy freedom in her life. It was finished, and so was some of me.

Our bedroom waited dimly at the end of the dark sterile hall. Giro's racetrack of a hall was spliced with light. My knees jerked as if I were walking away from a car accident. I made it to the edge of the bed and sat. No. Not the edge of a bed, I thought, the edge of a life. Perched alone in a rented bungalow bedroom, I saw Giro's final curtain begin to fall. Would I never hear the lone phone wire whine at four o'clock and run to see if it was my husband flying home; and run again and again in mounting fear, until at last a tiny crucifix hung in the pale green sky?

Or watch Katrina, slim and proud, in blue and scarlet like a mountain larrie, ride off along the strip, her toothbrush and nightclothes strapped on Bluebottle's impudent behind as she traveled off to Wonderful Dan's house?

Or see Melissa's hair whip into pale flames in a westerly, her color higher than it ever is in other places; her eyes more blue—from so much empty sky? Or hear the dingos bark under a monocle of moon and listen to the earth turning in their panting pauses—or. A vortex mind sucked me in and tried to prolong a last performance. That's what was wrong. At Giro I'd played with real people in real life. That was the kind of fire that burned you to a crisp.

Tears fattened my throat. I grimaced the way nobody lets you on film. Too ugly. The front door closed. Ran had gone somewhere. Where, I wondered. How many times I'd wondered that. I gasped and let the tears out. Oh, my God, beneath it all I was afraid. Afraid to come back. Afraid to face the battering rams of a civilization and a competition that had gone on swimmingly without me. I was in panic between the insanity of security and the insanity of escape. But the same people escape into life. I'd learned that. Step out on the stage and the fear goes away. Willy-nilly, Giro had been my stage and my life.

Giro, the King of Loneliness with a court of one, or was it two? Unsolvable, disquieting, cruel, bland, blind, blasé, as the moon is, but Circe nonetheless. I loved you. I'd always have a go at conquering you, sensing failure but unable to resist your flashy challenge. I suddenly saw myself dressed to the teeth in a stalled parade of phantasmagoric possibilities, finery and eyelashes drooping in a downpour. The thought amused and restored me. I was sure I heard an Aussie yell, "Hooray Giro!" In Australia the "Hooray" is like "Aloha"—it means "hello"— "good-bye"—"love"—"good luck" and "bully for you." Hooray Giro, Hooray. I salute you, damn you, and with you a verdant section of my life.

My neck hurt. I rolled my head around a few times, trying to ease it, and ended up chin down, staring at the phone. Slowly I reached for it and dialed—still enough of a hayseed to be impressed I didn't have to crank it like the one at home. My number rang like magic and was answered instantly and mellifluously. "Chasin Park Citron Agency?"

"Hi. This is Anne Baxter—is Mr. Park in?"

"Just a moment, please."

I waited, eyes fuzzed by focusing on nothing.

"Hello—Miss Baxter?" It was his efficient secretary.

"Yes."

"Mr. Park is in a meeting but I know he'll want to speak with you. Shall I tell him you're on the phone or can he call you back?"

"That's fine—it's not important. Just tell him I'm back."

HOUSE LIGHTS_DOWN
CURTAIN GOING UP: MARCH, 1963

384